His Infinite Variety

MAJOR SHAKESPEAREAN CRITICISM
SINCE JOHNSON

His Infinite Variety

MAJOR SHAKESPEAREAN CRITICISM

SINCE JOHNSON

Edited by Paul N. Siegel

LONG ISLAND UNIVERSITY

J. B. Lippincott Company
Philadelphia and New York

IN THIS ANTHOLOGY I have brought together some of the Shakespearean criticism which I believe to be of the greatest abiding value in contributing to the understanding and appreciation of Shakespeare. Unlike previous anthologies, it is not confined to the work of any particular time, but, although all historical periods are represented, the selections have been chosen on the basis of value rather than on the basis of their historical significance. It does not contain, therefore, tributes to Shakespeare's greatness that are not analytically critical, such as Ben Jonson's famous ode, or historical curiosities such as Thomas Rymer's comments on *Othello*. Nor does it contain works that are of interest mainly because of their own artistry, their author's place in literature, their representativeness, or their immediate influence. Dryden, Voltaire, Goethe, Heine, and Hugo are therefore absent from these pages. Furthermore, rather than to gain inclusiveness by having many brief passages, which can only be samplings, I have sought to give the critic space so that the reader may see his analysis in process. Instead of seeking to give a picture of the development of Shakespearean criticism through my selections, I have sought to provide such a picture in the editorial discussions, at least in broad outline, furnishing a background for the reader's understanding of the critics. A collection following these principles, I felt, would best be of value to students beginning their study of Shakespeare, of interest to many general readers, and of use to scholars, who will find it economical and convenient to have these works in a single volume.

The organization of the anthology, in keeping with its purpose, is not based on historical sequence but on subject matter. The first part of the anthology is concerned with Shakespeare's dramatic art in general, the succeeding parts with the various genres of Shakespeare's drama. The first selections in each of the parts dealing with the genres describe and analyze the general characteristics of that genre; the succeeding selections discuss plays representative of the genre, selections dealing with the same play being brought together. Within this framework the order is chronological. The anthology is rather heavily weighted with modern critics, for very often the successor who has elaborated upon the work of a pioneer has been chosen in preference to the pioneer himself.

Preceding each part is a brief introductory sketch, necessarily over-simplified in its generalization, of the trend of criticism on its subject. In the editorial introduction to each selection I have made brief comment on it and sought to "place" that critic in the history of Shakespearean criticism, stating his distinctive contribution and often pointing out relationships between critics. In reprinting the selections, I have dropped footnotes in many instances without any indication and renumbered the other footnotes accordingly. Where a selection has no title, I have given it one.

The bibliography lists some of the significant works of criticism on the subjects of each of the sections. The items in the bibliography contain brief descriptive comments so that the reader may readily find works that either follow the same line as a selection in the anthology, approach the play from another direction, or come in head-on collision with the selection. Works that mainly provide background material rather than engage in critical analysis have not, despite the light that they may cast, been included. The reader should remember that he may find other comments on the subjects of sections two to six by consulting the relevant portions of the works listed in the bibliography for the first section.

I wish to express my thanks to my colleagues, Ray C. Longtin and Hildreth Kritzer, who read the manuscript and made a number of helpful suggestions.

PAUL N. SIEGEL

New York, N.Y.
December 1, 1963

CONTENTS

CHANGE AND CONTINUITY IN SHAKESPEAREAN CRITICISM

H. H. FURNESS, thinking in 1886 that the point of diminishing returns in Shakespearean criticism had long been passed, exclaimed: "What numberless busy 'expositors,' high and low, wise and simple, learned and ignorant, clerk and lay, at home and abroad, have been, down to this hour, poring over every Act, and Scene, over every line, and syllable! Is there anything left for us to explore or to discover?" He went on to describe the critics of his day as geese cackling with joy over finding the few grains of wheat left in a field which had been harvested by the reapers and gleaners of past generations. Yet, following the sterile period of Shakespearean criticism after Edward Dowden, A. C. Bradley reaped a rich field.

So too Lily B. Campbell has described how after the publication of Bradley's *Shakespearean Tragedy* young graduate students felt something like futility. What more was there to be said? But there was a good deal more to be said about the tragedies which Bradley had discussed, to say nothing of the other plays. Research in Elizabethan intellectual history enabled critics to perceive more clearly the concept of hierarchical order of man, society, and the universe which

1

permeates the tragedies and, so at least many would say, the Christian overtones which reverberate through them. At the same time an intensified study of the imagery of the tragedies enhanced our understanding and appreciation of them. All of these things mark important advances in Shakespearean criticism. Yet, qualitatively different as they are in Bradley's successors, we can find anticipations of them in Bradley himself and in earlier critics.

How are we to explain this continuing process of discovery of what is not wholly new but which each time bears a fresh aspect? Francis Jeffrey's comment in reviewing Hazlitt's *Characters of Shakespear* in 1817 provides an answer:

> The beauties of Shakespeare are not of so dim or equivocal a nature as to be visible only to learned eyes— and undoubtedly his finest passages are those which please all classes of readers, and are admired for the same qualities by judges from every school of criticism.

The popularity of Shakespeare, however, and the universality of his appeal do not deprive the critic of his work, for he can show how Shakespeare has achieved the effects of which every one is conscious; and such a demonstration, performed with warmth and precision, is both pleasurable and instructive. But the critic can do more than explain how the broad effects have been achieved:

> In all works of original genius, there are a thousand retiring and less obtrusive graces, . . . a thousand slight and harmonizing touches, the merit and the effect of which are equally imperceptible to vulgar eyes. . . . In the exposition of these, there is room enough for originality.

Shakespeare, a dramatist writing for a broad audience, used firm, bold strokes for the basic designs of his plays so that those who ran could read—or rather, so that those who stood in the Globe playhouse throughout the course of the play could apprehend the design as it unrolled before them. His art is not the art of Ibsen in *The Wild Duck,* in which the righteous young idealist of the first act turns out to be in reality a destructively fatuous meddler and the villainous father against whom he is rebelling turns out to be a human being with virtues as well as faults. In Shakespeare the audience is not thus purposely misled: basic character is immediately established. Iago may deceive the other characters of the drama; but, although the frightening depths of his evil are not all at once plumbed, he is immediately revealed to the audience as a villain with sinister intentions towards Othello.

Within the firm outlines of Shakespeare's basic designs, however, there are all sorts of subtleties and complexities. If the critic, intent on the intricate internal patterns he sees or thinks he sees, does violence to the basic design, he has lost Shakespeare. This does not mean, however, that the critic must confine himself to demonstrating the technique of the basic design, although if he is not to go astray he must always be conscious of it. He can reveal the subtleties within the basic design, subtleties of which we need not assume Shakespeare himself was aware. Painstaking analysis reveals the constituent elements of what came to the poet in a flash as he was rendering his vision into words, but that Shakespeare was probably not aware, for instance, of the image clusters which critics have discovered in his work does not mean that the critic has substituted himself for the poet. The poet, as Robert Frost has sagely remarked, is entitled to everything the reader finds in him. The critic's job is to demonstrate that what he has "found" is indeed there, that it emerges from the work on close scrutiny rather than being imposed upon it by the suppression or distortion of elements of the work whose complexities cannot be fitted into the critic's superimposed pattern.

A new mode of analysis, a new angle of vision, reveals a different group of "slight and harmonizing touches," a different pattern hitherto only partially or dimly perceived. Each age develops its own modes of analysis and brings its own angles of vision. In Shakespearean criticism, as in literary history, we can use those convenient labels "neo-classical," "romantic," "Victorian," and "modern." Each period of Shakespearean criticism, with its own critical tenets and techniques, has seen Shakespeare differently. Speaking very broadly, for the neo-classical critics Shakespeare was an erratic genius whose plays were deficient in construction but who was unexcelled in the creation of scenes of passion faithful to human nature generally and appropriate to the dramatic characters. For the romantic critics Shakespeare was the infallible and god-like creator of characters living in a world of the imagination that operates by its own internal laws. For the Victorian critics Shakespeare was a moral philosopher who presented his changing view of life in plays which mirrored his emotional development. For modern critics he is an artist using the dramatic conventions, the poetic resources, and the ideas of his time.

But while each age has tended to see Shakespeare in its own way, it has at the same time assimilated the criticism of the past. Just about everyone today would agree with the neo-classical critics about Shakespeare's supremacy in scenes of passion, but most would add that other scenes have greater dramatic significance than the neo-classical critics attributed to them. Almost everyone would agree with the romantic critics about Shakespeare as a creator of character, but the concept of what constitutes character in drama has become refined and the differences between human beings in life and dramatic characters are more strongly emphasized. So too almost everyone regards Shakespearean drama as possessing organic unity, but the nature of that unity has become more complex so that the Porter's scene in *Macbeth,* which Coleridge rejected, is now seen as having an organic function. The modern critic tends to assume with the romantic critic that it is not Shakespeare who is careless but we who are unperceptive, but his manner is more like that of the neo-classical critic. He does not rhapsodize over Shakespeare's subtleties; he explains them. Like the romantic critic he sees a play as a self-contained universe which is not a mirror image of the real world, but unlike the romantic critic he will often also see it as a creation for the stage. Like the Victorian critic he sees Shakespearean drama as the representation of a view of life, but he usually regards that view of life not as Shakespeare's intensely personal response to his own immediate situation but as his bringing to intense artistic being the general ideas on life dominant in his time.

If, however, the history of Shakespearean criticism is not merely a display of the whirligig of taste, if critics not only react against their predecessors but assimilate them, the process of assimilation is accompanied by controversy about what is to be accepted, what is to be rejected, and what is to be modified and expanded upon so that it becomes something new. In this controversy every student of Shakespeare must make his choice, shrink though he may on occasion from acting as arbitrator when there is a battle of titans.

ON THE GENERAL CHARACTERISTICS OF SHAKESPEARE'S DRAMAS

FROM HIS OWN time the greatness of Shakespeare's dramas has not been challenged. The first attempt to analyze this greatness and not merely pay tribute to it was that of John Dryden. The neo-classical criticism of Shakespeare which he inaugurated was for the most part general. It found Shakespeare to be a highly irregular genius, unsurpassed at his greatest but with many weaknesses. Since then, the trend has been to explain these supposed weaknesses as deficiencies of understanding of critics blind to the art of his drama. Alexander Pope was the first to use the frequently repeated simile of Shakespeare's drama being like a Gothic cathedral, with its own kind of beauty not to be judged by the lines of classical architecture; it may be said that subsequent criticism has been concerned with explaining the complexities of Shakespeare's Gothic art. The romantic critics pointed out that his plays were not willful departures from the rules of drama but followed their own internal laws. While they regarded Shakespeare as infallible, they were ready, however, to throw out as not Shakespeare's those portions of his plays for which their sensibilities could find no warrant. The Victorian critics, continuing in the tradition of character analysis set by the romantics, tended to regard the plays as naturalistic. Accordingly, A. C. Bradley catalogued a list of Shakespearean faults, such as the characters addressing the audience in soliloquy, which would now be regarded as conventions of Elizabethan theatre that Shakespeare used for artistic purposes. The study of Shakespeare's use of stage convention and of his verse, itself a convention of his drama, has been a preoccupation of our own time. The complexity and denseness of his language, which repelled the neo-classical critics, has appealed to modern critics, who have particularly concerned themselves with his imagery. With the study of stage convention and of language has developed the study of symbolism.

SAMUEL JOHNSON
1709-1784

In his preface to his edition of Shakespeare, Johnson speaks as a liberal neo-classical critic. He follows Dryden, the father of Shakespearean criticism, and other neo-classical critics in making a judicious inventory of Shakespeare's virtues and his faults, concluding that, while there is no one equal to him at his greatest, his faults are "sufficient to obscure and overwhelm any other merit." The defects he finds in Shakespeare are lack of didacticism, looseness of plot construction, anachronism, grossness of language, bombast, obscurity of diction, and a frivolous playing with words regardless of propriety. However, he defends Shakespeare's use of comic scenes in tragedy against those who thought that tragedy and comedy are separate genres whose intermixture could only produce an idiot offspring, arguing that this "mingled drama" affords welcome variety and is faithful to life, which is a mixture of joy and sorrow. He likewise, in defending Shakespeare, attacks another of the rules which were thought to be inherent in the very nature of drama: the necessity for the scene to remain the same and the action to take place within one day so that the demands on the audience's imagination would not be too severe. To this Johnson retorts that since we really know all of the time that we are in a theatre the dramatist may just as well as not represent Alexandria in one scene and Rome in another. Johnson's argument, which perhaps does not do full justice to the complexity of the dramatic experience, was not new in his time; but, as William K. Wimsatt, Jr. says, if in attacking the unities he was kicking against a door that was already partly open, he did so with a vigor that insured that no carpenter could subsequently repair it. In shattering the rules, he helped to liberate a fuller appreciation of Shakespeare.

Johnson's notes to the plays are, as he says, "short strictures, containing a general censure of faults, or praise of excellence." They are pronouncements which often touch on the heart of the matter or raise fundamental questions. This is the spring from which later criticism flows, to whose clear, cool water it is useful to return. Although it may seem flat compared to the heady sparkling effervescence of the romantics, it has its merits. His remarks on the characters, couched in general terms, are the germ for later detailed character analyses.

In the passage here presented, Johnson lauds Shakespeare for the truth to life with which "his persons act and speak by the influence of those general passions and principles by which all minds are agitated." Thus, he remarks, echoing Aristotle's praise of the poet who makes the improbable seem real even when the events are extraordinary, the characters respond to them as people would respond if they did happen. When he says, "Shakespeare has no heroes," he means that he has none such as those in the neo-classical "heroic" tragedies, who exist merely as the mouthpieces for an absurdly vaunting rhetoric and oscillate mechanically between the opposing passions of love and honor. The romantic critics, however, were to point out that Shakespeare's protagonists are heroes greater than life-size. Charles Lamb in his essay on Shakespeare's tragedies (1811) regarded the passions there portrayed not as the easily recognizable superficial feelings of everyday life (he rejected contemptuously the customary adjective "natural" applied to Shakespeare in this sense) but as those springing from "a great or heroic nature, which is the only worthy object of tragedy." But if Shakespeare's heroes are greater than life-size, they are also, as Johnson says, life-like. As T. S. Eliot has expressed it:

> Shakespeare is one of the rarest of dramatic poets, in that each of his characters is most nearly adequate both to the requirements of the real world and to those of the poet's world.

SHAKESPEARE'S TRUTH TO LIFE

NOTHING CAN PLEASE many, and please long, but just representations of general nature. Particular manners can be known to few, and therefore few only can judge how nearly they are copied. The irregular combinations of fanciful invention may delight a-while, by that novelty of which the common satiety of life sends us all in quest; but the pleasures of sudden wonder are soon exhausted, and the mind can only repose on the stability of truth.

Shakespeare is above all writers, at least above all modern writers, the poet of nature; the poet that holds up to his readers a faithful mirrour of manners and of life. His characters are not modified by the

"Shakespeare's Truth to Life" is from the preface to Johnson's edition of Shakespeare (1765).

customs of particular places, unpractised by the rest of the world; by the peculiarities of studies or professions, which can operate but upon small numbers; or by the accidents of transient fashions or temporary opinions: they are the genuine progeny of common humanity, such as the world will always supply, and observation will always find. His persons act and speak by the influence of those general passions and principles by which all minds are agitated, and the whole system of life is continued in motion. In the writings of other poets a character is too often an individual; in those of *Shakespeare* it is commonly a species.

It is from this wide extension of design that so much instruction is derived. It is this which fills the plays of *Shakespeare* with practical axioms and domestick wisdom. It was said of *Euripides,* that every verse was a precept; and it may be said of *Shakespeare,* that from his works may be collected a system of civil and oeconomical prudence. Yet his real power is not shewn in the splendour of particular passages, but by the progress of his fable, and the tenour of his dialogue; and he that tries to recommend him by select quotations, will succeed like the pedant in *Hierocles,* who, when he offered his house to sale, carried a brick in his pocket as a specimen.

It will not easily be imagined how much *Shakespeare* excells in accommodating his sentiments to real life, but by comparing him with other authours. It was observed of the ancient schools of declamation, that the more diligently they were frequented, the more was the student disqualified for the world, because he found nothing there which he should ever meet in any other place. The same remark may be applied to every stage but that of *Shakespeare*. The theatre, when it is under any other direction, is peopled by such characters as were never seen, conversing in a language which was never heard, upon topicks which will never arise in the commerce of mankind. But the dialogue of this authour is often so evidently determined by the incident which produces it, and is pursued with so much ease and simplicity, that it seems scarcely to claim the merit of fiction, but to have been gleaned by diligent selection out of common conversation, and common occurrences.

Upon every other stage the universal agent is love, by whose power all good and evil is distributed, and every action quickened or retarded. To bring a lover, a lady and a rival into the fable; to entangle them in contradictory obligations, perplex them with oppositions of interest, and harrass them with violence of desires inconsistent with each other; to make them meet in rapture and part in agony; to fill their mouths with hyperbolical joy and outrageous sorrow; to distress them as nothing human ever was distressed; to deliver them as nothing human ever was delivered, is the business of a modern dramatist. For this probability is violated, life is misrepresented, and language is depraved. But love is only one of many passions; and as it has no great influence upon the sum of life, it has little operation in the dramas of a poet, who caught his ideas from the living world, and exhibited only what he saw before him. He knew, that any other passion, as it was regular or exorbitant, was a cause of happiness or calamity.

Characters thus ample and general were not easily discriminated and preserved, yet perhaps no poet ever kept his personages more distinct from each other. I will not say with *Pope,* that every speech may be assigned to the proper speaker, because many speeches there are which have nothing characteristical; but perhaps, though some may be equally adapted to every person, it will be difficult to find, any that can be properly transferred from the present possessor to another claimant. The choice is right, when there is reason for choice.

Other dramatists can only gain attention by hyperbolical or aggravated characters, by fabulous and unexampled excellence or depravity, as the writers of barbarous romances invigorated the reader by a giant and a dwarf; and he that should form his expectations of human affairs from the play, or from the tale, would be equally deceived. *Shakespeare* has no heroes; his scenes are occupied only by men, who act and speak as the reader thinks that he should himself have spoken or acted on the same occasion: Even where the agency is supernatural the dialogue is level with life. Other writers disguise the most natural passions and most frequent incidents; so that he who contemplates them in the book will not know them in the world: *Shakespeare* approximates the remote, and familiarizes the wonderful; the event which he represents will not happen, but if it were possible, its effects would probably be such as he has assigned; and it may be said, that he has not only shewn human nature as it acts in real exigencies, but as it would be found in trials, to which it cannot be exposed.

This therefore is the praise of *Shakespeare,* that his drama is the mirrour of life; that he who has mazed his imagination, in following

the phantoms which other writers raise up before him, may here be
cured of his delirious extasies, by reading human sentiments in human
language; by scenes from which a hermit may estimate the trans-
actions of the world, and a confessor predict the progress of the
passions.

His adherence to general nature has exposed him to the censure of
criticks, who form their judgments upon narrower principles. *Dennis*
and *Rhymer* think his *Romans* not sufficiently Roman; and *Voltaire*
censures his kings as not completely royal. *Dennis* is offended, that
Menenius, a senator of *Rome,* should play the buffoon; and *Voltaire*
perhaps thinks decency violated when the *Danish* Usurper is represented as a drunkard. But *Shakespeare* always makes nature pre-
dominate over accident; and if he preserves the essential character, is
not very careful of distinctions super-induced and adventitious. His
story requires Romans or kings, but he thinks only on men. He knew
that *Rome,* like every other city, had men of all dispositions; and
wanting a buffoon, he went into the senate-house for that which the
senate-house would certainly have afforded him. He was inclined to
shew an usurper and a murderer not only odious but despicable, he
therefore added drunkenness to his other qualities, knowing that kings
love wine like other men, and that wine exerts its natural power upon
kings. These are the petty cavils of petty minds; a poet overlooks the
casual distinction of country and condition, as a painter, satisfied with
the figure, neglects the drapery.

AUGUST WILHELM SCHLEGEL
1767-1845

PROFESSORIAL RATHER THAN rhapsodic in the manner
of the English romantic critics, Schlegel nevertheless
had a very great influence upon them. He presented
Shakespeare not as the wild genius of neo-classical
criticism, who always required apology even in the
midst of praise, but as the wise genius whose dramas

obey their own inner laws. Nicholas Rowe and Alexander Pope had argued in the eighteenth century that one cannot convict a man for not obeying the laws of which he is ignorant, but Schlegel does not plead ignorance on behalf of Shakespeare: he asserts that Shakespeare has a higher knowledge. In making this assertion, he throughout corrects Johnson, whom he makes the representative of a neo-classicism to be controverted.

In this selection Schlegel anticipates such modern critics as H. B. Charlton and S. L. Bethell in finding that Shakespeare captured the spirit of the historical periods he portrayed despite his anachronisms and that his anachronisms are artistic means by which he universalizes the contemporary. His defense of Shakespeare's figurative language, including its occurrence in scenes of passion, of his use of violence on the stage, and of his use of comedy in the midst of tragedy (not on Johnson's ground of truth to life but on the ground that it serves a thematic function as well as the function of relief from tension) is equally epoch-making and anticipatory of modern criticism. Likewise noteworthy are his observations that Shakespeare's characters embody the universal in the particular, that characters are subordinated to the total dramatic purpose, and that they act as foils to each other.

THE ART OF SHAKESPEARE'S ROMANTIC DRAMA

THE PROOFS OF his ignorance, on which the greatest stress is laid, are a few geographical blunders and anachronisms. Because in a comedy founded on a tale, he makes ships land in Bohemia, he has been the subject of laughter. But I conceive we should be very

"The Art of Shakespeare's Romantic Drama" is from *Lectures on Dramatic Art and Literature* (1808), tr. 1833.

unjust towards him, were we to conclude that he did not, as well as ourselves, possess the valuable but by no means difficult knowledge that Bohemia is no where bounded by the sea. He could never, in that case, have looked into a map of Germany, whereas he describes the maps of both Indies with the discoveries of the latest navigators.[1] In such matters Shakspeare is only faithful in the historical subjects of his own country. In the novels on which he worked, he avoided disturbing his audience to whom they were known, by the correction of errors in secondary things. The more wonderful the story, the more it ranged in a purely poetical region, which he transfers at will to an indefinite distance. These plays, whatever names they bear, took place in the true land of romance and in the century of wonderful love stories. He knew well that in the forest of Ardennes, there were neither the lions and serpents of the torrid zone, nor the shepherdesses of Arcadia: but he transferred both to it,[2] because the design and import of his picture required them. Here he considered himself entitled to the greatest liberties. He had not to do with a petty hypercritical age like ours, which is always seeking in poetry for something else than poetry; his audience entered the theatre, not to learn true chronology, geography, natural history, but to witness a vivid exhibition. I undertake to prove that Shakspeare's anachronisms are, for the most part, committed purposely, and after great consideration. It was frequently of importance to him to bring the subject exhibited, from the back ground of time, quite near to us. Hence in Hamlet, though avowedly an old northern story, there prevails the tone of modish society, and in every respect the costume of the most recent period. Without those circumstantialities it would not have been allowable to make a philosophical inquirer of Hamlet, on which however the sense of the whole is made to rest. On that account he mentions his education at a university, though in the age of the historical Hamlet there was not yet any university. He makes him study at Wittenberg, and no selection could be more suitable. The name was very popular: from the story of Dr. Faustus, of Wittenberg it was wonderfully well known; it was of particular celebrity in protestant England, as Luther had taught and written there shortly before, and the very name must have immediately suggested the idea of freedom in thinking. I cannot even consider it an anachronism that Richard the Third should speak

[1] *Twelfth Night, or What You Will*—Act. iii. Sc. ii.
[2] *As You Like It.*

of Macchiavel. The word is here used altogether proverbially: the contents of the book of the prince have been in existence even since the existence of tyrants; Macchiavel was merely the first to commit them to writing.

That Shakspeare has accurately hit the essential costume, namely, the spirit of ages and nations, is at least generally acknowledged by the English critics; but many sins against the external costume may be easily remarked. Here we must bear in mind that the Roman pieces were acted upon the stage of that day in the European dress. . . . The more early Christian painters represent the Saviour, the Virgin Mary, the Patriarchs, and Apostles in an ideal dress; but the subordinate actors or spectators of the action, in the dresses of their own nation and age. Here they were guided by a correct feeling: the mysteriously sacred ought to be kept in an awe-inspiring distance, but the human can only be properly understood when seen with the usual accompaniments. In the middle ages all heroical stories of antiquity, from Theseus and Achilles down to Alexander, were metamorphosed into true books of chivalry. What was related to themselves alone spoke an intelligible language to them; of differences and distinctions they did not wish to know. In an old manuscript of the Trojan war, I saw a miniature picture representing the funeral procession of Hector, where the coffin, hung with noble coats of arms, is carried into a Gothic church. It is easy to make ourselves merry with this piece of simplicity, but a reflecting mind will view the subject in a very different light. A powerful consciousness of the universal prevalency and the solid consistency of their manner of being, an undoubted conviction that it has always so been and will continue so to be in the world: these feelings of our ancestors were symptoms of the fresh fulness of life; they were the marrow of action in real life as well as in poetry. . . .

Many things in Shakspeare must be judged of according to the above principles, respecting the essential and the merely learned costume. . . .

So much with respect to the spirit of the age in which Shakspeare lived, and his peculiar cultivation and knowledge. To me he appears a profound artist, and not a blind and wildly luxuriant genius. I consider, generally speaking, all that has been said on this subject as a mere fabulous story, a blind and extravagant error. In other arts the assertion refutes itself; for in them acquired knowledge is an indispensable condition before anything can be performed. But even in such poets, as are usually given out for careless pupils of nature, without any art or school discipline, I have always found, on a nearer consideration, when they have really produced works of excellence, a distinguished cultivation of the mental powers, practice in art, and views worthy in themselves and maturely considered. This applies to Homer as well as Dante. The activity of genius is, it is true, natural to it, and in a certain sense unconscious; and consequently the person who possesses it is not always at the moment able to render an account of the course which he may have pursued; but it by no means follows that the thinking power had not a great share in it. It is from the very rapidity and certainty of the mental process, from the utmost clearness of understanding, that thinking in a poet is not perceived as something abstracted, does not wear the appearance of meditation (after thought). That idea of poetical inspiration, which many lyrical poets have brought into circulation, as if they were not in their senses, and like Pythia, when possessed by the divinity, delivered oracles unintelligible to themselves (a mere lyrical invention), is least of all applicable to dramatic composition, one of the productions of the human mind which requires the greatest exercise of thought. . . .

The English critics are unanimous in their praise of the truth and uniform consistency of his characters, of his heart-rending pathos, and his comic wit. Moreover, they extol the beauty and sublimity of his separate descriptions, images, and expressions. This last is the most superficial and cheap mode of criticising works of art. Johnson compares him, who should endeavour to recommend this poet by passages unconnectedly torn from his works, to the pedant in Hierocles, who exhibited a brick as a sample of his house. And yet he himself speaks so little, and so very unsatisfactorily, of the pieces considered as a whole! Let any man, for instance, bring together the short characters which he gives at the close of each play, and see if the aggregate will amount to that sum of admiration which he himself, at his outset, has stated as the correct standard for the appreciation of the poet. It was, generally speaking, the prevailing tendency of the time which preceded our own; a tendency displayed also in physical science, to consider what is possessed of life as a mere accumulation of dead parts, to separate what exists only in connexion and cannot otherwise be conceived, instead of penetrating to the central point and viewing all the parts as so many irradiations from it. Hence nothing is so rare as a critic who can elevate himself to the contemplation of an extensive work of art. Shakspeare's compositions, from the very depth of purpose displayed in them, have been exposed to the misfortune of being misunderstood. Besides, this prosaical species of criticism applies always the poetical form to the details of execution; but in so far as the plan of the piece is concerned, it never looks for more than the logical connexion of causes and effects, or some partial and trivial moral by way of application; and all that cannot be reconciled to this is declared a superfluous, or even a detrimental, addition. On these principles we must equally strike out the most of the choral songs of the Greek tragedies, which also contribute nothing to the development of the action, but are merely an harmonious echo of the impressions aimed at by the poet. In this they altogether mistake the rights of poetry and the nature of the romantic drama, which, for the very reason that it is and ought to be picturesque, requires richer accompaniments and contrasts for its main groupes. In all art and poetry, but more especially in the romantic, the fancy lays claims to be considered as an independent mental power governed according to its own laws.

In an essay on *Romeo and Juliet,* written a number of years ago, I went through the whole of the scenes in their order, and demonstrated the inward necessity of each with reference to the whole; I showed why such a particular circle of characters and relations was placed around the two lovers; I explained the signification of the mirth here and there scattered, and justified the use of the occasional heightening given to the poetical colours. From all this it seemed to follow unquestionably, that with the exception of a few plays of wit now become unintelligible or foreign to the present taste, (imitations of the tone of society of that day) nothing could be taken away, nothing added, nothing otherwise arranged, without mutilating and disfiguring the perfect work. I should be ready to undertake the same thing in all the pieces of Shakspeare produced in his maturer years, but this would require a separate book. Here I am reduced to confine my observations to the tracing of his great designs with a rapid pencil; but still I must previously be allowed to deliver my sentiments in a general manner on the subject of his most distinguishing properties.

Shakspeare's knowledge of mankind has become proverbial: in this his superiority is so great, that he has justly been called the master of the human heart. A readiness in remarking even the nicer involuntary demonstrations of the mind, and the expressing with certainty the meaning of these signs acquired from experience and reflection, constitutes the observer of men; acuteness in drawing still farther conclusions from them, and in arranging the separate observations according to grounds of probability in a connected manner, may be said to be knowing men. The distinguishing property of the dramatic poet who is great in characterization is something altogether different from this, which either, take it which way we will, includes in it this readiness, and this acuteness, or dispenses with both. It is the capability of transporting himself so completely into every situation, even the most unusual, that he is enabled, as plenipotentiary of the whole human race, without particular instructions for each separate case, to act and speak in the name of every individual. It is the power of endowing the creatures of his imagination with such self-existent energy, that they afterwards act in each conjuncture according to general laws of nature: the poet, in his dreams, institutes as it were experiments which are received with as much authority as if they had been made on real objects. The inconceivable in this, and what never can be learned, is, that the characters appear neither to do nor to say anything on account of the spectator; and yet that the poet, by means of the exhibition itself without any subsidiary explanation, communicates the gift of looking into the inmost recesses of their minds. Hence Goëthe has ingeniously compared Shakspeare's characters to watches with crystalline plates and cases, which, while they point out the hours as correctly as other watches, enable us at the same time to perceive the inward springs whereby all this is accomplished.

Nothing, however, is more foreign to Shakspeare, than a certain dissecting mode of composition, which laboriously enumerates to us all the motives by which a man is determined to act in this or that particular manner. This way of accounting for motives, the rags of many of the modern historians, might be carried at length to an extent which would abolish everything like individuality, and resolve all character into nothing but the effect of foreign or external influences, while we know that it frequently announces itself in the most decided manner in the earliest infancy. After all, a man acts so because he is so. And how each man is constituted, Shakspeare reveals to us in the most immediate manner: he demands and obtains our belief, even for what is singular, and deviates from the ordinary course of nature. Never perhaps was there so comprehensive a talent for characterization as Shakspeare. It not only grasps the diversities of rank, sex, and age, down to the dawning of infancy; not only do the king and the beggar, the hero and the pickpocket, the sage and the idiot, speak and act with equal truth; not only does he transport himself to distant ages and foreign nations, and portray in the most accurate manner, with only a few apparent violations of costume, the spirit of the ancient Romans, of the French in the wars with the English, of the English themselves during a great part of their history, of the Southern Europeans (in the serious part of many comedies), the cultivated society of that time, and the former rude and barbarous state of the North; his human characters have not only such depth and precision that they cannot be arranged under classes, and are inexhaustible even in conception: no, this Prometheus not merely forms men, he opens the gates of the magical world of spirits, calls up the midnight ghosts, exhibits before us his witches amidst their unhallowed mysteries, peoples the air with sportive fairies and sylphs; and these beings existing only in imagination possess such truth and consistency, that even when deformed monsters like Caliban, he extorts the assenting conviction, if there should be such beings they would so conduct themselves. In a word, as he carries with him the most fruitful and daring fancy into the kingdom of nature, on the other hand, he carries nature into the regions of fancy, lying beyond the confines of reality. We are lost in astonishment at seeing the extraordinary, the wonderful, and the unheard of, in such intimate nearness.

Pope and Johnson appear to contradict each other in a singular manner, when the first says, all the characters of Shakspeare are individuals, and the second, they are species. And yet perhaps these opinions may admit of reconciliation. Pope's expression is unquestionably the more correct. A character which should merely be a personification of a naked general idea could neither exhibit any great depth nor any great variety. The names of genera and species are well known to be merely auxiliaries for the understanding, that we may embrace the infinite variety of nature in a certain order. The characters which Shakspeare has thoroughly delineated possess undoubtedly a number of individual peculiarities, but at the same time a signification which is not applicable to them alone: they generally supply materials for a profound theory of their distinguishing property. But even with the above correction, this opinion must still have its limitation. Characterization is merely one ingredient of the dramatic art, and not dramatic poetry itself. It would be improper in the extreme, if the poet were to draw our attention to superfluous traits of character, when he ought to endeavour to produce other impressions. Whenever the musical or the fanciful preponderate, the characteristical is necessarily thrown into the back ground. Hence many of the figures of Shakspeare, exhibit merely external designations, determined by the place which they occupy in the whole: they are like secondary persons in a public procession, to whose physiognomy we seldom pay much attention; their only importance is derived from the solemnity of their dress and the object in which they are engaged. Shakspeare's messengers, for instance, are for the most part merely messengers, yet not common, but poetical messengers: the messages which they have to bring is the soul which suggests to them their language. Other voices too are merely raised as melodious lamentations or rejoicings, or reflections on what has taken place; and in a serious drama without chorus this must always be more or less the case if we would not have it prosaical.

If Shakspeare deserves our admiration for his characters, he is equally deserving of it for his exhibition of passion, taking this word in its widest signification, as including every mental condition, every tone from indifference or familiar mirth to the wildest rage and despair. He gives us the history of minds; he lays open to us, in a single word, a whole series of preceding conditions. His passions do not at first stand displayed to us in all their height, as is the case with so many tragic poets who, in the language of Lessing, are thorough masters of the legal style of love. He paints, in a most inimitable manner, the gradual progress from the first origin; "he gives," as Lessing says, "a living picture of all the most minute and secret artifices by which a feeling steals into our souls, of all the imperceptible advantages which it there gains, of all the stratagems by which every other passion is made subservient to it, till it becomes the sole tyrant of our desires and our aversions." Of all poets, perhaps, he alone has portrayed the mental diseases, melancholy, delirium, lunacy, with such inexpressible and, in every respect, definite truth, that the physician may enrich his observations from them in the same manner as from real cases.

And yet Johnson has objected to Shakspeare that his pathos is not always natural and free from affectation. There are, it is true, passages, though comparatively speaking very few, where his poetry exceeds the bounds of true dialogue, where a too soaring imagination, a too luxuriant wit, rendered the complete dramatic forgetfulness of himself impossible. With this exception, the censure originates only in a fanciless way of thinking, to which everything appears unnatural that does not suit its tame insipidity. Hence an idea has been formed of simple and natural pathos, which consists in exclamations destitute of imagery and nowise elevated above everyday life. But energetical passions electrify the whole of the mental powers, and will consequently, in highly favoured natures, express themselves in an ingenious and figurative manner. It has often been remarked that indignation gives wit; and as despair occasionally breaks out into laughter, it may sometimes also give vent to itself in antithetical comparisons. . . .

The objection that Shakspeare wounds our feelings by the open display of the most disgusting moral odiousness, harrows up the mind unmercifully, and tortures even our eyes by the exhibition of the most insupportable and hateful spectacles, is one of much greater importance. He has never, in fact, varnished over wild and bloodthirsty passions with a pleasing exterior, never clothed crime and want of principle with a false show of greatness of soul, and in that respect he is every way deserving of praise. Twice he has portrayed downright villains, and the masterly way in which he has contrived to elude impressions of too painful a nature may be seen in Iago and Richard the Third. I allow that the reading, and still more the sight, of some of his pieces are not advisable to weak nerves, any more than the *Eumenides* of Æschylus; but is the poet, who can only reach an important object by bold and hazardous means, to allow himself to be influenced by considerations for persons of this description? If the effeminacy of the present day is to serve as a general standard of what tragical composition may exhibit to human nature, we shall be forced to set very narrow limits to art, and everything like a powerful effect must at once be renounced. If we wish to have a grand purpose, we must also wish to have the means, and our nerves should in some measure accommodate themselves to painful impressions when, by way of requital, our mind is thereby elevated and strengthened.—The constant reference to a petty and puny race must cripple the boldness of the poet. Fortunately for his art, Shakspeare lived in an age extremely susceptible of noble and tender impressions, but which had still enough of the firmness inherited from a vigorous olden time, not to shrink back with dismay from every strong and violent picture. We have lived to see tragedies of which the catastrophe consists of the swoon of an enamoured princess: if Shakspeare falls occasionally into the opposite extreme, it is a noble error originating in the fulness of a gigantic strength. And this tragical Titan, who storms the heavens and threatens to tear the world from off its hinges, who, more fruitful than Æschylus, makes our hair stand on end, and congeals our blood with horror, possessed at the same time the insinuating loveliness of the sweetest poetry; he plays with love like a child, and his songs are breathed out like melting sighs. He unites in his existence the utmost elevation and the utmost depth; and the most foreign, and even apparently irreconcilable properties subsist in him peaceably together. The world of spirits and nature have laid all their treasures at his feet: in strength a demi-god, in profundity of view a prophet, in all-seeing wisdom a protecting spirit of the higher order, he lowers himself to mortals as if unconscious of his superiority, and is as open and unassuming as a child.

If the delineation of all his characters, separately considered, is inimitably firm and correct, he surpasses even himself in so combining and contrasting them, that they serve to bring out each other.—This is the very summit of dramatic characterization: for we can never estimate a man altogether abstractedly by himself according to his true worth; we must see him in his relations with others; and it is here that most dramatic poets are deficient. Shakspeare makes each of his principal characters the glass in which the others are reflected, and in which we are enabled to discover what could not be immediately revealed to us. . . .

The irony in Shakspeare has not merely a reference to the separate characters, but frequently to the whole of the action. Most poets who portray human events in a narrative or dramatic form take themselves a part, and exact from their readers a blind approbation or condemnation of whatever side they choose to support or oppose. The more zealous this rhetoric is, the more easily it fails of its effect. In every case we perceive that the subject does not come immediately before us, but that we view it through the medium of a different way of thinking. When, however, the poet, by a dexterous manœuvre, occasionally allows us a glance of the less brilliant reverse of the picture, he then places himself in a sort of secret understanding with the select circle of the intelligent among his readers or spectators; he shows them that he previously saw and admitted the validity of their objections; that he himself is not tied down by the subject represented, but soars freely above it; and that, if he chose, he could unrelentingly annihilate the beautiful and irresistibly attractive scenes which his magic pen has produced. Wherever the proper tragic enters, it is true, everything like irony immediately ceases; but from the avowed raillery of comedy, to the point where the subjection of mortal beings to an inevitable destiny demands the highest degree of seriousness, there are a multitude of human relations which unquestionably may be considered in an ironical view, without confounding the eternal line of separation between good and evil. This purpose is answered by the comic characters and scenes which are interwoven in the most of Shakspeare's pieces where romantic fables or historical events are made the subject of a noble and elevating exhibition. A determinate parody of the serious part is frequently not to be mistaken in them; at other times the connexion is more loose and arbitrary, and the more wonderful the invention of the whole, the more easily it becomes merely a light delusion of the fancy. The comic interruptions everywhere serve to prevent the play from being converted into an employment, to preserve the mind in the possession of its hilarity, and to keep off that gloomy and inert seriousness which so easily steals into the sentimental, but not tragical, drama. Most assuredly, Shakspeare did not wish in this to comply with the taste of the multitude contrary to his own better judgment: for in various pieces, and in considerable parts of others, especially when the catastrophe approaches, and the minds are consequently more on the stretch and no longer susceptible of any entertainment serving to divert their attention, he has abstained from all comic intermixtures. It was also an object with him, that the clowns or buffoons should not occupy a more important place than that which he had assigned them: he expressly condemns the extemporizing with which they loved to enlarge their parts.[3] Johnson founds the justification of their species of drama in which seriousness and mirth are mixed, on this, that in real life the vulgar is found close to the sublime, that the merry and the sad usually accompany and succeed one

[3] In Hamlet's directions to the players.

another. But it does not follow that because both are found together, they must not therefore be separated in the compositions of art. The observation is in no respect just, and this circumstance invests the poet with a power to proceed in that manner, because everything in the drama must be regulated by the conditions of theatrical probability; but the mixture of such dissimilar, and apparently contradictory, ingredients, in the same works, can only be justifiable on principles reconcilable with the views of art, which I have already described. In the dramas of Shakspeare the comic scenes are the antechamber of the poetry, where the servants remain; these prosaical associates must not give such an extension of their voice as to deafen the speakers in the hall itself; however, in those intervals when the ideal society has retired they deserve to be listened to; the boldness of their raillery, the pretension of their imitations, may afford us many a conclusion respecting the relations of their masters.

SAMUEL TAYLOR COLERIDGE
1772-1834

COLERIDGE, TOGETHER WITH Schlegel, dominated Shakespearean criticism until the time of Bradley despite the fact that he published only two short essays. His great influence in his lifetime came from his lectures, which, says Byron, were "a kind of rage." His notes and marginalia and the newspaper accounts of his lectures published at various times during the century kept his influence alive. Although Shakespeare's greatness had always been acknowledged, Coleridge's presentation of Shakespeare as a flawless and transcendant genius made Coleridge appear to be a prophet revealing for the first time the word of a hitherto unrecognized god. He was a prophet whose words delivered on high from the lecture platform effected a revolution.

In the twentieth century both the "historical" critics and the "new" critics have reacted against Coleridge's disciples, charging them with being subjective and given over to a character analysis which artificially detaches the characters from the drama. Coleridge, however, is a seminal critic whose scattered observations bear other seeds than those which produced the romantic and Victorian character analysts. As Alfred Harbage has pointed out:

It was Coleridge who outlined the program of the school of historical criticism, even though it was left to the twentieth century to carry out the program. He declared the need for a thorough knowledge of Elizabethan language, history, manners, theatres and minor dramatists, together with their, and Shakespeare's, literary sources. . . . He also, in details of his practice, forecast the so-called "new criticism"—in his assumption of complete integration in the artistic "construct," his textual scrutinies, his conviction of the significance of puns and word-play, and his concern with imagery.

In *Shakspeare's Judgment Equal to his Genius,* Coleridge uses the concept of organic form, which emerges from the work itself, as opposed to that of mechanic form, which is artificially imposed on it, to proclaim passionately the profound error of the animadversions not only of such extreme neo-classicists as Voltaire, against whom Johnson had defended Shakespeare, but of the entire neo-classical tradition.

In his *Recapitulation and Summary of the Characteristics of Shakspeare's Dramas* Coleridge states that while the unities of time and place are artificial, there is another unity, inherent in the very character of drama, which Shakespeare everywhere observes— "the unity of feeling," or, as we would say today, of over-all tone. Every drama of his has its own special atmosphere, its own "unity of feeling and character." He finds distinctive in Shakespearean drama the sense of dramatic inevitability ("expectation in preference to surprise") as against theatrical sensationalism ("independence of the dramatic interest on the plot") and novelty ("independence of the interest on the story"). He stresses, as recent critics have, that Shakespeare's is a poetic drama in which the poetry is integral to the work and not merely decorative. His statement about Shakespeare's essential morality is an implicit answer to Johnson's complaint about Shakespeare's lack of didactism and his grossness of language. Alfred Harbage's *As They Liked It* (1947) can be said to be in large part an expansion of this statement, just as his *Shakespeare and the Rival Traditions* (1952) can be said to be an expansion of Coleridge's contrast between Shakespeare and Beaumont and Fletcher. Coleridge's statement that the characters of Shakespeare's *dramatis personae,* like those of people in real life, have to be inferred from various indications had already been made by Maurice Morgann in his pioneering pre-romantic "Essay on the Dramatic Character of Sir John Falstaff" (1777). Coleridge's point, like Morgann's, is that the characters are complex creations who are not neatly labelled and that they have to be studied in the entire dramatic context—what is said about them and by whom and what they themselves say and do. Regardless of whether Morgann and Coleridge in practice ever extended this precept beyond its proper limits, it is not an excuse for inventing a life for the characters anterior to, concurrent with or subsequent to the stage-action without warrant in the text.

SHAKSPEARE'S JUDGMENT EQUAL TO HIS GENIUS

ARE THE PLAYS of Shakspeare works of rude uncultivated genius, in which the splendour of the parts compensates, if aught can compensate, for the barbarous shapelessness and irregularity of the whole?— Or is the form equally admirable with the matter, and the judgment of the great poet, not less deserving our wonder than his genius?—Or, again, to repeat the question in other words:—Is Shakspeare a great dramatic poet on account only of those beauties and excellencies which he possesses in common with the ancients, but with diminished claims to our love and honour to the full extent of his differences from them?—Or are these very differences additional proofs of poetic wisdom, at once results and symbols of living power as contrasted with lifeless mechanism—of free and rival originality as contradistinguished from servile imitation, or, more accurately, a blind copying of effects, instead of a true imitation of the essential principles?—Imagine not that I am about to oppose genius to rules. No! the comparative value of these rules is the very cause to be tried. The spirit of poetry, like all other living powers, must of necessity circumscribe itself by rules, were it only to unite power with beauty. It must embody in order to reveal itself; but a living body is of necessity an organized one; and what is organization but the connexion of parts in and for a whole, so that each part is at once end and means?—This is no discovery of criticism;—it is a necessity of the human mind; and all nations have felt and obeyed it, in the invention of metre, and measured sounds, as the vehicle and *involucrum* of poetry—itself a fellow-growth from the same life,—even as the bark is to the tree!

No work of true genius dares want its appropriate form, neither indeed is there any danger of this. As it must not, so genius cannot, be lawless; for it is even this that constitutes it genius—the power of acting creatively under laws of its own origination. How then comes it that not only single *Zoili,* but whole nations have combined in unhesitating condemnation of our great dramatist, as a sort of African nature, rich in beautiful monsters—as a wild heath where islands of fertility look the greener from the surrounding waste, where the love-

"Shakspeare's Judgment Equal to his Genius" is from Coleridge's *Lectures,* published in *Literary Remains,* 1836–39.

liest plants now shine out among unsightly weeds, and now are choked by their parasitic growth, so intertwined that we cannot disentangle the weed without snapping the flower?—In this statement I have had no reference to the vulgar abuse of Voltaire, save as far as his charges are coincident with the decisions of Shakspeare's own commentators and (so they would tell you) almost idolatrous admirers. The true ground of the mistake lies in the confounding mechanical regularity with organic form. The form is mechanic, when on any given material we impress a pre-determined form, not necessarily arising out of the properties of the material;—as when to a mass of wet clay we give whatever shape we wish it to retain when hardened. The organic form, on the other hand, is innate; it shapes, as it developes, itself from within, and the fulness of its development is one and the same with the perfection of its outward form. Such as the life is, such is the form. Nature, the prime genial artist, inexhaustible in diverse powers, is equally inexhaustible in forms;—each exterior is the physiognomy of the being within,—its true image reflected and thrown out from the concave mirror;—and even such is the appropriate excellence of her chosen poet, of our own Shakspeare,—himself a nature humanized, a genial understanding directing self-consciously a power and an implicit wisdom deeper even than our consciousness.

I greatly dislike beauties and selections in general; but as proof positive of his unrivalled excellence, I should like to try Shakspeare by this criterion. Make out your amplest catalogue of all the human faculties, as reason or the moral law, the will, the feeling of the coincidence of the two (a feeling *sui generis et demonstratio demonstrationum*) called the conscience the understanding or prudence, wit, fancy, imagination, judgment,—and then of the objects on which these are to be employed, as the beauties, the terrors, and the seeming caprices of nature, the realities and the capabilities, that is, the actual and the ideal, of the human mind, conceived as an individual or as a social being, as in innocence or in guilt, in a play-paradise, or in a war-field of temptation;—and then compare with Shakspeare under each of these heads all or any of the writers in prose and verse that have ever lived! Who, that is competent to judge, doubts the result?— And ask your own hearts,—ask your own common-sense—to conceive the possibility of this man being—I say not, the drunken savage of that wretched sciolist, whom Frenchmen, to their shame, have honoured before their elder and better worthies,—but the anomalous, the wild, the irregular, genius of our daily criticism! What! are we to have miracles in sport?—Or, I speak reverently, does God choose idiots by whom to convey divine truths to man?

RECAPITULATION AND SUMMARY OF THE CHARACTERISTICS OF SHAKSPEARE'S DRAMAS

THE GREEKS REARED a structure, which in its parts, and as a whole, filled the mind with the calm and elevated impression of perfect beauty and symmetrical proportion. The moderns also produced a whole, a more striking whole; but it was by blending materials and fusing the parts together. And as the Pantheon is to York Minster or West-minster Abbey, so is Sophocles compared with Shakspeare; in the one a completeness, a satisfaction, an excellence, on which the mind rests with complacency; in the other a multitude of interlaced materials, great and little, magnificent and mean, accompanied, indeed, with the sense of a falling short of perfection, and yet, at the same time, so promising of our social and individual progression, that we would not, if we could, exchange it for that repose of the mind which dwells on the forms of symmetry in the acquiescent admiration of grace. . . .

The law of unity, which has its foundations, not in the factitious necessity of custom, but in nature itself, the unity of feeling, is every where and at all times observed by Shakspeare in his plays. Read *Romeo and Juliet;*—all is youth and spring;—youth with its follies, its virtues, its precipitancies;—spring, with its odours, its flowers, and its transiency; it is one and the same feeling that commences, goes through, and ends the play. The old men, the Capulets and the Mon-tagues, are not common old men; they have an eagerness, a heartiness, a vehemence, the effect of spring; with Romeo, his change of passion, his sudden marriage, and his rash death, are all the effects of youth;—whilst in Juliet love has all that is tender and melancholy in the

"Recapitulation and Summary of the Characteristics of Shakspeare's Dramas" is from Coleridge's *Lectures.*

nightingale, all that is voluptuous in the rose, with whatever is sweet in the freshness of spring; but it ends with a long deep sigh like the last breeze of the Italian evening. This unity of feeling and character pervades every drama of Shakspeare.

It seems to me that his plays are distinguished from those of all other dramatic poets by the following characteristics:

1. Expectation in preference to surprise. It is like the true reading of the passage;—'God said, Let there be light, and there was *light*;'—not there *was* light. As the feeling with which we startle at a shooting star, compared with that of watching the sunrise at the pre-established moment, such and so low is surprise compared with expectation.

2. Signal adherence to the great law of nature, that all opposites tend to attract and temper each other. Passion in Shakspeare generally displays libertinism, but involves morality; and if there are exceptions to this, they are, independently of their intrinsic value, all of them indicative of individual character, and, like the farewell admonitions of a parent, have an end beyond the parental relation. Thus the Countess's beautiful precepts to Bertram, by elevating her character, raise that of Helena her favorite, and soften down the point in her which Shakspeare does not mean us not to see, but to see and to forgive, and at length to justify. And so it is in Polonius, who is the personified memory of wisdom no longer actually possessed. This admirable character is always misrepresented on the stage. Shakspeare never intended to exhibit him as a buffoon; for although it was natural that Hamlet,—a young man of fire and genius, detesting formality, and disliking Polonius on political grounds, as imagining that he had assisted his uncle in his usurpation,—should express himself satirically, —yet this must not be taken as exactly the poet's conception of him. In Polonius a certain induration of character had arisen from long habits of business; but take his advice to Laertes, and Ophelia's reverence for his memory, and we shall see that he was meant to be represented as a statesman somewhat past his faculties,—his recollections of life all full of wisdom, and showing a knowledge of human nature, whilst what immediately takes place before him, and escapes from him, is indicative of weakness.

But as in Homer all the deities are in armour, even Venus; so in Shakspeare all the characters are strong. Hence real folly and dulness are made by him the vehicles of wisdom. There is no difficulty for one being a fool to imitate a fool; but to be, remain, and speak like a wise man and a great wit, and yet so as to give a vivid representation of a veritable fool,—*hic labor, hoc opus est.* A drunken constable is not uncommon, nor hard to draw; but see and examine what goes to make up a Dogberry.

3. Keeping at all times in the high road of life. Shakspeare has no innocent adulteries, no interesting incests, no virtuous vice;—he never renders that amiable which religion and reason alike teach us to detest, or clothes impurity in the garb of virtue, like Beaumont and Fletcher, the Kotzebues of the day. Shakspeare's fathers are roused by ingratitude, his husbands stung by unfaithfulness; in him, in short, the affections are wounded in those points in which all may, nay, must, feel. Let the morality of Shakspeare be contrasted with that of the writers of his own, or the succeeding, age, or those of the present day, who boast their superiority in this respect. No one can dispute that the result of such a comparison is altogether in favour of Shakspeare; —even the letters of women of high rank in his age were often coarser than his writings. If he occasionally disgusts a keen sense of delicacy, he never injures the mind; he neither excites, nor flatters, passion, in order to degrade the subject of it; he does not use the faulty thing for a faulty purpose, nor carries on warfare against virtue, by causing wickedness to appear as no wickedness, through the medium of a morbid sympathy with the unfortunate. In Shakspeare vice never walks as in twilight; nothing is purposely out of its place;—he inverts not the order of nature and propriety,—does not make every magistrate a drunkard or glutton, nor every poor man weak, humane, and temperate; he has no benevolent butchers, nor any sentimental ratcatchers.

4. Independence of the dramatic interest on the plot. The interest in the plot is always in fact on account of the characters, not *vice versa,* as in almost all other writers; the plot is a mere canvass and no more. Hence arises the true justification of the same stratagem being used in regard to Benedict and Beatrice,—the vanity in each being alike. Take away from the *Much Ado About Nothing* all that which is not indispensable to the plot, either as having little to do with it, or, at best, like Dogberry and his comrades, forced into the service, when any other less ingeniously absurd watchmen and night-constables would have answered the mere necessities of the action;— take away Benedict, Beatrice, Dogberry, and the reaction of the former on the character of Hero,—and what will remain? In other

writers the main agent of the plot is always the prominent character; in Shakspeare it is so, or is not so, as the character is in itself calculated, or not calculated, to form the plot. Don John is the main-spring of the plot of this play; but he is merely shown and then withdrawn.

5. Independence of the interest on the story as the ground-work of the plot. Hence Shakspeare never took the trouble of inventing stories. It was enough for him to select from those that had been already invented or recorded such as had one or other, or both, of two recommendations, namely, suitableness to his particular purpose, and their being parts of popular tradition,—names of which we had often heard, and of their fortunes, and as to which all we wanted was, to see the man himself. So it is just the man himself, the Lear, the Shylock, the Richard, that Shakspeare makes us for the first time acquainted with. Omit the first scene in *Lear,* and yet every thing will remain; so the first and second scenes in the *Merchant of Venice.* Indeed it is universally true.

6. Interfusion of the lyrical—that which in its very essence is poetical—not only with the dramatic, as in the plays of Metastasio, where at the end of the scene comes the *aria* as the *exit* speech of the character,—but also in and through the dramatic. Songs in Shakspeare are introduced as songs only, just as songs are in real life, beautifully as some of them are characteristic of the person who has sung or called for them, as Desdemona's 'Willow,' and Ophelia's wild snatches, and the sweet carollings in *As You Like It.* But the whole of the *Midsummer Night's Dream* is one continued specimen of the drama-tized lyrical. And observe how exquisitely the dramatic of Hotspur;—

> Marry, and I'm glad on't with all my heart;
> I had rather be a kitten and cry—mew, &c.

melts away into the lyric of Mortimer;—

> I understand thy looks: that pretty Welsh
> Which thou pourest down from these swelling heavens,
> I am too perfect in, &c.
>
> Henry IV. part i. act iii. sc. i.

7. The characters of the *dramatis personae,* like those in real life, are to be inferred by the reader;—they are not told to him. And it is well worth remarking that Shakspeare's characters, like those in real

life, are very commonly misunderstood, and almost always understood by different persons in different ways. The causes are the same in either case. If you take only what the friends of the character say, you may be deceived, and still more so, if that which his enemies say; nay, even the character himself sees himself through the medium of his character, and not exactly as he is. Take all together, not omitting a shrewd hint from the clown or the fool, and perhaps your impression will be right; and you may know whether you have in fact discovered the poet's own idea, by all the speeches receiving light from it, and attesting its reality by reflecting it.

Lastly, in Shakspeare the heterogeneous is united, as it is in nature. You must not suppose a pressure or passion always acting on or in the character;—passion in Shakspeare is that by which the individual is distinguished from others, not that which makes a different kind of him. Shakspeare followed the main march of the human affections. He entered into no analysis of the passions or faiths of men, but assured himself that such and such passions and faiths were grounded in our common nature, and not in the mere accidents of ignorance or disease. This is an important consideration, and constitutes Shakspeare the morning star, the guide and the pioneer, of true philosophy.

WILLIAM HAZLITT
1778-1830

IN HAZLITT'S *Characters of Shakespear's Plays* (1817) English romantic Shakespearean criticism speaks out loud and bold. With a particularity of description and a vigor of expression, it seeks not only to discuss the characters but to communicate the experience of the plays; and it succeeds admirably.

In the selection from a lecture on Shakespeare and Milton which follows, Hazlitt extols Shakespeare's ability to identify himself with each of his characters at all times, that "negative capability" which Keats regarded as the mark of the poet. This is a point which had already been made, not only by Schlegel and Coleridge but by the late eighteenth-century critic William Richardson, who in the introduction to his book on Shakespeare's characters (1774) called Shakespeare the "Proteus of the drama" who "changes himself into every character, and enters easily into every condition of human nature." So too Hazlitt's "His plays alone are properly expressions of the passions, not descriptions of them" is similar to Lord Kames's statement in his *Elements of Criticism* (1762) that the speeches of Shakespeare's characters "appear the legitimate offspring of passion" while those of other dramatists are "descriptive only, and illegitimate." Hazlitt's statement that Shakespeare's characters are "real beings of flesh and blood; they speak like men, not like authors" similarly echoes Pope's "those [characters] of other Poets have a constant resemblance, which shews that they receiv'd them from one another . . . but every single character in *Shakespear* is as much an Individual, as those in Life itself." In short, romantic criticism not only reacted against neo-classical criticism but grew out of it. Hazlitt, however, in elaborating upon points made by neo-classical critics, writes with an ardor of his own and calls upon a wealth of illustration which makes his encomium come glowingly alive.

Hazlitt's description of Shakespeare's imagery and figures of speech as the product of an extraordinary imagination and command of language is, however, at variance with the neo-classical critical tradition, which accepted Dryden's statement in his preface to *Troilus and Cressida* (1679) that Shakespeare's style, unlike his depiction of characters and passions, was often unnatural: "To say nothing without a Metaphor, a Simile, an Image, or description, is I doubt to smell a little too strongly of the Buskin." Yet Hazlitt's "His language is hieroglyphical. It translates thoughts into visible images" was anticipated by Thomas Gray, when he wrote in a private letter (1742), "Every word in him is a picture."

Having followed the tradition of discussing such categories as character, passion, language, and versification, Hazlitt continues in the tradition by referring, in conclusion, to Shakespeare's faults. This conclusion is a much toned-down and more limited version of the neo-classical inventory of faults. It resolves itself down to the statement that Shakespeare is unduly careless (not grossly uneven) and rather too fond of puns (not enamoured of them to the sacrifice, in Johnson's words, of "reason, propriety and truth"). Although probably few today would exonerate Shakespeare of these faults completely (Juliet's well known string of puns on "eyes" on hearing of Romeo's supposed death is difficult to defend), contemporary critics place even less emphasis on them than did Hazlitt and discuss the artistic significance of Shakespeare's puns. A critic such as M. M. Mahood, whose excellent if sometimes over-ingenious *Shakespeare's Wordplay* (1957) is the closest study of the subject, finds that Shakespeare's punning is an aspect of that command over the language which Hazlitt praised. The pun is not, as Johnson said, "the fatal Cleopatra" for which Shakespeare "lost the world, and was content to lose it" but the Charmion attendant upon Shakespeare's real love, the English language, a love by which he gained the world rather than lost it.

SHAKESPEARE'S GENIUS

THE STRIKING PECULIARITY of Shakespeare's mind was its generic quality, its power of communication with all other minds—so that it contained a universe of thought and feeling within itself, and had no one peculiar bias or exclusive excellence more than another. He was just like any other man, but that he was like all other men. He was

"Shakespeare's Genius" is from Hazlitt's *Lectures on the English Poets,* 1818, 1819.

the least of an egotist that it was possible to be. He was nothing in himself, but he was all that others were, or that they could become. He not only had in himself the germs of every faculty and feeling, but he could follow them by anticipation, intuitively, into all their conceivable ramifications, through every change of fortune or conflict of passion, or turn of thought. He had 'a mind reflecting ages past' and present:—all the people that ever lived are there. There was no respect of persons with him. His genius shone equally on the evil and on the good, on the wise and the foolish, the monarch and the beggar. 'All corners of the earth, kings, queens, and states, maids, matrons, nay, the secrets of the grave,' are hardly hid from his searching glance. He was like the genius of humanity, changing places with all of us at pleasure, and playing with our purposes as with his own. He turned the globe round for his amusement, and surveyed the generations of men, and the individuals as they passed, with their different concerns, passions, follies, vices, virtues, actions, and motives—as well those that they knew, as those which they did not know, or acknowledge to themselves. The dreams of childhood, the ravings of despair, were the toys of his fancy. Airy beings waited at his call, and came at his bidding. Harmless fairies 'nodded to him, and did him curtesies:' and the night-hag bestrode the blast at the command of 'his potent art.' The world of spirits lay open to him, like the world of real men and women: and there is the same truth in his delineations of the one as of the other; for if the preternatural characters he describes could be supposed to exist, they would speak, and feel, and act, as he makes them. He had only to think of any thing in order to become that thing, with all the circumstances belonging to it. When he conceived of a character, whether real or imaginary, he not only entered into all its thoughts and feelings, but seemed instantly, and as if by touching a secret spring, to be surrounded with all the same objects, 'subject to the same skyey influences,' the same local, outward, and unforeseen accidents which would occur in reality. Thus the character of Caliban not only stands before us with a language and manners of its own, but the scenery and situation of the enchanted island he inhabits, the traditions of the place, its strange noises, its hidden recesses, 'his frequent haunts and ancient neighbourhood,' are given with a miraculous truth of nature, and with all the familiarity of an old recollection. The whole 'coheres semblably together' in time, place, and circumstance. In reading this author, you do not merely learn what his characters say,

—you see their persons. By something expressed or understood, you are at no loss to decipher their peculiar physiognomy, the meaning of a look, the grouping, the bye-play, as we might see it on the stage. A word, an epithet, paints a whole scene, or throws us back whole years in the history of the person represented. So (as it has been ingeniously remarked) when Prospero describes himself as left alone in the boat with his daughter, the epithet which he applies to her, 'Me and thy *crying* self,' flings the imagination instantly back from the grown woman to the helpless condition of infancy, and places the first and most trying scene of his misfortunes before us, with all that he must have suffered in the interval. How well the silent anguish of Macduff is conveyed to the reader, by the friendly expostulation of Malcolm:— 'What! man, ne'er pull your hat upon your brows.' Again, Hamlet, in the scene with Rosencrantz and Guildenstern, somewhat abruptly concludes his fine soliloquy on life by saying, 'Man delights not me, nor woman neither, though by your smiling you seem to say so.' Which is explained by their answer—'My lord, we had no such stuff in our thoughts. But we smiled to think, if you delight not in man, what lenten entertainment the players shall receive from you, whom we met on the way:'—as if while Hamlet was making this speech, his two old schoolfellows from Wittenberg had been really standing by, and he had seen them smiling by stealth, at the idea of the players crossing their minds. It is not 'a combination and a form' of words, a set speech or two, a preconcerted theory of a character, that will do this: but all the persons concerned must have been present in the poet's imagination, as at a kind of rehearsal; and whatever would have passed through their minds on the occasion, and have been observed by others, passed through his, and is made known to the reader.—I may add in passing, that Shakespeare always gives the best directions for the costume and carriage of his heroes. Thus to take one example, Ophelia gives the following account of Hamlet; and as Ophelia had seen Hamlet, I should think her word ought to be taken against that of any modern authority.

> *Ophelia.* My lord, as I was reading in my closet,
> Prince Hamlet, with his doublet all unbrac'd,
> No hat upon his head, his stockings loose,
> Ungartred, and down-gyved to his ancle,
> Pale as his shirt, his knees knocking each other,

> And with a look so piteous,
> As if he had been sent from hell
> To speak of horrors, thus he comes before me.
>   *Polonius.* Mad for thy love!
>   *Oph.* My lord, I do not know,
> But truly I do fear it.
>   *Pol.* What said he?
>   *Oph.* He took me by the wrist, and held me hard;
> Then goes he to the length of all his arm;
> And, with his other hand thus o'er his brow,
> He falls to such perusal of my face,
> As he would draw it: long staid he so;
> At last, a little shaking of my arm,
> And thrice his head thus waving up and down,
> He rais'd a sigh so piteous and profound,
> As it did seem to shatter all his bulk,
> And end his being. That done, he lets me go,
> And with his head over his shoulder turn'd,
> He seem'd to find his way without his eyes;
> For out of doors he went without their help,
> And to the last bended their light on me.
>
> Act II. Scene I.

How after this airy, fantastic idea of irregular grace and bewildered melancholy any one can play Hamlet, as we have seen it played, with strut, and stare, and antic right-angled sharp-pointed gestures, it is difficult to say, unless it be that Hamlet is not bound, by the prompter's cue, to study the part of Ophelia. The account of Ophelia's death begins thus:

> There is a willow hanging o'er a brook,
> That shows its hoary leaves in the glassy stream.—

Now this is an instance of the same unconscious power of mind which is as true to nature as itself. The leaves of the willow are, in fact, white underneath, and it is this part of them which would appear 'hoary' in the reflection in the brook. The same sort of intuitive power, the same faculty of bringing every object in nature, whether present or absent, before the mind's eye, is observable in the speech of Cleopatra, when conjecturing what were the employments of Antony in his absence:—'He's speaking now, or murmuring, where's my serpent of old Nile?' How fine to make Cleopatra have this consciousness of her own character, and to make her feel that it is this for which Antony is in love with her! She says, after the battle of Actium, when Antony has resolved to risk another fight, 'It is my birth-day; I had thought to have held it poor: but since my lord is Antony again, I will be Cleopatra.' What other poet would have thought of such a casual resource of the imagination, or would have dared to avail himself of it? The thing happens in the play as it might have happened in fact.— That which, perhaps, more than any thing else distinguishes the dramatic productions of Shakespeare from all others, is this wonderful truth and individuality of conception. Each of his characters is as much itself, and as absolutely independent of the rest, as well as of the author, as if they were living persons, not fictions of the mind. The poet may be said, for the time, to identify himself with the character he wishes to represent, and to pass from one to another, like the same soul successively animating different bodies. By an art like that of the ventriloquist, he throws his imagination out of himself, and makes every word appear to proceed from the mouth of the person in whose name it is given. His plays alone are properly expressions of the passions, not descriptions of them. His characters are real beings of flesh and blood; they speak like men, not like authors. One might suppose that he had stood by at the time, and overheard what passed. As in our dreams we hold conversations with ourselves, make remarks, or communicate intelligence, and have no idea of the answer which we shall receive, and which we ourselves make, till we hear it: so the dialogues in Shakespeare are carried on without any consciousness of what is to follow, without any appearance of preparation or premeditation. The gusts of passion come and go like sounds of music borne on the wind. Nothing is made out by formal inference and analogy, by climax and antithesis: all comes, or seems to come, immediately from nature. Each object and circumstance exists in his mind, as it would have existed in reality: each several train of thought and feeling goes on of itself, without confusion or effort. In the world of his imagination, everything has a life, a place, and being of its own! . . .

The passion in Shakespeare is of the same nature as his delineation of character. It is not some one habitual feeling or sentiment preying upon itself, growing out of itself, and moulding everything to itself; it is passion modified by passion, by all the other feelings to which the individual is liable, and to which others are liable with him; subject

to all the fluctuations of caprice and accident; calling into play all the
resources of the understanding and all the energies of the will; irritated
by obstacles or yielding to them; rising from small beginnings to its
utmost height; now drunk with hope, now stung to madness, now sunk
in despair, now blown to air with a breath, now raging like a torrent.
The human soul is made the sport of fortune, the prey of adversity:
it is stretched on the wheel of destiny, in restless ecstasy. The passions
are in a state of projection. Years are melted down to moments, and
every instant teems with fate. We know the results, we see the process.
Thus after Iago has been boasting to himself of the effect of his
poisonous suggestions on the mind of Othello, 'which, with a little
act upon the blood, will work like mines of sulphur,' he adds:—

> Look where he comes! not poppy, nor mandragora
> Nor all the drowsy syrups of the East,
> Shall ever medicine thee to that sweet sleep
> Which thou ow'dst yesterday.

And he enters at this moment, like the crested serpent, crowned with
his wrongs and raging for revenge! The whole depends upon the turn
of a thought. A word, a look, blows the spark of jealousy into a flame;
and the explosion is immediate and terrible as a volcano. The dialogues in *Lear,* in *Macbeth,* that between Brutus and Cassius, and
nearly all those in Shakespeare, where the interest is wrought up to
its highest pitch, afford examples of this dramatic fluctuation of
passion. . . .

Shakespeare's imagination is of the same plastic kind as his conception of character or passion. 'It glances from heaven to earth, from
earth to heaven.' Its movement is rapid and devious. It unites the
most opposite extremes; or, as Puck says, in boasting of his own feats,
'puts a girdle round about the earth in forty minutes.' He seems always
hurrying from his subject, even while describing it; but the stroke,
like the lightning's, is sure as it is sudden. He takes the widest possible
range, but from that very range he has his choice of the greatest
variety and aptitude of materials. He brings together images the most
alike, but placed at the greatest distance from each other; that is,
found in circumstances of the greatest dissimilitude. From the remoteness of his combinations, and the celerity with which they are effected,
they coalesce the more indissolubly together. The more the thoughts
are strangers to each other, and the longer they have been kept

asunder, the more intimate does their union seem to become. Their felicity is equal to their force. Their likeness is made more dazzling by their novelty. They startle, and take the fancy prisoner in the same instant. I will mention one or two which are very striking, and not much known, out of *Troilus and Cressida*. Æneas says to Agamemnon:

> I ask that I may waken reverence,
> And on the cheek be ready with a blush
> Modest as morning, when she coldly eyes
> The youthful Phœbus.

Ulysses urging Achilles to shew himself in the field, says—

> No man is the lord of any thing,
> Till he communicate his parts to others:
> Nor doth he of himself know them for aught,
> Till he behold them formed in the applause,
> Where they're extended! which, like an arch reverberates
> The voice again, or like a gate of steel
> Fronting the sun, receives and renders back
> Its figure and its heat.

Patroclus gives the indolent warrior the same advice:

> Rouse yourself; and the weak wanton Cupid
> Shall from your neck unloose his amorous fold,
> And like a dew-drop from the lion's mane
> Be shook to air.

Shakespeare's language and versification are like the rest of him. He has a magic power over words: they come winged at his bidding; and seem to know their places. They are struck out at a heat, on the spur of the occasion, and have all the truth and vividness which arise from an actual impression of the objects. His epithets and single phrases are like sparkles, thrown off from an imagination, fired by the whirling rapidity of its own motion. His language is hieroglyphical. It translates thoughts into visible images. It abounds in sudden transitions and elliptical expressions. This is the source of his mixed metaphors, which are only abbreviated forms of speech. These, however, give no pain from long custom. They have, in fact, become idioms in the language. They are the building, and not the scaffolding to thought. We take the meaning and effect of a well-known passage entire, and no more stop to scan and spell out the particular words and phrases than the syllables of which they are composed. In trying to recollect any other author, one sometimes stumbles, in case of failure, on a word as good. In Shakespeare, any other word but the true one, is sure to be wrong. If anybody, for instance, could not recollect the words of the following description,

> —————— Light thickens,
> And the crow makes wing to the rooky wood

he would be greatly at a loss to substitute others for them equally expressive of the feeling. These remarks, however, are strictly applicable only to the impassioned parts of Shakespeare's language, which flowed from the warmth and originality of his imagination, and were his own. The language used for prose conversation and ordinary business is sometimes technical, and involved in the affectation of the time. Compare, for example, Othello's apology to the Senate, relating 'his whole course of love,' with some of the preceding parts relating to his appointment, and the official dispatches from Cyprus. In this respect, 'the business of the state does him offence.'—His versification is no less powerful, sweet, and varied. It has every occasional excellence, of sullen intricacy, crabbed and perplexed, or of the smoothest and loftiest expansion—from the ease and familiarity of measured conversation to the lyrical sounds

> ————Of ditties highly penned,
> Sung by a fair queen in a summer's bower,
> With ravishing division to her lute.

It is the only blank verse in the language, except Milton's, that for itself is readable. It is not stately and uniformly swelling like his, but varied and broken by the inequalities of the ground it has to pass over in its uncertain course,

> And so by many winding nooks it strays,
> With willing sport to the wild ocean.

It remains to speak of the faults of Shakespeare. They are not so many or so great as they have been represented; what there are, are chiefly owing to the following causes:—The universality of his genius was, perhaps, a disadvantage to his single works; the variety of his resources sometimes diverting him from applying them to the most effectual purposes. He might be said to combine the powers of

Æschylus and Aristophanes, of Dante and Rabelais, in his own mind. If he had been only half what he was, he would perhaps have appeared greater. The natural ease and indifference of his temper made him sometimes less scrupulous than he might have been. He is relaxed and careless in critical places; he is in earnest throughout only in *Timon, Macbeth,* and *Lear.* Again, he had no models of acknowledged excellence constantly in view to stimulate his efforts, and, by all that appears, no love of fame. He wrote for the 'great vulgar and the small' in his time, not for posterity. If Queen Elizabeth and the maids of honour laughed heartily at his worst jokes, and the catcalls in the gallery were silent at his best passages, he went home satisfied, and slept the next night well. He did not trouble himself about Voltaire's criticisms. He was willing to take advantage of the ignorance of the age in many things, and if his plays pleased others, not to quarrel with them himself. His very facility of production would make him set less value on his own excellences, and not care to distinguish nicely between what he did well or ill. His blunders in chronology and geography do not amount to above half a dozen, and they are offences against chronology and geography, not against poetry. As to the unities he was right in setting them at defiance. He was fonder of puns than became so great a man. His barbarisms were those of his age. His genius was his own. He had no objection to float down with the stream of common taste and opinion: he rose above it by his own buoyancy, and an impulse which he could not keep under, in spite of himself, or others, and 'his delights did show most dolphin-like.'

S. L. BETHELL

MODERN CRITICS HAVE emphasized that Shakespeare's drama is a poetic drama, a form in which the poetry is not merely decorative but essential to the drama itself. As T. S. Eliot has phrased it: "A verse play is not a play done into verse, but a different kind of play: in a way more realistic than 'naturalistic drama,' because, instead of clothing nature in poetry," it exposes what lies underneath "the natural surface appearance." S. L. Bethell in his *Shakespeare and the Popular Dramatic Tradition* has analyzed the nature of Shakespeare's poetic drama. He has found it to be dependent on a conventionalism of which verse is an integral part, a conventionalism which applies to the handling both of character, in the frequent departures from representational depiction, and time, in the purposeful intermixing of the historical and the contemporary. Bethell explains this conventionalism by reference not only to dramatic history but to intellectual history, pointing out the importance of the medieval heritage in each case. Himself a Christian opposed to scientific rationalism, he holds that Shakespearean drama appeals to a form of response, "the ability to keep simultaneously in mind two opposite aspects of a situation," which the modern age, with its monistic thinking, has unfortunately largely lost. We need not accept everything he has to say about modern drama and modern thought to find his discussion of Shakespearean drama extremely fruitful.

Bethell's insistence on the non-realistic features of Shakespeare's depiction of character does not negate the neo-classical critics' praise of Shakespeare for his truth to nature but qualifies it. This qualification is a development of one previously made by Charles Lamb, who was well aware of the role of convention in art:

The form of *speaking,* whether it be in soliloquy or dialogue, is only a medium, and often a highly artificial one, for putting the reader or spectator into possession of that knowledge of the inner structure and workings of mind in a character, which he could otherwise never have arrived at *in that form of composition* by any gift short of intuition. We do here as we do with novels written in the *epistolary form.* How many improprieties, perfect solecisms in letter-writing, do we put up with in *Clarissa* and other books, for the sake of the delight which that form upon the whole gives us.

So too Bethell's "strip the poetry from a play of Shakespeare, and what is left" echoes Lamb's statement that *Hamlet,* rewritten as Banks or Lillo would have written it, "totally omitting all the poetry of it . . . in the poorest and most homely language of the servilest creeper after nature," would be a poor thing indeed. Bethell's book-length study may be said to be an exploration of what is implicit in these observations by Lamb.

In the extract which follows, Bethell analyzes the rich effect Shakespeare gains by calling the attention of the audience to the play as a play, as a dramatic illusion that is not reality but an image of it. We may note in this connection that the theatre of Shakespeare's company was called the Globe, a reference to the real world. The analogy between drama and life was almost as much a part of Elizabethan thinking as the analogy between the little world of man, the microcosm, and the universe, the macrocosm. It rose naturally from the Elizabethan habit of analogical thinking.

SHAKESPEARE'S PLANES OF REALITY

FROM TIME TO time and from place to place the drama varies its position on a scale between the two extremes of absolute conventionalism and absolute naturalism. At either extreme it would cease to be properly dramatic. Absolute conventionalism would work in symbols bearing no necessary relation to the things symbolized, and absolute naturalism would reproduce a "slice of life" with more than photographic fidelity. The former would be devoid of emotive power, like

"Shakespeare's Planes of Reality" is from S. L. Bethell, *Shakespeare and the Popular Dramatic Tradition* (Duke University Press, 1944), pp. 3–4, 5–9, 22–23, 29–42.

the symbols in algebra, whilst the latter would lack both intellectual and emotional organization. Actually the drama is never completely arbitrary in symbolism or completely and unselectively representational, although the difference, for example, between *Everyman* and *A Doll's House* is sufficient for the terms "conventional" and "naturalistic" to be applied to them respectively. *Everyman* represents allegorically the soul's conflict in its journey through life, and most of its characters personify abstract human qualities: Good Deeds, Knowledge, Strength, Discretion; but in *A Doll's House* everyday people are presented in everyday surroundings, the dialogue is conversational, and the action such as might take place in a contemporary household.

The position of Shakespeare is somewhere between these two practical extremes. His characters are not merely personified abstractions, but, on the other hand, they are not precisely like real people: for instance, they usually speak in verse. Conventionalism of this kind is so obvious, however, that nineteenth-century critics seem not to have reflected upon its implications; it was usual for them to treat Shakespeare as Ibsen is more appropriately treated: they fastened upon his characters as if they were historical personages, examining their psychology, weighing motives, allotting praise or blame to individual speeches and actions—even attempting to explain problems of character by imaginatively constructing the early life of Hamlet or Othello. There was no attempt to consider the historical anomaly by which a naturalistic drama could so quickly have arisen out of a conventional tradition. Behind the Elizabethan drama were generations of miracle plays and interludes, including "moralities" such as *Everyman;* they had not quite disappeared in the boyhood of Shakespeare himself. More recent investigation has accorded them their proper place as forerunners of the Elizabethan drama, which has been shown to have more in common with its conventional ancestry than used to be suspected. . . .

Psychological naturalism as the basis of Shakespearean criticism, reached its limits in A. C. Bradley's *Shakespearean Tragedy.* But already the physical conditions of Shakespeare's theater had been patiently investigated; and this new knowledge, coupled with the historical and comparative study of Shakespeare and his predecessors and contemporaries, was to produce among daring spirits a violent reaction against the psychological approach. Professor Schücking's treatise, translated as *Character Problems in Shakespeare's Plays,* shows how far even the presentation of character depends on stage convention rather than the direct representation of life. Apart from this seminal idea, however, the book is of doubtful value. Professor Schücking cannot appreciate the depth and subtlety of Shakespeare's verse, and though he claims Shakespeare as conventional rather than naturalistic, his sympathies seem to be with modern naturalism, so that he is also incapable of appreciating the dramatic subtleties made available by a conventional tradition. He speaks disparagingly of Shakespeare's "primitive" art-form and seems to confuse primitive technique with naïveté of thought and feeling. Believing in Shakespeare's naïveté, he misses all his deeper meaning, and endlessly multiplies conventions in order to account for everything he cannot understand. Professor Stoll, in his *Art and Artifice in Shakespeare,* has pushed the argument of Professor Schücking even farther, since to him Shakespeare's every tragic hero is built upon a contradiction impossible to psychology but rendered plausible by dramatic and poetic art: Shakespeare's object is "emotional illusion." However far we may feel Professors Schücking and Stoll to be from a profound and comprehensive view of Shakespeare, they have certainly revealed a body of dramatic conventions unsuspected by an earlier generation of critics. We are told that, on the Elizabethan stage, disguise was conventionally impenetrable, slander was conventionally believed, and characters conformed to type: the Avenger, the Machiavel, the Melancholy Man. The villain was conventionally—not cynically—aware of his own villainy, and the hero—without priggishness—of his own virtues. It is all useful knowledge, provided we remember that these are not rules but sweeping generalities, and certainly not true of every instance. We can be safe only in a close study of each individual text. The greatest contribution to Shakespearean criticism has not, in fact, come from the specialists, but from those general critics who have taught us to take his poetry seriously, and to realize that, in Shakespeare, poetry and drama are not separable ingredients, but that the drama is a poetic creation, existing in the poetry like a Thomist *universale in re.* The suggestions of Mr. T. S. Eliot and Dr. F. R. Leavis have been followed out by Miss Bradbrook and Dr. L. C. Knights: the time has gone by for anthologizing Shakespeare's "beauties," and the poetry has at last been accorded that fundamental position which it naturally holds. It is difficult to see how it can ever have been otherwise—how the poetry can ever have been treated as a decorative inessential. The immense superiority of *Antony and Cleopatra* over Dryden's *All for Love* is quite clearly a superiority in poetry. Indeed, strip the poetry from a play of Shakespeare, and what is left but a rather haphazard story about a set of vaguely outlined and incredibly "stagey" characters? There is no originality of plot, little subtlety of psychological analysis, no immediately accessible propaganda. Miss Bradbrook, uniting two lines of approach, has found pattern and convention in the poetry itself; and Professor Wilson Knight, by his "mystical" interpretation, again reminds us that Shakespeare was closer to *Everyman* than to *A Doll's House*. I am not attempting anything like a survey of recent criticism. I have said nothing of "verse tests," or of the tendency to split up nearly every play among a number of collaborators and to detect several layers of revision: under the influence of genuinely literary criticism the tide has turned against such misapplication of scientific method. My purpose has been to trace what I consider the most important developments in recent Shakespearean criticism, so as to show how my own work links with that of previous writers. Every approach to Shakespeare has something in it of value, but I am convinced of the fundamental importance of the words themselves—of the poetry—and of the great, though secondary, importance of a knowledge of Elizabethan stage conditions. My own particular approach, considered in these pages, can be undertaken only in the closest association with pure literary criticism and a consideration of Shakespeare's stagecraft.

I have stressed the element of convention in Shakespeare, since it is generally overlooked. But it is necessary also to insist that Shakespeare and his contemporaries worked to no thought-out conventional system; indeed, their conventions are successful just because they are traditional and unconscious. Moreover, being unconscious, they were by no means rigidly adhered to: the Elizabethan playwright varies his position on the scale between conventionalism and naturalism, even in the course of a single play. This rapidity of adjustment is a principal component in Shakespeare's remarkable subtlety. Lapses into naturalism are especially frequent in Shakespeare: they are probably a major cause of his continuous popularity on the stage, and provide color for a psychological approach which would have failed much more signally with, for example, Chapman or Tourneur. A single flash of natural dialogue, breaking the boundaries of convention, will reveal an intuitive understanding of human nature, unshared by his contemporaries. Othello, filled with the conflicting emotions of love and loathing, visits Desdemona in her chamber, and behaves there as if entering a brothel, calling upon Emilia to perform her "mystery" as doorkeeper. After a tense, but mannered and theatrical, display of passion, he makes an effective exit, still acting his abominable fiction:

> We have done our course; there's money for your pains:
> I pray you, turn the key and keep our counsel.
>
> (IV. ii. 93)

When he has gone out, Emilia addresses her mistress: "How do you, madam? how do you, my good lady?" (IV. ii. 96.) Desdemona's answer is surprising: " 'Faith, half asleep" (IV. ii. 97). Within the conventional framework of Elizabethan poetic drama, such a reply is unlikely, and on that account the more arresting. We expect an outburst in keeping with the tone set by Othello, but instead there has been a transition without warning to the plane of naturalism. Tragedy queens seldom complain of fatigue, though there is actually nothing so exhausting as a scene of tense emotion. This sudden revelation of ordinary womanhood in Desdemona engages the audience's sympathy when it is particularly needed, and also points a contrast between her sensible normality and the emotional exaggeration of Othello. . . .

Characters, without being themselves made up of incompatible qualities, may evoke distinct and separate responses from the audience. Thus Falstaff is (a) amusing, and (b) morally reprehensible; an Elizabethan audience would applaud his wit, but approve his final dismissal. Victorian critics, however, displayed bitter resentment, not only against Henry, but against Shakespeare himself, for refusing to sentimentalize. Where the Victorian critic laughs, he must love; but a popular audience is never under this necessity. In the miracle plays, humor was mainly provided by Herod and the fiends, characters held in abhorrence; similarly the Vice of the moralities was forerunner of the Shakespearean clown (does this account for a certain malignity in Feste?); and the pantomime audience today still laughs at the discomfiture of a comic devil. Not only character, but every aspect of the Elizabethan drama, is shot through with this quality of dual awareness. The mixture of conventionalism and naturalism demands a dual mode of attention. Awareness of the play as play implies the dual awareness of play world and real world: upon this depends the piquancy of a play-within-the-play, or of the situation in which a boy plays the part of a girl playing the part of a boy (Julia, Jessica, Rosalind, Viola, Imogen, Perdita). And the Elizabethan apparently enjoyed a song, when it broke the continuity of the play, perhaps criticizing the performer's voice ("A mellifluous voice" [*Twelfth Night,* II. iii. 54]) before taking up the play again where he dropped it for the counterattraction of music. . . .

The inability of the Elizabethan theater to produce an illusion of actuality was wholly to the good, as modern experimental theaters have shown. At a standard presentation of Ibsen, the audience remain passively receptive, whilst in another, two-dimensional world, beyond the orchestra pit, within a picture frame, and behind footlights, the actors create a vivid illusion of actual life. In the Elizabethan or the modern experimental theater, there is no illusion of actual life; but the audience are vividly aware of acting in progress and the communication, through their co-operative goodwill, of a work of dramatic art. If the one type of production is more realistic, the other is essentially more real.

Shakespeare, despite an occasional grumble at the inadequacy of his "wooden O" (*Henry V,* Prologue, 1. 13), wisely accepted the situation as it was, and turned it to good. Perhaps he would have welcomed the resources at Ibsen's command, but fortunately he was safe from temptation. I do not suggest that he had any conscious insight into the advantages of his own position; indeed, its strength lay partly in the unconscious acceptance, by both playwright and audience, of conditions as they found them. But Shakespeare did not merely acquiesce in those limitations which the physical conditions of his theater placed upon dramatic illusion; he actually exploited them, so that conventions in production are integrally related to conventions in the treatment of history, in the presentation of character, and in the verse. Moreover, he even draws attention to the play as play, overtly, in the dialogue itself, emphasizing verbally what the manner of production already implied: the co-existence of play world and real world in the minds of his audience. Perhaps when characters within a play referred to plays and players or noted that "All the world's a stage" (*As You Like It,* II. vii. 139), a certain piquancy in the situation may have been all that forced itself into conscious attention. Since they had never experienced naturalistic drama, the Elizabethans would not appreciate, as we do today, the nature of their own drama in distinction from it; just as it is impossible to appreciate a state of physical well-being until suffering has supplied us with a standard of comparison. But this double consciousness of play world and real world has the solid advantage of "distancing" a play, so that the words and deeds of which it consists may be critically weighed in the course of its performance. An Ibsen drama, attended to passively, is discussed afterwards in abstract terms; but in a Shakespearean play, criticism is an integral part of apprehension, and apprehension thereby becomes an activity of the whole mind. This is, of course, due mainly to the fact that the verse must be understood for a proper appreciation of the action; but the detachment necessary for attention to the verse is gained by insisting on the essential artificiality of the play world, and thus holding play world and real world before the mind simultaneously yet without confusion. Such an attitude has the advantage of accepting and exploiting the situation as it really is, whereas naturalism must engage in a constant effort to delude the audience into taking for actuality what they are bound to know, in their moments of critical alertness, to be only a stage performance. To gain a hearing, naturalism destroys the critical awareness necessary for appreciation; it is hardly surprising that a method thus divided against itself has produced little of permanent value.

When Malvolio appears before Olivia's household, cross-gartered and in "the trick of singularity" (*Twelfth Night,* II. v. 164), Signor Fabian has an interesting comment: "If this were played upon a stage now, I could condemn it as an improbable fiction" (III. iv. 140). It is, of course, an improbable fiction, and Shakespeare is employing a common enough literary device to cope with it. There are a great many novelists whose characters exclaim: "Why, it's just like a novel!" This sort of remark carries more than one layer of suggestion. Superficially it makes an improbable situation more plausible. If the characters displayed no consciousness of its improbability, we should be left with a rankling doubt; but since they react as we do to the situation, we are able to accept its improbability and incorporate it into the world of fiction. At the same time, whatever illusion may have been created has now been broken through: Shakespeare's mention of "playing upon a stage" forcibly reminds his audience of the nature of the spectacle before them. A naturalistic writer plays with fire when he attempts this sort of thing; but in the Elizabethan theater, with an audience continually aware of the two worlds of fiction and reality side by side, the effect is at the same time to justify an improbable situation and to underline the essential unreality of the play world. This latter function is much the more important: Shakespeare was not sufficiently concerned for probability and consistency to have inserted Fabian's comment merely for the sake of verisimilitude. It occurs at a significant juncture when the baiting of Malvolio is about to be carried to extremes. The passage continues:

Sir To.: His very genius hath taken the infection of the device, man.
Mar.: Nay, pursue him now, lest the device take air and taint.
Fab.: Why, we shall make him mad indeed.
Mar.: The house will be the quieter.
Sir To.: Come, we'll have him in a dark room and bound. . . .

(III. iv. 142)

The Victorians, who sympathized with Malvolio's sufferings to the extent of creating him a tragic hero, and who disdained the Elizabethan crudity which could enjoy Sir Toby's horseplay, failed to perceive that the Elizabethans were not in the habit of mistaking their comedies for real life. Shakespeare erected, through Fabian, a plain enough notice for his audience and for the Victorians too, if they had taken trouble with his text. We are reminded that the play is only a play, just when the reminder is needed to enable us to enjoy the comedy of Malvolio's imprisonment. The original audience would take such a hint unconsciously, but the Victorians, cut off from the popular tradition, preferred to discover the tragedy which Shakespeare was so careful not to write.

This explanation of Shakespeare's deeper—and surely unconscious —intention may seem far-fetched, and would never have occurred to me had I considered only the passage from *Twelfth Night.* But elsewhere there are similar reminders of the play as play without any ostensible design of rendering plausible an improbable incident. Indeed, in *Love's Labour's Lost,* the immediate intention is diametrically opposite: to excuse a naturalistic departure from the normal theatrical habit of ending a light comedy with wedding bells. *Love's Labour's Lost* is the most artificial of Shakespeare's comedies; the only note of ungarbled seriousness occurs at the end, when Biron is condemned to "jest a twelve-month in an hospital" (V. ii. 881), as a cure for levity and a preliminary to marriage. The unusual task imposed by Rosaline upon her knight breaks incongruously into the abstract gaiety of a simplified play world, bearing a sharp reminder of suffering and sorrow, ingredients of the real world hitherto unheeded through five acts of artificial wit-combat. This bitter reminder of the real world is underlined and at the same time distanced by the ensuing remarks of Biron and the King:

> *Biron:* Our wooing doth not end like an old play;
> Jack hath not Jill: these ladies' courtesy
> Might well have made our sport a comedy.
> *King:* Come, sir, it wants a twelvemonth and a day,
> And then 'twill end.
> *Biron:* That's too long for a play.
>
> (V. ii. 884)

The young Shakespeare, commenting in public on his technique, re-inforces the dual consciousness of play world and real world in the minds of his audience. A play so artificial may end quite appropriately with a reference from within to its own true nature. But, coming immediately after the hospital theme, this passage serves a more delicate purpose. With its reminder of reality, as distinguished from the play world, it underlines the reference to human suffering by taking us back to the real world where it is to be encountered. At the same time, by making explicit the nature of the play as play, it pre-serves a threatened poise: we remember that it is a stage personage only who is to "jest a twelvemonth in an hospital" and that personal sympathy would be misplaced. The intellectual position of the comedy has been strengthened, whilst its "artificiality" has been satisfactorily restored.

In plot and setting, *As You Like It* is every whit as artificial as *Love's Labour's Lost*. There is the same movement of lovers in pat-terned pairs (with two temporary triangles as an added complication in the later play); and the Masque of Hymen completes a general, if superficial, resemblance to the modern "musical comedy." The dia-logue is easy and relatively mature: Rosalind's prose in the Forest of Arden is so natural-seeming that as a character she "comes alive" mainly by this means; but Shakespeare is the more careful to provide a balance of artificiality in his verse and to indicate through his verse technique the varying degrees of actuality to which we are expected to adjust ourselves. This explains the antiphonal echoing of phrases between Orlando and Duke Senior, when the former bursts in upon the exiles with his demand for hospitality:

> *Orl.:* . . . If ever you have look'd on better days,
> If ever been where bells have knoll'd to church,
> If ever sat at any good man's feast,
> If ever from your eyelids wiped a tear
> And know what 'tis to pity and be pitied, ...
>   *Duke S.:* True is it that we have seen better days,
> And have with holy bell been knoll'd to church
> And sat at good men's feasts and wiped our eyes
> Of drops that sacred pity hath engender'd: . . . .
>
> (*As You Like It,* II. vii. 113)

This careful pattern of question and answer distances and tones down a scene where otherwise emotion might run too high. The tendency throughout is to pass lightly over whatever has the potentiality of heightened emotion, in order, presumably, to keep the intellect unclouded and to concentrate serious attention upon certain themes: court *versus* country, literary pastoral and the clodhopping rustic, tradition and innovation in rural economy. And so the love tangle resolves itself at a level of actuality similar to the average Gilbert and Sullivan opera. The lovers' repetitive phrases have the effect of "Three little maids from school":

> *Sil.:* It is to be all made of sight and tears;
> And so am I for Phebe.
>   *Phe.:* And I for Ganymede.
>   *Orl.:* And I for Rosalind.
>   *Ros.:* And I for no woman.
>
> (V. ii. 90)

In the next scene, the lovers pair off appropriately, and Rosalind is reunited to her father mostly in rhyme and as an integral part of the Masque of Hymen.

Apart from such obvious instances in which verse technique is used to distance the dramatic experience, it would be possible to grade all the verse in an ascending scale of artificiality, from the broken, vigorous dialogue of Duke Frederick to the near-burlesque of Silvius and Phebe. Duke Frederick has the sort of verse which develops in the tragedies:

> She is too subtle for thee; and her smoothness,
> Her very silence and her patience
> Speak to the people, and they pity her.
> Thou art a fool: she robs thee of thy name;

And thou wilt show more bright and seem more virtuous
When she is gone. Then open not thy lips:
Firm and irrevocable is my doom
Which I have passed upon her; she is banish'd.

(I. iii. 79)

Contrast:

> *Sil.:* Sweet Phebe, do not scorn me; do not, Phebe;
> Say that you love me not, but say not so
> In bitterness. The common executioner,
> Whose heart the accustom'd sight of death makes hard,
> Falls not the axe upon the humbled neck
> But first begs pardon: will you sterner be
> Than he that dies and lives by bloody drops?

(III. v. 1)

This is rhythmically more regular; the fourth and sixth lines have the pointless inversions of a strained "poetic" style; and the conceit has a certain obvious ingenuity typically Petrarchan. Between the extremes that I have quoted, lies a wide range of delicately perceptible differences in style, all indicating degrees of remoteness from actuality. At this time Shakespeare seems to have been serious in prose—there is more prose than verse in *As You Like It*—and to have used verse mainly to emphasize the conventional. This view of the matter is borne out in a significant remark of Jaques. Orlando enters and addresses Rosalind, who, as Ganymede, has been effectively ridiculing Jaques' melancholy:

> *Orl.:* Good day and happiness, dear Rosalind!
> *Jaq.:* Nay, then, God be wi' you, an you talk in blank verse.

(IV. i. 30)

The incident is, I suppose, explicable in naturalistic terms: Orlando utters an involuntary blank verse line, and the cynical Jaques seizes upon it to make his escape with an implied sneer against the lover. But, in any event, the mention of blank verse by a character draws attention to the play as play, in the same way as the remarks of Fabian and Biron, already discussed. Jaques' Parthian shot goes farther, however, by associating blank verse with the conventions of fashionable wooing, and thus suggesting that the play's artificiality is especially constituted by the verse. We have seen that this is, in fact, true of *As You Like It*.

Deliberate emphasis upon the unreality of the play world is uncommon nowadays. It is still, however, an habitual device of the Marx brothers, those excellent Hollywood comedians, who combine the wildest nonsense with a delicate satirical probing of the defective values in our modern civilization. Their methods are purely conventional, and they require above everything an alert audience, ready to grasp at every word and each significant gesture. It would be fatal for their purpose if the audience were to become emotionally involved in the thin line of romantic story which holds their performance together. In their best film, *Animal Crackers,* which appeared some years ago, there are two direct reminders of the film as film. Groucho forgets the name of the character he represents, and turning to the audience, demands a program: this is complicated by the reference back from film to "legitimate" stage, since programs are not provided in the motion picture theater. At another point in the film he reminds us after a feeble pun, that "You can't expect all the jokes to be good." The effect is the same as in Shakespeare; it reinforces the double consciousness of play world and real world, and at the same time it distances the play as play and produces intimacy with the audience for the actor as actor rather than as character.

It has already been observed that the acting of female parts by boys was further complicated by the frequency with which the story demanded a male disguise. It is usually said that the boy would welcome relief for a time from the embarrassment of his unaccustomed garments and would probably act the better for being unencumbered. Since the investigation of Elizabethan theatrical conditions opened a new field of conjecture, "practical" explanations of this kind have been carried to excess. A boy would soon learn to manage his skirts without thinking of them: girls do, and the talent is unlikely to be inherited. It is better to seek explanations in the nature of Shakespeare's sources and in the psychology of an audience to which the principle of multiconsciousness applies. Probably the situation of "boy playing girl playing boy" pleased in its suggestion of multiple planes of reality. It would, of course, be a pleasure entirely dependent upon the dual consciousness of play world and real world. I have seen, at a concert-party performance, a female impersonator (i.e., a man who habitually plays women's parts) playing the part of a woman in man's clothes. A popular audience clearly recognized and enjoyed the unusual situation. Cleopatra's objection to a Roman triumph:

> . . . I shall see
> Some squeaking Cleopatra boy my greatness
> I' the posture of a whore,
>
> (*Antony and Cleopatra,* V. ii. 219)

effects through dialogue a precisely similar complication in the planes of reality. Also, as a direct reference to acting, it performs the same function as the other passages I have considered, bringing forcibly to mind the duality of play world and real world. This passage is especially remarkable, since it occurs in a tragedy and at a moment of great emotional intensity. Moreover, *Antony and Cleopatra* comes at the end of the tragic period, when Shakespeare has learned all there is to learn about his art. An alert and critically detached audience is implied, and an attitude to tragedy very different from that to which we are accustomed.

Children are always fascinated by the notion of infinite regression. I remember a certain biscuit-tin which always gave me, as a small boy, a distinct sense of the "numinous." It had on it a picture of a boy holding a tin just like the real one, and on the tin the boy held was another picture of a boy holding a tin. The childish question "And who made God?" betrays a similar interest. The concern of Shakespeare and the Elizabethans with "planes of reality" shows not, of course, their childishness, but a healthy preoccupation with the questions men naturally ask when undeterred by the advances of civilization. The "play-within-the play," as in *A Midsummer Night's Dream* and *Hamlet,* or the device by which the main play is presented before a stage audience, as in *The Taming of the Shrew* or Kyd's *The Spanish Tragedy,* further illustrates the same preoccupation. An audience watches a stage audience watching a play and so becomes simultaneously aware of three planes of reality. Shakespeare carries the matter farther by his frequent metaphorical use of play and players. To Jaques "All the world's a stage . . ." (*As You Like It,* II. vii. 139), and to Macbeth

> Life's but a walking shadow, a poor player
> That struts and frets his hour upon the stage
> And then is heard no more.
>
> (*Macbeth,* V. v. 24)

Contemplation of regression, which produced the parlor games of Viola-Cesario and Hamlet's Mousetrap, has here assumed philosophical significance. The solidity of the first plane of reality, the plane of our terrestrial life, is seen to be illusory. It is significant that in the last fully Shakespearean play the planes of reality appear with most complexity. Prospero says of his Masque of Ceres:

> These our actors,
> As I foretold you, were all spirits and
> Are melted into air, into thin air.
> (The Tempest, IV. i. 148)

"On the actual stage," observes Dr. Tillyard, "the masque is executed by players pretending to be spirits, pretending to be real actors, pretending to be supposed goddesses and rustics." And immediately after the revels end, Prospero reminds us that, as his spirit actors have vanished, so

> The cloud-capped towers, the gorgeous palaces,
> The solemn temples, the great globe itself,
> Yea, all which it inherit, shall dissolve
> And, like this insubstantial pageant faded,
> Leave not a rack behind. We are such stuff
> As dreams are made on, and our little life
> Is rounded with a sleep.
> (IV. i. 152)

The world is seen as transient, and therefore insubstantial, whilst a reference to the dream world adds a further complication. It seems as if Shakespeare had deliberately crowded into a few moments of his last play all that can suggest the manifold mystery of experience. Both Jaques and Macbeth employed the play metaphor to express an attitude of cynicism: in Jaques, the cynicism which was a recognized ingredient of contemporary fashionable melancholy; in Macbeth, the cynicism of a hardened sinner, who, having rejected the laws of God and man, cut off from all sympathetic contact with the world outside himself, has become incapable of apprehending meaning in that world. But Prospero's speech begins:

> You do look, my son, in a moved sort,
> As if you were dismay'd: be cheerful, sir.
> (IV. i. 146)

To Prospero, whose "beating mind" (IV. i. 163) achieves at this moment an insight into reality, the transitoriness of this world is matter for cheerfulness. We are therefore justified in pushing the parallel farther, and remembering that, though the actors have faded, as invisible spirits they still exist; and that from sleep there is awakening. Sleep, in Shakespeare, is always regarded as remedial:

> Sleep that knits up the ravell'd sleave of care,
> The death of each day's life, sore labour's bath,
> Balm of hurt minds, great nature's second course,
> Chief nourisher in life's feast. . . .
>
> (*Macbeth,* II. ii. 37)

If, as seems likely, Prospero in his great speech voices Shakespeare's own conclusions, then this passage, far from proclaiming the agnosticism of a world-weary artist, clearly asserts, at the culmination of a lifelong and unique poetic experience, the existence of an eternal order behind the relatively trivial and impermanent phenomenal world, as the "real" world exists in comparative stability behind the shadow world of the theater. The survival of human persons after their sleep of death is incidentally implied. The final organization of Shakespeare's experience is thus functionally related to the dual consciousness of play world and real world, characteristic of Elizabethan playhouse psychology. If Shakespeare put the whole of life into his plays, he reciprocally interpreted life in terms of the theater.

ON SHAKESPEARE'S HISTORY PLAYS

THE NINETEENTH-CENTURY critics wrote comparatively few studies of the English history plays as a group. However, in the general surveys of Shakespeare the history plays were usually regarded as forming a national epic whose hero was the English nation. In our own time the history plays have been seen as being controlled by the Elizabethan philosophy of history and by the Elizabethan concept of the historical period depicted in them. The modern view gives them a higher degree of organic unity than the old idea of their constituting an epic in which the national spirit is expressed. They now seem to form a pattern of political crime and retribution with an immediate significance for Shakespeare's own day in their reminder of the dangers of the national disunity which human nature is constantly threatening to bring about.

E. M. W. TILLYARD
1889-1962

E. M. W. Tillyard was a scholar who used his scholarship for the purpose of criticism, in which he was as outstanding as he was in scholarship. Characteristically, his *The Elizabethan World Picture* (1943), an important analysis of the Elizabethan outlook, was written as a result of his study preparatory to his *Shakespeare's History Plays* (1944), in which Tillyard applied to an interpretation of these dramas the Elizabethan concept of the hierarchical society as part of the cosmic scheme of things. This concept was also explored by, among others, Hardin Craig and Theodore Spencer. Tillyard's other books on Shakespeare are *Shakespeare's Last Plays* (1938), *Shakespeare's Problem Plays* (1950), and *The Nature of Comedy and Shakespeare* (1958).

In this extract Tillyard shows the Tudor myth of history underlying the history plays, according to which the violation of order with the deposition of Richard II brought retribution to England until Richmond, God's agent, restored order. This pattern had been perceived by Schlegel, but Tillyard, in revealing the use of cosmic analogies and of conventions derived from the morality tradition, gives a greater richness to it. The degree to which the cycle derives its unity from a master plan which Shakespeare followed in detail may be exaggerated by Tillyard, as has been charged by Robert A. Law and others, but there is no doubting that the cycle has an over-all unity derived from a view of history and of life which governs all of the plays in it.

SHAKESPEARE'S PATTERN OF HISTORY

TEN PLAYS OF the First Folio have English history as their theme. They are distributed in a curious regularity. First there is a sequence of four closely linked plays: the three parts of *Henry VI* and *Richard III*. There follows an isolated play, *King John*. Then comes a second

"Shakespeare's Pattern of History" is from *Shakespeare's History Plays* by E. M. W. Tillyard. Copyright 1946 by The Macmillan Company. Reprinted with the permission of The Macmillan Company and Chatto & Windus Ltd.

sequence of four: *Richard II,* the two parts of *Henry IV,* and *Henry V.* And there is a second isolated play, *Henry VIII.* Disregarding the two isolated plays, we can say further that the two tetralogies make a single unit. Throughout the *Henry VI's* and *Richard III* Shakespeare links the present happenings with the past. We are never allowed to forget that, as Hall said in his preface, "King Henry the Fourth was the beginning and root of the great discord and division." For instance, in *1 Henry VI* the dying Mortimer says to his nephew, the future Duke of York:

> Henry the Fourth, grandfather to this king,
> Depos'd his nephew Richard, Edward's son,
> The first-begotten and the lawful heir
> Of Edward King, the third of that descent;
> During whose reign the Percies of the north,
> Finding his usurpation most unjust,
> Endeavour'd my advancement to the throne.

In *2 Henry VI* York, explaining his titles to Salisbury and Warwick, goes back to Edward III and his sons to the lucky number of seven, whom he solemnly enumerates, and fixes the mainspring of subsequent English history in the murder of Richard II:

> Edward the Black Prince died before his father
> And left behind him Richard, his only son:
> Who after Edward the Third's death reign'd as king,
> Till Henry Bolingbroke, Duke of Lancaster,
> The eldest son and heir of John of Gaunt,
> Crown'd by the name of Henry the Fourth,
> Seiz'd on the realm, depos'd the rightful king,
> Sent his poor queen to France, from whence she came,
> And him to Pomfret; where, as all you know,
> Harmless Richard was murder'd traiterously.

In *Richard III* Earl Rivers, awaiting execution in Pomfret Castle, links present with past by recalling the murder of Richard II:

> O Pomfret, Pomfret, O thou bloody prison,
> Fatal and ominous to noble peers!
> Within the guilty closure of thy walls
> Richard the Second here was hack'd to death.
> And for more slander of thy dismal seat
> We give thee up our guiltless blood to drink.

These are precisely the themes which Shakespeare repeated when he makes Henry V before Agincourt pray to God,

> Not to-day, O Lord,
> O not to-day, think not upon the fault
> My father made in compassing the crown.
> I Richard's body have interred new,
> And on it have bestow'd more contrite tears
> Than from it issued forced drops of blood.

Further, Shakespeare seems himself to declare the continuity of the two tetralogies when the Chorus at the end of *Henry V* makes a link with the next reign and refers back to the earlier written sequence.

> Henry the Sixth, in infant bands crown'd king
>   Of France and England, did this king succeed;
> Whose state so many had the managing,
>   That they lost France and made his England bleed:
> Which oft our stage hath shown; and for their sake
>   In your fair minds let this acceptance take.

The last line and a half mean: let the good success of my plays about *Henry VI* influence you in favour of the play you have just witnessed, *Henry V*. Shakespeare not only implies the continuity of the two tetralogies but expresses satisfaction with the one he had written in his youth. That he should, as it were, accept responsibility for all eight plays at the end of the last written one is important because it helps to confirm what even without this confirmation should be evident: that Shakespeare had in his early years disposed what for the Elizabethans was the most exciting and significant stretch of English history into a pattern; a pattern of such magnitude that it needed the space of eight plays and about ten years in the execution. The outlines of the pattern he derived from Hall, but the sustained energy of mind needed to develop them he got from his own ambitions and the example of other works, particularly of the *Mirror for Magistrates*.

There is no need to give details of Shakespeare's debt to Hall, as these can be found in articles by Edleen Begg and W. Gordon Zeeveld. But it is likely that Shakespeare got the hint of organising Hall's material into two tetralogies by taking for his culminating points the two reigns to which Hall had stuck specifically dramatic labels (the *Victorious acts of Henry V* and the *Tragical doings of*

Richard III) and which he had treated in a heightened way exceptional to the rest of his chronicle. Shakespeare can end with the reign
of Richard III because Richard's death both resolves the plot and
fulfils the title of Hall's history: *The Union of the two noble and
illustre Families of Lancaster and York.*

Why Shakespeare wrote the second half first we can only guess.
Perhaps, like others, he thought that vice was easier to picture than
virtue, hell than paradise, and that it would be safer to spend his
present energies on pictures of chaos and a great villain, leaving
the more difficult picture of princely perfection to his maturity. But
there is a very different explanation of what is after all a curious pro-
cedure. That it is hazardous and revolutionary should not preclude
its being seriously considered. In the nature of things so fluent an
author as Shakespeare probably wrote in his youth much that has
perished. He may well have written early versions of the plays of the
second tetralogy, *Richard II, Henry IV,* and *Henry V,* now lost but
recast in the plays we have. Further, the *Famous Victories of Henry V*
may well be an abridgement—a kind of dramatic Lamb's Tale—of
Shakespeare's early plays on the reigns of Henry IV and Henry V.
With the first version of the plays dealing with history from Henry VI
onwards Shakespeare would have been sufficiently content to for-
bear revision. And he is not ashamed to refer to them in his epilogue
to *Henry V.*

Shakespeare's first debt then in his earlier tetralogy is to Hall;
but this must not cause us to overlook the many different strains
Shakespeare here unites. It is indeed this masterly inclusiveness that
raises to greatness a series of plays which in the execution are sometimes immature and ineffective. I will recapitulate these strains and
illustrate them from the actual plays.

First, this tetralogy to an equal extent with the later tetralogy and
more powerfully than the most civilised of the Chronicle Plays shows
Shakespeare aware of order or degree. Behind all the confusion of
civil war, and the more precious and emphatic because of the confusion, is the belief that the world is a part of the eternal law and that
earthly mutability, as in Spenser's last cantos, is itself a part of a
greater and permanent pattern. Further, human events as well as
being subject to the eternal law are part of an elaborate system
of correspondences and hence the more firmly woven into the total
web of things. The very first words of the first of the four plays

will illustrate. They are spoken by the Duke of Bedford at the funeral procession of his brother Henry V.

> Hung be the heavens with black, yield day to night,
> Comets, importing change of times and states,
> Brandish your crystal tresses in the sky
> And with them scourge the bad revolting stars
> That have consented unto Henry's death!

Here the stars that have "consented unto," which means "conspired to procure," the death of Henry are intended to be the counterpart in the heavens of the English nobility who have already fallen into discord. The universe, in fact, was so much of a unity that the skies had to re-enact the things that happened in the human polity. It is the same correspondence that occurs in the speech on "degree" in *Troilus and Cressida*.

> But when the planets
> In evil mixture to disorder wander,
> What plagues and what portents, what mutiny,
> What raging of the sea, shaking of earth,
> Commotion in the winds, frights changes horrors,
> Divert and crack, rend and deracinate
> The unity and married calm of states
> Quite from their fixture!

In *Troilus and Cressida* Ulysses is maintaining the need for degree, and in *Henry VI* Bedford assumes as the righteous norm his brother Henry V, the strong upholder of order in his own kingdom.

The same play, though like the rest mainly occupied with revolt and disorder and misfortune, finds place for a positive example of the virtue of degree. It is where Henry VI, now in Paris for his coronation, accepts the homage of Talbot and rewards him with an earldom.

> *Tal.* My gracious prince and honourable peers,
> Hearing of your arrival in this realm,
> I have awhile given truce unto my wars,
> To do my duty to my sovereign:
> In sign whereof this arm, that hath reclaim'd
> To your obedience fifty fortresses,
> Twelve cities and seven wall'd towns of strength,
> Besides five hundred prisoners of esteem,

> Lets fall his sword before your highness' feet,
> And with submissive loyalty of heart
> Ascribes the glory of his conquest got
> First to my God and then unto your grace.
>   *Hen.* Welcome, brave captain and victorious lord!
> When I was young, as yet I am not old,
> I do remember how my father said
> A stouter champion never handled sword.
> Long since we were resolved of your truth,
> Your faithful service and your toil in war;
> Yet never have you tasted our reward
> Or been reguerdon'd with so much as thanks,
> Because till now we never saw your face.
> Therefore, stand up, and for these good deserts
> We here create you Earl of Shrewsbury;
> And in our coronation take your place.

Any Elizabethan would have perceived that the scene was a deliberate setting up of an ideal norm. Every detail suggests an exact and orderly disposition. God, the king, the peers, the captives are ranged in their degrees. Talbot, the last created earl, will take his proper place in the coronation. The very numbers of the things or persons captured suggest precise significances. Henry, in contrast to his usual practice, does exactly the right thing; and, in violent contrast to the facts of history (for he was only nine months old when Henry V died) is momentarily animated by the judgements of the perfect king, his father.

But the most effective statement of the principle of order occurs in the passage which largely by accident is the most famous of all three Henry VI plays, Henry's pathetic soliloquy where he regrets that he was born a king and not a shepherd.

> O God! methinks it were a happy life
> To be no better than a homely swain;
> To sit upon a hill, as I do now,
> To carve out dials quaintly, point by point,
> Thereby to see the minutes how they run,
> How many make the hour full complete;
> How many hours bring about the day;
> How many days will finish up the year;
> How many years a mortal man may live.
> When this is known, then to divide the times:

> So many hours must I tend my flock;
> So many hours must I take my rest;
> So many hours must I contemplate;
> So many hours must I sport myself;
> So many days my ewes have been with young;
> So many weeks ere the poor fools will ean;
> So many years ere I shall shear the fleece:
> So minutes hours days months and years,
> Pass'd over to the end they were created,
> Would bring white hairs unto a quiet grave.
> Ah, what a life were this, how sweet, how lovely!

It is a beautiful passage, justly famous. But it is famous partly because it is so easily anthologised and partly because it is almost omitted from the *True Tragedy of Richard Duke of York,* once thought to be the play on which Shakespeare founded the third part of *Henry VI* and now proved to be a pirated version of it. The passage thus appeared to be a clear addition to the old play, hence genuine Shakespeare, hence to be read without embarrassment. Actually its full meaning, its full pathos and irony, are quite hidden when it is taken as a mere Shakespearean afterthought, fit for a volume of beauties. The context is the Battle of Towton, where the Lancastrians suffered their bloodiest defeat and which Shakespeare selects from all the battles as most emphatically illustrating the full horrors of civil war. Henry has been "chidden from the field" by his terrible queen and the fierce Clifford, because he brings bad luck; but immediately after his soliloquy he witnesses two spectacles of the utmost horror, first a son discovering that he has killed his father and then a father discovering that he has killed his son. Henry's speech must be judged before this background of chaos. It signifies not, as naturally thought of out of its context, a little bit of lyrical escapism but Henry's yearning for an ordered life. This ordered life of the shepherd is a pitifully small thing compared with the majestic order he as a king should have been able to impose. Yet it stands for the great principle of degree, while bringing out Henry's personal tragedy: his admirable intentions and his utter inability to carry them out.

Another most explicit version of the same thing is the contrast between the lawlessness of Jack Cade and the impeccable moderation and discipline of the Kentish squire Iden, in *2 Henry VI.* Cade openly

boasts, "But then we are in order when we are most out of order."
All degree is to be levelled away:

> There shall be in England seven halfpenny loaves sold for a penny; the
> three-hooped pot shall have ten hoops; and I will make it a felony to
> drink small beer: all the realm shall be in common; and in Cheapside
> shall my palfrey go to grass . . . there shall be no money; all shall eat and
> drink on my score; and I will apparel them all in one livery that they
> may agree like brothers and worship me their lord.

Iden, who catches the fugitive Jack Cade in his garden and kills
him, is a flat symbolic character, beautifully contrasted with the
realism of the rebels. He is entirely content with his own station
in the social hierarchy, as smug as any eighteenth century moralist
over the virtues of the middle station of life. He introduces himself
to us by this soliloquy in his garden:

> Lord, who would live turmoiled in the court,
> Who may enjoy such quiet walks as these?
> This small inheritance my father left me
> Contenteth me, and worth a monarchy.
> I seek not to wax great by others' waning;
> Or gather wealth I care not, with what envy:
> Sufficeth that I have maintains my state
> And sends the poor well pleased from my gate.

This speech for all its smugness is perfectly serious in giving the
norm of order, upset by Cade.

As powerful as the theme of order in the tetralogy is the continual
insistence on cause and effect in the unfolding of history. Shakespeare
adopts the whole teaching of Hall and of the *Mirror for Magistrates*.
The passages about the death of Richard II quoted above serve to
illustrate this just as well as to illustrate the conceptual continuity
of the two tetralogies. But again and again, at any great happening,
Shakespeare seeks to bring out the concatenation of events. Thus in
2 Henry VI Gloucester, about to be murdered, sees his death the
cause of great misery to the land and of ruin to his king. He says
to Henry:

> I know their complot is to have my life,
> And if my death might make this island happy
> And prove the period of their tyranny,

> I would expend it with all willingness.
> But mine is made the prologue to their play;
> For thousands more, that yet suspect no peril,
> Will not conclude their plotted tragedy.

And, referring to his own services as Protector of the realm in Henry's minority, he adds:

> Ah, thus King Henry throws away his crutch
> Before his legs be firm to bear his body.
> Thus is the shepherd beaten from thy side
> And wolves are gnarling who shall gnaw thee first.
> Ah, that my fear were false, ah, that it were!
> For, good King Henry, thy decay I fear.

Again Margaret of Anjou is not merely a strong-minded and troublesome woman who prolongs the civil wars by her tenacity and fulfils the dramatic part of avenging fury; she has her precise place in the chain of events. Her marriage with Henry VI was from the first a disaster and brought to a head the troubles between Lancaster and York which otherwise would have lain quiet. Edward IV, in front of York, addresses these words to her about Henry's marriage:

> And had he match'd according to his state,
> He might have kept that glory to this day;
> But when he took a beggar to his bed
> And grac'd thy poor sire with his bridal day,
> Even then that sunshine brew'd a shower for him,
> That wash'd his father's fortunes forth of France
> And heap'd sedition on his crown at home.
> For what has broach'd this tumult but thy pride?
> Hadst thou been meek, our title still had slept;
> And we, in pity for the gentle king,
> Had slipp'd our claim until another age.

Many examples, and there are a great many, would be tedious. It is enough to mention the most elaborate of all. The ghosts that terrify and comfort the sleeps of Richard and Richmond on the night before Bosworth are not just enemies or friends but a convergence of causes leading to the defeat of Richard and to the issue of England's fortunes into prosperity through the union of the red rose and the white.

Shakespeare is more interested in the chain of cause and effect than in the ideas that history repeats itself and hence that we may apply to the present the exemplary lessons of the past. But these motives are not absent. For instance when in *Richard II* Queen Margaret breaks in on Richard making trouble with Queen Elizabeth's kindred she calls down curses on her enemies to correspond with the troubles she has had herself, as if this repetition of history were a probability. Addressing herself to Elizabeth, wife of Edward IV, she says:

> Edward thy son, which now is Prince of Wales,
> For Edward my son, which was Prince of Wales
> Die in his youth by like untimely violence;
> Thyself a queen, for me that was a queen,
> Outlive thy glory like my wretched self;
> Long mayst thou live to wail thy children's loss,
> And see another, as I see thee now,
> Deck'd in thy rights, as thou art stall'd in mine!

And behind all the unfolding of civil war there is the great lesson (implied always and rarely stated) that the present time must take warning from the past and utterly renounce all civil dissension. Here for instance is Sir William Lucy's comment on York's refusal to help Talbot on account of his jealousy of Somerset:

> Thus while the vulture of sedition
> Feeds in the bosom of such great commanders,
> Sleeping neglection doth betray to loss
> The conquest of our scarce cold conqueror,
> That ever living man of memory,
> Henry the Fifth. Whiles they each other cross,
> Lives, honours, lands, and all hurry to loss.

There is a short scene (II. 3) in *Richard III,* the kind of scene that is omitted from modern performance because it does not advance the plot and apparently can be spared, which in a brief space epitomises a number of Tudor commonplaces on history. It is a choric comment by three citizens on the death of Edward IV. The third citizen is a pessimist, who "looks to see a troublous world" and quotes the adage,

> Woe to that land that's govern'd by a child!

The other two are more optimistic, and the first citizen hopes that history will repeat itself in making the early years of Edward V prosperous like those of Henry VI when his uncles Bedford and Gloucester "enrich'd the land with politic grave counsel." But the third citizen denies the analogy: Edward's uncles are not at all like Henry VI's. He fears the worst, but adds

> All may be well. But if God sort it so,
> 'Tis more than we deserve or I expect.

In other words, the troubles of a country are God's punishment for its sins. His mixed sentiments are prophetic: God both punished the land and caused all to be well through the Earl of Richmond. Shakespeare is perfectly clear in making Richmond the emissary of God.

It is in the last two plays of the tetralogy that the prevalent high theme of the *Mirror for Magistrates,* the fall of an eminent and erring statesman, is most evident. In the first two plays Talbot and Humphrey of Gloucester are too individual and too virtuous to fit into the norm of that poem. But in the third play the tragedy of Richard Duke of York is solemnly enacted, and in *Richard III* the motive of the *Mirror* occurs with great power. Clarence perishes for his false oath, and in the fate of Buckingham Shakespeare may actually allude to the most famous portions of the *Mirror*: the contributions of Sackville. At the beginning of the fourth scene of the fourth act Queen Margaret says:

> So, now prosperity begins to mellow
> And drop into the rotten mouth of death.
> Here in these confines slily have I lurk'd
> To watch the warring of mine adversaries.
> A dire induction am I witness to,
> And will to France, hoping the consequence
> Will prove as bitter, black, and tragical.

The use of the words *induction* and *tragical* may well contain a hint of Sackville's *Induction* and his *Tragedy of Buckingham;* especially as Buckingham's fall is the theme of the next scene. And Buckingham confesses to his sin of treachery and to a false oath and admits the justice of his fate—

> Wrong hath but wrong, and blame the due of blame—

in a spirit entirely in accord with the morality of the *Mirror for Magistrates*.

So much for Shakespeare's use in his tetralogy of the conceptions of world order and the processes of history: the ideas that appear so little in the Chronicle Plays and seem to have been the property of a select and educated class, that ally Shakespeare with Chapman and Daniel and Sir John Hayward. His use of them illustrates the academic side of himself that was so prominent in his early years. It is to his History Plays what the Plautine form is to the *Comedy of Errors* and the Senecan and Ovidian elements and conventions to *Titus Andronicus*.

But Shakespeare was not only academic in his first historical tetralogy: he was a popular dramatist too. Not that the populace would have objected to his superior opinions on history; they would have been willing to be impressed if they also got the things they expected: which they most certainly did. And first, for this popular material, there is what I have called sometimes Higden and sometimes Holinshed: the mediation of sheer fact. For though Shakespeare did see history in an intelligible pattern he compressed into a popular and lively form an astonishing quantity of sheer historical fact. He can indeed be nearly as informative as the author of the *True Tragedy of Richard III*. This, for instance, is how York begins the genealogical statement on which he claims his title to the throne in *2 Henry VI*:

> Edward the Third, my lords, had seven sons:
> The first, Edward the Black Prince, Prince of Wales;
> The second, William of Hatfield, and the third,
> Lionel Duke of Clarence; next to whom
> Was John of Gaunt, the Duke of Lancaster;
> The fifth was Edmund Langley, Duke of York;
> The sixth was Thomas of Woodstock, Duke of Gloucester;
> William of Windsor was the seventh and last.

There seems to have been a genuine popular demand for this sheer information. And beyond presenting this unmitigated fact Shakespeare succeeded conspicuously in making palatable to his public a greater bulk of chronicle material than other dramatists were able to do.

Shakespeare also satisfied the popular taste in setting forth the great popular political theme, the horror of civil war, and in giving his plays the required chauvinist tone. Joan of Arc is a bad enough woman, Margaret of Anjou an intriguing enough queen; an Englishman is worth a sufficient number of Frenchmen; Frenchmen are sufficiently boastful and fickle, to satisfy every popular requirement.

Finally, Shakespeare occasionally satisfies the taste for the startling but irrelevant anecdote; the pieces of sensation that pleased the people but could be spared from the play. There is for example the scene in *1 Henry VI* (II. 3) where the Countess of Auvergne plots Talbot's death by inviting him to her house and he prevents her by summoning his men by a blast from his horn; and the scene in *2 Henry VI* (I. 4) where Bolingbroke the conjurer calls up spirits at the command of the Duchess of Gloucester.

In sum Shakespeare in his first effort could beat the writers of Chronicle Plays on their own ground.

Among the strains found in Tudor history was that akin to Froissart and shown in the work of More and Cavendish: a dramatic liveliness and a closeness to the event. This strain appears in Shakespeare's first historical tetralogy; but how much he owed to Berner's Froissart and to the lives of Richard III and Wolsey, and how much to his own dramatic inclinations, it is impossible to assess. However, it matters little whence he got the strain, but much more that it should be there. It is of course precisely this strain that the disintegrators have been after whenever they have wished to fish out any fragments of true Shakespeare from the general wreckage; and they have found it, for instance, in the first declaration of the feud between red and white rose in *1 Henry VI* and in the Jack Cade scenes in *2 Henry VI*. There is nothing wrong in praising these scenes and calling them typical of Shakespeare. But it is very wrong indeed to emphasise them and to make them the norm by which to judge the whole tetralogy. They enrich the tetralogy but on a balance they are exceptional to it.

To redress this wrong emphasis we must think of yet another strain in this tetralogy: that of formalism and stylisation. It is something archaic, inherited from the Morality Play. But it is the very feature through which the essential life of the poetry is expressed. When we encounter an unnatural and stylised balance of incident or an artificial pattern of speech we must not think that here is merely an archaic survival: we must accept them as things having contemporary vitality and must make them the norm of the play. We must in fact be good Aristotelians, for the moment, and believe that the soul of the play is in plot rather than in character. The realism of the Jack Cade scenes is not their main point but a subsidiary enrichment. Their main point is to make half a pattern, the other half being implied by the blameless orderliness of Iden. We are apt to praise the Cade scenes for being realistic and jeer at Iden for being a dummy, when we should merge praise and blame into the appreciation of a piece of stylisation which includes the whole. Similarly Henry VI's pathetic piece of nostalgia as he sits on the molehill watching the Battle of Towton has been isolated into a piece of poetic and "human" writing in a boring and inhuman context. Actually it loses most of its virtue apart from the context; apart from the terrible scene of the father killing his son and the son killing his father. That scene embodies a traditional motive; for these acts had been chosen by the authors of the Homilies, by Hall, and by the authors of the *Mirror for Magistrates* as the clearest symbol of the horrors of civil war. Shakespeare's fathers and sons here are as flat characters as Iden; and they have no business to be anything else. They stand as great traditional types, in whom realism would be impious. They enact a tableau; though they speak they are not far off a dumb-show: and their flatness adds enormous point to the ineffective humanity of the weak king. The most moving of all the scenes in the tetralogy, the ghosts visiting the sleeps of Richard III and Richmond in *Richard III,* is perhaps the most rigidly patterned and most grossly unrealistic of any. What could be remoter from actuality than the juxtaposition of the two tents and the liturgical chantings of each ghost as it passes? But to object to this scene on these grounds is as stupid as to blame the *Eumenides* of Aeschylus for being deficient in the realistic psychology of the *Electra* of Euripides. When this principle has been grasped and accepted the tetralogy comes out a much more assured and solid affair than it is generally thought to be.

But if the Morality Play prompted the formality of Shakespeare's first tetralogy it also supplied a single pervasive theme; one which overrides but in no way interferes with the theme he derived from Hall. In none of the plays is there a hero: and one of the reasons is that there is an unnamed protagonist dominating all four. It is England, or in Morality terms Respublica. Just as London, which appears only in the prologue, is the hero of Wilson's *Three Lords and three Ladies of London* (itself more a Morality Play than a developed Elizabethan drama), so England, though she is now quite excluded as a character, is the true hero of Shakespeare's first tetralogy. She is brought near ruin through not being true to herself; yielding to French witchcraft and being divided in mind. But God, though he punishes her, pities her and in the end through his grace allows the suppressed good in her to assert itself and restore her to health. I reserve the details of this scheme till the sections on the separate plays. How in the first three plays of his second tetralogy Shakespeare developed and enriched the Respublica theme will be described in due course.

Finally Shakespeare reinforces the structural unity which the themes of the Morality and of Hall create, by sowing in one play the seeds that are to germinate in the next and by constant references back from a later play to an earlier. In *1 Henry VI* he gives us modestly but with sufficient emphasis the first clash of York and Lancaster and the rivalry of Cardinal Beaufort with the good Protector, Humphrey Duke of Gloucester, which are to be a prevailing theme of the second play. In *2 Henry VI* Margaret of Anjou is important, yet she is kept subordinate to other characters in readiness to develop into a major character in the third play. Again, York begins faintly in the first play, gathers force in the second, and is cut off in the third, while the ruthlessness and hypocrisy of Richard Crookback begin faintly in the second play, grow big in the third, and overreach themselves to destruction in the last.

For all the inequality of execution, the vast crowding in of historical incident (some of it inorganic), Shakespeare planned his first historical tetralogy greatly, reminding one of Hardy in the *Dynasts*. When we consider how deficient his fellow-dramatists were in the architectonic power, we can only conclude that this was one of the things with which he was conspicuously endowed by nature. Far from being the untidy genius, Shakespeare was in one respect a born classicist. . . .

However large the apparent differences in style between *Richard II* and *Henry IV,* these plays are connected with a network of cross-references. On the other hand, although *Richard II* may have been written not long after *King John,* the connections are fitful and unimportant. *Richard II* looks forward; and Shakespeare conceived his second tetralogy as one great unit.

The matter is important and calls for substantiation.

First and most important, Richard and Prince Hal are deliberately contrasted characters; Richard being the prince in appearance rather than in reality, Hal being the prince in reality whose appearance at first obscures the truth. Richard's emblem was the sun of royalty emerging from a cloud, a piece of symbolism to which Bolingbroke refers when Richard appears on the walls of Flint Castle:

> See, see, King Richard doth himself appear
> As doth the blushing discontented sun
> From out the fiery portal of the east,
> When he perceives the envious clouds are bent
> To dim his glory and to stain the track
> Of his bright passage to the occident.

But Richard did not live up to his emblem, for he allowed the clouds, his evil advisers, to obscure his proper glory. It is Prince Hal who adopts and justifies in himself the emblem, according to his own declaration at the end of the second scene of *1 Henry IV*:

> Yet herein will I imitate the sun,
> Who doth permit the base contagious clouds
> To smother up his beauty from the world,
> That, when he please again to be himself,
> Being wanted he may be more wonder'd at
> By breaking through the foul and ugly mists
> Of vapours that did seem to strangle him.

If this were the one possible cross-reference between *Richard II* and *1 Henry IV* we might doubt its authenticity; being one of many it can hardly not be intentional.

Secondly, the whole theme of insurrection and civil war as developed in the plays is continuous, as if conceived as a whole. Carlisle's speech in Westminster Hall, for instance, prophesying civil war if Bolingbroke is crowned proclaims its sequel in future plays.

> My Lord of Hereford here, whom you call king,
> Is a foul traitor to proud Hereford's king.
> And if you crown him, let me prophesy:
> The blood of English shall manure the ground,
> And future ages groan for this foul act;
> Peace shall go sleep with Turks and infidels,
> And in this seat of peace tumultuous wars
> Shall kin with kin and kind with kind confound;
> Disorder horror fear and mutiny
> Shall here inhabit, and this land be call'd
> The field of Golgotha and dead men's skulls.

If these lines in the first play of the tetralogy look forward, Henry's prayer before Agincourt in the last one, that God should not visit on him the death of Richard, looks right back.

Thirdly, the Percies figure in *Richard II* in a way that suggests that they will figure even more prominently in the future. Northumberland is the main executant of Henry's rise; and Richard, informed by Northumberland that he must go to Pomfret Castle, warns him that one day he will think no reward sufficient for his services:

> Northumberland, thou ladder wherewithal
> The mounting Bolingbroke ascends my throne,
> The time shall not be many hours of age
> More than it is, ere foul sin gathering head
> Shall break into corruption. Thou shalt think,
> Though he divide the realm and give thee half,
> It is too little, helping him to all;
> And he shall think that thou, which know'st the way
> To plant unrightful kings, will know again,
> Being ne'er so little urg'd, another way
> To pluck him headlong from the usurped throne.

When Hotspur is airing his grievances to Blunt before the battle of Shrewsbury he recalls Bolingbroke's promise that he had returned from exile for no further purpose than to claim the Duchy of Lancaster. This was the promise conveyed by Northumberland to Richard in Flint Castle in the previous play:

> His coming hither hath no further scope
> Than for his lineal royalties and to beg
> Enfranchisement immediate on his knees,
> Which on thy royal party granted once,
> His glittering arms he will commend to rust.

A casual remark made by Green to the queen that Worcester (Northumberland's brother, who does not figure in *Richard II* in person) has broken his staff of office and resigned his stewardship is caught up in *1 Henry IV*, when before Shrewsbury Worcester tells Henry IV

> For you my staff of office did I break
> In Richard's time.

Lastly, to cut short an argument that could easily be prolonged, King Henry in *2 Henry IV* actually quotes from *Richard II*. He reminds Warwick of the words Richard spoke to Northumberland when about to be taken to Pomfret, and proceeds to quote some of them:

> 'Northumberland, thou ladder by the which
> My cousin Bolingbroke ascends my throne,'
> (Though then, God knows, I had no such intent,
> But that necessity so bow'd the state
> That I and greatness were compell'd to kiss)
> 'The time shall come' thus did he follow it,
> 'The time will come, that foul sin gathering head
> Shall break into corruption'; so went on,
> Foretelling this same time's condition
> And the division of our amity.

Shakespeare would never have quoted from the History Play before last unless he had thought his sequence an organic whole. That he misquotes (as can be seen by comparing the original passage from *Richard II* just quoted) shows that he was more mindful of big than of little things.

If then the plays of the second tetralogy are so closely connected, we must treat them as a single organism. Confronted with different styles in *Richard II* and *Henry IV,* we shall have to refrain from calling the first archaic and the second suddenly and miraculously mature, but shall be forced to admit that Shakespeare knew what he was doing from the start and deliberately planned this stylistic contrast. Once we accept this compulsion we shall be the gainers, finding that the plays form a great symphonic scheme. The first three at least will become not only easier to understand but finer works of art.

J. DOVER WILSON
1881-

J. DOVER WILSON is a bibliographer and an editor who is also a vigorous, delightful critic. As a critic he is an eclectic. In his *The Essential Shakespeare* (1932), he is concerned, in the Victorian tradition, with attempting to trace Shakespeare's life in the plays and with analyzing characters, but he brings to each task the learning of historical scholarship, a learning which he carries lightly. He has the unabashed enthusiasm of the romantic and is capable of bold speculation and over-ingenuity, yet he also has solid good sense and genial humor. In addition to *The Essential Shakespeare* and *The Fortunes of Falstaff* (1943), he is the author of *What Happens in Hamlet* (1935), *The Meaning of the Tempest* (1936), and of the introductions to five histories and four tragedies in the New Cambridge editions, of which he has been editor.

In *The Fortunes of Falstaff*, reacting against both the sentimentalized interpretation of Falstaff by A. C. Bradley and the historical realist interpretation of E. E. Stoll, Wilson avowedly returns to Samuel Johnson, who was conscious of the attraction of Falstaff without romanticizing him. Maurice Morgann in his celebrated essay on Falstaff had argued at length the paradoxical thesis that Falstaff is not a constitutional coward. This view affected subsequent criticism through the nineteenth century and then, as a result of Bradley's lecture "The Rejection of Falstaff" (1909), through a good part of the twentieth century. Against this interpretation Stoll trained the immense battery of his learning. For Stoll, Falstaff is a stage butt, a character of the braggart soldier type, whose witty elusiveness makes him all the more interesting a butt. Wilson refines upon this and shows Falstaff to be a highly complex creation derived not from one but many traditions. More than this, in discussing the function of Falstaff, he exhibits the morality pattern of the play, in good part not previously perceived. He slights, however, the relationship between the comic scenes and the rebellion scenes analyzed by Cleanth Brooks and Robert B. Heilman.

THE FALSTAFF MYTH

RIOT AND THE PRODIGAL PRINCE

Falstaff may be the most conspicuous, he is certainly the most fascinating, character in *Henry IV*, but all critics are agreed, I believe, that the technical centre of the play is not the fat knight but the lean prince. Hal links the low life with the high life, the scenes at Eastcheap with those at Westminster, the tavern with the battle-field; his doings provide most of the material for both Parts, and with him too lies the future, since he is to become Henry V, the ideal king, in the play that bears his name; finally, the mainspring of the dramatic action is the choice I have already spoken of, the choice he is called upon to make between Vanity and Government, taking the latter in its accepted Tudor meaning, which includes Chivalry or prowess in the field, the theme of Part I, and Justice, which is the theme of Part II. Shakespeare, moreover, breathes life into these abstractions by embodying them, or aspects of them, in prominent characters, who stand, as it were, about the Prince, like attendant spirits: Falstaff typifying Vanity in every sense of the word, Hostpur Chivalry, of the old anarchic kind, and the Lord Chief Justice the Rule of Law or the new ideal of service to the state.[1]

Thus considered, Shakespeare's *Henry IV* is a Tudor version of a time-honoured theme, already familiar for decades, if not centuries, upon the English stage. Before its final secularization in the first half of the sixteenth century, our drama was concerned with one topic, and one only: human salvation. It was a topic that could be represented in either of two ways: (i) historically, by means of miracle plays, which in the Corpus Christi cycles unrolled before spectators' eyes the whole scheme of salvation from the Creation to the Last Judgement; or (ii) allegorically, by means of morality plays, which exhibited the process of salvation in the individual soul on its road between birth and death, beset with the snares of the World or the

"The Falstaff Myth" is from John Dover Wilson, *The Fortunes of Falstaff* (Cambridge University Press, 1961), pp. 17–35, 43–48. By permission of the publisher.

[1] In what follows I develop a hint in Sir Arthur Quiller-Couch's *Shakespeare's Workmanship*, 1918, p. 148: 'The whole of the business [in *Henry IV*] is built on the old Morality structure, imported through the Interlude. Why, it might almost be labelled, after the style of a Morality title, *Contentio inter Virtutem et Vitium de anima Principis.*'

wiles of the Evil One. In both kinds the forces of iniquity were allowed full play upon the stage, including a good deal of horse-play, provided they were brought to nought, or safely locked up in Hell, at the end. Salvation remains the supreme interest, however many capers the Devil and his Vice may cut on Everyman's way thither, and always the powers of darkness are withstood, and finally overcome, by the agents of light. But as time went on the religious drama tended to grow longer and more elaborate, after the encyclopaedic fashion of the middle ages, and such development invited its inevitable reaction. With the advent of humanism and the early Tudor court, morality plays became tedious and gave place to lighter and much shorter moral interludes dealing, not with human life as a whole, but with youth and its besetting sins.

An early specimen, entitled *Youth* and composed about 1520, may be taken as typical of the rest. The plot, if plot it can be called, is simplicity itself. The little play opens with a dialogue between Youth and Charity. The young man, heir to his father's land, gives insolent expression to his self-confidence, lustihood, and contempt for spiritual things. Whereupon Charity leaves him, and he is joined by Riot, that is to say wantonness, who presently introduces him to Pride and Lechery. The dialogue then becomes boisterous, and continues in that vein for some time, much no doubt to the enjoyment of the audience. Yet, in the end, Charity reappears with Humility; Youth repents; and the interlude terminates in the most seemly fashion imaginable.

No one, I think, reading this lively playlet, no one certainly who has seen it performed, as I have seen it at the Malvern Festival, can have missed the resemblance between Riot and Falstaff. The words he utters, as he bounces on to the stage at his first entry, give us the very note of Falstaff's gaiety:

> Huffa! huffa! who calleth after me?
> I am Riot full of jollity.
> My heart is as light as the wind,
> And all on riot is my mind,
> Wheresoever I go.

And the parallel is even more striking in other respects. Riot, like Falstaff, escapes from tight corners with a quick dexterity; like Falstaff, commits robbery on the highway; like Falstaff, jests immediately afterwards with his young friend on the subject of hanging; and like Falstaff, invites him to spend the stolen money at a tavern, where, he promises, 'We will drink diuers wine' and 'Thou shalt haue a wench to kysse Whansoeuer thou wilte'; allurements which prefigure the Boar's Head and Mistress Doll Tearsheet.

But Youth at the door of opportunity, with Age or Experience, Charity or Good Counsel, offering him the yoke of responsibility, while the World, the Flesh, and the Devil beckon him to follow them on the primrose way to the everlasting bonfire, is older than even the medieval religious play. It is a theme to which every generation gives fresh form, while retaining its eternal substance. Young men are the heroes of the Plautine and Terentian comedy which delighted the Roman world; and these young men, generally under the direction of a clever slave or parasite, disport themselves, and often hoodwink their old fathers, for most of the play, until they too settle down in the end. The same theme appears in a very different story, the parable of the Prodigal Son. And the similarity of the two struck humanist teachers of the early sixteenth century with such force that, finding Terence insufficiently edifying for their pupils to act, they developed a 'Christian Terence' by turning the parable into Latin plays, of which many examples by different authors have come down to us. In these plot and structure are much the same. The opening scene shows us Acolastus, the prodigal, demanding his portion, receiving good counsel from his father, and going off into a far country. Then follow three or four acts of entertainment almost purely Terentian in atmosphere, in which he wastes his substance in riotous living and falls at length to feeding with the pigs. Finally, in the last act he returns home, penniless and repentant, to receive his pardon. This ingenious blend of classical comedy and humanistic morality preserves, it will be noted, the traditional ratio between edification and amusement, and distributes them in the traditional manner. So long as the serious note is duly emphasized at the beginning and end of the play, almost any quantity of fun, often of the most unseemly nature, was allowed and expected during the intervening scenes.

All this, and much more of a like character, gave the pattern for Shakespeare's *Henry IV*. Hal associates Falstaff in turn with the Devil of the miracle play, the Vice of the morality, and the Riot of the interlude, when he calls him 'that villainous abominable misleader of Youth, that old white-bearded Satan,'[2] 'that reverend Vice, that grey Iniquity, that father Ruffian, that Vanity in years,'[3] and 'the tutor and the feeder of my riots.'[4] 'Riot,' again is the word that comes most readily to King Henry's lips when speaking of his prodigal son's misconduct.[5] And, as heir to the Vice, Falstaff inherits by reversion the functions and attributes of the Lord of Misrule, the Fool, the Buffoon, and the Jester, antic figures the origins of which are lost in the dark backward and abysm of folk-custom. We shall find that Falstaff possesses a strain, and more than a strain, of the classical *miles gloriosus* as well. In short, the Falstaff-Hal plot embodies a composite myth which had been centuries amaking, and was for the Elizabethans full of meaning that has largely disappeared since then: which is one reason why we have come so seriously to misunderstand the play.

Nor was Shakespeare the first to see Hal as the prodigal. The legend of Harry of Monmouth began to grow soon after his death in 1422; and practically all the chroniclers, even those writing in the fifteenth century, agree on his wildness in youth and on the sudden change that came upon him at his accession to the throne. The essence of Shakespeare's plot is, indeed, already to be found in the following passage about King Henry V taken from Fabyan's *Chronicle* of 1516:

This man, before the death of his fader, applyed him unto all vyce and insolency, and drewe unto hym all ryottours and wylde disposed persones; but after he was admytted to the rule of the lande, anone and suddenly he became a newe man, and tourned al that rage into sobernesse and wyse sadnesse, and the vyce into constant vertue. And for he wolde contynewe the vertue, and not to be reduced thereunto by the familiarytie of his olde nyse company, he therefore, after rewardes to them gyuen, charged theym upon payne of theyr lyues, that none of theym were so

---

[2] Pt. I, 2. 4. 450 (508); cf. l. 435 (491): 'Thou art violently carried away from grace, there is a devil haunts thee in the likeness of an old fat man.' [Wilson follows the line-enumeration of "The New Shakespeare," adding that of "The Globe Shakespeare" in parentheses where the two differ.]

[3] *Ibid.* 2. 4. 442 (500).

[4] Pt. II, 5. 5. 63 (66).

[5] Cf. Pt. I, 1. 1. 85: 'Riot and dishonour stain the brow / Of my young Harry'; Pt. II, 4. 4. 62: 'His headstrong riot hath no curb,' 4. 5. 135: 'When that my care could not withhold thy riots, / What wilt thou do when riot is thy care?'

hardy to come within x. myle of such place as he were lodgyd, after a day by him assigned.

There appears to be no historical basis for any of this, and Kingsford has plausibly suggested that its origin may be 'contemporary scandal which attached to Henry through his youthful association with the unpopular Lollard leader' Sir John Oldcastle. 'It is noteworthy,' he points out, 'that Henry's political opponents were Oldcastle's religious persecutors; and also that those writers who charge Henry with wildness as Prince find his peculiar merit as King in the maintaining of Holy Church and destroying of heretics. A supposed change in his attitude on questions of religion may possibly furnish a partial solution for his alleged "change suddenly into a new man".' The theory is the more attractive that it would account not only for Hal's conversion but also for Oldcastle's degradation from a protestant martyr and distinguished soldier to what Ainger calls 'a broken-down Lollard, a fat old sensualist, retaining just sufficient recollection of the studies of his more serious days to be able to point his jokes with them.'

Yet when all is said, the main truth seems to be that the fifteenth and early sixteenth centuries, the age of allegory in poetry and morality in drama, needed a Prodigal Prince, whose miraculous conversion might be held up as an example by those concerned (as what contemporary political writer was not?) with the education of young noblemen and princes. And could any more alluring fruits of repentance be offered such pupils than the prowess and statesmanship of Henry V, the hero of Agincourt, the mirror of English kingship for a hundred years? In his miracle play, *Richard II,* Shakespeare had celebrated the traditional royal martyr; in his morality play, *Henry IV,* he does the like with the traditional royal prodigal.

He made the myth his own, much as musicians adopt and absorb a folk-tune as the theme for a symphony. He glorified it, elaborated it, translated it into what were for the Elizabethans modern terms, and exalted it into a heaven of delirious fun and frolic; yet never, for a moment, did he twist it from its original purpose, which was serious, moral, didactic. Shakespeare plays no tricks with his public. He did not, like Euripides, dramatize the stories of his race and religion in order to subvert the traditional ideals those stories were first framed to set forth. Prince Hal is the prodigal, and his repentance is not only to be taken seriously, it is to be admired and commended. Moreover, the story of the prodigal, secularized and modernized as it might be, ran the same course as ever and contained the same three principal characters: the tempter, the younker, and the father with property to bequeath and counsel to give. It followed also the fashion set by miracle, morality and the Christian Terence by devoting much attention to the doings of the first-named. Shakespeare's audience enjoyed the fascination of Prince Hal's 'white-bearded Satan' for two whole plays, as perhaps no character on the world's stage had ever been enjoyed before. But they knew, from the beginning, that the reign of this marvellous Lord of Misrule must have an end, that Falstaff must be rejected by the Prodigal Prince, when the time for reformation came. And they no more thought of questioning or disapproving of that finale, than their ancestors would have thought of protesting against the Vice being carried off to Hell at the end of the interlude.

The main theme, therefore, of Shakespeare's morality play is the growing-up of a madcap prince into the ideal king, who was Henry V; and the play was made primarily—already made by some dramatists before Shakespeare took it over—in order to exhibit his conversion and to reveal his character unfolding towards that end, as he finds himself faced more and more directly by his responsibilties. It is that which determines its very shape. Even the 'fearful symmetry' of Falstaff's own person was welded upon the anvil of that purpose. It is probably because the historical Harry of Monmouth 'exceeded the meane stature of men,' as his earliest chronicler tells us; 'his necke . . . longe, his body slender and leane, his boanes smale,'—because in Falstaff's words he actually was a starveling, an eel-skin, a tailor's yard, and all the rest of it—that the idea of Falstaff himself as 'a huge hill of flesh' first came to Shakespeare. It was certainly, at any rate in part, in order to explain and palliate the Prince's love of rioting and wantonness that he set out to make Falstaff as enchanting as he could.[6] And he succeeded so well that the young man now lies

---

[6] Cf. H. N. Hudson, *Shakespeare: his Life, Art and Characters* (ed. 1888), ii. p. 83: 'It must be no ordinary companionship that yields entertainment to such a spirit [as Prince Hal's] even in his loosest moments. Whatever bad or questionable elements may mingle with his mirth, it must have some fresh and rich ingredients, some sparkling and generous flavour, to make him relish it. Anything like vulgar rowdyism cannot fail of disgusting him. His ears were never organized to that sort of music. Here then we have a sort of dramatic

under the stigma, not of having yielded to the tempter, but of disentangling himself, in the end, from his toils. After all, Falstaff *is* 'a devil . . . in the likeness of an old fat man', and the Devil has generally been supposed to exercise limitless attraction in his dealings with the sons of men. A very different kind of poet, who imagined a very different kind of Satan, has been equally and similarly misunderstood by modern critics, who no longer believing in the Prince of Darkness have ceased to understand him. For, as Professor R. W. Chambers reminded us in his last public utterance, when Blake declared that Milton was 'of the Devil's party without knowing it,' he overlooked the fact, and his many successors have likewise overlooked the fact, that, if the fight in Heaven, the struggle in Eden, the defeat of Adam and Eve, and the victory of the Second Adam in *Paradise Regained,* are to appear in their true proportions, we must be made to realize how immeasurable, how indomitable, is the spirit of the Great Enemy. It may also be noted that Milton's Son of God has in modern times been charged with priggishness no less freely than Shakespeare's son of Bolingbroke.

Shakespeare, I say, translated his myth into a language and endued it with an atmosphere that his contemporaries would best appreciate. First, Hal is not only youth or the prodigal, he is the young prodigal *prince,* the youthful heir to the throne. The translation, then, already made by the chroniclers, if Kingsford be right, from sectarian terms into those more broadly religious or moral, now takes us out of the theological into the political sphere. This is seen most clearly in the discussion of the young king's remarkable conversion by the two bishops at the beginning of *Henry V.* King Henry, as Bradley notes, 'is much more obviously religious than most of Shakespeare's heroes,' so that one would expect the bishops to interpret his change of life as a religious conversion. Yet they say nothing about religion except that he is 'a true lover of the holy church' and can 'reason in divinity;' the rest of their talk, some seventy lines, is concerned with learning and statecraft. In fact, the conversation of these worldly prelates demonstrates that the conversion is not the old repentance for sin

---

necessity for the character of Falstaff. To answer the purpose it was imperative that he should be just such a marvellous congregation of charms and vices as he is.' See also A. H. Tolman, *Falstaff and other Shakespearian Topics,* 1925, and W. W. Lawrence, *Shakespeare's Problem Comedies,* 1931, p. 64 (an interesting contrast between Hal and Falstaff, Bertram and Parolles).

and amendment of life, which is the burden, as we have seen, of Fabyan and other chroniclers, but a repentance of the renaissance type, which transforms an idle and wayward prince into an excellent soldier and governor. Even King Henry IV, at the bitterest moments of the scenes with his son, never taxes him with sin, and his only use of the word refers to sins that would multiply in the country, when

> the fifth Harry from curbed licence plucks
> The muzzle of restraint.[7]

If Hal had sinned, it was not against God, but against Chivalry, against Justice, against his father, against the interests of the crown, which was the keystone of England's political and social stability. Instead of educating himself for the burden of kingship, he had been frittering away his time, and making himself cheap, with low companions

> that daff the world aside
> And bid it pass.

In a word, a word that Shakespeare applies no less than six times to his conduct, he is guilty of Vanity. And Vanity, though not in the theological category of the Seven Deadly Sins, was a cardinal iniquity in a young prince or nobleman of the sixteenth and seventeenth centuries; almost as heinous, in fact, as Idleness in an apprentice.

I am not suggesting that this represents Shakespeare's own view. Of Shakespeare's views upon the problems of conduct, whether in prince or commoner, we are in general ignorant, though he seems to hint in both *Henry IV* and *Henry V* that the Prince of Wales learnt some lessons at least from Falstaff and his crew, Francis and his fellow-drawers, which stood him in good stead when he came to rule the country and command troops in the field. But it is the view that his father and his own conscience take of his mistreadings; and, as the spectators would take it as well, we must regard it as the thesis to which Shakespeare addressed himself.

When, however, he took audiences by storm in 1597 and 1598 with his double *Henry IV* he gave them something much more than a couple of semi-mythical figures from the early fifteenth century,

[7] Pt. II, 4. 5. 131.

brought up to date politically. He presented persons and situations at once fresh and actual. Both Hal and Falstaff are denizens of Elizabethan London. Hal thinks, acts, comports himself as an heir to the Queen might have done, had she delighted her people by taking a consort and giving them a Prince of Wales; while Falstaff symbolizes, on the one hand, all the feasting and good cheer for which Eastcheap stood, and reflects, on the other, the shifts, subterfuges, and shady tricks that decayed gentlemen and soldiers were put to if they wished to keep afloat and gratify their appetites in the London underworld of the late sixteenth century. It is the former aspects of the old scoundrel that probably gave most pleasure to those who first saw him on the stage; and, as they are also those that we moderns are most likely to miss, I make no apology for devoting most of the rest of this chapter to an exposition of them.

SWEET BEEF

Riot invites Youth, it will be remembered, to drink wine at a tavern, and tavern scenes are common in other interludes, especially those of the Prodigal Son variety. But Shakespeare's tavern is more than a drink-shop, while his Riot is not only a 'huge bombard of sack' but also a 'roasted Manningtree ox with the pudding in his belly.'

The site of the Boar's Head tavern in Eastcheap is now as deep-sunk in the ooze of human forgetfulness as that of the palace of Haroun. But it was once a real hostelry, and must have meant much to Londoners of the reigns of Elizabeth and James. Records are scanty, but the very fact that Shakespeare makes it Falstaff's head-quarters suggests that it was the best tavern in the city. And the further fact that he avoids mentioning it directly, though quibbling upon the name more than once,[8] suggests, on the one hand, that he kept the name off the stage in order to escape complications with the proprietors of the day, and on the other that he could trust his audience to jump to so obvious an identification without prompting. In any event, no other tavern in Eastcheap is at all likely to have been intended, and as Eastcheap is referred to six times in various scenes, there can be little real doubt that what Falstaff once calls 'the king's tavern' is the famous Boar's Head, the earliest known reference

[8] V. Pt. I, 2. 4. 107 (122): 'That damned brawn'; Pt. II, 1. 1. 19: 'Harry Monmouth's brawn'; 2. 2. 143 (159): 'Doth the old boar feed in the old frank? / At the old place, my lord, in Eastcheap'; and 2. 4. 224 (250): 'Thou whoreson little tidy Bartholomew boar-pig.'

to which occurs in a will dating from the reign of Richard II. Whether there is anything or not in Skeat's conjecture that the Glutton in *Piers Plowman* made it the scene of his exploits like Falstaff, it was a well-known house of entertainment more than two hundred years before Shakespeare introduced it into his play, and had come therefore by his day to be regarded as a historic hostelry, for which reason it was probably already associated in popular imagination with the floating legends of the wild young prince. What, however, seems to have escaped the attention of modern writers is that the house, with a name that symbolized good living and good fellowship above that of any other London tavern, was almost certainly even better known for good food than for good drink.

Eastcheap, there is plenty of evidence to show, was then, and had long been, the London centre at once of butchers and cookshops. Lydgate, writing in the reign of Henry V, puts the following words in the mouth of his *London Lyckpenny:*

> Then I hyed me into Estchepe;
>   One cries 'rybbes of befe and many a pye';
> Pewter pots they clattered on a heap;
>   There was a harp, pype, and minstrelsy.

The street was famed, in short, not only for meat and drink, but also for the 'noise' of musicians, which belonged to 'the old Tauerne in Eastcheap' in *The Famous Victories,* and which 'Mistress Tearsheet would fain hear' in Part II of *Henry IV.*[9] As for 'rybbes of befe,' though we never see or hear of Falstaff eating, or desiring to eat, anything except Goodwife Keech's dish of prawns[10] and the capon, anchovies and halfpenny worth of bread recorded with 'an intolerable deal of sack' in the bill found upon him while asleep,[11] Shakespeare none the less contrives to associate him perpetually with appetizing food by means of the imagery that plays about his person. For the epithets and comparisons which Hal and Poins apply to him, or he himself makes use of, though at times connected with his consumption of sack, are far more often intended to recall the chief stock-in-trade of the victuallers and butchers of Eastcheap, namely meat of all kinds, and meat both raw and roast.

[9] Pt. II, 2. 4. 11–12.
[10] *Ibid.* 2. 1. 94 (102) ff.
[11] Pt. I, 2. 4. 523–7 (584–90).

Falstaff is once likened to a 'huge bombard,'[12] once to a 'hogshead,'[13] once to a 'tun,'[14] and twice to a 'hulk,' that is, to a cargo boat; the nature of the cargo being specified by Doll, who protests to Mistress Quickly, 'There's a whole merchant's venture of Bourdeaux stuff in him, you have not seen a hulk better stuffed in the hold.'[15] But beyond these there is little or nothing about him in the vintner's line. When, on the other hand, Shakespeare promises the audience, through the mouth of his Epilogue in Part II, to continue the story, with Sir John in it, 'if you be not too much cloyed with fat meat,' the phrase sums up the prevailing image, constant in reference though ever-varying in form, which the physical characteristics of Falstaff presented to his mind's eye, and which he in turn was at pains to keep before the mind's eye of his public. Changes in London, and even more, changes in the language, have obliterated all this for the modern reader, so that what was intended, from the first, as little more than a kind of shimmering half-apprehended jest playing upon the surface of the dialogue, must now be recovered as a piece of archaeology, that is, as something long dead. The laughter has gone out of it; yet I shall be disappointed if the reader does not catch himself smiling now and again at what follows.

'Call in Ribs, call in Tallow' is Hal's cue for Falstaff's entry in the first great Boar's Head scene; and what summons to the choicest feast in comedy could be more apt? For there is the noblest of English dishes straightaway: Sir John as roast Sir Loin-of-Beef, gravy and all. 'Tallow,' a word often applied to him, generally in approbrium, is not rightly understood, unless two facts be recalled: first, that it meant to the Elizabethans liquid fat, as well as dripping or suet or animal fat rendered down; second, that human sweat, partly owing perhaps to the similarity of the word to 'suet,' was likewise thought of as fat, melted by the heat of the body. The most vivid presentation of Falstaff served up hot, so to say, is the picture we get of him sweating with fright in Mistress Page's dirty linen basket, as it was emptied by her servants into the Thames; and though *The Merry Wives* does not strictly belong to the Falstaff canon, the passage may be quoted here, as giving the clue to passages in *Henry IV* itself. For however different in character the Windsor Falstaff may be from his namesake of Eastcheap, he possesses the same body, the

---

[12] *Ibid.* 2. 4. 440 (497).   [13] Pt. II, 2. 4. 59 (69).
[14] Pt. I, 2. 4. 436 (494).   [15] Pt. II, 2. 4. 59–61 (69–71).

body that on Gad's Hill 'sweats to death, and *lards* the lean earth, as he walks along.'[16]

'And then,' he relates to the disguised Ford,

to be stopped in, like a strong distillation, with stinking clothes that fretted in their own grease! Think of that, a man of my kidney! think of that—that am as subject to heat, as butter; a man of continual dissolution and thaw; it was a miracle to 'scape suffocation. And in the height of this bath, when I was more than half stewed in grease, like a Dutch dish, to be thrown into the Thames, and cooled, glowing-hot, in that surge, like a horse-shoe. Think of that—hissing hot: think of that, Master Brook![17]

The 'greasy tallow-catch,'[18] again, to which the Prince compares him, much to the bewilderment of commentators, betokens, I believe, nothing more mysterious than a dripping-pan to catch the fat as the roasting joint turned upon the spit before the fire. Or take the following scrap of dialogue:

L. Chief Justice. What, you are as a candle, the better part burnt out.

Falstaff. A wassail candle, my lord, all tallow—if I did say of wax, my growth would approve the truth.

L. Chief Justice. There is not a white hair on your face, but should have his effect of gravity.

Falstaff. His effect of gravy, gravy, gravy.[19]

Falstaff's repeated 'gravy' is a quibble, of course. But it is not just a feeble jest upon his table manners, as seems to be usually assumed: it follows upon the mention of 'tallow' and refers to the drops of sweat that never cease to stand upon his face. In fact, to use a seventeenth-century expression, applicable to one bathed in perspiration, he may be said perpetually to 'stew in his own gravy.'

Indeed, he glories in the fact. Was it not, according to the physiological notions of the time, the very warrant of his enormous vitality? Never is he more angered to the heart than when the Prince likens him one day to a dry withered old apple-john. His complexion is merely sanguine; heat and moisture mingle to form the element he moves in; except in moods of mock-repentance he leaves to baser earth the cold and dry of melancholy.

[16] Pt. I, 2. 2. 106 (115).
[17] *Merry Wives of Windsor*, 3. 5. 103–12 (114–24).
[18] Pt. I, 2. 4. 223 (252).   [19] Pt. II, 1. 2. 155–61 (182–4).

Once we have the trick of it, all sorts of other allusions and playful terms of abuse are seen to belong to the same category, while the analogy between that vast carcase, as a whole or in its parts, and roasts of various kinds is capable of almost infinite elaboration. 'Chops,' for instance, as he is twice called,[20] carries the double significance of 'fat cheeks' and 'cutlets'; 'guts,' the Elizabethan word for 'tripe,' is an epithet that occurs no less than five times;[21] and 'sweet beef' as a term of endearment[22] requires no explaining. Nor is he only served up as beef; pork, still more appropriate to the Boar's Head, though brought in less often, provides some magnificent examples. The term 'brawn,' which means a large pig fattened for the slaughter, is applied to him on two occasions;[23] on his return from Wales the Prince, enquiring of Bardolph, 'Is your master here in London? . . . Where sups he? doth the old boar feed in the old frank?'[24] refers to the familiar inn-sign; Falstaff himself declares that he walks the streets followed by the diminutive page 'like a sow that hath overwhelmed all her litter but one';[25] last, and best of all, when Doll salutes him between her 'flattering busses' as her 'whoreson little tidy Bartholomew boar-pig,'[26] she is alluding to the tender sweet-fleshed little sucking-pigs which formed the chief delicacy at Bartholomew Fair.

The mention of Bartholomew Fair, the most popular annual festivity of Elizabethan and Jacobean London, may be linked with two other comparisons, which take us beyond the confines of Eastcheap and help to bestow on Falstaff that 'touch of infinity' which Bradley discovers in him, associating him, as they do, with feasting on a vast and communal scale. The first, already quoted above, is the Prince's description of him as a 'Manningtree ox with the pudding in his belly,'[27] in other words, as an ox roasted whole and stuffed with sausages, after the fashion of the annual fairs at Manningtree, an Essex town famed for the exceeding fatness of its beasts. But the extremest inch of possibility is reached by Poins when he asks Bardolph 'How doth the Martlemas, your master?'[28] Martlemas, or the

[20] Pt. I, 1. 2. 131 (151); Pt. II, 2. 4. 211 (234).
[21] Pt. I, 2. 4. 222, 252, 440 (251, 286, 498); *ibid.* 3. 3. 152, 155 (173, 176).
[22] Pt. I, 3. 3. 176 (198).
[23] Pt. I, 2. 4. 107 (122); Pt. II, 1. 1. 19.
[24] Pt. II, 2. 2. 143 (169).   [25] *Ibid.* 1. 2. 11–12 (13-14).
[26] *Ibid.* 2. 4. 224–5 (250).   [27] Pt. I, 2. 4. 441 (498).
[28] Pt. II, 2. 2. 100 (110).

feast of St Martin, on 11 November, was in those days of scarce fodder the season at which most of the beasts had to be killed off and salted for the winter, and therefore the season for great banquets of fresh meat. Thus it had been for centuries, long before the coming of Christianity, and thus it remained down to the introduction of the cropping of turnips in the eighteenth century. In calling him a 'Martlemas' Poins is at once likening Falstaff's enormous proportions to the prodigality of fresh-killed meat which the feast brought, and acclaiming his identity with Riot and Festivity in general. But perhaps the best comment upon Falstaff as Martlemas comes from Spenser's procession of the seasons in the Book of Mutabilitie. His November might almost be Falstaff himself, though the dates prove that the two figures must be independent:

> Next was Nouember, he full grosse and fat,
> As fed with lard, and that right well might seeme;
> For, he had been a fatting hogs of late,
> That yet his browes with sweat did reek and steem,
> And yet the season was full sharp and breem.

One might go to the other end of the scale and point out that the objects Falstaff chooses as a contrast to his person, objects excessively thin, wizened or meagre, are likewise often taken from the food-shops. There is, for instance, the shotten herring, the soused gurnet, the bunch of radish, the rabbit-sucker or poulter's hare, and wittiest of all perhaps, the carbonado—the rasher of bacon, we should say—which he will only allow Hotspur to make of him, if he is foolish enough to come in his way.[29] But enough to have shown that by plying his audience with suggestions of the choicest food that London and Eastcheap had to offer, whenever the person of Falstaff is mentioned, Shakespeare lays as it were the physical foundations of his Falstaff myth.

The prodigiously incarnate Riot, who fills the Boar's Head with his jollity, typifies much more, of course, than the pleasures of the table. He stands for a whole globe of happy continents, and his laughter is 'broad as ten thousand beeves at pasture.'[30] But he is Feasting first, and his creator never allows us to forget it. For in this way he not only perpetually associates him in our minds with appetizing images, but contrives that as we laugh at his wit our souls shall be satisfied

[29] Pt. I, 5. 3. 57 (58).
[30] George Meredith, *The Spirit of Shakespeare*.

as with marrow and fatness. No one has given finer expression to this satisfaction than Hazlitt, and I may fitly round off the topic with words of his:

> Falstaff's wit is an emanation of a fine constitution; an exuberance of good-humour and good-nature; an overflowing of his love of laughter and good-fellowship; a giving vent to his heart's ease, and over-contentment with himself and others. He would not be in character, if he were not so fat as he is; for there is the greatest keeping in the boundless luxury of his imagination and the pampered self-indulgence of his physical appetites. He manures and nourishes his mind with jests, as he does his body with sack and sugar. He carves out his jokes, as he would a capon or a haunch of venison, where there is *cut and come again;* and pours out upon them the oil of gladness. His tongue drops fatness, and in the chambers of his brain 'it snows of meat and drink.' He keeps perpetually holiday and open house, and we live with him in a round of invitations to a rump and dozen. . . . He never fails to enrich his discourse with allusions to eating and drinking, but we never see him at table. He carries his own larder about with him, and is himself 'a tun of man.'

MONSIEUR REMORSE

Like all great Shakespearian characters Falstaff is a bundle of contradictions. He is not only Riot but also Repentance. He can turn an eye of melancholy upon us, assume the role of puritan sanctimony, and when it pleases him, even threaten amendment of life. It is, of course, *mock*-repentance, carried through as part of the untiring 'play extempore' with which he keeps the Prince, and us, and himself, entertained from beginning to end of the drama. And yet it is not mere game; Shakespeare makes it more interesting by persuading us that there is a strain of sincerity in it; and it almost completely disappears in Part II, when the rogue finds himself swimming on the tide of success. There is a good deal of it in Part I, especially in the earliest Falstaff scenes.

> But, Hal, I prithee, trouble me no more with vanity. I would to God thou and I knew where a commodity of good names were to be bought.
> Thou hast done much harm upon me, Hal—God forgive thee for it: before I knew thee, Hal, I knew nothing, and now am I, if a man should speak truly, little better than one of the wicked: I must give over this life, and I will give it over: by the Lord, an I do not, I am a villain. I'll be damned for never a king's son in Christendom.[31]

[31] Pt. I, 1. 2. 80–2, 90–6 (91–2, 102–10).

One of his favourite poses is that of the innocent, beguiled by a wicked young heir apparent; he even makes it the burden of his apologia to the Lord Chief Justice at their first encounter. It serves too when things go wrong, when resolute men who have taken £1000 on Gad's Hill are left in the lurch by cowardly friends, or when there's lime in a cup of sack:

> There is nothing but roguery to be found in villainous man, yet a coward is worse than a cup of sack with lime in it. A villainous coward! Go thy ways, old Jack, die when thou wilt, if manhood, good manhood, be not forgot upon the face of the earth, then am I a shotten herring. . . . There live not three good men unhanged in England, and one of them is fat, and grows old. God help the while! a bad world, I say. I would I were a weaver—I could sing psalms or anything.[32]

But beside this talk of escaping from a wicked world and the toils of a naughty young prince, there is also the pose of personal repentance. At his first entry Poins hails him as Monsieur Remorse, an indication that this is one of his recognized roles among Corinthians and lads of mettle. And we may see him playing it at the opening of act 3, scene 3, when there is no Hal present to require entertaining.

> Well, I'll repent, and that suddenly, while I am in some liking. I shall be out of heart shortly, and then I shall have no strength to repent. An I have not forgotten what the inside of a church is made of, I am a peppercorn, a brewer's horse. The inside of a church! Company, villainous company, hath been the spoil of me.

Such passages, together with the habit of citing Scripture, may have their origin, I have said, in the puritan, psalm-singing, temper of Falstaff's prototype—that comic Lollard, Sir John Oldcastle in the old *Henry IV*. But, if so, the motif, adapted and developed in Shakespeare's hands, has come to serve a different end. In this play of the Prodigal Prince it is Hal who should rightly exhibit moods of repentance; and on the face of it, it seems quite illogical to transfer them to Falstaff, the tempter. Yet there are reasons why Hal could not be thus represented. In the first place, as already noted, repentance in the theological sense, repentance for sin, is not relevant to his case at all, which is rather one of a falling away from political virtues, from the duties laid upon him by his royal vocation. And in

[32] *Ibid*. 2. 4. 121–29 (137–47).

the second place, since Henry V is the ideal king of English history, Shakespeare must take great care, even in the days of his 'wildness,' to guard him from the breath of scandal. As has been well observed by a recent editor: 'His riots are mere frolics. He does not get drunk and is never involved in any scandal with a woman.'[33] And there is a third reason, this time one of dramatic technique not of morals, why the repentance of the Prince must be kept in the background as much as possible, viz. that as the only satisfactory means of rounding off the two parts, it belongs especially to the last act of the play.

Yet Monsieur Remorse is a good puppet in the property-box of the old morality, and may be given excellent motions in the fingers of a skilful showman, who is laying himself out, in this play especially, to make fun of the old types. Why not shape a comic part out of it, and hand it over to Falstaff, who as the heir of traditional medieval 'antics' like the Devil, the Vice, the Fool, Riot and Lord of Misrule, may very well manage one more? Whether or not Shakespeare argued it out thus, he certainly added the ingredient of melancholy, and by so doing gave a piquancy to the sauce which immensely enhances the relish of the whole dish. If only modern actors who attempt to impersonate Falstaff would realize it!

Falstaff, then, came to stand for the repentance, as well as the riotous living, of the Prodigal Son. And striking references to the parable, four of them, seem to show that his creator was fully aware of what he was doing. 'What, will you make a younker of me? shall I not take mine ease in mine inn but I shall have my pocket picked?'[34] Sir John indignantly demands of Mistress Quickly, on discovering, or pretending to discover, the loss of his grandfather's seal-ring. The word 'younker' calls up a scene from some well-known representation of the parable, in picture or on the stage, a scene to which Shakespeare had already alluded in the following lines from *The Merchant of Venice*:

> How like a younker or a prodigal
> The scarfèd bark puts from her native bay,
> Hugged and embracèd by the strumpet wind!

[33] *V*. p. xi of 1 *Henry IV*, ed. by G. L. Kittredge (Ginn & Co.). I fancy Hal is just a little tipsy at the beginning of Pt. I, 2. 4; but the point is, in general, sound enough, and the more striking that the chroniclers do not hide the fact that Prince Henry was given to sexual intemperance.

[34] Pt. I, 3. 3. 80–3 (90–3). 'The alternative title for the Prodigal Son was the "younger," as the alternative for the good brother was the "elder" ' (Richmond Noble, *Shakespeare's Biblical Knowledge*, p. 277).

How like a prodigal doth she return,
With over-weathered ribs and ragged sails,
Lean, rent, and beggared by the strumpet wind![35]

Equally vivid is Falstaff's description of the charge of foot he led into battle at Shrewsbury as so 'dishonourable ragged' that 'you would think that I had a hundred and fifty tattered prodigals lately come from swine-keeping, from eating draff and husks.'[36] And seeing that he calls them in the same speech 'slaves as ragged as Lazarus in the painted cloth, where the Glutton's dogs licked his sores,' we may suppose that, here too, he is speaking right painted cloth, from whence he had studied his Bible; an inference which seems borne out by his third reference, this time from Part II. Having, you will remember, already honoured Mistress Quickly by becoming indebted to her for a hundred marks, that is for over £65, he graciously condescends to borrow £10 more from her. And when she protests that to raise the sum she must be fain to pawn both her plate and the tapestry of her dining-chambers, he replies: 'Glasses, glasses, is the only drinking—and for thy walls, a pretty drollery or the story of the Prodigal or the German hunting in waterwork is worth a thousand of these bed-hangers and these fly-bitten tapestries.'[37] This is not just the patter of the confidence-trickster; Falstaff, we must believe, had a real liking for the Prodigal Son story, or why should that tactful person, mine Host of the Garter Inn, have gone to the trouble of having it painted, 'fresh and new,' about the walls of the chamber that he let to the greasy philanderer who assumed the part of Sir John, in Windsor.[38] Not being a modern critic, the good man could not know that his guest was an impostor.

But jollification and mock-repentance do not exhaust Falstaff's roles. For most of *Henry IV* he plays the soldier, taking a hand in a couple of campaigns, the first culminating in the death of Hotspur at Shrewsbury, and the other in the encounter between Prince John and the Archbishop of York at Gaultree Forest, where the rebels are finally overthrown. In both of these he performs the useful dramatic function of supplying the light relief, and in so doing he exhibits himself as at once the supreme comic soldier of English literature and a variation of a time-worn theme, the *miles gloriosus* of Plautus. . .

[35] *The Merchant of Venice*, 2. 6. 14–19; cf. 3 *Henry VI*, 2. 1. 24: 'Trimmed like a younker, prancing to his love.'
[36] Pt. I, 4. 2. 32–3 (37–9).   [37] Pt. II, 2. 1. 143–7 (155–9).
[38] *The Merry Wives*, 4. 5. 7.

THE BELLOWING BULL-CALF

We laugh at Falstaff in act 1, scene 2, at his bland evasion of Hal's successive attacks upon his character, at his whimsical melancholy, sanctimony, and fits of repentance, at his complaints of the moral contagion of keeping company with a wicked young prince, and at the alacrity with which all this is gaily cast aside upon a mere hint of purse-taking. But it is his next appearance which provides Shakespeare with the earliest opportunity of making comic capital out of his chief visible asset: Falstaff's weight begins to tell first of all upon Gad's Hill. For there we see the 'tun of man' in action; a crescendo of action, in which both legs and lungs are more and more brought into play, and more and more surprisingly. He enters puffing and blowing, as he painfully drags himself afoot uphill, Poins having removed his horse and tied him he knows not where. Clearly, that mountain of flesh and that broken wind are incapable of further exertion. And yet, no sooner do the travellers appear than he begins shouting threats, brandishing his sword, and dancing with rage, on the fringe of the scuffle, while Bardolph, Peto and Gadshill deal with the victims. Lastly, when the robbers are in turn attacked by the men in buckram, we have him striking a hasty blow or two, turning tail, and in terror of their sword-points which prod him from behind, scurrying off as nimbly and bellowing as loudly, as ever bull-calf ran and roared at a bull-baiting. And if the varying speed at which he carries along his guts under this varying stimulus is the source of most of the comic action in the scene, reflections upon his bulk provide the theme for much of the wit. Two of Shakespeare's happiest inventions in this kind belong here: to Hal's suggestion that he should put his ear to the ground and listen for the approaching travellers Falstaff retorts, 'Have you any levers to lift me up again, being down?' and Hal adds the final touch to our vision of the fat knight in flight with the immortal words,

> Falstaff sweats to death,
> And lards the lean earth as he walks along.

Critics who tell us that Prince Henry lacks wit, forget that mighty stroke; critics who insist that Falstaff always has the best of it, ignore the fact that the fun, from beginning to end of this delicious episode, is at Falstaff's expense.

But most modern critics, as everyone knows, taking their cue from Maurice Morgann, go much farther than this: they deny that Falstaff is a coward at all. They cannot square an exhibition of genuine cowardice with 'the impression,' to use Morgann's words, 'which the *whole* character of Falstaff is calculated to make on the minds of an unprejudiced audience.' And though Andrew Bradley admits 'that Falstaff sometimes behaves in what we should generally call a cowardly way,' he continues, 'but that does not show that he was a coward; and if the word means a person who feels painful fear in the presence of danger, and yields to that fear in spite of his better feelings and convictions, then assuredly Falstaff was no coward.' What the 'better feelings and convictions' of a Falstaff may be I cannot tell, but it is unquestionable that, if we rely upon our 'impressions' of his behaviour in this scene alone, he must be pronounced an absolute coward, seeing that the audience is clearly intended to derive all possible pleasure from the agonized cries and precipitate flight of 'a person'—and such a person!—'who feels painful fear in the presence of danger, and yields to that fear.' Morgann, again, does not say what he means by 'an unprejudiced audience,' but it looks very much as if he meant an audience which had never watched this scene! In any case, both Morgann and Bradley handle the scene with what may be called extreme circumspection, if not a Falstaffian discretion.

Equally weak is their treatment of the Prince's explicit comparison, two scenes later, of Falstaff's running and roaring to the terrified bellowing of a young bull baited in the ring.[39] The image is clearly intended by Shakespeare as a vivid reminder to us of the intensely amusing action upon the stage, the spectacle, that is, of this colossal old man, quivering with fright and roaring for his

---

[39] Morgann attempts 'to account for and excuse' Falstaff's conduct on the absurd pretext that the sole testimony we have of the running and roaring is the word of the prejudiced Poins, that the Prince's comparison with the bull-calf two scenes later is merely a jesting exaggeration of Poins's statement, and that 'if he did roar for mercy, it must have been a very inarticulate sort of roaring, for there is not a single word set down for Falstaff from which this roaring may be inferred.' Bradley faces the issue more squarely, as might be expected from so honest a critic, but with scarcely more courage. 'It is to be regretted,' runs his footnote, 'that in carrying his guts away so nimbly he "roared for mercy"; for I fear we have no ground for rejecting Henry's statement to that effect, and I do not see my way to adopt the suggestion (I forget whose it is) that Falstaff spoke the truth when he swore that he knew Henry and Poins as well as he that made them.' The 'suggestion' he speaks of is, I think, H. N. Hudson's.

life, as he flies from what he takes to be pitiless assailants, though they mean him no harm beyond the tickling of his catastrophe with their swords. Had not all this happened before the eyes of the audience, the words would have been pointless. They are, as a matter of fact, little more than a repetition of words uttered by Poins immediately after Falstaff's precipitate exit on Gad's Hill. 'How the fat rogue roared!' he exclaims, as the Prince and he split their sides with laughter.[40]

Morgann, Bradley, and the rest cannot admit such conduct, because it lowers Falstaff in their esteem. How can they reconcile ignominious cowardice like this with the complete self-possession they find him displaying on all other occasions? What of that 'inexplicable touch of infinity' which Bradley in particular discovers and acclaims in him? To these questions there are two excellent answers. In the first place, the critics are, as usual, reading the play backwards. Before the Gad's Hill scene the only thing an audience knows about Falstaff is that he is an old reprobate who is at once very funny and very fat. They cannot share the reverence for him which Morgann and Bradley profess, because, unlike them, they have had no opportunity of reading both parts of the play and meditating upon them. They perceive, then, nothing at all incongruous or disturbing in the running and roaring. And if it be urged that this is only to postpone the problem, that once spectators have learnt to think of Falstaff as a butt and a coward, they can never afterwards entertain the respect and admiration which a consideration of his character as a whole shows to be his due, I counter with my second point, viz. that the critics, again as usual, are confusing stage-performance with real life. Under the conditions of theatrical illusion all sorts of things, which would seem incredible or impossible in the world of fact, may be enacted and will be accepted without question. A good actor, for example—and it may be presumed that Shakespeare, a man of the theatre, had such an actor in mind, or he would hardly have gone to the trouble of creating Falstaff—is perfectly capable of exhibiting

---

[40] Professor Kittredge (*op. cit.*) having made up his mind that 'Falstaff is not a coward in fact' gets rid of the roaring by declaring that Poins is here referring 'to the vociferous swaggering' as Falstaff attacks the travellers. Thus is a fine and independent judgement corrupted by romantic tradition. For nothing is more certain than that Poins's words at the end of 2. 2 and the Prince's about the bull-calf in 2. 4. 254 (287) refer to the same incident.

extreme terror and complete self-possession at one and the same time.

If anyone doubts this I invite his attention to the words of that inveterate play-goer and theatre-lover, Charles Lamb, whose essay on *Stage Illusion* furnishes an illustration remarkably apt to our purpose. After speaking of the tacit understanding which a great comic player habitually establishes with his audience, he continues:

> The most mortifying infirmity in human nature, to feel in ourselves, or to contemplate in another, is, perhaps, cowardice. To see a coward *done to the life* upon a stage would produce anything but mirth. Yet we most of us remember Jack Bannister's cowards. Could any thing be more agreeable, more pleasant? We loved the rogues. How was this effected but by the exquisite art of the actor in a perpetual sub-insinuation to us, the spectators, even in the extremity of the shaking fit, that he was not half such a coward as we took him for? We saw all the common symptoms of the malady upon him; the quivering lip, the cowering knees, the teeth chattering; and could have sworn 'that man was frightened.' But we forgot all the while—or kept it almost a secret to ourselves—that he never once lost his self-possession; that he let out by a thousand droll looks and gestures—meant at *us,* and not at all supposed to be visible to his fellows in the scene, that his confidence in his own resources had never once deserted him. Was this a genuine picture of a coward? or not rather a likeness, which the clever artist contrived to palm upon us instead of an original; while we secretly connived at the delusion for the purpose of greater pleasure than a more genuine counterfeiting of the imbecility, helplessness, and utter self-desertion, which we know to be concomitants of cowardice in real life, could have given us?

What was within the compass of John Bannister at Drury Lane towards the end of the eighteenth century was assuredly not beyond that of Will Kempe or some other comedian on an Elizabethan stage. As I have said, the whole conception of Falstaff was probably built up in Shakespeare's mind round 'the exquisite art' of such an actor. We need not doubt then that the original impersonator of Falstaff was capable of exhibiting 'all the common symptoms of the malady' of cowardice, while he persuaded the spectators at the same time 'that he had never once lost his self-possession.'

And when Lamb exclaims 'we loved the rogues' he tells us what an audience feels, or should feel if the part is properly played, about Falstaff, as their laughter dies away with the noise of his roaring. What he leaves behind is not jeering contempt for a butt or a coward, but affection; an affection compounded of many simples: laughing sympathy for one who has 'more flesh than another man, and therefore more frailty,' astonishment at the quick dexterity with which he nevertheless carries his guts away, merriment at the turning of the tables upon him, delight in the sheer absurdity of his predicament, and above all—quite illogically, though inextricably, blended with the rest—gratitude to the player for the cleverness of the whole entertainment. There is tenderness in Hal's

> Were't not for laughing, I should pity him,

a touch of admiration in Poins's

> How the fat rogue roared!

Morgann and Bradley had no need to run away from Falstaff's running away. In its proper setting, which is the theatre, that stone of stumbling is seen to be the true foundation of the affectionate mirth with which we follow his drolleries and his wit for the remainder of the play.

ON SHAKESPEARE'S ROMANTIC COMEDIES

FEW CRITICS SINCE Samuel Johnson have shared his opinion that Shakespeare's comedies are superior to his tragedies. The romantic critics, not given to humor, neglected them in favor of the tragedies; and this neglect has, comparatively speaking, fairly well continued to the present day. To the Victorian critics, profiting from the studies of the literary and textual scholars of the period, goes the credit of separating the romantic comedies from the satiric comedies and the tragi-comic romances. The Victorians continued to expatiate on the themes of Hazlitt that "the poetical and impassioned passages are the best part of his comedies" and that Shakespeare's is a sympathetic rather than a satiric comedy, sometimes extending sympathy to characters like Malvolio and Shylock whom many modern critics would find unsympathetic. The women in the romantic comedies constituted a favorite topic. Modern critics have concerned themselves more with the integration of romance and comedy than the Victorians did, but they have had fewer sharp differences of opinion with their predecessors in writing about this genre than in others. A number have expressed the feeling that the romantic comedies present the richest field for further criticism.

EDWARD DOWDEN
1843-1913

EDWARD DOWDEN'S *Shakspere, A Critical Study of his Mind and Art* (1874) was for a generation the standard work, and his *Shakspere, A Primer* (1877) the standard introduction. Succeeding generations were, however, not so ready to follow Dowden in his inferences concerning the mind and moods of Shakespeare from the development of his art. His designations for the four periods which scholars concerned with the study of the chronology of Shakespeare's plays had worked out—"In the Workshop," "In the World," "In the Depths," "On the Heights"—are nowadays often referred to with amusement. However, Dowden, now perhaps rather neglected, remains a sensitive and lucid critic, whatever reservations we may have concerning his biographical speculation. Bradley, whose *Shakespearean Tragedy,* despite some reaction against it some years ago, remains very influential, is greatly indebted to him.

Although a number of critics have written on the subject, Shakespearean comedy has not received the kind of philosophical analysis which Shakespearean tragedy received in the first two chapters of Bradley's book. Dowden's essay, a portion of which follows, furnishes some of the materials for such an analysis. He explores the relationship between plot, character, and chance in Shakespeare's comedy, as Bradley explored it in his tragedy, finding that the law of his comedy is a law of greater liberty than that of his tragedy, with conversions or moral transformations frequent in comedy's realm of fantasy.

THE ESSENTIALS OF SHAKESPEARE'S COMEDY

PERHAPS IT IS impossible to include under any single general conception works which differ from each other as widely as *The Comedy of Errors, Measure for Measure,* and *The Tempest;* but if we cannot seize it as a whole, we may see from a little distance this side and that of comedy as understood by Shakespeare. Its vital centre is not an idea, an abstraction, a doctrine, a moral thesis, but something concrete—persons involved in an action. When philosophical critics assure us that the theme of *The Merchant of Venice* is expressed by the words *Summum jus, summa injuria,* or that it exhibits "man in relation to money," we admire the motto they discovered in their nut, and prefer the kernel in our own. The persons and the action are placed in some region, which is neither wholly one of fantasy nor yet one encumbered with the dross of actuality. Aery spirits, an earth-born Caliban, Robingoodfellow, the king and queen of Faery, may make their incursion into it, yet it is in the truest sense the haunt and home of "human mortals." The finer spirit of the poet's own age is forever present, but he makes no laborious effort to imitate life in the lower sense of reproducing contemporary manners. He turns away from his own country. Once—by command—Sir John Falstaff makes love to the laughing bourgeois wives of Windsor; but to comply with the necessity Shakespeare's comedy descends from verse to prose. Ben Johnson's invention is at home in Cob's Court and Picthatch, in the aisle of Paul's, or among the booths of Bartholomew Fair; having disguised the characters of his first important play under Italian names, he rightly christened them anew as Londoners. Shakespeare's imagination, throwing off the burden of the actual, disported itself in the Athenian moonlit wood and on the yellow sands of the enchanted island, under green boughs in Arden, in the garden at Belmont, in the palace of Illyria, at the shepherd's festival in Bohemia.

The action corresponds with the environment. In the great tragedies Shakespeare may on rare occasions demand certain postulates at the outset. These having been granted, the plot evolves itself within the bounds of the credible. In *King Lear* the opening scene puts some strain upon our imaginative belief, but Shakespeare received the

"The Essentials of Shakespeare's Comedy" is from "Shakespeare as a Comic Dramatist" in *Representative English Comedies,* edited by Charles Mills Gayley.

legend as it had been handed down to him, and all that follows the opening scene—though the action is vast and monstrous—obeys an order and logic which compel our acquiescence. It is not always so, if we refuse its claims to fancy, in Shakespearian comedy. In a region which borders on the realm of fantasy we must be prepared to accept many happy surprises. Our desire for happiness inclines our hearts to a pleasant credulity; if chance at the right moment intervenes, it comes as our own embodied hope. When all and every one in Arden wood, save Jaques, are on their way to wedlock, like couples coming to the ark, we are not disposed to question the reality of that old religious man upon the borders of the forest who suddenly converts the usurping Duke, and turns back the mighty power which he had set on foot. We are grateful for such hermits and such convertites.

The characters again correspond in comedy with the environment and with the action. In tragedy character is either from the first fully formed and four-square, or, if it is developed by events, it develops in accordance with an internal law. Passion runs its inevitable course, like a great wave driven of the wind, and breaks with thunder upon the shoal of death. The human actors disappear; only the general order of the world and the eternal moral law endure. But in comedy the individual must be preserved, and must at the close enter into possession of happy days; if he has erred through folly or vice, his error has not been mortal; he may in the last scene of the fifth act swiftly change his moral disposition as he would change his outward garb. The traitor Proteus is suddenly restored to his better mind, and Valentine is generous enough to resign to the repentant traitor all his rights in Silvia. Bertram, who almost to the last entangles himself in a network of dastardly lies, is rescued from his dishonesty and foolish pride by a successful trick, and becomes the loyal husband of Helena. The Duke Orsino transfers his amorous homage from his "fancy's queen" Olivia to his "fancy's queen" Viola with a most convenient facility. Angelo discovers his own baseness in the moment when he perceives it is discovered by the world, and is straightway virtuous enough to bring the happiness required by a fifth act to the wronged Mariana. Even Iachimo—the Iago of a comedy—makes sorrowful confession of his villainy, and restores the purloined bracelet and the ill-won ring. Such transformations as these indicate that even as regards character the law of comedy is a law of liberty. When it suits Shakespeare's purpose, the study of character can be profound and veracious; when occasion requires it, incident becomes all-important, and character yields to the requirements of the situation.

In truth, while it may be said that in Shakespearian tragedy character is fate, in Shakespearian comedy, among the contrasts and surprises which form so abundant a source of its vivacity, not the least effective contrast is that of character set over, as it were, against itself, not the least effective surprise is that of character entering upon new phases under the play of circumstance. The unity and logic of character may not in reality be impaired, but the unity is realized in and through diversity. In punning, a word is made to play a double part; it jostles its other self, and laughter ensues. What is so single and indivisible as personality? But if John is mistaken for Thomas, accident seems to triumph over law, and the incongruity arises of a doubled personal identity—the apparent and the real. Antipholus, of Syracuse, like the little woman of the nursery rhyme, whose sense of personality was dependent on the length of her petticoats, is almost persuaded that he is other than himself. If Viola disguises in doublet and hose, she secures by anticipation the victory of Sebastian over Olivia's heart, while in her own heart she endures a woman's hidden love for the Duke. One man in his brief time on Shakespeare's comic stage may play many parts. The ascetic scholars of Navarre are transformed into the most gallant of lovers and the most ingenious of sonneteers. Katherine the curst becomes more resolute in her wifely submission than she had been in her virgin *sauvagerie*. Signior Benedick, who challenged Cupid at the flight, in due time alters to Benedick, the married man; my dear Lady Disdain, in pity for him, and a little in pity for herself, has yielded upon great persuasion. If, as Montaigne teaches us, man is the most variable of animals, perhaps we learn as important a truth about human nature from Shakespeare's comedies as from his more profound study of the fatality of character and passion in the tragedies.

The essentials of Shakespearian comedy at its best are, after all, simple and obvious enough—a delightful story, conducted, in some romantic region, by gracious and gallant persons, thwarted or aided by the mirthful god, Circumstance, and arriving at a fortunate issue. Such would not serve as a description of the comedies of Ben Jonson. He is pleased to keep us during the greater part of five laborious acts in the company of knaves and gulls, and at the close, poetic justice is satisfied with the detection of folly and a general retribution descending on evil-doers. Shakespeare, in comedy, is no such remorseless justicer. Don John, the bastard, is reserved for punishment, but it shall be upon the morrow, and the punishment shall be such as the mirthful Benedick may devise. Parolles escapes lightly with the laughter of Lafeu, and mockery, qualified by a supper, will not afflict him beyond endurance. Lucio is condemned to marry the mother of his child, which is so dire an evil that all other forfeits are remitted. Sir John Falstaff will join the rest by Mistress Page's country fire in jesting at his own discomfiture. Even Shylock is not wholly overwhelmed; he shall have godfathers and a godmother at his baptism, and remain in possession of half his worldly goods. Sebastian may live and discover that he is morally superior to Caliban, the thief, and Stephano, the drunkard. Iachimo kneels and receives the free forgiveness of Posthumus.

But if Shakespeare, in comedy, is niggard of punishment, he is liberal in rewards. And since almost all the stories he chooses for his comic stage are stories of love and lovers, what grand reward can be reserved for the fifth act so fitting as the reward of love? In the seventeenth century masque amid all its mythological, fantastic, or humorous diversities, one point, or pivot, of the action remained fixed—the incidents must give occasion to a dance of the masquers. So in Shakespearian comedy we may, with almost equal certainty, reckon upon a marriage, or more marriages than one, in act, or in immediate prospect, before the curtain closes. Or, if not a marriage, for the lovers may be wedded lovers at the opening, then, after division, or separation of husband and wife, what we may call a remarriage, with misunderstandings cleared up and faults forgiven. When Shakespeare wrote his earlier plays he was himself young, and his gaze was fixed upon the future; exultant lovers begin their new life, and the song of joy is an epithalamium. When he wrote his latest plays, he was no longer young, and he thought of the blessedness of recovering the happy past, of knitting anew the strained or broken bonds of life, of connecting the former and the latter days in natural piety. Youth still must have its rapture; Florizel must win his royal shepherdess, queen of curds and cream; the nuptials of Ferdinand and Miranda, "these, our dear-beloved," must be duly solemnized at Naples; but Shakespeare's temper is no longer the temper of youth; he is of the company of Hermione and Prospero, and the music of the close is a grave and spiritual harmony.

Between the first scene and the last the path in comedy is beset with obstacles and dangers, past which love must find a way—"the course of true love never did run smooth." These may be either internal—some difficulty arising from character, or external—difference of blood or of rank, the choice of friends, slanderous tongues, rival passions, the spite of fortune. The resolution of the difficulty must be of a corresponding kind; temper, or rash determination, must yield to the predominance of love, or the external obstacles must be removed by well-directed effort, or by a happy turn of events. The young king of Navarre and his fellow-students are immured by their ascetic vow of culture; Isabella is all but ceremonially pledged to the life of religion; Olivia is secluded by her luxury of sentimental sorrow; Beatrice, born to be a lover, is at odds with love through her pride of independence and wilful mirth; Bertram has the young colt's pleasure in freedom, refuses to be ranged, and suffers from the haughty blindness of youth, which cannot recognize its own chief need and highest gain. All such rebels against love will be subdued in good time. On the other hand, it is her father who has decreed that Hermia shall be parted from Lysander; both father and mother have rival designs for marring the destiny of sweet Nan Page; a false friend and fickle lover separates Valentine and Silvia; a malignant plotter, who would avenge on all happy creatures the wrong of his own base birth, strikes down Hero with the blow of slander as she stands before the altar. But love has on its side gallantry and resource, loyalty and valour, the good powers of nature and the magic of the moonlit faery wood; and so, over the mountains and over the waves, love at last finds out a way.

Love being the central theme of Shakespearian comedy, laughter cannot be its principal end, and cruel or harsh laughter is almost necessarily excluded. But the laughter of joy rings out in the earlier and middle comedies, and a smile, beautiful in its wisdom and serenity, illuminates the comedies of his closing period. If satire is present, it is only on rare occasions a satire of manners; it deals rather with something universal, a satire of the fatuity of self-lovers, of the power which the human heart has of self-deception, or it is a genial mockery of the ineptitude of brainless self-importance, or the little languid lover's amorous endeavours, or the lumbering pace of heavy-witted ignorance, which cannot catch a common meaning, even by the tail; at its average rate of progress the idea whisks too swiftly from the view of such slow gazers.

The dramatis personæ form a large and varied population, ranging in social rank from the king to the tinker and the bellows-mender. Princes, dukes, courtiers, pages, dissolute gallants, soldiers, sailors, shepherds, clowns, city mechanicals, the country justice, the constable and head-borough, the schoolmaster, the parson, the faithful old servant, the lively waiting-maid, roysterers, humourists, light-fingered rogues, foreign fantasticoes, middle-class English husbands and wives, Welshman, Frenchman, Spaniard, Italian, Jew, noble and gracious ladies, country wenches, courtesans, childhood, youth, manhood, old age, the maiden, the wife, the widow—all sorts and conditions of human mortals occupy the scene, while on this side enters Caliban, bearing his burden of pine-logs, and Ariel flies overhead upon the bat's back, on the other, the offended king of faery frowns upon Titania, and claims his pretty Eastern minion.

The characters are ordinarily ranged, with an excellent effect on dramatic perspective, in three groups or divisions. The lovers and their immediate friends or rivals occupy the middle plane. Above them are persons of influence or authority by virtue of age or rank, on whom in some measure the fortunes of the lovers depend. Below them are the humbler aiders and abettors of their designs, or subordinate figures lightly attached to the central action, yet sometimes playing into the hands of benevolent Chance, and always ready to diversify the scene, to enliven the stage, to afford a breathing-space between passages of high-wrought emotion, to fill an interval with glittering word-play or unconscious humour, to save romance from shrill intensity or too aerial ascension by the contact of reality. Shakespeare in comedy was hardly quite happy until he had found his Duke and his clown; then he had the space in which he could move at ease; love remains his central theme, but it is love which rises out of life; his principal figures are rendered more distinct, are seen more in the round, because they stand out from a rich and various background.

GEORGE GORDON
1881-1942

GEORGE GORDON DID not publish much, but he lectured frequently on Shakespeare during his twenty-five years at Leeds, Oxford, and Cambridge; and his colleagues brought together a volume of his lectures after his death. He was at his best in his witty talks on the comedies.

In one of them he has some remarks on Shakespeare's clowns, an important part of the comedies but little discussed by Dowden or by Gordon in the lecture here reprinted, which should be quoted:

> I think the best division of the professional comic men in Shakespeare's plays . . . would be this: (1) those who play with words; and (2) those who are played with by them—those, that is, who are sufficiently masters of the English language to make fun out of it; and those who are so mastered by it as to give fun unconsciously. I don't know what you think: but with one or two exceptions—Touchstone perhaps, at his best—I find the second, the helpless class, more amusing, and of a more lasting humour, than the first. (1) In the first class come all the professional Fools, headed by Touchstone, with Feste, and such court-bred attendants as Moth—that "tender juvenal." In the same class, though touching on the second, come the men servants, the roguish valets, like Speed, and Launce, and Launcelot. They see the fun well enough, but, sometimes, through illiterate ambition, they take a fall. (2) In the second class come rustics like Costard, artisans like Bottom, and officials like Dogberry, Verges, and Dull. The amusement they cause is at their own expense. They are complacent, vain, and adorably stupid. . . . There is nothing in Shakespeare more certainly the work of genius than the *mettled* nonsense, the *complacent* nonsense, the perfectly contented and ideal inanity which Shakespeare, in some of these characters, has presented to us.

The verbal combats led by the fools, he points out, was a fashion which has become dated, and most of it is now dead: "We have to read a commentary to see the joke: a test which few jokes survive." Dogberryism is, however, immortal: "We have still Town Councillors and Mayors and Tribunes of the People who try to make their language climb to the height of their great vocation."

As Gordon states in the lecture which follows, comedy exists coterminously with romance: the world of Shakespearean comedy is really two worlds—the world of poetic romance and the world of comic realism. The artistically used anachronism, which Bethell finds in the histories and the tragedies, Gordon finds in the romantic comedies in the "alternations between Nowhere and England." These two worlds, however, interpenetrate each other to a greater extent than Gordon says. Bethell's "principle of multiconsciousness" holds here too. The laughers and the sighers do not merely, as Gordon says, live side by side without competing for attention at the expense of each other. The laughers often level a jest at the sighers. Touchstone's description of his love-struck behavior in courting Jane Smile parodies the love of Orlando and Rosalind without puncturing it. The danger that true love runs of being ridiculous is not always avoided. We often smile at the lovers (in *A Midsummer Night's Dream* we laugh at them), even as we sympathize with them. Moreover, true love is not always serious. The lovers engage in wit combats in the manner of Castiglione's court of Urbino, in which love is a game as well as an ideal. This comedy, like Dogberryism, is immortal: lovers are still prone to tender badinage. Finally, as stated in the discussion of Dowden's "The Essentials of Shakespeare's Comedy," the lovers at the conclusion of the play return from the world of poetic romance to the normal world of society. Although Gordon has well pointed out the ingredients of the mixture of comedy and romance in Shakespeare, the blend, therefore, is more complex than he indicates.

THE WORLD OF THE COMEDIES

THERE ARE TWO groups of characters in Shakespeare's comedies:

(1) The young men and women, who dwell in that romantically devised world, of youth, and dreams, and laughter, of which he possessed, and retains, the secret; and

(2) The workaday people, who keep things going—ploughmen, shepherds, servingmen, stewards, waiting-maids—with the unconverted drinkers, jesters, rogues, and odd fellows in a kind of limbo between the two regions—between upstairs and down—all plodding, stepping, tripping, and staggering along in a world of the four elements —of food and drink and sleep and labour. You may study this double world in any of these comedies: very fruitfully in *Much Ado* and *As You Like It:* most clearly, perhaps, in *Twelfth Night*. Like all these romantic comedies *Twelfth Night* is partly serious, and partly comic: a mixture of love and fun. The love story is the plot: it is serious, southern, and poetical. The comic story is the under-plot. It is not at all serious; it is anything but southern; and it is in prose. We don't at first know where we *are* when the play opens, and we very soon understand that it doesn't in the least matter. We are in the Utopia of lovers, where there is much despair, but no broken hearts.

All these plays are sweet with music: it is a part of this fairyland, the food of love. The Young Duke, being then in perfect health, sitting among his equally healthy lords, breathes out his luxurious agonies to the God of Love. It is a picture of eternal youth, framed in a setting of music, and poetry, and cushions, and flowers. What then, is the *climate* of these sweet tortures? Do we care? Viola comes to land.

> *Viola.* What country, friends, is this?
> *Captain.* This is Illyria, lady.

We are on those Adriatic coasts where the East and West lie so neighbourly—in Illyria—one of the Elysiums of fiction—and to most of us even now—as to almost all Elizabethans—not much more real than Ruritania. We hear in a distant sort of way of Candy and Crete,

"The World of the Comedies" is from George Gordon, *Shakespearean Comedy* (Oxford University Press, 1944), pp. 45–51. By permission of the publisher.

and ships named the *Tiger* and the *Phoenix;* and of a place called Messaline, which by some trifling oversight of Nature seems never to have existed. It has been searched for (though you will hardly believe it) by scholars, and rechristened Metelin, for Mitylene—because, I suppose, Mitylene is a real place. As if that mattered! This game has rules: and really, as visitors, we must allow the dramatist to pour out his own tea, and pull his own curtains!

I receive almost annually, from America and Germany, printed attempts to discover the 'source,' as it is called, of *The Tempest,* and to locate Prospero's island in the Mediterranean or the Atlantic. The authors of these investigations are gentlemen for whom Utopias were not intended. There is an entrance fee to this club of good Utopians, which they cannot pay; of which they do not even understand the currency. Their children (who, by the way, get in for nothing)—their children could teach them better. Because, if you think of it, to imagine, even if it could be shown to be true, that anything is gained by knowing that Prospero's island was Lampedusa, and lay between Malta and the African coast—or that it was Corcyra, as another critic is equally prepared to prove—is to declare the play, on the whole, a failure. If the Island does not convince us, and convince us without any argument, that it lies precisely nowhere, it has missed its purpose, and the ideal impression which the dramatist was all along attempting to make upon us has not been made. The island has neither latitude nor longitude, because Shakespeare gave it none: and this will still be true, even if the moles should triumph: if the lost story which Shakespeare read should be unearthed; and some paltry original island be produced with a name and a place on the map.

Being an *idle* world, this world of romantic Comedy of which I am speaking: there are therefore students in it—but no lectures. There are a number of university students in Shakespeare: it was one of the choices of Elizabethan youth:

> Some to the wars, to try their fortunes there:
> Some to discover islands far away
> Some to the studious Universities.

Young Walter Raleigh was so thorough an Elizabethan that he had done all three—fought, sailed, and studied—before he was twenty. The most notable of all the young students in Shakespeare, and, one would guess, by far the most studious, is Hamlet; but he is outside our range. The Prince and his friends in *Love's Labour's Lost* are nearer our mark; or that bright spark Lucentio in *The Taming of the Shrew*. Lucentio was a graduate of the University of Rheims, and is supposed by his confiding relations to have entered on a post-graduate course at the University of Padua. I regret to say that there is no evidence that he even matriculated there, or, if he matriculated, that he ever did any work: unless you call it work disguising himself as a language-master, and teaching Bianca to misconstrue Ovid. 'Where left we last,' says Bianca coolly.

> *Luc.* Here, madam:
> > *Hic ibat Simois; hic est Sigeia tellus;*
> > *Hic steterat Priami regia celsa senis.*
> *Bian.* Construe them.
> *Luc. Hic ibat,* as I told you before, *Simois,* I am Lucentio, *hic est,* son unto Vincentio of Pisa, *Sigeia tellus,* disguised thus to get your love; *Hic steterat,* and that Lucentio that comes a wooing, *Priami,* is my man Tranio, *regia,* bearing my port, *celsa senis,* that we might beguile the old pantaloon.

A young puppy, you see!

> *Bian.* Now let me see if I can construe it: *Hic ibat Simois,* I know you not, *hic est Sigeia tellus,* I trust you not; *Hic steterat Priami,* take heed he hear us not, *regia,* presume not; *celsa senis,* despair not.

A nice pair! As Grumio says in the same play: 'See, to beguile the old folks, how the young folks put their heads together!' It has been the same since Menander. Lucentio's father, we are told, had his misgivings about his son, and they were not ill-founded. But the young man takes risks for love, and Shakespeare, therefore, sees him through.

In this climate of Romance, it is, of course, the rule that all the lovers shall love at once, and love absolutely. Nothing else, in this world, is to be permitted. One glance at Olivia, and no work need be expected from Orsino for some time to come. Olivia herself, *grande dame* though she is, succumbs in one interview: they are all struck from heaven. Only two of these couples have the temerity to stand off for a time, and assume, at any rate, the postures of defence—I mean Rosalind and Biron, and Benedick and Beatrice—and there are special reasons for that. This Utopian Love is what the Elizabethans called *Fancy:* bred neither in the head nor in the heart, but in the eyes. We call it 'love at first sight'—and, really, I have never heard that it wears worse than any other. The eyes are not the *least* intelligent agents either of the head or of the heart. It has, of course, some disadvantages, this remorseless way of loving, from the point of view of the performers: (1) it must be acknowledged to be extremely open to ridicule; (2) if everybody did it, there would be an end of all society. The trouble is, that true love alone can never make a comedy. True love is serious, and Comedy should amuse. It is exclusive—most terribly so—and Comedy should be friendly. It is unsocial—it cannot be hidden from you how very unsocial two lovers can be!—but the subject of Comedy is Society. Comedy is a plump figure, and holds its sides; Love is lean, and holds a hand upon its heart.

What is to be done? Is *Romantic* Comedy, then, impossible? Must either the laughers or the sighers be given up? But which? *Not* the laughers, surely! Does true Comedy mean no more cakes and ale? Shall there be no Comedy but Mr. Shaw's? But then—a play *all* laughter? What is to be done?

Shakespeare proceeded, as he always does, by compromise. If Comedy laughs, Romance is not to be offended; if Love sighs, Comedy promises to put up with it—to a point! to a point! If the jokes are good, and the sighs are true, there would appear, on this undertaking, to be no reason in literature why they should quarrel. In Romantic Comedy, therefore, the laughers and the sighers live side by side, like good neighbours: on only *one* condition: that neither shall commit excess, or compete for attention at the expense of the other. And this is sound. For what is more wearisome than the uninterrupted spectacle of lovemaking in which we have no share? Or more awful than the gravity which falls upon a company that has laughed too much, or giggled too intellectually? The law, therefore, is one of decency and measure. The solemnity of Love is relieved by the generosity of Laughter, and the irresponsibility of Laughter by the seriousness of Love. This is the principle of Romantic Comedy, and for a compromise—how admirably it works! No one ever managed it so well as Shakespeare. The words of Mercury need not be harsh after the songs of Apollo.

I don't know a better or more convincing demonstration of this compact than to pass from Orsino and Viola in the first two scenes of *Twelfth Night* to Sir Toby and Maria in the third—from Illyria to the Buttery Hatch. The first two scenes pitch their language high. Romance is to be secured on her throne before Comedy comes in. Olivia being in mourning for her brother's death, Orsino has sent a messenger with kind inquiries. Maria very properly refuses to admit him, and informs him that her mistress does not intend either to put off mourning or go into society for seven years. This is how Valentine reports to Orsino:

> So please my lord, I might not be admitted;
> But from her handmaid do return this answer:
> The element itself, till seven years' heat,
> Shall not behold her face at ample view;
> But, like a cloistress, she will veiled walk,
> And water once a day her chamber round
> With eye-offending brine; all this, to season
> A brother's dead love, which she would keep fresh
> And lasting in her sad remembrance.

I am quite sure this is not how Maria said it, or anybody but an actor. The style goes on. Since Viola has escaped drowning herself, there is a hope that her brother may have escaped also, especially as the Captain saw him tied to a mast. This is how it is put:

> Mine own escape unfoldeth to my hope,
> Whereto thy speech serves for authority,
> The like of him.

These are phrases neither of men nor of angels: only actors ever spoke them. Viola and the Captain now walk off: a door seems to open: we step into the Buttery: and a voice cries 'What a plague means my niece to take the death of her brother thus? I am sure care's an enemy to life.' With what a comfortable sense of shock we encounter this underworld. This is the very tune of unconverted man, and every ear is ready for it. It is the dialect of life. The etiquette of Romance is exacting: how pleasant it is to step downstairs! How snug it is. A different syntax controls the speech of these quarters. The air seems to change. It is Illyrian no longer. These strayed revellers, fools, and drinkers, who raise the owl at midnight, and burn sack to bring in the morning (because it is too late to go to bed), and talk of Puritans and weavers, and count the bells of St. Bennet—one, two, three— were never bred on the Adriatic. Every member of the audience, and every reader, knows that he is at home again—in the paradise of humorists and odd fellows—in England—among friends. The blood of the living Falstaff is in Sir Toby Belch; Sir Andrew might have sat on the same bench with Justice Silence; and Feste, the third man and best singer in the trio, is no other than Will Kempe, fool-in-ordinary to the company of the Chamberlain's Servants.

This was well understood by Shakespeare's audience: there was a tacit understanding at that time between audience and the stage that the entrance of the comic characters indicated a temporary suspension of the romantic or historical fiction on which the serious action was based; that the assumption of a strange country or a different period of history had been dropped. This is the practical explanation of several liberties in more serious plays and even in Tragedies. Such was the Porter in *Macbeth,* with his jokes about Garnett the Jesuit and last year's harvest. No one supposed him to be a porter of ancient Scotland. Here was a primitive convention which Shakespeare maintained.

It is in his power over these two worlds, in his ostensible alternations between Nowhere and England, that Shakespeare's romantic comedies excel all others.

NORTHROP FRYE
1912-

IN HIS HIGHLY acclaimed *Anatomy of Criticism* (1957), Northrop Frye, displaying a remarkable erudition, sought to classify literature in accordance with an ambitious system of his construction based on mythic themes.

In this essay Frye's subject is the nature of comedy in general, but he makes constant reference to Shakespeare, presenting much that is suggestive in his wide-ranging manner. Frye's description of the "green world" of Shakespearean romantic comedy as typically bounded on both sides by a normal world, with the comic resolution of the problems of the normal world being effected on the characters' passage through this green world, had been hinted at in Dowden's "love has on its side . . . the good powers of nature and the magic of the moonlit faery wood." Frye, however, traces the green world to the survivals in England of pagan ritual and to the drama derived from these survivals. The theme of the green world, the "triumph of life over the waste land," he indicates, is one which has an archetypal appeal. So too Frye's discussion of the relation between tragedy and comedy is implicit in G. Wilson Knight's remarks on the theme of renewal, redemption and resurrection in pagan and Christian ritual concluding in the statement: "In the world of Shakespearian tragedy this unique act of the Christ sacrifice can . . . be felt as central . . . Shakespeare's final plays celebrate . . . the resurrection and renewal, that in the Christian story . . . succeed the sacrifice." Frye, however, widens and deepens Knight's remarks.

The danger of the critic's use of mythic themes in the discussion of literature is that he may fail to distinguish properly between different works or types of works making use of the same themes. Frye, in dealing with mythic sources and implications, differentiates even as he is pointing out similarities: the problem comedies lack a green world; the nature-myth in the romances, having cracked the conventions of Elizabethan drama in which it was confined in the romantic comedies, emerges full-blown; the comic Saturnalia of Falstaff is a temporary escape from the normal world, which it does not affect, while the characters' passage through the green world of the romantic comedies results in a change in the normal world. Moreover, Frye's discussion serves to illuminate the individual work: his comments on the senex and the humors character corroborates Stoll's interpretation of Shylock.

Other works of Shakespearean criticism making use of the study of myth and ritual include J. I. M. Stewart's *Character and Motive in Shakespeare* (1947), C. L. Barber's *Shakespeare's Festive Comedy* (1951) and John Holloway's *The Story of the Night* (1961).

THE ARGUMENT OF COMEDY

THE GREEKS PRODUCED two kinds of comedy, Old Comedy, represented by the eleven extant plays of Aristophanes, and New Comedy, of which the best known exponent is Menander. About two dozen New Comedies survive in the work of Plautus and Terence. Old Comedy, however, was out of date before Aristophanes himself was dead; and today, when we speak of comedy, we normally think of something that derives from the Menandrine tradition.

New Comedy unfolds from what may be described as a comic Oedipus situation. Its main theme is the successful effort of a young man to outwit an opponent and possess the girl of his choice. The opponent is usually the father (*senex*), and the psychological descent of the heroine from the mother is also sometimes hinted at. The father frequently wants the same girl, and is cheated out of her by the son, the mother thus becoming the son's ally. The girl is usually a slave or courtesan, and the plot turns on a *cognitio* or discovery of birth which makes her marriageable. Thus it turns out that she is not under an insuperable taboo after all but is an accessible object of desire, so that the plot follows the regular wish-fulfillment pattern. Often the central Oedipus situation is thinly concealed by surrogates or doubles of the main characters, as when the heroine is discovered to be the hero's sister, and has to be married off to his best friend. In Congreve's *Love for Love,* to take a modern instance well within the Menandrine tradition, there are two Oedipus themes in counterpoint: the hero cheats his father out of the heroine, and his best friend violates the wife of an impotent old man who is the heroine's guardian. Whether this analysis is sound or not, New Comedy is certainly concerned with the maneuvering of a young man toward a young woman, and marriage is the tonic chord on which it ends. The normal comic resolution is the surrender of the *senex* to the hero, never the reverse. Shakespeare tried to reverse the pattern in *All's Well That Ends Well,* where the king of France forces Bertram to marry Helena, and the critics have not yet stopped making faces over it.

New Comedy has the blessing of Aristotle, who greatly preferred it to its predecessor, and it exhibits the general pattern of Aristotelian

"The Argument of Comedy" is from *English Institute Essays, 1948,* ed. D. A. Robertson, Jr., (Columbia University Press, 1949). By permission of the publisher.

causation. It has a material cause in the young man's sexual desire, and a formal cause in the social order represented by the *senex,* with which the hero comes to terms when he gratifies his desire. It has an efficient cause in the character who brings about the final situation. In classical times this character is a tricky slave; Renaissance dramatists often use some adaptation of the medieval "vice"; modern writers generally like to pretend that nature, or at least the natural course of events, is the efficient cause. The final cause is the audience, which is expected by its applause to take part in the comic resolution. All this takes place on a single order of existence. The action of New Comedy tends to become probable rather than fantastic, and it moves toward realism and away from myth and romance. The one romantic (originally mythical) feature in it, the fact that the hero or heroine turns out to be freeborn or someone's heir, is precisely the feature that trained New Comedy audiences tire of most quickly.

The conventions of New Comedy are the conventions of Jonson and Molière, and a fortiori of the English Restoration and the French rococo. When Ibsen started giving ironic twists to the same formulas, his startled hearers took them for portents of a social revolution. Even the old chestnut about the heroine's being really the hero's sister turns up in *Ghosts* and *Little Evolf.* The average movie of today is a rigidly conventionalized New Comedy proceeding toward an act which, like death in Greek tragedy, takes place offstage, and is symbolized by the final embrace.

In all good New Comedy there is a social as well as an individual theme which must be sought in the general atmosphere of reconciliation that makes the final marriage possible. As the hero gets closer to the heroine and opposition is overcome, all the right-thinking people come over to his side. Thus a new social unit is formed on the stage, and the moment that this social unit crystallizes is the moment of the comic resolution. In the last scene, when the dramatist usually tries to get all his characters on the stage at once, the audience witnesses the birth of a renewed sense of social integration. In comedy as in life the regular expression of this is a festival, whether a marriage, a dance, or a feast. Old Comedy has, besides a marriage, a *komos,* the processional dance from which comedy derives its name; and the masque, which is a by-form of comedy, also ends in a dance.

This new social integration may be called, first, a kind of moral norm and, second, the pattern of a free society. We can see this more clearly if we look at the sort of characters who impede the progress of the comedy toward the hero's victory. These are always people who are in some kind of mental bondage, who are helplessly driven by ruling passions, neurotic compulsions, social rituals, and selfishness. The miser, the hypochondriac, the hypocrite, the pedant, the snob: these are humors, people who do not fully know what they are doing, who are slaves to a predictable self-imposed pattern of behavior. What we call the moral norm is, then, not morality but deliverance from moral bondage. Comedy is designed not to condemn evil, but to ridicule a lack of self-knowledge. It finds the virtues of Malvolio and Angelo as comic as the vices of Shylock.

The essential comic resolution, therefore, is an individual release which is also a social reconciliation. The normal individual is freed from the bonds of a humorous society, and a normal society is freed from the bonds imposed on it by humorous individuals. The Oedipus pattern we noted in New Comedy belongs to the individual side of this, and the sense of the ridiculousness of the humor to the social side. But all real comedy is based on the principle that these two forms of release are ultimately the same: this principle may be seen at its most concentrated in *The Tempest*. The rule holds whether the resolution is expressed in social terms, as in *The Merchant of Venice*, or in individual terms, as in Ibsen's *An Enemy of the People*.

The freer the society, the greater the variety of individuals it can tolerate, and the natural tendency of comedy is to include as many as possible in its final festival. The motto of comedy is Terence's "Nothing human is alien to me." This may be one reason for the traditional comic importance of the parasite, who has no business to be at the festival but is nevertheless there. The spirit of reconciliation which pervades the comedies of Shakespeare is not to be ascribed to a personal attitude of his own, about which we know nothing whatever, but to his impersonal concentration on the laws of comic form.

Hence the moral quality of the society presented is not the point of the comic resolution. In Jonson's *Volpone* the final assertion of the moral norm takes the form of a social revenge on Volpone, and the play ends with a great bustle of sentences to penal servitude and the galleys. One feels perhaps that the audience's sense of the moral norm does not need so much hard labor. In *The Alchemist,* when Lovewit returns to his house, the virtuous characters have proved so weak and the rascals so ingenious that the action dissolves in laughter. Whichever is morally the better ending, that of *The Alchemist* is more concentrated comedy. *Volpone* is starting to move toward tragedy, toward the vision of a greatness which develops *hybris* and catastrophe.

The same principle is even clearer in Aristophanes. Aristophanes is the most personal of writers: his opinions on every subject are written all over his plays, and we have no doubt of his moral attitude. We know that he wanted peace with Sparta and that he hated Cleon, and when his comedy depicts the attaining of peace and the defeat of Cleon we know that he approved and wanted his audience to approve. But in *Ecclesiazusae* a band of women in disguise railroad a communistic scheme through the Assembly, which is a horrid parody of Plato's *Republic,* and proceed to inaugurate Plato's sexual communism with some astonishing improvements. Presumably Aristophanes did not applaud this, yet the comedy follows the same pattern and the same resolution. In *The Birds* the Peisthetairos who defies Zeus and blocks out Olympus with his Cloud-Cuckoo-Land is accorded the same triumph that is given to the Trygaeus of the *Peace* who flies to heaven and brings a golden age back to Athens.

Comedy, then, may show virtue her own feature and scorn her own image—for Hamlet's famous definition of drama was originally a definition of comedy. It may emphasize the birth of an ideal society as you like it, or the tawdriness of the sham society which is the way of the world. There is an important parallel here with tragedy. Tragedy, we are told, is expected to raise but not ultimately to accept the emotions of pity and terror. These I take to be the sense of moral good and evil, respectively, which we attach to the tragic hero. He may be as good as Caesar, and so appeal to our pity, or as bad as Macbeth, and so appeal to terror, but the particular thing called tragedy that happens to him does not depend on his moral status. The tragic catharsis passes beyond moral judgment, and while it is quite possible to construct a moral tragedy, what tragedy gains in morality it loses in cathartic power. The same is true of the comic catharsis, which raises sympathy and ridicule on a moral basis, but passes beyond both.

Many things are involved in the tragic catharsis, but one of them is a mental or imaginative form of the sacrificial ritual out of which tragedy arose. This is the ritual of the struggle, death, and rebirth of a

God-Man, which is linked to the yearly triumph of spring over winter. The tragic hero is not really killed, and the audience no longer eats his body and drinks his blood, but the corresponding thing in art still takes place. The audience enters into communion with the body of the hero, becoming thereby a single body itself. Comedy grows out of the same ritual, for in the ritual the tragic story has a comic sequel. Divine men do not die: they die and rise again. The ritual pattern behind the catharsis of comedy is the resurrection that follows the death, the epiphany or manifestation of the risen hero. This is clear enough in Aristophanes, where the hero is treated as a risen God-Man, led in triumph with the divine honors of the Olympic victor, rejuvenated, or hailed as a new Zeus. In New Comedy the new human body is, as we have seen, both a hero and a social group. Aristophanes is not only closer to the ritual pattern, but contemporary with Plato; and his comedy, unlike Menander's, is Platonic and dialectic: it seeks not the entelechy of the soul but the Form of the Good, and finds it in the resurrection of the soul from the world of the cave to the sunlight. The audience gains a vision of that resurrection whether the conclusion is joyful or ironic, just as in tragedy it gains a vision of a heroic death whether the hero is morally innocent or guilty.

Two things follow from this: first, that tragedy is really implicit or uncompleted comedy; second, that comedy contains a potential tragedy within itself. With regard to the latter, Aristophanes is full of traces of the original death of the hero which preceded his resurrection in the ritual. Even in New Comedy the dramatist usually tries to bring his action as close to a tragic overthrow of the hero as he can get it, and reverses this movement as suddenly as possible. In Plautus the tricky slave is often forgiven or even freed after having been threatened with all the brutalities that a very brutal dramatist can think of, including crucifixion. Thus the resolution of New Comedy seems to be a realistic foreshortening of a death-and-resurrection pattern, in which the struggle and rebirth of a divine hero has shrunk into a marriage, the freeing of a slave, and the triumph of a young man over an older one.

As for the conception of tragedy as implicit comedy, we may notice how often tragedy closes on the major chord of comedy: the Aeschylean trilogy, for instance, proceeds to what is really a comic resolution, and so do many tragedies of Euripides. From the point of Christianity, too, tragedy is an episode in that larger scheme of redemption and resurrection to which Dante gave the name of *commedia*. This conception of *commedia* enters drama with the miracle-play cycles, where such tragedies as the Fall and the Crucifixion are episodes of a dramatic scheme in which the divine comedy has the last word. The sense of tragedy as a prelude to comedy is hardly separable from anything explicitly Christian. The serenity of the final double chorus in the St. Matthew Passion would hardly be attainable if composer and audience did not know that there was more to the story. Nor would the death of Samson lead to "calm of mind all passion spent" if Samson were not a prototype of the rising Christ.

New Comedy is thus contained, so to speak, within the symbolic structure of Old Comedy, which in its turn is contained within the Christian conception of *commedia*. This sounds like a logically exhaustive classification, but we have still not caught Shakespeare in it.

It is only in Jonson and the Restoration writers that English comedy can be called a form of New Comedy. The earlier tradition established by Peele and developed by Lyly, Greene, and the masque writers, which uses themes from romance and folklore and avoids the comedy of manners, is the one followed by Shakespeare. These themes are largely medieval in origin, and derive, not from the mysteries or the moralities or the interludes, but from a fourth dramatic tradition. This is the drama of folk ritual, of the St. George play and the mummers' play, of the feast of the ass and the Boy Bishop, and of all the dramatic activity that punctuated the Christian calendar with the rituals of an immemorial paganism. We may call this the drama of the green world, and its theme is once again the triumph of life over the waste land, the death and revival of the year impersonated by figures still human, and once divine as well.

When Shakespeare began to study Plautus and Terence, his dramatic instinct, stimulated by his predecessors, divined that there was a profounder pattern in the argument of comedy than appears in either of them. At once—for the process is beginning in *The Comedy of Errors*—he started groping toward the profounder pattern, the ritual of death and revival that also underlies Aristophanes, of which an exact equivalent lay ready to hand in the drama of the green world. This parallelism largely accounts for the resemblances to Greek ritual which Colin Still has pointed out in *The Tempest*.

The Two Gentlemen of Verona is an orthodox New Comedy except for one thing. The hero Valentine becomes captain of a band of outlaws in a forest, and all the other characters are gathered into this forest and become converted. Thus the action of the comedy begins in a world represented as a normal world, moves into the green world, goes into a metamorphosis there in which the comic resolution is achieved, and returns to the normal world. The forest in this play is the embryonic form of the fairy world of *A Midsummer Night's Dream*, the Forest of Arden in *As You Like It*, Windsor Forest in *The Merry Wives of Windsor*, and the pastoral world of the mythical sea-coasted Bohemia in *The Winter's Tale*. In all these comedies there is the same rhythmic movement from normal world to green world and back again. Nor is this second world confined to the forest comedies. In *The Merchant of Venice* the two worlds are a little harder to see, yet Venice is clearly not the same world as that of Portia's mysterious house in Belmont, where there are caskets teaching that gold and silver are corruptible goods, and from whence proceed the wonderful cosmological harmonies of the fifth act. In *The Tempest* the entire action takes place in the second world, and the same may be said of *Twelfth Night*, which, as its title implies, presents a carnival society, not so much a green world as an evergreen one. The second world is absent from the so-called problem comedies, which is one of the things that makes them problem comedies.

The green world charges the comedies with a symbolism in which the comic resolution contains a suggestion of the old ritual pattern of the victory of summer over winter. This is explicit in *Love's Labour's Lost*. In this very masque-like play, the comic contest takes the form of the medieval debate of winter and spring. In *The Merry Wives of Windsor* there is an elaborate ritual of the defeat of winter, known to folklorists as "carrying out Death," of which Falstaff is the victim; and Falstaff must have felt that, after being thrown into the water, dressed up as a witch and beaten out of a house with curses, and finally supplied with a beast's head and singed with candles while he said, "Divide me like a brib'd buck, each a haunch," he had done about all that could reasonably be asked of any fertility spirit.

The association of this symbolism with the death and revival of human beings is more elusive, but still perceptible. The fact that the heroine often brings about the comic resolution by disguising herself as a boy is familiar enough. In the Hero of *Much Ado About Nothing* and the Helena of *All's Well That Ends Well*, this theme of the withdrawal and return of the heroine comes as close to a death and revival as Elizabethan conventions will allow. The Thaisa of *Pericles* and the Fidele of *Cymbeline* are beginning to crack the conventions, and with the disappearance and revival of Hermione in *The Winter's Tale,* who actually returns once as a ghost in a dream, the original nature-myth of Demeter and Proserpine is openly established. The fact that the dying and reviving character is usually female strengthens the feeling that there is something maternal about the green world, in which the new order of the comic resolution is nourished and brought to birth. However, a similar theme which is very like the rejuvenation of the *senex* so frequent in Aristophanes occurs in the folklore motif of the healing of the impotent king on which *All's Well That Ends Well* is based, and this theme is probably involved in the symbolism of Prospero.

The conception of a second world bursts the boundaries of Menandrine comedy, yet it is clear that the world of Puck is no world of eternal forms or divine revelation. Shakespeare's comedy is not Aristotelian and realistic like Menander's, nor Platonic and dialectic like Aristophanes', nor Thomist and sacramental like Dante's, but a fourth kind. It is an Elizabethan kind, and is not confined either to Shakespeare or to the drama. Spenser's epic is a wonderful contrapuntal intermingling of two orders of existence, one the red and white world of English history, the other the green world of the Faerie Queene. The latter is a world of crusading virtues proceeding from the Faerie Queene's court and designed to return to that court when the destiny of the other world is fulfilled. The fact that the Faerie Queene's knights are sent out during the twelve days of the Christmas festival suggests our next point.

Shakespeare too has his green world of comedy and his red and white world of history. The story of the latter is at one point interrupted by an invasion from the comic world, when Falstaff *senex et parasitus* throws his gigantic shadow over Prince Henry, assuming on one occasion the role of his father. Clearly, if the Prince is ever to conquer France he must reassert the moral norm. The moral norm is duly reasserted, but the rejection of Falstaff is not a comic resolution. In comedy the moral norm is not morality but deliverance, and we certainly do not feel delivered from Falstaff as we feel delivered from Shylock with his absurd and vicious bond. The moral norm does not carry with it the vision of a free society: Falstaff will always keep a bit of that in his tavern.

Falstaff is a mock king, a lord of misrule, and his tavern is a

Saturnalia. Yet we are reminded of the original meaning of the Saturnalia, as a rite intended to recall the golden age of Saturn. Falstaff's world is not a golden world, but as long as we remember it we cannot forget that the world of *Henry V* is an iron one. We are reminded too of another traditional denizen of the green world, Robin Hood, the outlaw who manages to suggest a better kind of society than those who make him an outlaw can produce. The outlaws in *The Two Gentlemen of Verona* compare themselves, in spite of the Italian setting, to Robin Hood, and in *As You Like It* Charles the wrestler says of Duke Senior's followers: "There they live like the old Robin Hood of England: they say many young gentlemen flock to him every day, and fleet the time carelessly, as they did in the golden world."

In the histories, therefore, the comic Saturnalia is a temporary reversal of normal standards, comic "relief" as it is called, which subsides and allows the history to continue. In the comedies, the green world suggests an original golden age which the normal world has usurped and which makes us wonder if it is not the normal world that is the real Saturnalia. In *Cymbeline* the green world finally triumphs over a historical theme, the reason being perhaps that in that play the incarnation of Christ, which is contemporary with Cymbeline, takes place offstage, and accounts for the halcyon peace with which the play concludes. From then on in Shakespeare's plays, the green world has it all its own way, and both in *Cymbeline* and in *Henry VIII* there may be suggestions that Shakespeare, like Spenser, is moving toward a synthesis of the two worlds, a wedding of Prince Arthur and the Faerie Queene.

This world of fairies, dreams, disembodied souls, and pastoral lovers may not be a "real" world, but, if not, there is something equally illusory in the stumbling and blinded follies of the "normal" world, of Theseus' Athens with its idiotic marriage law, of Duke Frederick and his melancholy tyranny, of Leontes and his mad jealousy, of the Court Party with their plots and intrigues. The famous speech of Prospero about the dream nature of reality applies equally to Milan and the enchanted island. We spend our lives partly in a waking world we call normal and partly in a dream world which we create out of our own desires. Shakespeare endows both worlds with equal imaginative power, brings them opposite one another, and makes each world seem unreal when seen by the light of the other. He uses freely both the heroic triumph of New Comedy and the ritual resurrection of its predecessor, but his distinctive comic resolution is different from either: it is a detachment of the spirit born of this reciprocal reflection of two illusory realities. We need not ask whether this brings us into a higher order of existence or not, for the question of existence is not relevant to poetry.

We have spoken of New Comedy as Aristotelian, Old Comedy as Platonic and Dante's *commedia* as Thomist, but it is difficult to suggest a philosophical spokesman for the form of Shakespeare's comedy. For Shakespeare, the subject matter of poetry is not life, or nature, or reality, or revelation, or anything else that the philosopher builds on, but poetry itself, a verbal universe. That is one reason why he is both the most elusive and the most substantial of poets.

E. E. STOLL
1874-1959

E. E. STOLL, a redoubtable polemicist, directed heavy blows at impressionistic criticism throughout his long life. His books include *Othello* (1915), *Hamlet* (1919), *Shakespeare Studies* (1927), *Poets and Playwrights* (1930), *Art and Artifice in Shakespeare* (1933), *Shakespeare's Young Lovers* (1937), *Shakespeare and Other Masters* (1940), and *From Shakespeare to Joyce* (1944). The cudgel which he used seems to have become more gnarled and his prose more knotty through the years. He was concerned with elucidating Shakespeare through the study of the history of dramatic technique and of Elizabethan convention and was one of the first to call attention to the non-realistic elements in Shakespeare. However, the disciples of G. Wilson Knight who joined Stoll in attacking those who engaged in the psychological analysis of Shakespeare's characters as though they were human beings also directed their fire against Stoll. Stoll early in his career had announced as his credo: "To criticize is not merely or primarily to analyze one's own impression of a work of art, as the impressionistic critics aver, but to ascertain, if possible, the author's intention, and to gauge and measure the forces and tendencies of his time." Knight, on the other hand, writing twenty years later at the outset of his own career, had affirmed in his credo that the intentions of the artist, stated in terms of intellectual discourse, furnish a poor guide to his work, which is the product of his imagination, and that the study of supposed forces and tendencies is of no help in interpretation. "The intellectual mode . . . with its army of 'intentions,' 'causes,' 'sources' . . . . works havoc with our minds, since it is trying to impose on the vivid reality of art a logic totally alien to its nature." Ironically, then, while Bradley's reputation has recovered from the attacks made against it two decades ago, partly perhaps as a result of Knight's 1947 statement in a new edition of *The Wheel of Fire* that when he had attacked character analysis he had not meant to repudiate Bradley, Stoll's reputation seems to be in a state of decline.

The tendency among many now is to regard Stoll as having performed a useful negative service in his demolition work, but that is all; the historical critic has merely served an historical function. There is some truth here, but it is an exaggeration. Stoll's value does not reside solely in his attacks on error. Although his statement of his credo, like Knight's statement, was extreme (the job of the critic, it would seem, is indeed primarily to analyze his own impression of a work of art—but only after he has possessed himself as much as he can of the attitudes and expectations of the author's contemporaries), Stoll was a sensitive critic as well as an enormously erudite scholar.

An essay such as the one on Shylock, only small portions of which follow, is an historical reconstruction that requires not only the special knowledge by which the restorer of a painting by an old master removes centuries of incrustation from it. It requires also the taste and judgment of the art critic. This reconstruction is, to be sure, not universally accepted as authentic, although, directly or indirectly, it has strongly influenced subsequent discussions of the portrait. Perhaps the dominant view today regards Shylock as the comical villain pictured by Stoll but holds that Shakespeare, with his genius for identifying himself with his characters, caused him to speak for himself so that, at least for a moment, we see things from his view rather than from that of the aristocratic characters. For Stoll this is a distortion of the play, a last, desperate attempt to save Shakespeare from being a man of his age. In any case it would seem that we can laugh at Shylock's comic rigidity and shiver at his villainy, that we can respond to the contrast between his harshly grotesque world of the Rialto, now comical and now picturesquely diabolic, and Portia's poetically romantic world of Belmont, without accepting as our own the medieval stereotype of the Jew, just as we can respond to the vision of universal chaos in the tragedies without accepting as our own the notion of interrelated hierarchies. "The great poets," as R. W. Chambers has said, defending Shakespeare's use of the substituted bride story, "speak to all time only through the language, conventions, and beliefs of their own age." In the theatre, however, our enjoyment will be impaired as long as, racial prejudice continuing, we must wonder if our laughter will be misinterpreted or if our neighbor's laughter is a manifestation of his own bias.

SHYLOCK A COMICAL VILLAIN

To GET AT Shakespeare's intention (after a fashion) is, despite all, not hard. As with popular drama, great or small, he who runs may read—he who yawns and scuffles in the pit may understand. The time is past for speaking of Shakespeare as utterly impartial or in-

"Shylock a Comical Villain" is from Edgar Elmer Stoll, *Shakespeare Studies* (Macmillan, 1927), pp. 262–269, 311–320, 324–327, 329–336.

scrutable: the study of his work and that of his fellows as an expression of Elizabethan ideas and technique is teaching us better. The puzzle whether the *Merchant of Venice* is not meant for tragedy, for instance, is cleared up when, as Professor Baker suggests, we forget Sir Henry Irving's acting, and remember that the title—and the hero—is not the 'Jew of Venice' as he would lead us to suppose; that this comedy is only like others, as *Measure for Measure* and *Much Ado,* not clear of the shadow of the fear of death; and that in closing with an act where Shylock and his knife are forgotten in the unravelling of the mystery between the lovers and the crowning of Antonio's happiness in theirs, it does not, from the Elizabethan point of view, perpetrate an anti-climax, but, like many another Elizabethan play, carries to completion what is a story for story's sake. 'Shylock is, and always has been the hero,' says Professor Schelling. But why, then, did Shakespeare drop his hero out of the play for good before the fourth act was over? It is a trick which he never repeated—a trick, I am persuaded, of which he was not capable.

Hero or not, Shylock is given a villain's due. His is the heaviest penalty to be found in all the pound of flesh stories, including that in *Il Pecorone,* which served as model for the play. Not in the Servian, the Persian, the African version, or even that of the *Cursor Mundi,* does the money-lender suffer like Shylock—impoverishment, sentence of death, and an outrage done to his faith from which Jews were guarded even by decrees of German emperors and Roman pontiffs. It was in the old play, perhaps, source of the present one; but that Shakespeare retained it shows his indifference, at least, to the amenities, as regards either Jews or Judaism. In not a single heart do Shylock's griefs excite commiseration; indeed, as they press upon him they are barbed with gibes and jeers. Coriolanus is unfortunate and at fault, but we know that the poet is with him. We know that the poet is not with Shylock, for on that point, in this play as in every other, the impartial, inscrutable poet leaves little or nothing to suggestion or surmise. As is his custom elsewhere, by the comments of the good characters, by the methods pursued in the disposition of scenes, and by the downright avowals of soliloquy, he constantly sets us right.

As for the first of these artifices, all the people who come in contact with Shylock except Tubal—among them being those of his own house, his servant and his daughter—have a word or two to say on the subject of his character, and never a good one. And in the same breath they spend on Bassanio and Antonio, his enemies, nothing but words of praise. Praise or blame, moreover, is, after Shakespeare's fashion, usually in the nick of time to guide the hearer's judgment. Lest at his first appearance the Jew should make too favorable an impression by his Scripture quotations, Antonio is led to observe that the devil can cite Scripture for his purpose; lest the Jew's motive in foregoing interest (for once in his life) should seem like the kindness Antonio takes it to be, Bassanio avows that he likes not fair terms and a villain's mind; and once the Jew has caught the Christian on the hip, every one, from Duke to Gaoler, has words of horror or detestation for him and of compassion for his victim.

As for the second artifice, the ordering of the scenes is such as to enforce this contrast. First impressions, every playwright knows (and no one better than Shakespeare himself), are momentous, particularly for the purpose of ridicule. Launcelot and Jessica, in separate scenes, are introduced before Shylock reaches home, that, hearing their story, we may side with them, and, when the old curmudgeon appears, may be moved to laughter as he complains of Launcelot's gormandizing, sleeping, and rending apparel out, and as he is made game of by the young conspirators to his face. Here, as Mr Poel has noticed, when there might be some danger of our sympathy becoming enlisted on Shylock's side because he is about to lose his daughter and some of his property, Shakespeare forestalls it. He lets Shylock, in his hesitation whether to go to the feast, take warning from a dream, but nevertheless, though he knows that they bid him not for love, decide to go in hate, in order to feed upon the prodigal Christian. And he lets him give up Launcelot, whom he has half a liking for, save that he is a huge feeder, to Bassanio—'to one that I would have him help to waste his borrowed purse.' Small credit these sentiments do him; little do they add to his pathos or dignity. Still more conspicuous is this care when Shylock laments over his daughter and his ducats. Lest then by any chance a stupid or tender-hearted audience should not laugh but grieve, Salanio reports his outcries—in part word for word —two scenes in advance, as matter of mirth to himself and all the boys in Venice. It is exactly the same method as that employed in *Twelfth Night,* Act III, scene ii, where Maria comes and tells not only Sir Toby, Sir Andrew, and Fabian, but, above all, the audience, how ridiculously Malvolio is acting, before they see it for themselves. The art of the theatre, but particularly the art of the comic theatre, is the art of preparations, else it is not securely comic. But the impression first of all imparted to us is of Shylock's villainy—an impression which, however comical he may become, we are not again allowed to lose. In the first scene in which he appears, the third in the play, there is one of the most remarkable instances in dramatic literature of a man saying one thing but thinking another and the audience made to see this. He prolongs the situation, keeps the Christians on tenterhooks, turns the terms of the contract over and over in his mind, as if he were considering the soundness of it and of the borrower, while all the time he is hoping, for once in his life, that his debtor may turn out not sound but bankrupt. He casts up Antonio's hard usage of him in the past, defends the practice of interest-taking, is at the point of stipulating what the rate this time shall be, and then— decides to be friends and take no interest at all. He seems, and is, loath to part for a time with three thousand ducats—' 'tis a good round sum!'—but at the bottom of his heart he is eager.

And as for the third artifice, that a sleepy audience may not make the mistake of the cautious critic and take the villain for the hero, Shakespeare is at pains to label the villain by an aside at the moment the hero appears on the boards:

> I hate him for he is a Christian,
> But more for that in low simplicity
> He lends out money gratis, and brings down
> The rate of usance here with us in Venice.

Those are his motives, later confessed repeatedly;[1] and either one brands him as a villain more unmistakably in that day, as we shall see, than in ours. Of the indignities which he has endured he speaks also, and of revenge; but of none of these has he anything to say at the trial. There he pleads his oath, perjury to his soul should he break it, his 'lodged hate,' or his 'humour'; further than that, 'I can give no reason nor I will not,'—for some reasons a man does not give; but

[1] *M. V.* I, iii, 43 f.; III, i, 55 f., 133; III, iii, 2—'the fool that lends out money gratis'; and compare Antonio, line 22 f.:—

> I oft delivered from his forfeitures
> Many that have at times made moan to me:
> Therefore he hates me.

here to himself and later to Tubal—'were he out of Venice I can make what merchandise I will'—he tells, in the thick of the action, the unvarnished truth. As with Shakespeare's villains generally—Aaron, Iago, or Richard III—only what they say concerning their purposes aside or to their confidants can be relied upon; and Shylock's oath and his horror of perjury are, as Dr Furness observes, belied by his clutching at thrice the principal when the pound of flesh escapes him, just as is his money-lender's ruse of[2] pretending to borrow the cash from 'a friend' (avowed as such by Moses in the *School for Scandal*) by his going home 'to purse the ducats straight.'

His arguments, moreover, are given a specious, not to say a grotesque colouring. Similar ones used by the Jew in Silvayn's *Orator* (1596), probably known to Shakespeare, are there called 'sophistical.' But Hazlitt and other critics strangely say that in argument Shylock has the best of it.

> What if my house be troubled with a rat
> And I be pleas'd to give ten thousand ducats
> To have it ban'd?

This particular rat is a human being; but the only thing to remark upon, in Shylock's opinion, is his willingness to squander ten thousand ducats on it instead of three. 'Hates any man the thing,' he cries (and there he is ticketed), 'he would not kill!' Even in Hazlitt's time, moreover, a choice of 'carrion flesh' in preference to ducats could not be plausibly compared as a 'humour'—the Jew's gross jesting here grates upon you—with an aversion to pigs or to the sound of the bag-pipe, or defended as a right by the analogy of holding slaves; nor could the practice of interest-taking find a warrant in Jacob's pastoral trickery while in the service of Laban; least of all in the day when Sir John Hawkins, who initiated the slave-trade, with the Earls of Pembroke and Leicester and the Queen herself for partners, bore on the arms which were granted him for his exploits a demi-Moor, proper, in chains, and in the day when the world at large still held interest-taking to be robbery. Very evidently, moreover, Shylock is discomfited by Antonio's question 'Did he take interest?' for he falters and stumbles in his reply—

[2] In Silvayn's *Orator* (Furness, 311); *L'Avare*, II, i; and it is employed also by Isaac of York.

> No, not take interest, not, as you would say,
> Directly, interest,—

and is worsted, in the eyes of the audience if not in his own, by the repeated use of the old Aristotelian argument of the essential barrenness of money, still gospel in Shakespeare's day, in the second question,

> Or is your gold and silver ewes and rams?

For his answer is meant for nothing better than a piece of complacent shamelessness:

> I cannot tell: I make it breed as fast.

Only twice does Shakespeare seem to follow Shylock's pleadings and reasonings with any sympathy—'Hath a dog money?' in the first scene in which he appears, and 'Hath not a Jew eyes?' in the third act—but a bit too much has been made of this. Either plea ends in such fashion as to alienate the audience. To Shylock's reproaches the admirable Antonio, 'one of the gentlest and humblest of all the men in Shakespeare's theatre,'[3] praised and honoured by every one but Shylock, retorts, secure in his virtue, that he is just as like to spit on him and spurn him again. And Shylock's celebrated justification of his race runs headlong into a justification of his villainy: 'The villainy which you teach me I will execute, and it shall go hard but I will better the instruction.' 'Hath not a Jew eyes?' and he proceeds to show that your Jew is no less than a man, and as such has a right, not to respect or compassion, as the critics for a century have had it, but to revenge. Neither large nor lofty are his claims. The speech begins with the answer to Salanio's question about the pound of flesh. 'Why, I am sure, if he forfeit, thou wilt not take his flesh. What's that good for?' 'To bait fish withal,' he retorts in savage jest; 'if it will feed nothing else it will feed my revenge'; and he goes on to complain of insults, and of thwarted bargains to the tune of half a million, and to make a plea for which he has already robbed himself of a hearing. Quite as vigorously and (in that day) with as much reason, the detestable and abominable Aaron defends his race and colour, and Edmund, the dignity of bastards. The worst of his villains Shakespeare allows to

---

[3] Cf. J. W. Hales, *English Historical Review,* ix, p. 652, f., especially p. 660 for an accumulation of the evidence for his goodness and amiableness. 'A kinder gentleman treads not the earth.'

plead their cause: their confidences in soliloquy or aside, if not (as here) slight touches in the plea itself, sufficiently counteract any too favourable impression. This, on the face of it, is a plea for indulging in revenge with all its rigours; not a word is put in for the nobler side of Jewish character; and in lending Shylock his eloquence Shakespeare is but giving the devil his due . . .[4]

To the comic effect of Jonson's *Silent Woman,* not only in Shakespeare's day but long after, there is abundant and authoritative testimony—to the comic effect of the 'heartless raging of harmless old Morose,' whose only shortcomings were a 'tight purse and extreme tranquillity.' These may have offended the *beau monde* as smacking of the bourgeois, the Puritan. But to laugh and jeer at Shylock would have been less cruel, more human, in its inhumanity.

However that be, lest our own laughter should fail—we here approach the last principle—the situation has been hedged about with the most explicitly comic technique and apparatus. There is in Shakespeare's comedy comparatively little, as we have seen, which squares with the rationale of it in Monsieur Bergson's book; little of that highly developed, formal comic technique, which somewhat reminds you of the structure of music, abounding in Molière; but an exception is to be found in the scenes where Shylock appears. Here, quite apart from the social and racial prejudices brought so directly to bear

---

[4] It is in these passages, no doubt, that, according to Mr [W. H.] Hudson, the racial feeling rises superior to Shylock's greed and personal ferocity, and Shylock becomes an impressive, tragic figure. I dislike to disagree with a critic with whom I have found myself, unawares, so often agreeing; but I think that at this point Mr Hudson has not quite shaken off the spell of the *Zeitgeist,* of which, as he himself confesses, it is hard to rid the mind. As I show below, *passim,* these appeals did not reach the hearts of the Elizabethans as they reach ours. Mr Hudson explains them, like Professor Wendell, as moments where Shylock 'got too much for Shakespeare,' and said what he liked. But that dark saying I cannot comprehend—not in itself and still less on the lips of a critic who protests, so justly, against treating the characters of Shakespeare as if they were real people in a real world. What else are Mr Hudson and Mr Wendell doing when they let the poet be inspired by those whom he himself had inspired, and so say things in a spirit of racial sympathy beyond his ken? 'Shylock spoke as Shylock would speak'—not Shakespeare—'spoke so simply because of the life which had been breathed into him.' Granting that, Mr Hudson surrenders all the ground he had gained for historical criticism. Shylock is thereupon free to say, regardless of his maker, whatever it comes into the head of the critic to have him say; and here is the entering in of the wedge for all those modernizing tendencies which Mr Hudson, like a scholar, abhors.

upon him, are the comic devices of repetition and inversion, as well as others less easily designated.

By repetition I mean, as in chapter iv, not the repetition of words or phrases at happy junctures (often comically used by Elizabethans like Dekker, as well as by dramatists so different and remote from one another as Plautus, Molière, and Ibsen) but the repetition of a *motif,* as in the daughter-ducats dialogue with Tubal, and in this case it takes the form of alternation:

> *Tubal.* One of them showed me a ring that he had of your daughter for a monkey.
>
> *Shylock.* Out upon her. Thou torturest me, Tubal. It was my turquoise; I had it of Leah when I was a bachelor. I would not have given it for a wilderness of monkeys.

This, most critics assert, the great historian of the drama almost alone dissenting,[5] is pathos: it is not the ducats behind the turquoise ('a diamond gone, cost me two thousand ducats in Frankfort!') but the thought of Leah that wrings his heart. 'What a fine Hebraism is implied in this expression!' cries Hazlitt. 'He has so deep a veneration for his dead wife,' says Hawkins, with impenetrable gravity, 'that a wilderness of monkeys would not compensate for the loss of the ring she had given him in youth.'[6] More Elizabethan fun running to waste! We may not be used to laughing at a man as he mourns the flight of his daughter, the memory of his wife, or the theft of his ducats; but neither are we used, any more than Salanio or the boys of Venice, to the manner of his mourning.

> I never heard a passion so confus'd,
> So strange, outrageous, and so variable.

Shylock is a puppet, and Tubal pulls the strings. Now he shrieks in grief for his ducats or his daughter, now in glee at Antonio's ruin. In his rage at the trading of a turquoise for a monkey, he blurts out, true to his native instincts, 'not for a wilderness of monkeys!' and the Elizabethan audience, as well as some few readers to-day, have the heart—or the want of it—to think the valuation funny. The rest may find it hard to laugh at this, as in the opinion of Rousseau, Taine, Mantzius, and many another candid spirit, it is nowadays hard to

---

[5] Creizenach. *Geschichte des Dramas* (1909), iv, pp. 279–80.
[6] Quoted by Furness, Variorum ed., p. 433.

laugh at the plight of George Dandin or Arnolphe, or, to come nearer home, as it is hard to laugh at the torments of Malvolio; but the invitation to hilarity is in all these instances plain and clear. The true Molière has been pretty well restored not only to the stage but also to his right status in criticism; but in lands where people see (however more profoundly) less clearly, Shylock's love for Leah moves men to tears, and Mr Sothern can elicit sympathy for Olivia's stately steward pleading in a madman's chains to be set free. But Mr Granville Barker, at the Savoy a few years ago, and Monsieur Copeau, at the Vieux Colombier, produced the latter play surely as Shakespeare intended it to be, and forebore to spoil and thwart his purely comic scene.

The mistake of the critics is in some measure that of viewing the text piecemeal and not as a whole. Wrenched from the context, there are phrases, even sentences, that may, indeed, seem pathetic. But Shakespeare, as soon as Tubal enters, lets Shylock strike up the tune of 'my daughter—my ducats,' and, adhering to the method of comic alternation throughout the scene, plays the familiar dramatic trick of taking the audience in for a moment and of then clapping upon the seemingly pathetic sentiment a cynical, selfish, or simply incongruous one:—

Two thousand ducats in that; and other precious, precious jewels. I would my daughter were dead at my foot—and the jewels in her ear! Would she were hears'd at my foot—and the ducats in her coffin.

The dashes are my own, replacing commas in the quartos and folios; they are necessary, according to modern usage, to carry out what seems the manifest intention of the author. Such quick afterthoughts and comical anticlimaxes as we have here are to be found elsewhere in Shakespeare and in comic dialogue to this day. In *Le Malade imaginaire* Béline, his designing second wife, is bid by the dying Argan to take the money out of the cupboard—

Non, non, je ne veux point de tout cela. Ah!—combien dites-vous qu'il y a dans votre alcôve?

Falstaff, taking account of his slender stock of virtues, recalls that he had paid back money that he borrowed—'three or four times'; Sir Peter Teazle, speaking of Charles, declares to Joseph that never in life had he denied him—'my advice'; Bob Acres, replying to Jack

Absolute as he reassures Sir Lucius ('He generally kills a man a week
—don't you, Bob?') cries, 'Aye—at home'; and old Eccles, in the
presence of the young folk, vows that 'there is nothing like work—for
the young.' So Shylock cannot wish that his daughter were dead at his
foot (if that really be pathos) without, at the same time, wishing that
the jewels were in her ear, the ducats in her coffin;[7] he cannot hear
that there is no news of them without bewailing what has been 'spent
in the search'; he cannot think of Launcelot's kindness, as he parts
with him, without also thinking—'a huge feeder!'—of his appetite;
and when he hears of his turquoise exchanged for a monkey, thoughts
of Leah, his bachelorhood, and a wilderness of monkeys come clatter-
ing through his brain. Here is pathos side by side with laughter, but
not—according to Mr Schelling's thought—the grotesqueness bordering on laughter, the pathos bordering on tears. The nuance, the
harmony is lacking—in true Elizabethan style, there is glaring contrast instead. The pathos is a pretense, a moment's illusion; the
laughter alone is real. Nor is it restrained—it is nothing less than a
roar; the grotesqueness passes over the border of laughter—perhaps of
tears.

I have used above the figure of the puppet and the string; and
surely nowhere else in Shakespeare do we get so distinctly as here that
effect of the human being turned mechanical—automaton, or jack-
in-the-box—which is frequent in comedy, as Monsieur Bergson has
shown. We are familiar, as I have said, with such comically mechanical effects in ordinary life, when, for instance (to employ the vernacu-
lar) we 'take a rise out of' a person. We speak the provocative
word—pull the string or press the spring,—and, behold, the effect
expected! Shakespeare does that through the comfortable Tubal's
alternate method of imparting his news, though he only continues the
alternation set at work when first Shylock learned of his double loss:
—Tubal pulls the strings of a puppet already in motion. The situation
is thus instinct with comedy, pathos could not possibly live in its
midst. The same situation indeed was already established on the
stage as comic, as 'pathétique plaisant,' for the outcries of robbed
misers had entertained 'hard-hearted' audiences since the days of

[7] Professor Jastrow and Dr Honigmann, like Heine (*mirabile dictu!*) before them, see no fun here. Racial sympathy hinders them. 'He would prefer
burying his child and his gold,' says the former [*Penn Monthly*, 1880], 'to knowing them to be in the possession of the Christian fools.' If Shylock buried it he
would not forget the spot.

Euclio. Marlowe's Barabas had displayed even the same jumble of emotions, as he gloated over his girl and his gold, and probably there had been others too. A little later Cyrano de Bergerac, in the scene of *Le Pédeant joué,* noticed above, presents comically, like Molière and Shakespeare, the pangs of paternal affection contending with avarice, but attains a climax not to be found in either. Unlike Géronte, Granger does not yet know the amount of the ransom demanded to save his son from hanging; but when he hears that it is a hundred pistoles, the scale then and there ceases to balance and kicks the beam. 'Go, Corbineli, tell him to be hanged and have done with it.' Here is the same grotesque, and (for the hard-hearted) comical, pref-erence of the loss of a child to a worse thing that might befall him, that we find afterwards in *L'Avare,* when Harpagon declares that the fact that Valére (charged with having stolen his casket of treasure) had saved his daughter's life, is nothing, and tells her 'it were much better to have let you drown than have done what he has done.' 'Would she were hears'd at my foot—and the ducats in her coffin!' Harpagon, we remember, used to be misinterpreted, as Shylock still is; but Coquelin *cadet* changed that, and now again, as when Molière played him—and as when to Robinet he wrote of the playing—'d'un bout à l'autre il fait rire.'

Then there is inversion, the tables turned. 'L'histoire du persécuteur victime de sa persécution, du dupeur dupé, du voleur volé, fait le fond de bien des comédies.' The trial scene is an example. To most critics Shylock has here seemed to be more or less pathetic, despite the fact that, as I take it, Shakespeare has employed almost every possible means to produce a contrary, quite incompatible effect.

Professor Baker holds that Shakespeare evinces a sense of dramatic values in presenting Shylock's disappointment as tragic in his own eyes, amusing in Gratiano's. How is the tragic value presented? By the miser and usurer's prostrate prayer to the Duke to take his life if he would take his wealth, or by the plea that he is not well? The biter bitten, is the best gibe cast at him at the end of *Il Pecorone;* and that, exactly, is the spirit of the scene. It is the same spirit and almost the same situation as at the close of Sheridan's *Duenna,* where another Jew, not nearly so culpable as Shylock, having now been fast married to the dragon herself, not, as he thinks, to the maiden that she guards, is jeered at for it, while one of the characters gives the reason,—that 'there is not a fairer subject for contempt and ridicule than a knave become the dupe of his own art.' Shylock's disappointment is tragic to him, but good care is taken that it shall not be to us. Shakespeare is less intent on values than on the conduct and direction of our sympathies through the scene. This he manages both by the action and the comment. The scene is a rise and a fall, a triumph turned into a defeat, an apparent tragedy into a comedy; and the defeat is made to repeat the stages of the triumph so as to bring home to us the fact—the comic fact—of retribution. When fortune turns, almost all the steps of the ladder whereby Shylock with scales and knife had climbed to clutch the fruit of revenge he must now descend empty-handed and in bitterness; and what had been offered to him and refused by him, he is now, when he demands it again, refused. With the course of the action the comment is in perfect accord and unison, marking and signalizing the stages of Shylock's fall. The outcries against the Jew and his stony heart, of the Duke, Bassanio, and Gratiano—protested against by Antonio as futile—give place to the jeers of Gratiano and the irony of the fair judge. Gratiano is not the only one to crow. 'Thou shalt have justice, more than thou desir'st —Soft! The Jew shall have all justice—Why doth the Jew pause? Take thy forfeiture—Tarry, Jew; the law hath yet another hold on you—Art thou contented, Jew? What dost thou say?' Aimed at Shylock as he pleads and squirms, these words fall from lips which had a moment before extolled the heavenly qualities of mercy! But for more than the meagre mercy which Shylock is shown there is neither time nor place, the crowing fits the latter part of the action as perfectly as the indignant comment had fitted the earlier, and we must equally accept it or divest the scene of meaning and sense. The Jew's very words are echoed by Portia and Gratiano as they jeer, and at every turn that the course of justice takes (welcomed by Shylock, while it was in his favour, with hoarse cries of gloating and triumph) there are now peals and shouts of laughter, such laughter as arises when Tartuffe the hypocrite is caught by Orgon,—'un rire se lève de tous les coins de la salle, un rire de vengeance si vous voulez, un rire amer, un rire violent.'[8] The running fire assails him to the very moment —and beyond it—that Shylock says he is not well, and staggers out, amid Gratiano's jeers touching his baptism, to provoke in the audience the laughter of triumph and vengeance in his own day and bring

[8] Sarcey, *Quarante ans,* ii, 132.

tears to their eyes in ours. How can we here for a moment sympathize with Shylock unless at the same time we indignantly turn, not only against Gratiano, but against Portia, the Duke, and all Venice as well? But Shakespeare's scene it is—Shakespeare's comedy,—not ours or Hazlitt's.

One reason why the critics have, despite all, even in this scene, found pathos in Shylock, is that they well know that comic effects may keep company with the pathetic, in Shakespeare as in Dostoevsky and Chekhov. They remember Mercutio's last words, Mrs Quickly's report of Falstaff's death, or the Fool's babblings in *King Lear*. Laughter may indeed blend with tears when the character is treated tenderly; but here and in the daughter-ducats scene it is, as I have said, only the laughter of derision. In the judgment scene, moreover, there is— very clearly marked—the spirit of retaliation; it is a harsh and vindictive laughter; and if Shakespeare had here intended any minor and momentary pathetic effects such as critics nowadays discover, he simply overwhelms them. Professor Matthews says that Shakespeare meant the spectators to hate Shylock and also to laugh at him, and yet made him pathetic—supremely pathetic too. The combination seems to me impossible, at least in a comedy, and Professor Matthews seems to me to be talking metaphysics and forgetting the stage which he knows so well. If hateful, Shylock would provoke in the audience the *rire de vengeance,* an echo of Gratiano's jeer; if pathetic also, he would—and should—provoke no laughter (at least of such kind as is known to me) at all. In comedy, at any rate, things must be simple and clear-cut; a character which is to provoke laughter cannot be kept, like Buridan's ass, in equilibrium, exciting, at the same time, both sympathy and hatred. For then the audience will keep its equilibrium too.

The crowing is not indispensable to the process of comic inversion, or the turning of the tables. Even without it, Shylock could quite well have been made to swallow the medicine, drop by drop, and be now refused what he had earlier been offered. Portia's words about justice, the forfeiture, and the bond, whereby she reverses the machinery that had been set in motion, might have been enough. Gratiano's crowing is, then, a bit of formal comic technique, added to make the effect unmistakable and secure. What pains comic dramatists take, and yet, in a century, they may be futile! Gratiano—and Portia also when she

turns against Shylock—makes the audience in the court laugh, that in
the theatre they may be certain to laugh too. The twitting and crowing
when the tables are turned is to be found serving this same purpose
elsewhere in Shakespeare, as in *Love's Labour's Lost, Much Ado,
Twelfth Night,* and *Henry IV;* indeed (where there is no inversion)
the merry report by Salanio and Salarino of Shylock's 'strange' and
'variable' lamentations, and of the outcries of all the boys in Venice, is
introduced for a similar end. Sarcey, as he discusses *Les Femmes
savantes* and *Le Monde où l'on s'ennuie,* observes that in these alike
there is one method because there is no other:

> Le public n'y sent le ridicule des mœurs qui sont traduites sur la
> scène, que par l'étonnement que provoquent ces mœurs chez un
> personnage en scène. Il s'en amuse en les entendant railler; il rit par
> contre-coup,—*Quarante ans,* vi, p. 312.

The comic effect in the theatre is the echo and reduplication of that on
the stage—somewhat as the shudder of wonder at the supernatural
spreads and is caught up by the spectators from Horatio, Brutus, or
Macbeth. Laughter, we all know, is contagious—in an instant the
electric spark circles the house, explodes the magazine.

There are still other comic devices, such as the anti-climaxes and
prompt miserly afterthoughts of Shylock, comical on the face of them,
and the whetting of his knife. All together, there is in the Shylock
scenes such an array of these as is nowhere else to be found in Shakespeare save in the *Comedy of Errors* or in the *Taming of the Shrew.*
As Mr Woodbury says, and Booth had recognized, Shakespeare 'did
not hesitate to let the exhibition of these low qualities [avarice, cunning, and revenge] approach the farcical.' In general the comedy in
Shakespeare is more a comedy of character than of situation, and the
situations, as I have said, are seldom worked out and developed to
the full; but here we have repetition and inversion, crowing and anti-
climaxes, as in Molière; and in a comic tune wrought out so elaborately and emphatically that one wonders how any pathetic note could
possibly find a place in it, save for the moment, and then only to
contribute to the prevailing effect. . . .

The speech that to-day moves us most is 'Hath not a Jew eyes?'
etc., discussed above. This, again, is the speech not so much of a
comic character as of a villain; and like other villains in Shakespeare,
as we have seen, he is given his due—a full chance to speak up and to

make a fair showing for himself—while he holds the floor. But it seems quite impossible to take it as pathetic, so hedged about is it with prejudice, beginning on a note of thwarted avarice and of revengefulness, and ending on one of rivalry in revenge, of beating the Christians at what, however justly, he chooses to think their own game. Certainly it is not the plea for toleration that it has generally been taken to be,— here in the third act, after all this cloud of prejudice has been raised up against him, and after his avowals of ignoble hatred, on which he is harping still:

> He was wont to lend money for a Christian courtesy; let him look to his bond. . . . He hath disgraced me and hindered me half a million, laughed at my losses, mocked at my gains, etc.

As Dr Furness and others have observed, Shakespeare managed in this play very strangely if he meant to stand up for the Jews; but even the human appeal is deliberately thwarted.

We are alienated, not by Shylock's avarice and revengefulness alone —he seems just before his defence fairly to be hungering for the pound of flesh that shall 'feed' his revenge,[9] to him more profitable (for all that he says that it is not) than the flesh of muttons, beefs, or goats,—but also by the comic circumstances. Here is a remarkable case of comic preparations and precautions, of 'isolation.' This is the 'daughter-ducats' scene, in which Shylock first appears after the ludicrous report given, in Act II, scene viii, by Salanio to Salarino, of his strange and variable lamentations; and to whom is he talking but to these two merry gentlemen at this moment? If in the theatre it is to be pathos, he should be speaking to some one more responsive on the stage; at every word he is expected to burst out in his 'daughter-ducats' vein once more; and presently so he does. Though we do not laugh at Shylock when he asks, 'Hath not a Jew senses, affections, passions?' good care has been taken that we shall not weep.

Indeed, I cannot but think that even this speech has for generations been misread, simply taken, like the other supposedly pathetic pas-

---

[9] It must be remembered that Shakespeare is skirting the fringes of a horrible superstitious prejudice—the notion that the Jews, not only crucified Christian children, but, when they had a chance, ate of a Christian's flesh. In John Day's *Travels of Three English Brothers* (1607), the Jew Zariph says:

> Now by my soule 'twould my sprits much refresh
> To tast a banket all of Christian's flesh.—p. 54.
> Sweet gold, sweete Iewell! but the sweetest part
> Of a Iewes feast is a Christian's heart.—p. 60.

sages, out of its context, and a meaning superimposed. Not only does
every one forget how it begins and how it ends, but every one fails to
see the thread running through it, the idea, not that Jews have been
inhumanly treated but that from a Jew mistreated you may expect the
same as from a Christian—revenge, though in a richer measure. 'And
what's his reason?' he begins, 'I am a Jew.' And then and there, we,
with our humanitarian impulses, jump the track—at once we are, one
and all, over on Shylock's side. But Shylock's answer is not meant to
have such a disconcerting effect; we must remember the cry of the
London mob when Lopez paid the penalty, and Antonio's words, 'I
am like to call thee so again'; we must remember Luther, Coke, Bishop
Hall, James Howell, Jeremy Taylor, Robert Smith, William Prynne,
the Elizabethan dramatists, Shakespeare himself throughout his play.

> A perfect Judge will read each work of Wit
> With the same spirit that its author writ.

For *Jew,* read *German,* time, 1914–18, place, Belgium or France,
England or America, and we have, with greater provocation, that
spirit approximately. Shakespeare does not jump the track himself.
Hath not a Jew eyes? Hath not a Jew hands? and he proceeds to show
that a Jew, having the wit to perceive an injury, the hand to avenge
it, quite the same organs, senses, and passions, in fact, as a Christian
has, he will when hurt do all that a Christian will do, and a good bit
besides. 'Let him look to his bond.' There is no suggestion that
Christians should no longer do any hurt to the Jews, and we make
Shylock overstate his case. He is only defending himself in what he
intends to do; we make him defend his race against all that has been
done to it. He is putting in a plea for the right of revenge; we turn
it into a plea for equal treatment at the outset.

Of itself, to be sure, provided we can forget both beginning and end
and the far from mitigating circumstances, this celebrated defence
might touch us. In this regard it is, as we have seen, like other
speeches of Shylock's, that about Leah and the turquoise, that about
Launcelot's 'kindness,' and the last speech of all, at the trial—they
too would touch us were it not for the context and situation. That is,
Shakespeare's method is not the ordinary method of caricature. He
does not distort or grossly exaggerate the Jew's features, but flings a
villainous or comic light upon them,—does not turn him into a gar-
goyle or hobgoblin like Barabas, but gives him, to an extraordinary

degree, the proportions and lineaments of humanity and of his race, scoundrel though he be. . . .

There is much besides that is comical in him, details of his miserliness and his 'Jewishness' which should tickle the risible senses of any ordinary audience, Elizabethan or modern: a touch more rare is in the strait and rigid way that his mind and heart are cooped up within the confines of the law and the letter of it. 'Then must the Jew be merciful,' says Balthazar. 'On what compulsion must I?' It is Greek to him, not Hebrew, these words and the following ones:—'Have by some surgeon, Shylock.'—(Is it so nominated in the bond?)—'It is not so express'd; but what of that? 'Twere good you do so much for charity.'—But only half does he hear what she is saying; and he pores over the writing—'I cannot find it; 'tis not in the bond.' Surely he is not feigning; and though some may rather think it tragic, this spiritual blindness—and indeed the tragic crisis is not yet past;—the contrast contrived and the repetition employed seem calculated deliberately to bring home to us that rigidity, or 'raideur,' of the human spirit which Monsieur Bergson finds essential to comedy. The mercy must be down in black and white, signed and sealed. He is after all pretty much of a piece, a thorough grotesque; and in his quaint antique fashion business is business to him, a contract is a contract, a bargain a bargain. Everything is a bargain to him, good or bad, and it is often with a subtle and unobtrusive hand that Shakespeare makes this apparent. We have noticed his rage over the exchange of a turquoise for a monkey; but it is droller still to see how the contract for the pound of flesh is to him a good bargain even while with gruesome jesting he makes it out a bad one.

> . . . what should I gain
> By the exaction of the forfeiture?
> A pound of man's flesh taken from a man
> Is not so estimable, profitable neither,
> As flesh of muttons, beefs, or goats.

Literal-minded still! He might have said to Bassanio, 'Only a formality; a contract is not a contract without interest or forfeit?' But he cannot shake off his inveterate materialism, or the language of the market; and must needs look upon the forfeit as a precious commodity, flesh like other flesh (though in his chaffering, higgling way he vows that it is not), of which the price is high. ''Tis a good round sum.'

And what of Shylock at the very end, in the last act, where no one speaks or thinks of him, and the spirit of romance is once more regnant? Professor Baker asks why, 'if Shakespeare wished to create laughter by Shylock, he kept him out of the fifth act, thus losing the many opportunities which his forlorn, defeated condition would have given to delight the Jew-baiters.' But that would have been to make a point of the matter, and to raise the Jewish question in a play where the Jew's story is, and is meant to be, but an episode. That question, or the slavery question, which Professor Jastrow[10]—not Shylock—raises, or the sex question, or any other, as has been seen, had for Shakespeare, or his brother playwrights, no existence. To him things were solid and settled; and in his plays he held no brief, followed no program. The Jews he made comical not because he himself had a grudge against them, but, as he made London citizens, Puritans, Frenchmen, and Welshmen comical, because, as he might have said, they were so. He took the world as he found it, and in no respect more than in the matters of mirth. He was no Rabelais, Montaigne, Swift, or Voltaire, Bernard Shaw or Anatole France, who have found out precious new things to laugh at.

I have been at pains to ascertain and define the attitude of the author and his public, and so interpret the play. I have found in Shylock the comic villain, and though finely and delicately done, nothing really and sincerely pathetic in him at all. Pains wasted, some present-day writers of the eminence of Professor Matthews will say; though the number of them is relatively fewer than it used to be. What Shakespeare intended does not much matter—what matters is what he did—and we have as good a right as Shakespeare to our opinion of Shylock, though 'the comic aspects of Shylock have disappeared from our modern vision and the pathetic interest of the desolate figure is now most obvious.'[11] Art then ceases to be a means of communication from soul to soul, the author and his meaning are a matter of indifference, and there is really no work of interpretation, but only of expatiation, to do. Apart from Shakespeare's opinion, what Shylock is there? one wonders, bewildered. There is, we are assured, an

---

[10] p. 737:—'The Jew reproaches the Christian with his sinful traffic in human flesh.' Surely not; that would have spoiled Shylock's argument from analogy; and here we have a neat example of reading with modern spectacles, and by sentences rather than by speeches, by speeches rather than by scenes.

[11] *Shakespeare as a Playwright,* p. 151.

Elizabethan Shylock and—'even though Shakespeare might himself protest'—a modern one, equally legitimate, though for us the modern is the real. And Shylock then is ambiguous, Janus-faced. Professor Matthews well knows what it is for an actor to misinterpret his part, to play it *à contresens;* but it is permissible in actor and critic too, it seems, when the play is three hundred years old. It is impossible, rather, for in that space of time a new meaning—mysteriously, but legitimately—develops, somewhat as a beard can grow in the grave, or as razors sharpen in the drawer.

   Such a prodigious ambiguity—ranging between the satiric and the pathetic—would, I think, be a serious defect in a character; but I do not believe it is there. The mistake, as I conceive it, of Professor Matthews and other modernizing critics is that they either ignore the intention of the author or establish such an antinomy between what the author intended and what he did. There are cases, no doubt, where an author fails in his intention, but there is no opposition or discrepancy between intention and achievement here; for his intention we gather from what he did, and by that we mean the emphasis, the arrangement, the preparations and fulfillment, the comment, the villain's attempt and the turning of the tables upon him,—all that larger meaning which is to be found not so much in the letter of the text as in the spirit of it and in the structure of the whole. To this the modernizing critics do not rightly attend; they read the text but they read it to suit themselves,—they read the lines or pages, not the play. Yet the intention—all this pervading spirit and purpose—is as important as the wording itself;—the intonation and accent and gesture of a spoken sentence convey as much of the meaning as the mere words do;—and to attend to these last alone is to do violence to the author and his work. What this means Professor Matthews also knows—for Macready and Barrett to cut the piece down to a Shylock play in three acts, ending with the trial, he says, is 'plainly a betrayal of Shakespeare's intent.'[12] Is it less a betrayal to keep the text intact, indeed, but read into half of it what to his intent is directly opposed?
   In insisting on the historical aspect of the question—that is, to the effect of asserting our right to be modern, to be what we are—Professor Matthews and the others are really confusing the issue. The considerations of historical character which we have been urging are

[12] Ibid., p. 145.

secondary: the primary consideration is the technical—that of the emphasis, the arrangement, the comment, and the like, just mentioned above, which convey the author's meaning—and the historical considerations serve but to make that meaning more clear. That done, the figure stands before us, not a 'scientific curiosity,' or a bit of hopelessly old-fashioned Elizabethan stage-furniture, but (though handled roughly) a human being; and it has the considerable advantage of being real, whereas the modern is a chimæra, a myth. It is not resident in the faraway Elizabethan age any more than in ours, but in the mind of Shakespeare. The history, if it troubles us, can be quite forgotten. Treat Shakespeare as if a modern, and yet our reasoning applies. Read 'Ibsen' for 'Shakespeare' in the opinion rendered: 'What *Ibsen* intended does not much matter—and we have as good a right as *Ibsen* to our opinion of Rebecca West.' To that, I know, Professor Matthews and some of the others would demur. But by this same method of ignoring the author's intention or misreading his text, Mr Huneker makes of that unscrupulous but unmalignant woman (who lures indeed Beata to her death but only in order to enable Beata's husband to attain to his high destiny) a monster, a Medusa. She is a Real-politiker, is *jenseits von Gut und Böse,* is (though terribly) enlightened. But Mr Huneker has a right to his Rebecca if Professor Matthews has a right to his Jew. And Ibsen? He has nothing to say!

It is only a question of clear thinking, of knowing what we are doing (or not doing) and freely and honestly admitting it. On the popular stage, to be sure, Shylock must be played pretty much as Irving played him (though, like Irving himself, we should at the same time remember that this is not Shakespeare's Shylock at all); but criticism, unlike acting, has to do with the truth alone. If in reading the play we find a tear in Shakespeare's eye shall we not like Sainte-Beuve catch ourselves, and if we cannot find it in our hearts to dry the tear, at least candidly acknowledge that it is we ourselves who put it there? It is the French who see straight. As I have had occasion repeatedly to notice they have brushed away the Romantic cobwebs and moonshine from Molière, and on the stage and in criticism he is himself again; whereas Professor Matthews does to Molière much as he does to Shakespeare, finds George Dandin and Arnolphe, too, pathetic, is inclined to find *L'Avare* and *Le Tartuffe* tragic, and blurs the fine sharp outlines of the master's comedy. . . .

Not only is the modern meaning foreign to Shakespeare but it is, as we have suggested, superfluous. Critics speak as if it were impossible for Shylock to mean anything to us unless thus sentimentalized and tragicalized. Indeed, as we moderns have done with many another rough customer in history, literature, or holy writ, we have tamed and domesticated the 'dog Jew,' and drawn his 'fangs.' 'He will speak soft words unto us,' he no longer grins and he cannot bite. But Shakespeare and the Elizabethans, as we have seen, shuddered at him and laughed at him; and except at popular performances, where racial antipathy is rather to be allayed than fomented, so should we, as much as in us lies, do to-day. Thus we shall come into sympathy with the manifest intention of the poet, with the acting of the part on the Elizabethan stage, with the conception of the money-lending Jew in the contemporary drama, character-writing, and ballad, and with the lively prejudice of the time. A villain and a butt, 'une simple figure à gifles,' as Francisque Sarcey shrewdly observes, 'un monstrueux grotesque, sur le nez de qui tombent à l'envi d'effroyables nasardes,'[13] (only, as we have seen, he is not a monster, not a caricature);—such, save for the happily human elements and lineaments of his make-up, and for the splendour of poetry, shed like the rain and the light of heaven, on the just and the unjust, is the impression which Shylock makes after he has been duly restored to the sixteenth century, an impression in which pathos has no place, and with which our notions of justice and social responsibility, on the one hand, or of ironical art, on the other, have, so far as they are merely modern, nothing to do. So he is not lost to us. That Hebraic and picturesque figure will be remembered long after he has retreated from the warm circle of our sentiments, and be visited again and again, by an exhilarating sally of the imagination, in the midst of the harsh and sturdy life to which he belongs.

[13] *Quarante ans de théâtre: Shylock.*

ON SHAKESPEARE'S SATIRIC COMEDIES

SAMUEL JOHNSON FOUND Bertram, the hero of *All's Well That Ends Well,* to be an ungrateful wretch; Coleridge confessed puzzlement over *Troilus and Cressida* and thought *Measure for Measure* to be Shakespeare's only painful play; Hazlitt regarded *Troilus and Cressida* as unsuccessful and *Measure for Measure* as distasteful. However, only in Victorian times were these three plays segregated as a group having special characteristics in common. For the Victorians these were the "dark" comedies, written at a time when the sunniness of Shakespeare's previous comedies was being clouded over by the mood which produced the tragedies. In our time there has been a revolution in the way in which these plays have been regarded, and *Measure for Measure* and *Troilus and Cressida* stand higher in critical estimation than ever before. There have been three new lines of interpretation: what had been regarded as unpleasant in these plays had come from taking realistically romantic folk material; *Measure for Measure* and *All's Well That Ends Well* have Christian implications not previously perceived; *Measure for Measure* and *Troilus and Cressida* are to be appreciated as "comical satires."

OSCAR JAMES CAMPBELL
1874-

OSCAR JAMES CAMPBELL is a scholar who in his two books, *Comicall Satyre and Shakespeare's Troilus and Cressida* (1938) and *Shakespeare's Satire* (1943), discusses the satirical element in Shakespeare's plays in relation to intellectual and literary trends of the time. He is the editor of an anthology of Shakespeare, *The Living Shakespeare* (1949), whose introductions are both stimulating and sane, fresh and learned.

Campbell sees *Troilus and Cressida* and *Measure for Measure* as comical satire, a dramatic form devised by Jonson and Marston. The two commentators who are conventional in this form, the moral, satiric observer and the scurrilous cynic, are, he finds in this extract, represented by the Duke and Lucio in *Measure for Measure*. In an earlier chapter he found them to be represented by Ulysses and Thersites in *Troilus and Cressida*. Oddly, he does not discuss *All's Well That Ends Well*. Here, it might be pointed out, Lafeu and, at least for a moment, Parolles are representative of these two types of commentators. In each of the three plays the social milieu is one of degeneration and corruption, as in the other Elizabethan comical satires.

Campbell may, as Theodore Spencer and others have charged, force the plays somewhat to fit the categories he has established. He may fail to come to grips with the interpretations of G. Wilson Knight and R. W. Chambers, which discuss the theme of redemption in *Measure for Measure*. However, his elucidation of the structure and the temper of the satiric comedies remains important.

SHAKESPEARE'S UNION OF COMEDY
AND SATIRE

THE VILLAINY OF Angelo and the cowardice of Claudio, set in a Vienna morally rotten from top to bottom, form a strange basis for any sort of merriment. Nor does calling *Measure for Measure* a 'dark' comedy, or recognizing it as the product of a pessimistic spirit, provide a chart for safe aesthetic sailing. E. K. Chambers solves the problem no more successfully by sagely remarking that the structure of the play 'indicates uncertainty of dramatic invention.' Mark Van Doren begins his analysis of the play by admitting that it is unsatisfactory, though certainly not from a lack of serious attention on Shakespeare's part. 'The reason is rather that it goes against his grain to make comedy out of such matter.' But one may well ask why Shakespeare should ever deliberately write a play 'against his grain.' Surely so experienced a playwright would hardly labor to create a comedy out of material he felt unadapted to the dramatic form. Later in his essay Mr. Van Doren himself gives a strange answer to this question. 'Perhaps,' he suggests, 'in this year [1604] Shakespeare was not up to tragedy'—although he was almost surely at work on *Othello* at about the time when he was fashioning *Measure for Measure*.

The following paragraphs offer a different explanation of the aesthetic confusion caused by the drama, an explanation which does not attribute mythical woes to the author or find in him resented inner or outer compulsions to fashion a comedy out of unsuitable material. It is simply that *Measure for Measure* is Shakespeare's second attempt to adapt to his genius some of the conventions of comical satire.

According to this view Angelo was first designed as clearly as Malvolio or Troilus to serve as an object of ridicule. The Duke was as certainly a satiric and moral commentator as were similar figures in earlier dramas of Jonson or Marston. Isabella's first duty, then, was to serve as the main agent in the exposure and derision of Angelo. The Viennese background of corruption and moral filth is as harmonious with the sin of the principal culprit as was the disorganization of the Greek and Trojan hosts with the passion which destroyed Troilus and Cressida.

"Shakespeare's Union of Comedy and Satire" is from Oscar James Campbell, *Shakespeare's Satire* (Oxford University Press, 1943), pp. 124–130, 139–140. By permission of the publisher.

This satiric structure is now obscure because Isabella completely outgrew the role in which she was first cast. A modern audience is properly much more concerned for her fate than for her success in laying bare the hypocrisy of Angelo. Consequently the play does not end as a satire should. Angelo is exposed but not ejected from the play with a final burst of derision. Instead he is shown as purged of his sin, repentant, and ready to make atonement for it. This fact enables Shakespeare to put into Isabella's mouth a final plea for the mercy for which she has stood during the entire drama. Once the Duke has granted this prayer, Shakespeare has lost his chance for an effective denouement. So he falls back upon the conventional ending of romantic comedy, a marriage for both the deserving and undeserving. This offers no proper resolution of the emotions aroused by the characters and is a perfunctory and aesthetically unsatisfactory close to the complicated action. For Angelo deserves not a wife, but scornful ridicule. The nature of Isabella and of her problems on the other hand have carried us to the deepest springs of human conduct. They have all along trembled on the verge of tragedy. Her promised marriage to the Duke provides a completely unsatisfactory conclusion to such a dramatic career.

Let us examine then the fundamental satiric structure and temper of the drama. As in *Troilus and Cressida* the social world in which the characters live is in a state of chaos and for the same reason: 'The specialty of rule hath been neglected.' The Duke, as he himself confesses, has disregarded his plain duties as magistrate:

> We have strict statutes and most biting laws
> (The needful bits and curbs to headstrong steeds),
> Which for this fourteen years we have let sleep,
> Even like an o'ergrown lion in a cave,
> That goes not out to prey. Now, as fond fathers,
> Having bound up the threat'ning twigs of birch,
> Only to stick it in their children's sight
> For terror, not to use, in time the rod
> Becomes more mock'd than fear'd; so our decrees,
> Dead to infliction, to themselves are dead,
> And liberty plucks justice by the nose;
> The baby beats the nurse, and quite athwart
> Goes all decorum.
>   (I. iii. 19–31)

The last lines of this speech are strikingly like some in Ulysses' famous speech describing the chaos that overtakes a society in which 'degree is shaked':

> Strength should be lord of imbecility
> And the rude son should strike the father dead.
>
> (I. iii. 114–15)

The social disintegration in *Measure for Measure* is of a somewhat different sort from that depicted in the earlier drama. Here the Duke's incompetence has resulted in moral chaos. Mr. Van Doren's trenchant description of the poisonous immorality of Vienna cannot be improved. 'The city,' he writes, 'stews in its vices; bawds and pimps swarm in the streets, the prisons are crowded with moral vermin, and the gentle folk have lost their goodness. Goodness exists; Isabella, if one likes, is a saint; but it is forced to be unwholesomely conscious of itself, and the universal consciousness of evil puts a certain bitter perplexity into everyone's voice.' The serious-minded are sore perplexed, but the careless and thoughtless are cynical and irresponsible in the face of the vice and license which flourish around them. Shakespeare, following the earlier satiric dramatists, obeyed a sound aesthetic instinct in setting the characters whose vices he satirizes in a morally chaotic milieu.

The Duke, fearing to be thought tyrannical if he should now begin to correct his people, has chosen Angelo to be his deputy. He disguises himself as a friar in order to observe Angelo's actions. Indeed he intends to conduct a kind of experiment on the fellow in the hope of discovering if his cloistered virtue and untried purity will remain unchanged under the stress of real temptation. The Duke's subsequent actions, however, show that his real dramatic purpose is not to probe Angelo's nature but to expose the man's unconscious hypocrisy and to hold it up for derision.

John Marston had made conventional the casting of a deposed and disguised Duke in the role of satiric commentator. Malevole, who plays this part in *The Malcontent* (1600), is Altofronto, the deposed Duke of Genoa. In *The Fawn* (1602) the ironic commentator is Hercules, the disguised Duke of Ferrara, who has followed his son abroad to watch the young man's wooing of the Princess Dulcimel and to manipulate events as he chooses. The first commentator which Marston introduced into one of his plays was Feliche. He appears in

Antonio and Mellida (1599), not, to be sure, as a disguised duke, but as no less of a hanger-on at the court. He, like Altofronto, seems to hold a roving commission to ferret out the evils of life there. Now the Duke in *Measure for Measure* bears a close relationship to these figures of Marston. He is also a commentator, one who utters the condemnations of his author as clearly as do Marston's characters. He too, like Hercules in *The Fawn,* manipulates events in such a way as to drive the derided figures into exaggerated displays of their follies.

The Duke, playing the part of a friar, appropriately couches his denunciations of vice in the solemn and elevated language of a churchman. He lashes the bawd Pompey in a tone of suitable indignation:

> Fie, sirrah! a bawd, a wicked bawd!
> The evil that thou causest to be done,
> That is thy means to live. Do thou but think
> What 'tis to cram a maw or clothe a back
> From such a filthy vice. Say to thyself
> 'From their abominable and beastly touches
> I drink, I eat, array myself, and live.'
> Canst thou believe thy living is a life
> So stinkingly depending?
>
> (III. ii. 20–28)

His comments on the rancid condition of his city maintain the critical and sinister tone that Shakespeare desires his play to possess. It is the proper atmosphere for a satiric drama.

> There is so great a fever on goodness, that the dissolution of it must cure it. Novelty is only in request; and it is as dangerous to be aged in any kind of course, as it is virtuous to be constant in any undertaking. There is scarce truth enough alive to make societies secure; but security enough to make fellowship accurst. Much upon this riddle runs the wisdom of the world.
>
> (III. ii. 235–42)

At the end of the play, just as he is about to remove his disguise, the Duke returns to this general condemnation of the social corruption in Vienna:

> . . . My business in this state
> Made me a looker-on here in Vienna,
> Where I have seen corruption boil and bubble

> Till it o'errun the stew; laws for all faults,
> But faults so countenanc'd that the strong statutes
> Stand like the forfeits in a barber's shop,
> As much in mock as mark.
>
> (v. i. 318–24)

This is sound comment, grave and reverent.

To keep laughter awake, even though it be the sneering sort proper to satire, Shakespeare associates with the Duke a rogue named Lucio, a representative of the second or buffoonish commentator who had become conventional in satiric plays. Lucio is a gay and ribald cynic like Carlo Buffone and all his successors. His talk bristles with extravagant and bawdy figures of speech, and his satiric portrait of Angelo is a scurrilous and unsavory caricature:

> LUCIO. A little more lenity to lechery would do no harm in him. Something too crabbed that way, friar.
> DUKE. It is too general a vice, and severity must cure it.
> LUCIO. Yes, in good sooth, the vice is of a great kindred—it is well allied; but it is impossible to extirp it quite, friar, till eating and drinking be put down. They say this Angelo was not made by man and woman after the downright way of creation. Is it true, think you?
> DUKE. How should he be made then?
> LUCIO. Some report a sea-maid spawn'd him; some, that he was begot between two stockfishes. But it is certain that, when he makes water, his urine is congeal'd ice; that I know to be true. And he is a motion generative; that's infallible.
> DUKE. You are pleasant, sir, and speak apace.
>
> (III. ii. 103–20)

Lucio is a much more credible human being than any of Ben Jonson's buffoonish commentators, and much more credible than Thersites, whose censure is frank calumny. Though a gentleman, Lucio has contact with the bawdy underworld, which frequently erupts into the main action. Sexual promiscuity to Lucio is a joke, and a merry one. This attitude lends to all his comments a careless and cynical tone appropriate to a buffoonish satirist.

In creating this figure Shakespeare seems again to be indebted to John Marston. In his play *What You Will* (1601) Marston presented as an ideal satiric commentator a character called Quadratus [Four Square], a keen-minded debauchee, a gay ribald fellow of whom

Pietro Aretino was the prototype and patron. Marston believed that the satiric attitude of his Quadratus was a happy union of the traditionally severe spirit of correction with the traditional gaiety of comedy. Lucio in these respects clearly resembles Quadratus, but he has a more secure place in the plot than Marston's commentator. His appetite for cleverly expressed detraction leads him to slander the Duke to his disguised face and to keep it up with perverse insistence. 'The Duke had crotchets in him,' he confidentially informs the Friar. 'He would be drunk, too, that let me inform you . . . The Duke, I say to thee again, would eat mutton on Fridays. He's not past it yet: and I say to thee, he would mouth with a beggar, though she smelt brown bread and garlic. Say that I said so. Farewell.' (III. ii. 134–6, 190–95.)

The Duke leads Lucio on, to the amusement of the audience, with the clear purpose of exposing him. When Lucio plucks off the Friar's hood and discovers the Duke, the impudent buffoon also accomplishes his own exposure. He then tries to sneak unobtrusively away, but is arrested and held before the Duke for sentence. Although threatening Lucio with whipping and hanging after he has married the punk whom he has got with child, the Duke relents and remits all the 'forfeits' except his marriage with the courtesan. This deflation of the careless cynic and liar is in exactly the right key. An audience which has been entertained by this genial rascal throughout the play would have been outraged to see him severely punished. But it would accept the libertine's forced marriage to the harlot as an excellent joke. Moreover the sentence arouses in nice proportions the laughter of both comedy and satire. . . .

We can perhaps best understand *Measure for Measure* if we regard it as a form of comical satire designed for a popular audience, as *Troilus and Cressida* was the version of the type suited to the taste of an intelligent audience of barristers. The two plays are alike in possessing a background of social disintegration which forms an appropriate milieu for the individuals who are to be satirized. They are alike in attacking lust, the vice against which all the satirists directed most of their barbed shafts. They are alike in the method by which the central figures are presented to the audience.

However, the dramas are in some ways as unlike as the different spectators for which they were written. The complicated structure of

Troilus and Cressida and the many long passages devoted to the elaboration of ethical and social theory were too heavy for a popular audience. Consequently Shakespeare made the plot which exposes Angelo simple in structure and contrived the philosophical speeches of the Duke and Isabella in such a way that they too advance the plot. Moreover, an ending like that of *Troilus and Cressida* would have confused a popular Elizabethan audience, as it has confused almost every modern reader, just because it is so resolutely consistent with the temper of satire.

Shakespeare took no such chance of perplexing his spectators with the denouement of *Measure for Measure*. Instead of ending it on a note of savage scorn, he gave the drama a conventional close, one that forces satire to effect a self-effacing compromise with comedy. It ends with the inevitable three marriages. None of these is a logical consummation of any part of the story, nor does any one of them give off the slightest aroma of romance. The marriages merely announce to the audience in familiar terms that the play is finished. This pseudo-romantic denouement ought not to divert intelligent spectators from their interest in the exposure and humiliation of Lucio and Angelo. An attentive audience should continue to recognize the correction of the knave and the scamp as the central theme of the drama.

R. W. CHAMBERS
1874-1942

R. W. CHAMBERS was a medievalist, not a professional Shakespearean. His study of medieval literature, however, helped him to produce two notable lectures which have enabled us to understand better Shakespeare's use of themes and conventions. He united sober scholarship with sensitive criticism.

In this lecture to the British Academy, written with

good-natured urbane humor, Chambers's tone is personal, not oracular like that of G. Wilson Knight, whom he does not mention and whose work he apparently did not know, but what he has to say corroborates Knight's symbolist criticism in his essay "*Measure for Measure* and the Gospels" in *The Wheel of Fire*. Like Knight he sees the theme of *Measure for Measure* as "Judge not: for with what measure ye mete it shall be measured to you again," and the Duke as suggestive of divine providence. He is also aware that the Duke's withholding from Isabella the knowledge that her brother lives, not to be defended on psychological grounds, is necessary preparation not only for the theatrical effect of the dénouement but for the symbolic action of Isabella's kneeling in behalf of Angelo. Chambers, however, is able to defend his reading of the play by reference to Shakespeare's use of his source and to Elizabethan convention.

Oscar James Campbell disagrees with Chambers concerning the conclusion of *Measure for Measure,* which he finds unsuccessful, perhaps because it does not conform to that of the genre of comical satire. For the rest, he focuses on elements which Chambers ignores, so that they seem to be talking of two different plays. However, the two interpretations are not irreconcilable. Campbell emphasizes the corruption of the social milieu and the castigation of evil, and Chambers emphasizes the theme of redemption; but it is precisely a corrupt society which stands in need of being redeemed, and castigation may be a preliminary to forgiveness. The tradition of popular religious satire traced by John Peter in *Complaint and Satire in Early English Literature* (1956), an influence apart from that of formal satire discussed by Campbell, would seem to explain the difference between *Measure for Measure* and the comical satires of the private playhouses and to account for those elements in the play which Chambers has lighted up.

MEASURE FOR MEASURE

IN *Measure for Measure* Shakespeare took as his source an old play, *Promos and Cassandra,* written by George Whetstone a quarter of a century before. Now, just as certainly as *Hamlet* was a story of revenge, so was *Promos and Cassandra* a story of forgiveness. In this play Cassandra (like Isabel) pleads for her brother, who (like Claudio) had been condemned to death for unchastity. The judge, Promos (like Angelo) will grant pardon only if Cassandra yield to his passion. Cassandra at last does so. That is the essential difference between the old plot, and Shakespeare's play. Nevertheless, Promos orders Cassandra's brother to be beheaded, and the head to be presented to her. Cassandra complains to the King; the King gives judgment that Promos first marry Cassandra, then lose *his* head. But, this marriage solemnized, Cassandra, now tied in the greatest bonds of affection to her husband, suddenly becomes an earnest suitor for his life. In the end it appears that the kindly gaoler has in fact released the brother, and presented Cassandra with a felon's head instead. So, to renown the virtues of Cassandra, the King pardons both brother and judge, and all ends well.

The story shows the violence of much Elizabethan drama. John Addington Symonds says, in *Shakespeare's Predecessors,* that the sympathies of a London audience were like 'the chords of a warrior's harp, strung with twisted iron and bull's sinews, vibrating mightily, but needing a stout stroke to make them thrill.' The playwrights 'glutted their audience with horrors, cudgelled their horny fibres into sensitiveness.'

Now mark how Shakespeare treats this barbarous story. According to Professor Dover Wilson, at the time when he wrote *Measure for Measure* Shakespeare 'quite obviously believed in nothing; he was as cynical as Iago, as disillusioned as Macbeth, though he still retained, unlike the first, his sensitiveness, and, unlike the second, his hatred of cruelty, hypocrisy, and ingratitude.'[1] According to Sir Edmund Chambers, in *Measure for Measure* his 'remorseless analysis' 'probes the

---

"*Measure for Measure*" is from R. W. Chambers, "The Jacobean Shakespeare and *Measure for Measure,*" *Man's Unconquerable Mind* (Jonathan Cape Ltd., 1939). Reprinted by permission.

[1] J. DOVER WILSON, *The Essential Shakespeare,* p. 122.

inmost being of man, and strips him naked.' 'It is the temper of the inquisitor:' 'you can but shudder.'[2]

Prepare then to shudder, as you observe William Iago Torquemada Shakespeare at work. Shakespeare, for all the 'self-laceration,' 'disgust,' and 'general morbidity'[3] which is supposed to have obsessed him and his Jacobean contemporaries, removes from the play the really morbid scene of the heroine kissing the severed head of her supposed brother. Then, he divides the sorrows of the heroine between two characters, Isabel and Mariana. And the object of this duplication is, that, whatever their spiritual anguish, neither of them shall be placed in the 'really intolerable situation'[4] of poor Cassandra. Mariana has been contracted to Angelo formally by oath. It is vital to remember that, according to Elizabethan ideas, Angelo and Mariana are therefore man and wife. But Angelo has deserted Mariana. Now I grant that according to our modern ideas, it is undignified for the deserted Mariana still to desire union with the husband who has scorned her. *We* may resent the elegiac and spaniel-like fidelity of Mariana of the Moated Grange. *But is that the attitude of the year 1604?* The tale of the deserted bride seeking her husband in disguise is old, approved, beloved. It is a mere anachronism to assume that Shakespeare, a practical dramatist, told this tale with some deep cynical and self-lacerating intention unintelligible to his audience, but now at last revealed to modern criticism. Shakespeare made Mariana gentle and dignified. She, in all shadow and silence, visits her husband in place of Isabel, to save Claudio's life.

And our twentieth-century critics are scandalized over the tale. This surprises me, a Late Victorian, brought up on the Bible and Arthurian story. I did not know that our modern age was so proper. A Professor to-day cannot deliver a series of lectures on 'The Application of Thought to Textual Criticism' without its being reported as 'The Application of Thought to Sexual Criticism.' Yet this sex-obsessed age of ours is too modest to endure the old story of the substituted bride. I learnt at my Early Victorian mother's knee, how Jacob served seven years for Rachel: 'And it came to pass, that in the morning, behold, it was Leah,' and Jacob had to serve another seven years for his beloved. I did not exclaim: 'Oh, my mother, you are lacer-

[2] *Shakespeare: A Survey,* p. 213.
[3] J. DOVER WILSON, *op. cit.,* pp. 117, 118.
[4] *Works of Shakespeare,* ed., G. L. KITTREDGE, p. 97.

ating my feelings with this remorseless revelation of patriarchal polygamy.' A child could grasp the story of Jacob's service for Rachel, which 'seemed unto him but a few days, for the love he had to her.'

Sir Edmund Chambers is entitled to say that the story of the substituted bride 'does not commend itself to the modern conscience.' Jaques was entitled to say that he did not like the name of Rosalind. And Orlando was entitled to say, 'There was no thought of pleasing you when she was christened.' In the sixteenth century the story was a commonplace of romance, and Shakespeare used it in order to make more gentle one of the quite horrible situations of the pre-Shakespearean drama. There was a time when Shakespeare had not shrunk from staging the grossest horrors. It is to avoid them, that he now introduces the substitution which offends 'the modern conscience.'

It may be objected that Shakespeare is 'not for an age, but for all time,' and that therefore he ought not to have condescended to use stories which, although current in his day, and although he made them less horrible, nevertheless would not appeal to future ages. But the great poets, Homer, Aeschylus, Sophocles, Dante, Shakespeare, speak to all time only through the language, conventions, and beliefs of their own age. How else?

A second fault of the old play is the crudity of the change from Cassandra's thirst for vengeance to her prayer for forgiveness. Shakespeare had permitted himself similar crudities in the past. Now he sets to work to make the plot consistent: he does this by making it turn, from first to last, on the problem of punishment and forgiveness. It is Shakespeare's addition to the story that the Duke is distressed by this problem. Fearing lest his rule has been too lax, he deputes his office to Angelo, whilst remaining, disguised as a friar, to 'visit both prince and people.' And here critics, among them Sir Walter Raleigh[5] and Sir Arthur Quiller-Couch,[6] object. It is not seemly for a Duke to 'shirk his proper responsibility, and steal back incognito to play busybody and spy on his deputy.'

I am reminded of one of the first essays ever shown up to me, by a Japanese student, some thirty-five years ago. He objected to *The Merchant of Venice.* 'Sir Bassanio,' he said, 'did not bring doctor in

[5] *Shakespeare,* p. 167.
[6] New Cambridge Shakespeare, *Measure for Measure,* p. xxxiv.

order that he tie up wound of friend. He did not recognize own spouse in masculine raiment.'

There was every reason for a Japanese student to be puzzled when suddenly introduced to the world of western romance, just as we in our turn are puzzled, when we first try to understand a translation of one of the *No* plays. But why do English critics to-day bring against *Measure for Measure* this kind of objection? They would be ashamed to bring it against Shakespeare's earlier comedies, or later romances.

Disguise and impersonation and misunderstanding are the very life of romantic comedy. The disguised monarch, who can learn the private affairs of his humblest subject, becomes a sort of earthly Providence, combining omniscience and omnipotence. That story has always had its appeal. 'Thus hath the wise magistrate done in all ages;'[7] although obviously to introduce into our daily life this ancient habit of the benevolent monarch would be to incur deserved satire.

When Professor Raleigh complains that the Duke 'shirks his public duties,' and when he likens him to a head of a college who 'tries to keep the love of the rebels by putting his ugly duties upon the shoulders of a deputy,' is he not falling into the mistake which he deplores in other critics, that of being so much more moral than Shakespeare himself? Is he not substituting for Shakespeare's Duke another, and a quite different one? Bernard Shaw has rewritten the last act of *Cymbeline*, as Shakespeare might have written it, if he had been post-Ibsen and post-Shaw. And that is a legitimate thing to do, compared with the modern habit of keeping Shakespeare's text, but putting upon it a construction which is post-Ibsen and post-Shaw; imposing an outlook and a morality not Shakespeare's.

Obviously, it is wrong for the Master of a College deliberately to put his unpopular duties upon the Vice-Master; and it would be most improper for him to watch the result from the Porter's Lodge, disguised as a scout. It would be equally improper for a young lady to intervene in a law suit, by personating a K.C.; and in this way we might moralize amiss every one of Shakespeare's romantic plays. The question is not how Shaw might have satirized the Duke, had he rewritten *Measure for Measure*. The question is how Shakespeare meant us to see the Duke; and since the Duke controls the whole action of the play, we must see him as Shakespeare meant us to do, or misunderstand the play.

[7] JONSON, *Bartholomew Fair*, II, i.

Shakespeare makes the Duke describe himself as one who has ever loved the life removed; one who does not relish well the loud applause of the people. Under his Friar's disguise, the Duke is stung by Lucio's slanders into defending himself as one who, by the business he has helmed, 'shall appear to the envious a scholar, a statesman and a soldier.' To make it quite clear that we must take this seriously, Shakespeare makes Escalus, immediately after, confirm the Duke's words by describing him as

One that, above all other strifes, contended especially to know himself. Rather rejoicing to see another merry, than merry at anything which professed to make him rejoice: a gentleman of all temperance.

Isabel, in her moment of direst distress, remembers him as 'the good Duke.' To Mariana he is, in his Friar's disguise, 'a man of comfort,' who has often stilled her 'brawling discontent.' (This, of course, violates chronology, but Shakespeare never bothered about that.) Angelo, in his moment of deepest humiliation, addresses the Duke with profound reverence and awe. If our moderns prefer to follow the 'fantastic' Lucio, and to regard the Duke cynically, they should remember that Lucio was but speaking according to the trick, and himself suggested a whipping as adequate punishment.

Shakespeare puts into the Duke's mouth a speech on Death which might have been uttered by Hamlet; and Shakespeare seems to have meant us to regard him as a man of Hamlet's thoughtful, scholarly type, but older, with much experience of government and of war: no longer 'courtier, soldier, scholar,' but 'statesman, soldier, scholar'; yet still rather melancholy and distrustful of himself. Shakespeare, however, did not depict him with that intensity which makes his greatest characters come alive. The Duke remains somewhat impersonal, a controlling force; we never think of him by his name, Vincentio. But, though hardly a fully-realized character, he seems more than 'a puppet, cleverly painted and adroitly manipulated.'[8] Rather, he is the god in the machine: and we may concede that sometimes the machine creaks. But the Jacobeans did not mind if the machinery of their masques creaked a little, provided only it worked. And the Duke works: he is the source of the action of the play. Very truly he has been described as rather a power than a character.[9] So

[8] W. W. LAWRENCE, *Shakespeare's Problem Comedies,* 1931, p. 112.
[9] *The Times Literary Supplement,* 16 July 1931, p. 554.

far from 'shirking his proper responsibility,' he controls the fate of all the characters in the play.

The Duke is deeply distressed because, after fourteen years of his rule, his subjects are still no better than they ought to be. To the moralists who say that he ought to have announced publicly and personally his intention of himself inflicting a little experimental decapitation, it is answer enough that thereby the plot, which needs the Duke as a power in reserve, would have been wrecked. In the world of romantic story, in which alone he moves, the Duke has the long-established right of adopting a disguise and appointing a deputy; who will, as he knows, elect to exercise his office with severity.

Perhaps there may be a touch of irony when Shakespeare makes the Duke, who is to end as the lover of Isabel, begin by declaring that the dribbling dart of love cannot pierce a complete bosom. But there is nothing unfriendly in such irony. Of course it is part of the fun of the story (and good fun too) that the Duke has to listen to slander upon himself; has to keep his end up by giving himself a handsome testimonial; is frustrated by Lucio's 'Nay, friar, I am a kind of burr, I shall stick,' when he tries to escape from his tormentor. But such are the inevitable misfortunes of the monarch in disguise; we do not honour King Alfred the less, because we enjoy his confusion when scolded for burning the cakes. Yet so great is the effect of persistent denigration, that even a wise critic, who is effectively defending the Duke, concedes to his detractors that he 'punished Lucio merely for poking fun at him behind his back.'[10] But that is not what Shakespeare wrote. Lucio, in the old days, had escaped marrying the mother of his child, by denying his parentage. The Duke, when he learns the truth, merely carries out his original plan of making Lucio marry the woman to whom he had promised marriage.[11] The Duke markedly does *not* punish Lucio for his slanders: the suggestion that he does so is merely one more instance of the extraordinary prejudice which critics cherish against all the people in this play. They christen it 'a dark comedy,' and then darken the characters to justify their classification.

Not only does the Duke control the fate of all the characters; he profoundly alters the very nature of one: Angelo. The deputy, An-

[10] THALER, *Shakespeare's Silences*, p. 88.
[11] III. ii. 210, etc.; IV. iii. 180, etc.

gelo, is not so called for nothing. He *is* 'angel on the outward side'—
an ascetic saint in the judgment of his fellow citizens, and despite the
meanness of his spirit, nay, because of it, a saint in his own esteem.
His soliloquies prove this, and Isabel at the end gives him some
credit for sincerity.

Now Claudio and Juliet have lived together as man and wife, although their contract has been secret: it has 'lacked the denunciation
of outward order.' (The contract between Angelo and Mariana, on
the other hand, had been public, and so had undoubtedly given them
the rights of man and wife.) Angelo's puritanical revival of an ancient law, fourteen years out of date, renders Claudio's life forfeit.
This Viennese law seems strange, but the Duke says the law is such.
If we allow Portia to expound the even stranger law of Venice to the
Duke and Magnificoes, we may surely allow the Duke of Vienna to
understand the law of his own state. It is a postulate of the story.

Critics speak as if Shakespeare had imagined Claudio a self-
indulgent boy, a 'poor weak soul.'[12] Yet it is only Angelo's retrospec-
tive revival which makes Claudio's offence capital. 'He hath but as
offended in a dream,' says the kindly Provost. He 'was worth five
thousand of you all,' says Mistress Overdone to Lucio and his friends.
Claudio is first introduced, bearing himself with dignity under his sudden arrest. He sends his friend Lucio to his sister in her cloister, to
beg her to intercede for him, because, he says,

> in her youth
> There is a prone and speechless dialect,
> Such as move men; beside, she hath prosperous art
> When she will play with reason and discourse,
> And well she can persuade.

Such descriptions of characters before they appear—perhaps before
Shakespeare had written a word for them to speak—have surely a
great weight. They show how Shakespeare wished the audience to
see them. Isabel's characteristic when she does appear is exactly this
mixture of winning silence with persuasive speech.

But before she can reach Angelo, his colleague Escalus has already interceded for Claudio, urging that, had time cohered with
place, and place with wishing, Angelo might himself have fallen.
Angelo replies:

[12] E. K. CHAMBERS, *op. cit.*, p. 209.

> When I, that censure him, do so offend,
> Let mine own judgment pattern out my death,
> And nothing come in partial. Sir, he must die.

Isabel begins her pleading slowly and with characteristic silences: then she grows eloquent, and to Angelo's stern refusal she at last replies:

> I would to Heaven I had your potency,
> And you were Isabel! Should it then be thus?
> No; I would tell what 'twere to be a judge,
> And what a prisoner.

Isabel has no notion as yet of the depth of sin which may have to be pardoned in Angelo. But there is 'dramatic irony' behind these two speeches, and we can forecast that in the end the places will be reversed: the fate of the convicted Angelo depending upon Isabel.

The phrase 'dramatic irony' may be misunderstood. Shakespeare, like Sophocles, puts into the mouths of his characters words which they speak in all sincerity, but which, as the play proceeds, will be found to have a deeper meaning than the speaker knew. Dramatic irony does *not* mean that, at every turn, we are justified in suspecting that Shakespeare may have meant the reverse of what he makes his characters say. When he does that ('honest Iago') he leaves us in no doubt. As a great American critic has put it: 'However much the *dramatis personae* mystify each other, the audience is never to be perplexed.'[13]

It is a marked feature of the plays which Shakespeare was producing about the same time as *Measure for Measure,* that their early scenes contain 'ironical,' ominous lines, forecasting the conclusion:

BRABANTIO. She has deceived her father, and may thee.
OTHELLO. My life upon her faith. Honest Iago . . .

(Othello, I. ii)

LADY MACBETH. A little water clears us of this deed.

(Macbeth, II. i)

This is meant to forecast her later:

'What, will these hands ne'er be clean?'

(Macbeth, V. i)

EDMUND. Sir, I shall study deserving.
GLOSTER. He hath been out nine years, and away he shall again.

(Lear, I. i)

---

13 *Works of Shakespeare,* ed. G. L. KITTREDGE, p. 20.

But before Gloster can send him out again, Edmund lies dying with
the words 'The wheel is come full circle.'

To Angelo and to Isabel the wheel will come full circle. Will Isabel
then remember the pleas which she now pours forth? 'Well she can
persuade.' Her marvellous and impassioned pleadings, unsurpassed
anywhere in Shakespeare, are based on her Christian faith, and upon
the Sermon on the Mount: all men are pardoned sinners, and *must*
forgive:

> Why, all the souls that were, were forfeit once;
> And he that might the vantage best have took
> Found out the remedy.

'Judge not, that ye be not judged. For with what measure ye mete,
it shall be measured to you again.' *Measure for Measure*. But how is
the Sermon on the Mount to be reconciled with the practical necessities of government? That is the problem which puzzles people—
and particularly perhaps young people—so much to-day. In the
Tudor Age men met it by exalting Government. The King is 'the
image of God's majesty': to him, and to his Government, the divine
office of rule and punishment is committed. The private man must
submit and forgive. Accordingly, Angelo appeals to his 'function':
and there is real force in his answers to Isabel—if we remember, as
we always must, that, for the purposes of the play, Claudio is supposed guilty of a capital offence.

Never does Shakespeare seem more passionately to identify himself with any of his characters than he does with Isabel, as she pleads
for mercy against strict justice:

> O, it is excellent
> To have a giant's strength; but it is tyrannous
> To use it like a giant. . . .
>   man, proud man,
> Drest in a little brief authority . . .
>   like an angry ape
> Plays such fantastic tricks before high heaven
> As make the angels weep. . . .

'Man, proud man' is the man who, 'drest in authority,' condemns
his fellow men. The 'fantastic tricks' which such an unforgiving man
plays 'like an angry ape' make the angels weep; because it is the
function of angels to rejoice over one sinner that repenteth. Yet

portions of these lines are constantly quoted,[14] divorced from their context, as if they were Shakespeare's generalization about all actions of all mankind, when, in fact, they are the words he gives to a distressed sister pleading before a hard-hearted, proud, self-righteous authoritarian. To Shakespeare, we are told, 'man is now no more than "an angry Ape." ' And so, Isabel's protest against the proud self-righteous man who condemns his fellow men, is turned by the critics into Shakespeare's proud, self-righteous condemnation of his fellow men.

But the unforgiving Angelo is himself about to fall, though not without a sincere struggle. More than one of Isabel's pleadings find a mark which she never meant:

> Go to your bosom;
> Knock there, and ask your heart what it doth know
> That's like my brother's fault . . .
> Hark how I'll bribe you . . .

Angelo has thought himself superior to human weakness, because he is free from the vulgar vices of a Lucio. And the 'beauty of mind' of a distressed, noble woman throws him off his balance.[15] If we fail to see the nobility of Isabel, we cannot see the story as we should. The plot is rather like that of Calderon's *Magician,* where the scholarly, austere Cipriano is overthrown by speaking with the saintly Justina. Cipriano sells himself literally to the Devil to gain his end by magic. Angelo tempts Isabel in a second dialogue, as wonderful as the first. In her innocence Isabel is slow to see Angelo's drift, and it is only her confession of her own frailty that gives him a chance of making himself clear. 'Nay,' Isabel says,

> call us ten times frail;
> For we are soft as our complexions are,
> And credulous to false prints.

If Shakespeare is depicting in Isabel the self-righteous prude which some critics would make of her, he goes strangely to work.

But when she perceives Angelo's meaning, Isabel decides without hesitation. Now whatever we think of that instant decision, it is certainly not un-Christian. Christianity could never have lived through

---

[14] E. K. CHAMBERS, *op. cit.,* p. 213; J. DOVER WILSON, *op. cit.,* p. 213; U. M. ELLIS-FERMOR, *The Jacobean Drama,* p. 261.

[15] Cf. JOHN MASEFIELD, *William Shakespeare,* p. 179.

its first three hundred years of persecution, if its ranks had not been stiffened by men and women who never hesitated in the choice between righteousness and the ties to their kinsfolk. We may call this fanaticism: but it was well understood in Shakespeare's day. Foxe's *Martyrs* was read by all; old people could still remember seeing the Smithfield fires; year after year saw the martyrdoms of Catholic men (and sometimes of Catholic women like the Ven. Margaret Clitherow). It was a stern age—an age such as the founder of Christianity had foreseen when he uttered his stern warnings. 'He that loveth father or mother more than me . . .' 'If any man come to me, and hate not his father, and mother, . . . and brethren and sisters, . . . he cannot be my disciple.'

It is recorded of Linacre, the father of English medicine, that, albeit a priest, he opened his Greek New Testament for the first time late in life, and came on some of these hard sayings. 'Either this is not the Gospel,' he said, 'or we are not Christians,' and refusing to contemplate the second alternative, he flung the Book from him and returned to the study of medicine. Now it is open to us to say that we are not Christians: it is not open to us to say that Isabel is un-Christian. She goes to her brother, not because she hesitates, but that he may share with her the burden of her irrevocable decision. Claudio's first reply is, 'O heavens! it cannot be;' 'Thou shalt not do't.' But the very bravest of men have quailed, within the four walls of a prison cell, waiting for the axe next day. I am amazed at the way critics condemn Claudio, when he breaks down, and utters his second thoughts, 'Sweet sister, let me live.' Isabel overwhelms him in the furious speech which we all know. And I am even more amazed at the dislike which the critics feel for the tortured Isabel. But when they assure us that their feeling towards both his creatures was shared by the gentle Shakespeare, I am then most amazed of all.

It is admitted that no greater or more moving scenes had appeared on any stage, since the masterpieces of Attic drama ceased to be acted. Yet our critics tell us that Shakespeare wrote them in a mood of 'disillusionment and cynicism,' 'self-laceration' and, strangest of all, 'weariness.'[16] 'A corroding atmosphere of moral suspicion'[17] hangs about this debate between 'the sainted Isabella, wrapt in her selfish chastity,' and 'the wretched boy who in terror of death is ready to

---

[16] J. DOVER WILSON, *op. cit.*, pp. 116, 117.
[17] E. K. CHAMBERS, *op. cit.*, p. 214.

sacrifice his sister's honour.'[18] Isabel's chastity, they say, is 'rancid,' and she is 'not by any means such a saint as she looks';[19] her inhumanity is pitiless, her virtue is self-indulgent, unimaginative, and self-absorbed.[20]

And yet, think of Rose Macaulay's war-poem, 'Many sisters to many brothers,' and let us believe that a sister may suffer more in agony of mind than the brother can suffer in physical wounds or death. Shakespeare has made Isabel say to Claudio,

> O, were it but my life,
> I'ld throw it down for your deliverance
> As frankly as a pin.

It is standing the play on its head,[21] to say that Shakespeare wrote those words in irony and cynicism. How did he convey that to his audience? If such assumptions are allowed, we can prove anything we like, 'eight years together, dinners and suppers and sleeping-hours excepted.'

Isabel then, as Shakespeare sees her and asks us to see her, would frankly, joyously, give her life to save Claudio: and *'greater love hath no man than this.'* And now Claudio is asking for what she cannot give, and she bursts out in agony. Have the critics never seen a human soul or a human body in the extremity of torment? Physical torture Isabel thinks she could have stood without flinching. She has said so to Angelo:

> The impression of keen whips I'ld wear as rubies,
> And strip myself to death, as to a bed
> That longing have been sick for, ere I'ld yield
> My body up to shame.

To suppose that Shakespeare gave these burning words to Isabel so that we should perceive her to be selfish and cold, is to suppose that he did not know his job. The honour of her family and her religion are more to her than mere life, her own or Claudio's.

---

[18] J. DOVER WILSON, *op. cit.,* p. 116.

[19] New Cambridge Shakespeare, *Measure for Measure,* p. xxx.

[20] U. M. ELLIS-FERMOR, *op. cit.,* pp. 261, 262.

[21] I borrow this very excellent phrase from W. W. Lawrence (p. 70). The brevity of a lecture compels me to pass over many points that a critic may think should have been more fully argued, but I do this the more cheerfully, because they have been already so fully discussed by Lawrence in his *Shakespeare's Problem Comedies,* 1931, and their moral emphasized in an excellent leading article in *The Times Literary Supplement* of 16 July 1931.

There are those, like Sir George Greenwood, who prefer to the character of Isabel that of the heroine of the original story—Cassandra, who was willing to endure all shame to save her brother's life. The New Cambridge Shakespeare quotes this dictum of Sir George with more approval than it would give to his other dicta. And we may agree that from such a story a noble, if harrowing, tragedy might be made. There is no need to play the moralist, and to condemn either Cassandra or Isabel. 'Wisdom is justified of all her children.' Faced by a dire choice, different souls may make different decisions, which for each may be the right decision. Shakespeare has chosen to depict Isabel as one who cannot yield. And most of those who have criticized her, from Hazlitt downwards, agree that she cannot. And she has got to make that clear to Claudio. It is just here that her critics quarrel with her. Sir Arthur Quiller-Couch digs out Mrs. Charlotte Lennox from the obscurity of the mid-eighteenth century to tell us how the scene should have been written. Isabel, Charlotte says,

should have made use of her superior understanding to reason down Claudio's fears, recall nobler ideas to his mind, teach him what was due to her honour and his own, and reconcile him to his approaching death by arguments drawn from that religion and virtue of which she made so high a profession.

'To reason down Claudio's fears!' 'By arguments drawn from religion and virtue!' Why, the Duke had just preached to Claudio the most eloquent Sermon Against the Fear of Death that has ever been written since Lucretius completed his Third Book. Claudio had expressed himself convinced; and then the Duke's discourse had shrivelled like a thread in the flame of Claudio's longing for life.

How will pi-jaw help Claudio? Shakespeare imagined Claudio as a good lad, but not, like his sister, devout; he doesn't keep devout company, exactly. Isabel 'well can persuade.' She is one of a few women in Shakespeare who can persuade. (Not Portia: 'The quality of mercy is not strain'd,' produces no persuasion in the soul of Shylock.) Volumnia is a special case. The other great persuaders are: Isabel, Beatrice and Lady Macbeth. And they all use the same arguments—the arguments which, I expect, the first Cave-woman, when in dire straits, used to her Cave-man: You are a coward; You have no love or respect for me; I have no love for you.

Isabel is the most vehement of the three. Sisterly technique has its own rules; there is a peculiar freedom about the talk of those who have known each other from babyhood. And Isabel can appeal to the honour of the family. Escalus, when he first pleaded for Claudio, remembered his 'most noble father.' Isabel had exclaimed, when she first found Claudio firm,

> there my father's grave
> Did utter forth a voice.

And now she cries,

> Heaven shield my mother play'd my father fair.

Isabel appeals to the passion which, in an Elizabethan gentleman, may be presumed to be stronger than the fear of death—pride in his gentle birth and in the courage which should mark it. Don't people see that there are things about which we cannot argue calmly? The fierceness of Isabel's words is the measure of the agony of her soul. 'The fortress which parleys, the woman who parleys, is lost.' I grant that, at the end of a lifetime's training, a saint like Thomas More could smile on his daughter when she tempted him. 'What, Mistress Eve?' But the young martyrs are apt to be more stern, whether it be Cordelia or Antigone, the spitfire St. Eulalia, or St. Juliana putting the fear of death upon the Devil. Who but a pedant would blame them? And it is our fault if we don't see that Isabel is suffering martyrdom none the less because her torment is mental, not physical.

One of the most significant of Shakespeare's alterations of his original is to make the heroine a 'votarist of St. Clare.' At the root of the movement of St. Francis and St. Clare was the intense remembrance of the sufferings of Christ, in atonement for the sins of the whole world—the 'remedy' of which Isabel in vain reminds Angelo. Isabel, as a novice, is testing herself to see whether she is called to that utter renunciation which is the life of the 'poor Clare.' Whether she remains in the Convent or no, one who is contemplating such a life can no more be expected to sell herself into mortal sin, than a good soldier can be expected to sell a stronghold entrusted to him.

Imagine an officer and his subaltern commanded to hold to the uttermost a fortified post against rebels. In a sortie the rebels capture the subaltern, and threaten to shoot him unless the fort surrenders. The subaltern breaks down, and implores his commandant to save his life. I can imagine that the commandant would reply, firmly but gently, that surrender is impossible. But suppose the subaltern were his beloved younger brother, or his only son. I can imagine that then the commandant would reply to his son's appeal by passionate denunciation, telling him that he is a disgrace to his family. To discuss the matter calmly would lead to the surrender which he knows he must not make: his instinct would tell him that. So, at least, it seems to me in my ignorance. And when I find Shakespeare in his wisdom depicting the matter so, I don't see anything cynical about it.

Those who dislike the vehemence of Isabel would do well, in Ben Jonson's phrase, to 'call forth Sophocles to us,' and to ponder on the *Philoctetes*. In that play Neoptolemus is asked to sell his honour and betray his father's friend by a base lie, for the good of his country, and for the ultimate good of the friend who is to be deceived. Neoptolemus refuses indignantly, but he lets himself be drawn into discussion, and so sells his honour and his friend. But the anticipated good does not follow, and Neoptolemus has to make amends to his friend, though this means treason to the Greek army. The play is ending, with Neoptolemus deserting the army, and even contemplating war against his own countrymen, when the god appears from the machine to solve the knot. All this follows because Neoptolemus listens and debates when he hears the voice of the tempter: 'Now give thyself to me for one short, shameless day, and then, for the rest of thy time, be called of all mortals the most righteous.' We cannot argue with the tempter, when our own desires are already so much enlisted on his side. We can only refuse, instinctively, vehemently.

It is precisely the alternation of vehemence with silence which gives Isabel her individuality. When she first understands the drift of Angelo's temptation, the poor child flies at him with a pathetic attempt at blackmail: 'Sign me a present pardon for my brother, or . . . I'll tell the world . . .' When she is told that Angelo has slain Claudio, she exclaims:

O, I will to him and pluck out his eyes!

Shakespeare sometimes puts his heroines in pairs, coupling the fierce, vehement girl with the gentle, swooning girl: Hermia with Helena, Beatrice with Hero, Isabel with Mariana. For all her silence and modesty, Isabel has the ferocity of the martyr. Yet I don't think Shakespeare disliked his vixens. Hermia has nails which can reach her enemy's eyes. Benedick foresaw a predestinate scratched face for the husband of Beatrice. Yet would any of us take Hero in to dinner, if we could get Beatrice, or go hiking through the Athenian forest with Helena, if we could get Hermia?

Critics ask, as does Sir Edmund Chambers, whether Isabel too 'has not had her ordeal, and in her turn failed,' whether she was 'wholly justified in the eyes of her creator.' They are entitled to ask the question. But they ought to wait for the answer. The Duke enters, takes Claudio aside, and tells him there is no hope for him. And we find that Claudio, who before Isabel's outburst had been gripped by the mortal fear of death, is now again master of his soul:

> Let me ask my sister pardon. I am so out of love with life, that I will sue to be rid of it.

'Hold you there,' says the Duke. Claudio does. Later, we see him quiet and self-possessed when the Provost shows him his death-warrant. To the Provost he is 'the most gentle Claudio': and to Shakespeare, the word 'gentle' is a word of very high praise, not consistent with any want of spirit. 'Gentle' and 'most gentle' is how his worthy friends and fellows—Ben Jonson, Heminge, Condell—described Shakespeare. Claudio, 'most gentle' in his prison, has passed his ordeal well, showing quiet courage equally removed from the hilarity of a Posthumus and the insensibility of a Barnardine.

Mrs. Lennox says that Isabel ought to have taught Claudio what is due to her honour and his own. She has.

Now, if Isabel's speech had been intended to depict a 'cold' and 'remorseless' woman, 'all for saving her own soul,' acting cruelly to her brother in the 'fiery ordeal' which (we are told) 'his frail soul proves ill-fitted to endure,' why does Shakespeare show Claudio, far from resenting his sister's reproaches, only wishing to ask her pardon, and henceforth courageous and resolute? Why, above all, does Shakespeare make the Duke, when he overhears Isabel's whole speech, comment on the beauty of her goodness? This is intelligible only if Shakespeare means Isabel's speech to be an agonized outcry, working on her brother as no calm reasoning could have done. If Shakespeare's critics think they could have written the scene better, they are welcome to try; but it does not follow that Shakespeare was a disillusioned cynic because he did not write Isabel's speech as Charlotte Lennox would have done.

When the Duke suggests that Isabel may yet be able to save her brother, she replies, 'I have spirit to do any thing that appears not foul in the truth of my spirit.' And now Isabel's critics disapprove of her because of the 'businesslike' way in which she sets about saving her brother and assisting the Duke's plot. If Shakespeare's Jacobean audiences were as perverse as his modern critics, I can well understand how 'gloom and dejection' may have driven the poor man 'to the verge of madness,' as critics assert that it did. That Shakespeare imagined Isabel as businesslike, should be clear to any one who studies with care her words in the earlier scenes. She is a sensible Elizabethan girl, with no nonsense about her, and she knows that it is no sin to bring husband and wife together.

So Mariana takes Isabel's place, to save Claudio's life.

Again, if Shakespeare meant us to regard Isabel cynically, why did he picture her not only as touching by her goodness both Angelo and the Duke, though to different issues, but even as awing the frivolous Lucio into sobriety and sympathy? To Lucio she is 'a thing ensky'd and sainted,'

> an immortal spirit;
> And to be talk'd with in sincerity,
> As with a saint.

Sir Arthur disqualifies Lucio's evidence because Lucio is a sensualist, and sensualists, he says, habitually divide women into angels and those who are 'their animal prey.'[22] Even if that be true, could Shakespeare seriously expect his audience to grasp such a subtlety? Critics see Isabel 'hard as an icicle.'[23] If Shakespeare meant that why did he make Lucio see her differently: 'O pretty Isabella, I am pale at mine heart to see thine eyes so red.'[24] Even a sensualist can tell when people's eyes are red.

Angelo's own words make it clear that it is his conviction of the innocence and goodness of Isabel which overthrows him.

As for Claudio—the critics may despise him, but Angelo knows better. He knows that Claudio is a plucky lad who, 'receiving a dishonour'd life with ransom of such shame,' might take his revenge in time to come. So he commands Claudio's execution. The Duke, of

[22] New Cambridge Shakespeare, p. xxvii.
[23] U. M. ELLIS-FERMOR, *op. cit.,* p. 262.
[24] IV. iii. 158.

course, prevents it, and continues to weave his toils round Angelo, till the moment when he will fall on him, and grind him to powder.

And, immediately, Angelo's remorse begins. He realizes what he really is: 'This deed unshapes me quite.' Yet his state is more gracious now, when he believes himself to be a perjured adulterer, than it was a few days before, when he believed himself to be a saint.

I pass over the agonies of Angelo's repentance. 'Dull to all proceedings,' he fights to maintain all that is left him, the 'credent bulk' of a public esteem which has become a mockery to him. When Lucio brings the struggle to an end, by tearing the Friar's hood off the Duke, Angelo realizes that his master is one from whom no secrets are hid:

> DUKE. Hast thou or word, or wit, or impudence,
> That yet can do thee office? . . .
>   ANGELO.   O my dread lord,
> I should be guiltier than my guiltiness,
> To think I can be undiscernible,
> When I perceive your Grace, like power divine,
> Hath looked upon my passes.

A cold-hearted, self-righteous prig is brought to a sense of what he is, in the sight of his Master. A few hours before, Angelo had turned a deaf ear to the plea 'Why, all the souls that were, were forfeit once.' But now he can conceive no depth of guilt so deep as his own. 'Guiltier than my guiltiness.' It is like the repentance of Enobarbus, 'I am alone the villain of the earth,' or of Posthumus,

>   it is I
> That all the abhorred things o' the earth amend
> By being worse than they.

For Angelo, as for Enobarbus and for Posthumus, nothing remains save a passionate prayer to be put out of his misery:

>   Then, good prince,
> No longer session hold upon my shame,
> But let my trial be mine own confession:
> Immediate sentence then, and sequent death,
> Is all the grace I beg.

Surely it is concerning repentance like this that it is written, 'There is joy in the presence of the angels of God.'

The ninety and nine just persons which need no repentance naturally think otherwise. Coleridge began the outcry against *Measure for Measure,* which he found 'the most painful—say rather the only painful—part' of Shakespeare's genuine works. The pardon of Angelo, he says, 'baffles the strong indignant claim of justice—(for cruelty, with lust and damnable baseness, cannot be forgiven, because we cannot conceive them as being morally repented of).'[25] Swinburne endorsed this judgment at great length. Justice, he said, 'is buffeted, outraged, insulted, struck in the face.'[26] 'We are tricked out of our dole, defeated of our due, lured and led on to look for some equitable and satisfying upshot, defrauded and derided and sent empty away.' Hazlitt could not allow Mariana to love Angelo 'whom we hate.'[27] To enumerate the ninety-six other just persons would be to write a bibliography of *Measure for Measure,* which is no part of my intention. Rather I turn to Mariana as she implores pardon for her husband. Coleridge thought the pardon and marriage of Angelo not only unjust, but degrading to the character of woman. Yet repentance, intercession and forgiveness are the stuff of Christianity and of the old stories of Christendom. In the story which Calderon used, Cipriano, after selling himself to the Devil in order to win Justina to his will, repents and dies a martyr at her side, comforted by her words: 'So many stars has not the Heaven, so many grains of sand the sea, not so many sparks the fire, not so many motes the sunlight, as the sins which He forgives.'

But the Duke again and again rejects Mariana's plea for mercy. She turns at last to Isabel:

> Sweet Isabel, take my part;
> Lend me your knees and all my life to come
> I'll lend you all my life to do you service.

Isabel stands silent.

It is many years ago that I saw acted, within this building where we are now met, Calderon's *Life is a Dream,* in the version of Edward Fitzgerald. In that play Basilio, King of Poland, has learnt from his study of the stars that his new-born son will end by trampling on his father's head. So Prince Segismund is kept, from his birth, in a cruel prison, not knowing who he is. But his father, relenting,

[25] *Notes on Shakespeare.*
[26] *Study of Shakespeare.*
[27] *Characters of Shakespeare's Plays.*

determines to test whether he has read the stars aright: so he brings Segismund drugged to the palace. There Segismund awakes to find himself heir to the throne of Poland; but he abuses his one day of power, and is carried back in sleep again to his prison, to be told that all that he has seen and done that day has been a dream. Yet later the mutinous army releases him. Segismund marches at the head of the army, not knowing whether he dreams or no, and his victories end with the King Basilio kneeling humbled at the feet of his wronged son.

What will Segismund now do? Has he learnt how to forgive, the greatest thing that can be learnt from the Dream which is called Life?

It is not often that one can see a classical masterpiece acted without knowing how it will end. Whether it was the acting of Miss Margaret Halstan, who took the part of the boy-prince, or the stage production of Mr. Poel, I have never since felt the suspense of a great scene as I felt that. I like to think that those who first saw Shakespeare's play acted at the Christmas revels of 1604 may perhaps have felt such a suspense. The title, *Measure for Measure,* gave them no clue as to the ending.

A second time Mariana appeals:

> Isabel,
> Sweet Isabel, do yet but kneel by me;
> Hold up your hands, say nothing, I'll speak all.

Still Isabel stands silent, whilst Mariana pleads on pitifully:

> They say, best men are moulded out of faults;
> And, for the most, become much more the better
> For being a little bad: so may my husband.

At her third appeal,

> O Isabel, will you not lend a knee?

Isabel kneels at the feet of the Duke.

While Isabel is pleading for his life, Angelo is longing for death. Escalus turns to him, regretting his fall. Angelo only says:

> I am sorry that such sorrow I procure:
> And so deep sticks it in my penitent heart,
> That I crave death more willingly than mercy;
> 'Tis my deserving, and I do entreat it.

The wheel is come full circle.

Only two days before, Angelo had rejected the plea of mercy for Claudio with the words

> When I, that censure him, do so offend,
> Let mine own judgment pattern out my death.

And Isabel had longed for the potency of Anglo that she might 'tell what 'twere to be a judge, and what a prisoner.' Later we have seen Angelo 'unshaped' by his remorse, though still confident that he will escape undetected, whilst Isabel longs to 'pluck out his eyes,' and is promised revenges to her heart on 'this wretch' who has murdered her brother. And now Angelo, publicly shamed, longing for death, faces an Isabel who can bring herself to say, after an agony of silent struggle, 'let him not die.' It was not in a spirit of 'weariness, cynicism, and disgust' that the Master Craftsman made the whirligig of time bring in revenges like these.

Isabel's sufferings are over. The Provost produces the muffled Claudio. Sister meets brother with that 'prone and speechless dialect' which moves, or should move, men.

Sir Edmund Chambers asks, Why does the Duke conceal from Isabel in her grief the knowledge that her brother yet lives? Sir Walter Raleigh asked the same question thirty years ago. His answer was that the reason is dramatic; the crisis must be kept for the end. And, as a piece of stagecraft, the ending justifies itself; it is magnificent. But Sir Edmund Chambers is surely right when he says that a play dealing seriously with the problems of life must be taken seriously; the Duke, he thinks, symbolizes the workings of Providence. Is not such treatment of Providence, then, he asks, ironical?

The Duke certainly reminds us of the ways of Providence. And we feel so in the great final scene, where Mariana is imploring the silent Isabel to intercede for Angelo. Why, then, does the Duke gather up all his authority, as former Friar and present Monarch, and crash it, with a lie, in the path Isabel must tread?

> Should she kneel down in mercy of this fact,
> Her brother's ghost his paved bed would break,
> And take her hence in horror.

Yet all this time the Duke is keeping her brother in reserve, to produce him when Isabel shall have fulfilled her destiny, by making intercession for the man she most hates.

If we are thinking of the Duke as a character in the play, this is difficult to understand. Equally difficult is it to understand the Hermione of the last scene in the *Winter's Tale*. We cannot imagine the wronged queen of the first three acts shamming death, and tormenting her husband with sixteen years of remorse. There is, of course, the dramatic effect; but is there not also something more? Is there not something symbolic of a mysterious power, when, in the *Alcestis,* Heracles seems to torment Admetus before he restores his wife to him?

> It was the crowning grace of that great heart,
> To keep back joy, procrastinate the truth.[28]

If it be said that this torturing of Isabel,

> To make her heavenly comforts of despair
> When it is least expected,

is unbearably cruel, I can only reply that life undoubtedly *is* sometimes like that. There are some souls (Isabel is one) for whom it is decreed that no trial, however agonizing, no pain, however atrocious, is to be spared them. Nevertheless, it is also true that there is no trial so agonizing, no pain so atrocious, but that some souls can rise above it, as Isabel does when, despite the Duke's stern warning, she kneels at his feet to intercede for Angelo.

Is it then true, as Sir Arthur Quiller-Couch says, that Isabel writes no lesson on the dark walls, and that they teach none to her soul? Or is it true when Sir Edmund Chambers echoes the complaint of Coleridge, and says that *Measure for Measure* 'just perplexes and offends,' because there is no poetic justice? Is it true that 'to no profit of righteousness has Isabella's white soul been dragged through the mire'?

I know that many readers find a stumbling-block in this culminating scene, in Isabel's pleading for Angelo. Why should she plead, they ask, for her brother's murderer?

We must be prepared to accept the postulates of Shakespeare's plays, as we do, for example, of Sophocles' *Oedipus Tyrannus*. And, generally, we are so prepared: we accept the caskets and the pound of flesh, King Lear's love test and Prospero's art. It is a postulate of our story that Claudio has committed a capital offence. Angelo has not committed a crime in letting the law take its course upon

---

[28] BROWNING, *Balaustion's Adventure.*

Claudio; he has not committed a crime in his union with Mariana, to whom he has been publicly betrothed; those are assumptions on which the play is based. Angelo would be despicable if he put forward any such plea for himself, and he does not. But the fact remains that Angelo's sin has been, not in act, but in thought, and human law cannot take cognizance of thought: 'thoughts are no subjects.' Besides, Isabel is conscious that, however innocently, she herself has been the cause of Angelo's fall:

> I partly think
> A due sincerity govern'd his deeds,
> Till he did look on me; since it is so,
> Let him not die.

And Angelo is penitent. There can be no doubt what the words of the Sermon on the Mount demand: 'Judge not, and ye shall not be judged.' That had been Isabel's plea for Claudio. It is a test of her sincerity, if she can put forward a plea for mercy for her dearest foe, as well as for him whom she dearly loves.

Criticism of *Measure for Measure,* from Coleridge downwards, has amounted to this: 'There is a limit to human charity.' 'There is,' says Chesterton's Father Brown, 'and that is the real difference between human charity and Christian charity.' Isabel had said the same:

> O, think on that;
> And mercy then will breathe within your lips
> Like man new made.

Shakespeare has so manipulated the story as to make it end in Isabel showing more than human charity to Angelo, whilst at the same time he has avoided, by the introduction of Mariana, the error, which he found in his crude original, of wedding Isabel to Angelo.

Yet we are told that in *Measure for Measure* 'the evidence of Shakespeare's profound disillusionment and discouragement of spirit is plain enough,' that 'the searchlight of irony is thrown upon the paths of Providence itself.'[29]

The way in which the Duke, an earthly Providence, tortures Isabel till he wrings her agonized forgiveness out of her, reminds us of the way in which, in Shakespeare's contemporary tragedies, Providence seems to ordain that no suffering is spared to Lear or Cordelia, to Othello or Desdemona. It is very terrible. But it cannot be called, as it

29 E. K. CHAMBERS in the *Encyclopaedia Britannica* (1911), xxiv, 785.

often is called, un-Christian, or 'an indictment of man's maker,' or 'a definite arraignment of the scheme of things,' or 'the final victory of evil.'[30] For in that case the representation would leave us desperate or rebellious. And it does not. Lear and Othello, Cordelia and Desdemona rise 'superior to the world in which they appear.'[31] That wise critic, A. C. Bradley, has said:

> The extremity of the disproportion between prosperity and goodness first shocks us, and then flashes on us the conviction that our whole attitude in asking or expecting that goodness should be prosperous is wrong; that, if only we could see things as they are, we should see that the outward is nothing and the inward is all.[32]

It is a thought which is difficult to express, and Bradley felt his own statement to be 'exaggerated and too explicit.' But the thought that 'Whosoever will lose his life shall find it,' or, as Kent in the stocks puts it, 'Nothing almost sees miracles but misery,' was, perhaps, more generally understood by the Englishmen of Shakespeare's day than it is now. Mr. Bettenham, Reader of Gray's Inn, was wont to say 'that virtuous men were like some herbs and spices, that gave not their sweet smell, till they be broken and crushed.' And Francis Bacon, of the same Inn, put this doctrine into his Essay *Of Adversity,* to show that 'Prosperity is the blessing of the Old Testament; adversity is the blessing of the New, which carrieth the greater benediction, and the clearer revelation of God's favour.'

And I heard A. E. Housman, who, of all men I have known, was sternest in refusing to break his proud reserve, say in his first lecture:

> Fortitude and continence and honesty are not commended to us on the ground that they conduce, as on the whole they do conduce, to material success, nor yet on the ground that they will be rewarded hereafter: those whose office it is to exhort mankind to virtue are ashamed to degrade the cause they plead by proffering such lures as these.

Forty-one years later, in his last great public utterance, in which he bade us 'Farewell for ever,' he quoted: 'Whosoever will save his life shall lose it, and whosoever will lose his life shall find it.' 'That,' he said, 'is the most important truth which has ever been uttered, and the greatest discovery ever made in the moral world; but I do not find in it anything which I should call poetical.'[33]

---

[30] Idem, *Shakespeare: A Survey,* pp. 215, 220, 231, 247.
[31] A. C. BRADLEY, *Shakespearean Tragedy,* p. 324.
[32] *Ibid.,* p. 326.
[33] *Introductory Lecture,* 1892, p. 36; *Name and Nature of Poetry,* 1933, p. 36.

Now it would take me altogether out of my depth, to discuss whether there is anything poetical in those words. But it can surely be contended that Shakespearean tragedy is an expression *in poetry* of that 'most important truth which has ever been uttered.' And so, equally, is *Measure for Measure* an expression of 'the greatest discovery ever made in the moral world': the highly unpleasant discovery that there are things more important, for oneself and for others, than avoiding death and pain.

That, of course, is not a Christian discovery. One of the founders of modern Japan uttered it in two lines of Chinese verse, as he was led to execution, speaking with a loud voice, so that he might take farewell of his friend without implicating him by turning his head:

> It is better to be a crystal and be broken
> Than to remain perfect like a tile upon the housetop.

It is not Christian: but it is a foundation upon which Christianity, in common with every other religion worth the name, is built.

Measure for Measure is a play of forgiveness, more distinctly even than *The Tempest*. Isabel forgives in her moment of direst loss: Prospero only when he has recovered his Dukedom. Isabel urges forgiveness because a Christian must forgive: Prospero forgives because he does not condescend to torment his enemies further. And the contrast applies also to those forgiven. Angelo longs for death, because the Duke, *'like power divine,'* has seen his sinfulness. Sebastian and Antonio learn from Prospero, when he forgives them, that besides their crimes against him, he knows also how they have plotted to kill their king; to the pardoned Sebastian, just as to Angelo, there naturally seems to be something superhuman in such knowledge; but Sebastian expresses his conviction differently from Angelo:

> The devil speaks in him.

'No!' says Prospero; and then he turns to his brother Antonio:

> For you, most wicked Sir, whom to call brother
> Would even infect my mouth, I do forgive
> Thy rankest fault . . .

Antonio makes no answer to this forgiveness. But he and Sebastian, unabashed, continue their joyless jests to the end.

Now, when we mark how evil, and its forgiveness, is depicted in *Measure for Measure* in 1604, can we agree that Shakespeare's philosophy about 1604 was 'obviously not a Christian philosophy'? On the contrary, it seems to me more definitely Christian than that of *The Tempest,* though I don't deny that the philosophy of the Romances can also be called Christian. I would not deny that, on the whole, Shakespeare's last plays *are* 'happy dreams,' 'symbols of an optimistic faith in the beneficent dispositions of an ordering Providence.'[34] But I see no ground to believe that there is any 'complete breach' between the mood of 1604 and that of 1611, or that we must assume a 'conversion,' caused by 'a serious illness which may have been a nervous breakdown, and on the other hand may have been merely the plague.'[35]

We are told that the low-comedy characters of *Measure for Measure* are 'unwholesome company': that whereas Shakespeare, in Falstaff and his associates, had represented sin as 'human,' he now represents it as 'devilish.'[36] But is this really so? Surely the answer was given by Sir Walter Raleigh years ago. These characters in *Measure for Measure* 'are live men, pleasant to Shakespeare.' Pompey is 'one of those humble, cheerful beings, willing to help in anything that is going forward, who are the mainstay of human affairs . . . Froth is an amiable, feather-headed young gentleman—to dislike him would argue an ill-nature, and a small one . . . This world of Vienna, as Shakespeare paints it, is not a black world; it is a weak world, full of little vanities and stupidities, regardful of custom, fond of pleasure, idle, and abundantly human.'[37]

As to Barnardine, his creator came to love him so much that he had not the heart to decapitate him, although Barnardine was only created to be decapitated.

In *Measure for Measure* sin is not represented as 'devilish': it is represented as sinful, and that is necessitated by the serious and earnest character of the whole play. Yet the sinners do not altogether forfeit our sympathy. And when the unmasked Duke finally taxes Lucio with his slanders, he is not unequal to the occasion:

> Faith, my lord, I spoke it but according to the trick. If you will hang me for it, you may; but I had rather it would please you I might be whipt.

[34] E. K. CHAMBERS in the *Encyclopaedia Britannica* (1911), xxiv, 785.
[35] Idem, *William Shakespeare,* 1930, i, 86, 274.
[36] Idem, *Shakespeare: A Survey,* 1935, p. 211.
[37] *Shakespeare,* p. 166.

This, then, is how Shakespeare treats the barbarous old story of *Promos and Cassandra*, removing its morbid details, harmonizing its crudities, giving humanity and humour to its low characters, turning it into a consistent tale of intercession for sin, repentance from and forgiveness of crime. Yet *Measure for Measure* is adduced as the supreme proof that, about 1603, Shakespeare was in a mood of 'self-laceration, weariness, discord, cynicism, and disgust.'[38] He has been in that mood for the two years since the execution of Essex, and will remain in it for another four or five. This dominant mood of gloom and dejection will bring him on one occasion to the verge of madness, and lead him to write dramas greater than any other man ever wrote save Aeschylus and Sophocles alone. Then in 1608 Sir Edmund Chambers will cure him of his seven years of 'profound disillusionment and discouragement of spirit' by giving him either the plague, or (alternatively) a nervous break-down.

I hear a gentle voice from Stratford murmur

Good frend, for Jesus sake forbeare.

Yet the critics have one final kick at *Measure for Measure*. More Papistical than the Pope, they feel outraged that Isabel should 'throw her noviate headdress over the mill'[39] and marry the Duke. Even the sober A. C. Bradley thought that here Shakespeare lent himself to 'a scandalous proceeding.'[40] Yet Isabel is a novice, and her business as a novice is to learn her Creator's intentions for her future. Whether she ought to return to the cloister from which she has been so urgently summoned rests with her creator—William Shakespeare. And he leaves her silent, and us guessing. For myself, I am satisfied that Isabel will do her duty in that state of life unto which it shall please William Shakespeare to call her, whether as abbess or duchess.

Yet in Shakespeare's greatest plays, his greatest characters, for all their individuality, have also an imaginative, a symbolic suggestion. It is so in *The Tempest*, it is so in *Hamlet*. Thus also in the person of Lear, not only a helpless old man, but Paternity and Royalty are outraged; and 'Glamis hath murder'd Sleep.' No woman in Shakespeare is more individual than Isabel: silent yet eloquent, sternly righteous yet capable of infinite forgiveness, a very saint and a very vixen. But,

[38] J. DOVER WILSON, *op. cit.*, p. 117.
[39] New Cambridge Shakespeare, p. xxxi.
[40] *Shakespearean Tragedy*, p. 78.

first and last, she 'stands for' mercy. The Duke is first shown to us as a governor perplexed about justice, puzzled in his search for righteousness, seeking above all things to know himself; and he becomes the arbiter of the destinies of everyone in the play. Is it altogether fanciful to remember once again that *Measure for Measure* was acted before the court at Christmas, 1604: that when Isabel at the beginning urges her plea for mercy (which she also makes good at the end) it is on the ground that

> He that might the vantage best have took
> Found out the remedy.

The day before *Measure for Measure* was acted, the finding out of that remedy was being commemorated. All sober criticism must remember the part which the accepted theology played in the thought of Shakespeare's day; that the Feast of the Nativity was—is—the union of Divine Mercy and of Divine Righteousness, and was—is—celebrated in the Christmas psalm:

> Mercy and truth are met together: righteousness and peace have kissed each other.

Shakespeare's audience expected a marriage at the end: and, though it may be an accident, the marriage of Isabel and the Duke makes a good ending to a Christmas play.

But I hear my Japanese student objecting: 'I imagine Lady Duchess can not be other than embarrassed, when she welcome Mr. Angel to marriage meal.'

We have no business to imagine any such thing. The play is over. But, if we must go by imaginations, I will imagine with you. I imagine that, as they moved off the stage two and two, the Duke and Isabel, Claudio and Juliet, Angelo and Mariana, Abhorson and Barnardine bringing up the rear, Isabel broke silence, and said softly to the Duke, 'Give me your pardon that I, your vassal, should now beseech that you do intend the Lord Angelo for your swift ambassador to London. England is the place where the poor man will suffer least embarrassment, for in England they are such prudes that they rarely read and more rarely act *Measure for Measure;* although, my Duke'—and here Isabel turns to him with her 'heavenly and yielding'[41] smile—'al-

---

[41] W. W. LAWRENCE, *Shakespeare's Problem Comedies,* p. 107. And may I here, once again, express my indebtedness to that great American scholar.

though you and I are agreed that, to us, it is the wisest of all Shakespeare's comedies.'

And, to conclude. I have no excuse, save a love of Shakespeare, for trespassing on the specialist field of Shakespeare study. But it was a high adventure to leave Beowulf alone for a while in his contest with Grendel and the Dragon and to do battle on behalf of pretty Isabel. Further, I have sought to rescue William Shakespeare from his seven years' imprisonment in the pestiferous Cave of Despair, albeit thereby I have had to joust against Sir Arthur and Sir Edmund and the Lady Una Britomartis Ellis-Fermor, backed by all those spells which the Wizard professor of the North, the Prince of the Power of the Air, can weave from his chair amid the mists of high Dunedin. I realize how deeply fixed, by generations of repetition, is the dogma of Shakespeare's disillusioned early Jacobean period, 'in the Depths.' That is my excuse for venturing to repeat the protest, eloquently made in this place three years ago by Professor Sisson, in his discourse on 'The Mythical Sorrows of Shakespeare.'

I submit that *Measure for Measure*, whilst it is akin to the tragedies with which it is contemporary, has also a likeness to those 'Romances' with which Shakespeare crowned his work. It is, indeed, for the continuity of Shakespeare that I am pleading. 'Shakespeare's career is the career of an artist.' Let us study his plays as the works of art which we know them to be, rather than weave baseless conjectures concerning details of a biography which we can never know. No one formula can summarize Shakespeare's life for us. Yet instead of always seeing him as suddenly plunged into the Depths, then raised by some convulsion to the Heights, might we not sometimes think of his career as a continuous progress to the Heights? We can trace the steady advance of Shakespeare's art, from *Henry VI* and *Richard III* to *Othello, Lear,* or *Macbeth;* or from the *Two Gentlemen* to *The Tempest*. We can also trace, I believe, the growth of a faith in the power of goodness, the growth of a belief that even in the valley of the shadow of death souls like Cordelia or Desdemona need fear no evil, that the beauty of such souls is Truth. It may be that Shakespeare felt the shadow closing upon him, when he made Prospero return to his Milan where

Every third thought shall be my grave.

Yet no one has rightly felt *The Tempest* to be pessimistic or gloomy.

That is all we know, and all we need to know. The real story is so wonderful that we can only mar it by groundless biographical conjectures. Our knowledge 'can only be increased by minute and patient study, by the rejection of surmise about him, and by the constant public playing of his plays, in the Shakespearean manner, by actors who will neither mutilate nor distort what the great mind strove to make just.'[42]

I deprecate attempts to define Shakespeare's theological beliefs or unbeliefs. But from his earliest plays to his latest, he shows a belief in forgiveness as the virtue by which human goodness draws nearest to the divine:

> Who by repentance is not satisfied
> Is nor of heaven nor earth, for these are pleased.[43]

And so far from agreeing that when he wrote *Measure for Measure* 'he quite obviously believed in nothing,' I submit that it is precisely the depth of his belief in forgiveness which has puzzled, in their judgment of that play, so many of his greatest critics, from Coleridge and Hazlitt and Swinburne, down to the present day. *Measure for Measure* shows 'the drama of strong characters taking up and transforming the fanciful products of an earlier world, the inventions of minds not deeply or especially interested in character.' The great poet (in the words of Aristotle, quoted by W. P. Ker) 'gets over the unreason by the grace and skill of his handling.'[44] Grace and skill have transformed *Promos and Cassandra* into a noble drama on the theme 'Judge not: for with what measure ye mete it shall be measured to you again.' It is that which matters, rather than any surviving traces of the original 'unreason.'

This series of Academy Shakespeare lectures was initiated by the great ambassador of France, Jusserand, who crossed the Atlantic from Washington in 1911 to tell us 'What to expect of Shakespeare.' He gave me (it is twenty-six years ago) the copy of his inaugural lecture now on the table before me. It is inscribed 'To R. W. Chambers, who knows how to fight a good fight.' I have tried to fight a good fight this afternoon. I believe that *Measure for Measure* and *The Tempest* are Shakespeare's greatest plays of forgiveness. It is

---

[42] JOHN MASEFIELD, *William Shakespeare,* p. 251.
[43] *Two Gentlemen of Verona,* v. iv. 79.
[44] *Epic and Romance,* p. 37.

for forgiveness I would ask, if I have hurt the feelings of any of the great English scholars from whom I have ventured to differ. And I shall receive it, for I know their generosity.

> As you from crimes would pardon'd be,
> Let your indulgence set me free.

THEODORE SPENCER
1902-1949

THEODORE SPENCER'S *Shakespeare and the Nature of Man* (1942) is an admirable exposition of what E. M. W. Tillyard, in his book* published almost at the same time, called the Elizabethan world picture. Spencer's work is also a survey of the plays which lucidly shows how this world-picture is contained in them. It has so opened our eyes to the use of microcosm-macrocosm, human body-body politic, king-sun and other such analogies in Shakespeare that they now seem to be self-evident. It does more, however, than to treat the plays as intellectual documents, for it shows how Shakespeare used the conflict between the traditional view of man, society, and the universe and the new views of them for artistic purposes.

In this selection Spencer analyzes *Troilus and Cressida,* which has been called Shakespeare's most puzzling play, in the light of this conflict. As a result, he is able to correct Campbell, pointing out that Troilus is no mere dissolute rake but an idealistic young man whose betrayal by Cressida shatters the universe for him.

One note may be appended to Spencer's discussion of the scene in which Cressida submits to Diomed. An

* *The Elizabethan World Picture,* 1943.

examination of the dialogue reveals that Thersites not only comments on the action and words of Cressida, as Spencer says, but on the conversation of Troilus and Ulysses, which he evidently is likewise in a position to overhear. Of the three commentators on the action, representing passion, reason, and cynicism, it is the cynical commentator who has the last word in this drama.

TROILUS AND CRESSIDA AS DRAMATIC EXPERIMENT

Troilus and Cressida is a puzzling play, both in execution and intention, and the uncertainty of the Folio editors as to where to place it (at the last minute they squeezed it between the Histories and the Tragedies) has been reflected ever since in the comments of the critics.[1] If we are to have a clear view of it, we must first remember three things; that it was in all probability written for a special audience of law students, that it was very probably influenced by the contemporary fashion for dramatic satire, and that Shakespeare was dealing with a story more familiar to his audience than, say, the story of Hamlet, and that he was therefore less free to change the outline of its events. This last fact is particularly important when we think of the end of the play. The old story, as Chaucer and many other writers had told it, was unsatisfactory for tragedy because its conclusion was so indefinite: Cressida keeps on living as Diomed's mistress, and Troilus keeps on fighting the Greeks until he is eventually

"*Troilus and Cressida* as Dramatic Experiment" is from Theodore Spencer, *Shakespeare and the Nature of Man*. Copyright 1942, 1949 by The Macmillan Company. Reprinted with permission of the publisher.
[1] In discussing the play I am indebted to W. W. Lawrence, *Shakespeare's Problem Comedies*, New York, 1931, to O. J. Campbell, *Comicall Satyre and Shakespeare's Troilus and Cressida*, San Marino, California, 1938, and to my own article (with which I no longer entirely agree), "A Commentary on Shakespeare's *Troilus and Cressida*," *Studies in English Literature*, Tokyo, XVI (1936), 1 ff. See also J. E. Phillips, Jr., *The State in Shakespeare's Greek and Roman Plays*, New York, 1940.

killed by Achilles in an irrelevant way that has nothing to do with his previous actions. Shakespeare was too close to his audience to be able to change—as Dryden later was able to change—this undramatic trailing-off of the sequence of events, and it is this trailing-off which more than anything else has made the play seem unsatisfactory. Death was the essence of tragedy to an Elizabethan audience, but to follow the old story of Troilus and Cressida meant to keep them alive at the end. Yet, if, as modern critics have pointed out, "Shakespeare's picture of the Troy story is an experiment in the middle ground between comedy and tragedy,"[2] the traditional ending could be very useful. If we examine the play more closely we shall discover that, governed by these facts which I have mentioned, Shakespeare was in all probability experimenting with a new kind of dramatic form.

There are two main themes in the play: the theme of war and the theme of love. The first is represented by Hector, the second by Troilus, and the climax of the action is that both these heroes are destroyed. At the end Hector removes his armor, and Achilles, not even single-handed, but accompanied by a gang of Myrmidons, attacks him in the most cowardly fashion and he is killed without a chance for self-defense. Cressida, the object of Troilus' passionate devotion, after swearing to him that she will be forever true, betrays him the very first night after their separation. The result is that we have, in the case of Troilus, a worse kind of tragedy than death, the tragedy of continued existence after everything that matters has been destroyed. There is nothing here of that inevitability which ennobles the end of *Hamlet*.

The two dastardly climaxes of the action, the murder of Hector and the betrayal of Troilus, are all the more shocking because of the way Shakespeare planned the play. For in *Troilus and Cressida,* almost more elaborately than anywhere else, Shakespeare sets up a standard of conduct which the main action of the play violates. In the first act, when the Greeks are discussing among themselves why it is that their siege is unsuccessful, Ulysses delivers that long and magnificent speech on order with which we are already familiar, and which is the finest expression in Shakespeare's work of the traditional view of the state and of Nature. The "specialty of rule"—the special art of government—says Ulysses, has been neglected in the Greek camp, and that specialty, namely the maintenance of order and degree, must be enforced if the state, and also the heavens, the ele-

[2] O. J. Campbell, *op. cit.,* p. 187.

ments, society and the individual, are to fulfill their proper functions. The argument is one that must have been recognized at once by the law-students before whom the play was probably first performed. But what we see on the stage is a complete violation of the whole traditional belief. Instead of order we have anarchy, instead of degree there is violent personal rivalry. Both Ajax and Achilles stand out as petulant and proud individualists, and Ulysses, who acts throughout as the voice of common sense and practical wisdom, learns that there is nothing he can do which will enforce the standards of order and perseverance which he so eloquently describes. The action of the war ends in chaos; the fifth act, apart from the scene describing Cressida's betrayal, is a series of brutal combats ending with a curse.

The Trojans, though they may seem to be nobler than the Greeks as far as their action in war is concerned, are equally ineffective. Like the Greeks they too have a debate (act ii, scene 2) among themselves, in which a proper standard of action is set up, and then dismissed for a less rational course. The point at issue is whether or not they shall return Helen to Menelaus; Hector thinks they should, Troilus passionately argues that they should not, since honor demands that they keep what they have taken. Paris, naturally enough, supports him, but Hector rebukes both of them for the superficiality of their views—they cannot determine between right and wrong because their arguments come from "the hot passion of distemper'd blood." The right lies on the opposite side, and, Hector says:

> Nature craves
> All dues be render'd to their owners: now,
> What nearer debt in all humanity
> Than wife is to the husband? if this law
> Of nature be corrupted through affection,
> And that great minds, of partial indulgence
> To their benumbed wills, resist the same,
> There is a law in each well-order'd nation
> To curb those raging appetites that are
> Most disobedient and refractory.
> If Helen then be wife to Sparta's king,
> As it is known she is, these moral laws
> Of nature, and of nations, speak aloud
> To have her back return'd: thus to persist
> In doing wrong extenuates not wrong,
> But makes it much more heavy. Hector's opinion
> Is this, in way of truth—

This is the traditional view, and all rational opinion would support it; to do otherwise is to go against Nature. But what happens? Hector immediately switches to the opposite, irrational side, and supports the argument of passion:

> Hector's opinion
> Is this, in way of truth; yet, ne'ertheless,
> My spritely brethren, I propend to you
> In resolution to keep Helen still;
> For 'tis a cause that hath no mean dependence
> Upon our joint and several dignities.

It would be hard to find a more lame and impotent conclusion than this, and though we may say that Shakespeare was forced by the familiar story to end the argument in such a fashion (for the Trojans did keep Helen, as everyone knew), nevertheless he need not have introduced the argument in the first place. Having done so, and having made Hector reach a conclusion which only too clearly implies that the Trojans are staking their lives on a cause which violates the law of reason, of Nature and of nations, he gives us only the feeblest kind of confidence in the validity of their enterprise and in the success of its outcome. In another fashion, but just as clearly, the Trojans, like the Greeks, are doomed to disintegration.

But Shakespeare does not rely merely on the violation of the conventional standards to give his picture of disruption, he uses another feature of the old story, the character of Thersites, to act as a reviling and denigrating chorus to the whole action. In many previous versions of the story, dramatic and otherwise, Thersites had been described as a railer, and in making him rail, Shakespeare was only giving the members of his audience what they expected. But they can never before have heard such effectively corrosive railing as this. Thersites' entrance is carefully prepared for by several mentions of his name, and when he first appears with Ajax, at the beginning of the second act, his violence makes everything he thinks of either bestial or diseased. "Agamemnon," he begins—and we must remember that as the leader of the Greek state Agamemnon should be, in Ulysses' words of the previous scene, like the hive "to whom the foragers shall all repair"—"Agamemnon," says Thersites, "how if he had boils? full, all over, generally? And those boils did run? Say so, did not the general run then? were not that a botchy core?"

There are plenty of disease images in *Hamlet*,[3] in fact more than in any other play, but Thersites speaks with a destructive venom that is peculiar to himself. "A botchy [an ulcerous] core" does not promise a healthy fruit, nor does a king who is running with boils promise a healthy state. And as Thersites and Ajax curse one another while Ajax beats Thersites with his fists, image after image is piled up of corruption and bestiality: in fifty lines they call each other *dog, bitch-wolf's son, horse, toadstool, porpentine, whoreson cur, ass,* and *camel;* they speak of diseases like the murrain, the scab, and the scurvy—all is degradation and corruption. This is the tone of Thersites throughout: he can see only "Lechery, lechery; still, wars and lechery: nothing else holds fashion."

For he is not merely a commentator on the warriors, he is a commentator on the lovers too, and he adds his harsh, grating emphasis to the peculiar bitterness which is so deeply a part of Troilus' emotion. Troilus is a very different kind of lover from Romeo—the difference shows even in the texture of his speech. When Romeo addresses Juliet, his images are the conventional images of romantic love (ii, 2, 10):

> It is my lady; O! it is my love:
> O! that she knew she were.
> She speaks, yet she says nothing: what of that?
> Her eye discourses; I will answer it.
> I am too bold, 'tis not to me she speaks:
> Two of the fairest stars in all the heaven,
> Having some business, do intreat her eyes
> To twinkle in their spheres till they return.
> What if her eyes were there, they in her head?
> The brightness of her cheek would shame those stars
> As daylight doth a lamp; her eyes in heaven
> Would through the airy region stream so bright
> That birds would sing and think it were not night.

But when Troilus speaks of his love for Cressida (i, 1, 51), we have no such exalted language. Romeo's images are full of lightness, bright-

---

[3] See Caroline Spurgeon, *Shakespeare's Imagery*, New York, 1936, p. 316. But in discussing *Hamlet* Miss Spurgeon fails to point out the interesting fact that the great majority, about 85 per cent, of these images of disease appear after the middle of the third act; in other words Shakespeare uses images from the decay of the body of man with increasing frequency as his plot shows the decay, under Claudius as king, of the body of the state.

ness—*stars, daylight, lamp, heaven, airy region,* birds singing. They
are images that lead us upward. But the images of Troilus lead us
down; they are violent and harsh. As Troilus speaks of love he uses
such words as *drown'd, deep, indrench'd, mad, ulcer, ink, ploughman's
hand, gash, knife.* When we listen carefully the effect is very striking:

> O Pandarus! I tell thee, Pandarus,—
> When I do tell thee, there my hopes lie drown'd,
> Reply not in how many fathoms deep
> They lie indrench'd. I tell thee I am mad
> In Cressid's love: thou answer'st, she is fair;
> Pour'st in the open ulcer of my heart
> Her eyes, her hair, her cheek, her gait, her voice;
> Handlest in thy discourse, O! that her hand,
> In whose comparison all whites are ink,
> Writing their own reproach; to whose soft seizure
> The cygnet's down is harsh, and spirit of sense
> Hard as the palm of ploughman: this thou tell'st me,
> As true thou tell'st me, when I say I love her;
> But, saying thus, instead of oil and balm,
> Thou lay'st in every gash that love hath given me
> The knife that made it.
>
> (i, 1, 50)

In Troilus' love for Cressida there is a strong element of sensuality,
though his love is not, as some critics[4] would have it, sensuality and
nothing else. He thinks a great deal of the physical fruition of his passion:

> I am giddy, expectation whirls me round.
> The imaginary relish is so sweet
> That it enchants my sense.
>
> (iii, 2, 17)

But he has also exalted the worthless Cressida into an ideal, and we
know, from the debate about Helen, that he is a worshipper of
honor. He tells us himself, somewhat priggishly perhaps, that he is

---

[4] For example, O. J. Campbell, *op. cit.,* pp. 210 ff. Mr. Campbell reduces
the stature of Troilus' character to that of Cressida; they are "two virtuosi in
sensuality." Mr. Campbell has to adopt this view in order to fit the play into
the type of "Comicall Satyre" which he sets out to describe. As a result his
otherwise excellent discussion minimizes and distorts the great speeches of
Troilus.

                     as true as truth's simplicity,
            And simpler than the infancy of truth.
                          (iii, 2, 176)

And Ulysses, whose words are always meant to be trusted, speaks
very highly of him indeed:

> The youngest son of Priam, a true knight:
> Not yet mature, yet matchless; firm of word,
> Speaking in deeds and deedless in his tongue;
> Not soon provok'd, nor being provok'd soon calm'd:
> His heart and hand both open and both free;
> For what he has he gives, what thinks he shows;
> Yet gives he not till judgment guide his bounty,
> Nor dignifies an impure thought with breath. . . .
> Thus says Aeneas; one that knows the youth
> Even to his inches, and with private soul
> Did in great Ilion thus translate him to me.
>   (iv, 5, 96)

This is obviously someone to respect, and it is an error in criticism
not to see at least as much idealism as sensuality in Shakespeare's
conception of Troilus' character. Therefore when he discovers Cressida's betrayal, her surrender to Diomed on the very first night after
her separation from him, the evil reality under her apparently true
protestations of eternal fidelity nearly breaks him apart. The scene
in which this happens is an admirable example of the dramatic
experimentation which is one of the chief characteristics of the play
(v, 2). We have just had Thersites' speech about Diomed—

> They say he keeps a Trojan drab,[5] and uses the traitor Calchas' tent.
> I'll after. Nothing but lechery! all incontinent varlets—

when the scene opens in front of Calchas' tent. From the purely
technical point of view I know nothing like this scene in previous
Elizabethan drama. We see the situation from no fewer than four

---

[5] One of the striking differences between Chaucer's version of the story and
Shakespeare's is that in Shakespeare everyone seems to know all about Cressida's affairs, whereas in Chaucer they are kept secret. The medieval convention of privacy and honor has disappeared, and as a result the sordidness of
Cressida's character is emphasized, as anything is emphasized the more it is
talked about. In the same way Achilles' love affair with Polixena is well known,
to Achilles' surprise. "Ha! known!" he exclaims, when Ulysses refers to it (iii,
3, 195).

angles—it should be imagined on the Elizabethan stage for its full effect to be conveyed. At the back on the inner stage, are Cressida and Diomed, the main focus of attention; on one side of the front stage are Troilus and Ulysses; Thersites is on the other. Cressida and Diomed talk, she strokes his cheek, and their talk and action are interpreted for us by Troilus—emotional, agonized, incredulous—by Ulysses, rationally trying to control Troilus, and by Thersites, to whom all is lechery. Passion, reason and cynicism form the discordant chorus to action; they are three emotional mirrors which reflect the demonstration of the evil reality, Cressida's whorishness, under what had seemed so fair an appearance.

After she has left the stage, mildly and unconvincingly self-reproachful, we see the full effect of her behavior on Troilus. Throughout the play we have felt a sense of strain, of pressure, in the complex of his emotion toward Cressida—"This is the monstruosity in love, lady, that the will is infinite, and the execution confined; that the desire is boundless, and the act a slave to limit (iii, 2, 84)." There is not much in common between Hamlet and Troilus, but they do share one characteristic: they are aware, in what is perhaps a peculiarly masculine way, of the inexplicable, the almost incomprehensible gap between what the mind can think and desire, and what the body can perform. And when Cressida's faithlessness is revealed to him this peculiar tension in Troilus' mind produces an outburst of what can only be called metaphysical anguish.

> Never did young man fancy
> With so eternal and so fix'd a soul—

But his devotion is now a chaos.

For like every Elizabethan he feels that with the destruction of one element in his universe, the whole structure is in pieces. Because the appearance and what he believes to be the reality do not fit, the very concept of unity itself, on which the whole Elizabethan vision of the world was based, lacks order and rule. What he has just seen makes reason and its opposite, the loss of reason, seem the same thing; and something which cannot be separated, his view of Cressida combined with Cressida as she really is, is at the same time split in two and an indivisible unity. The thought is almost more than he can bear, and the difficulty he faces almost strains comprehension. Professor Campbell, writing of this speech, says that "Troilus, in attempting to preserve his characteristic self-deceit in the face of contradictory objective fact, forces his logical machine to perform feats of prestidigitation that make it creak ridiculously."[6] I cannot believe the speech should be interpreted in this fashion. On the contrary, its rhythm beats with emotional torture, and the intellectual effort, as in metaphysical poetry elsewhere, only increases and stiffens the tension.

> This she? no, this is Diomed's Cressida.
> If beauty have a soul, this is not she;
> If souls guide vows, if vows be sanctimonies,
> If sanctimony be the gods' delight,
> If there be rule in unity itself,
> This is not she. O madness of discourse,
> That cause sets up with and against itself;
> Bi-fold authority! where reason can revolt
> Without perdition, and loss assume all reason
> Without revolt: this is, and is not, Cressid.
> Within my soul there doth conduce a fight
> Of this strange nature that a thing inseparate
> Divides more wider than the sky and earth;
> And yet the spacious breadth of this division
> Admits no orifice for a point as subtle
> As Ariachne's broken woof to enter.
> Instance, O instance! strong as Pluto's gates;
> Cressid is mine, tied with the bonds of heaven:
> Instance, O instance! strong as heaven itself;
> The bonds of heaven are slipp'd, dissolv'd, and loos'd;
> And with another knot, five-finger-tied,
> The fractions of her faith, orts of her love,
> The fragments, scraps, the bits, and greasy reliques
> Of her o'er-eaten faith, are bound to Diomed.

After this he can do nothing but rage against the Greeks, and take his fruitless part in the general turmoil of fighting and betrayal with which the play concludes.

From the beginning his passion had been under a cloud, for the only way he could communicate with Cressida was through Pandar, and Shakespeare describes Pandar as a very coarse, worldly character, who speaks a vulgar prose, and who surrounds the love story, as Thersites in a different way surrounds the war story, with his sor-

[6] *Op. cit.*, p. 216.

did, chorus-like comments on the physical aspects of love. In fact Pandar, groaning with the pox, speaks the last lines of the play—an address to those people in the audience who are, like himself, "traders in the flesh."

When Troilus discovers that the object of his passionate, strained love is no better than her uncle, no wonder his reason almost cracks, and the coarse images of food[7] with which his speech ends are an indirect reflection of what he now knows to be Cressida's true nature. Thersites' comment is justified: "Lechery, lechery; still, wars and lechery; nothing else holds fashion."

Troilus and Cressida, though it follows *Hamlet* chronologically, is obviously not an improvement on it as a play. But it is not the ambiguous failure it has often been thought to be. Indeed, so far as our subject is concerned, it marks an extension of awareness in Shakespeare's presentation of man's nature. Whatever name we give it, whether we call it a tragedy, or a history, a comedy or a "comicall satyre," it describes in a new way the difference between man as he ought to be and man as he is. He ought to be part of an ordered state in an ordered universe; he ought to act according to reason and not according to passion. But these ideals are expounded only to be refuted by example after example: Achilles is a proud and selfish individualist who, when he is finally roused, acts like a bully; Cressida is a whore; and the nobility of Troilus, shining through his own sensuality and the murky lustfulness of his environment, is disillusioned and betrayed. The conflict between the two views of man which was implicit in Shakespeare's age is presented in concrete terms through the medium of the old story, and without that conflict the story could not have taken such a vivid, if bitter and disillusioned, form. *Troilus* is the kind of experiment which was necessary before *King Lear* could be written.

[7] Miss Spurgeon (*op. cit.,* pp. 320 ff.) points out that there are 42 images of food, cooking, etc., in *Troilus;* twice as many as in any other play: a reflection, she rightly suggests, of the coarseness embedded in the whole action.

ON SHAKESPEARE'S TRAGEDIES

NEO-CLASSICAL CRITICS saw Shakespeare's tragedies as faithful depictions of human passions in the face of catastrophe. Romantic critics saw these passions as the titanic emotions of extraordinary characters. The character analysis of their followers, however, often reduced the size of the tragic heroes. The great Victorian critics were concerned with formulating the view of life expressed in the tragedies. Dowden and Bradley found life to be presented as a painful mystery, but a mystery made tolerable by the presence of love and virtue. Swinburne, on the other hand, found in *King Lear* unrelieved darkness. But each found Shakespearean tragedy to be basically secular. Many critics in our time, however, find Shakespearean tragedy—at least, *Hamlet, Othello, Macbeth* and *King Lear*—to be basically Christian, although they differ in their emphases and interpretations. But this view has been contested, and the difference of opinion is probably the chief controversy in Shakespearean criticism today.

A. C. BRADLEY
1851-1935

THE ROMANTIC–VICTORIAN tradition culminates in A. C. Bradley's *Shakespearean Tragedy*. The reaction against this tradition also brought a reaction against Bradley, of which L. C. Knights's satirically titled essay *How Many Children Had Lady Macbeth?* (1933) is the best known example. In fact, so influential was this essay that it has been stated a number of times in print that the question was asked by Bradley, Knights's parody of Bradley being confused with Bradley himself. Actually, Bradley had said: "It may be that Macbeth had many children or that he had none. We cannot say, and it does not concern the play."

Knights, under the influence of G. Wilson Knight, stated that the analysis of characters practiced by Bradley splits up the unity of the play. The characters, abstracted from the play, are analyzed without regard for the "system" which "gives emotional coherence to the play." "The system [in *Macbeth*] will remain obscured if we concentrate our attention upon 'the two great terrible figures, who dwarf all the remaining characters of the drama.' " Knights, however, was being inaccurate and unfair to Bradley. Bradley had seen more than "the two great terrible figures"; he had seen the dramatic universe, with its own peculiar atmosphere, of which they were an integral part.

From this murky background stand out the two great terrible figures, who dwarf all the remaining characters of the drama. . . . They are never detached in imagination from the atmosphere which surrounds them and adds to their grandeur and terror. It is, as it were, continued into their souls. . . . The way to be untrue to Shakespeare here, as always, is to relax the tension of imagination, to conventionalize, to conceive Macbeth, for example, as a half-hearted cowardly criminal, and Lady Macbeth as a wholehearted fiend.

Nor did Bradley, as Knights said, judge characters by the moral canons of real life. In his opening chapter he wrote:

> When we are immersed in a tragedy, we feel towards dispositions, actions, and persons such emotions as attraction and repulsion, pity, wonder, fear, horror, perhaps hatred; but we do not *judge*. This is a point of view which emerges only when, in reading a play, we slip, by our own fault or the dramatist's from the tragic position, or when, in thinking about the play afterwards, we fall back on our everyday legal and moral notions.

This is not far distant from G. Wilson Knight's "where one person within the drama is immediately apparent as morally good and another as bad, we will note the difference: but we should follow our dramatic intuitions," that is, we should be guided by the feelings elicited if we give ourselves up to the play rather than by ordinary moral canons.

In reality, Bradley, although he might on occasion have fallen briefly into the error of leaving the dramatic universe which he so well apprehended, was true to what Knight has called "the quality of the original poetic experience." It is because of this that his book remains a great work, as, the reaction against him spent, now seems to be generally recognized. He is, moreover, unlike the extreme adherents of the study of Shakespeare's language as the only valid approach to him, aware that Shakespeare's poetic dramas are dramas as well as poems, although his insufficient realization of the functioning of Elizabethan dramatic convention sometimes weakens his analysis. At the same time his sensitivity to the play's atmosphere caused him to anticipate contemporary studies of Shakespeare's imagery.

Bradley's chapter on the nature of Shakespearean tragedy, which follows, shows not only a great ability to respond to the tragedies and to hold true to the experience of each of them but to compare, to extract

the common salient characteristics, to generalize. All
subsequent critics must to some degree base themselves
on it. Many of his perceptions have been corroborated
by modern scholarship. Thus his description of how
Shakespearean tragedy includes the medieval view of
tragedy but goes beyond it receives historical warrant
from Willard Farnham's *The Medieval Heritage of
Elizabethan Tragedy* (1936), which traces how
tragedy developed from the medieval belief that mortal
life is inherently subject to irrational vicissitudes to
an acceptance of tragic justice which links character
and event. Other portions of his analysis may need
to be modified in the light of what we have learned
about the thought and emotion of the Elizabethan age,
but his analysis in turn has cast light upon that thought
and emotion by illuminating the tragedies which were
a product of the age.

In the portion of the chapter before our selection,
Bradley has analyzed Shakespearean tragedy as a story
of "human actions producing exceptional calamity and
ending in the death" of "a man in high estate." The
deeds which produce this calamity are characteristic
of the person performing them, and, although abnormal conditions of mind, the supernatural and
chance play a part in the action, the dominant factor
is these deeds by which men bring upon themselves
their own misfortunes. This action involves conflict,
not only between the hero and those opposed to him
but also within the hero.

THE SUBSTANCE OF
SHAKESPEAREAN TRAGEDY

LET US NOW turn from the 'action' to the central figure in it; and, ignoring the characteristics which distinguish the heroes from one another, let us ask whether they have any common qualities which appear to be essential to the tragic effect.

One they certainly have. They are exceptional beings. We have seen already that the hero, with Shakespeare, is a person of high degree or of public importance, and that his actions or sufferings are of an unusual kind. But this is not all. His nature also is exceptional, and generally raises him in some respect much above the average level of humanity. This does not mean that he is an eccentric or a paragon. Shakespeare never drew monstrosities of virtue; some of his heroes are far from being 'good'; and if he drew eccentrics he gave them a subordinate position in the plot. His tragic characters are made of the stuff we find within ourselves and within the persons who surround them. But, by an intensification of the life which they share with others, they are raised above them; and the greatest are raised so far that, if we fully realise all that is implied in their words and actions, we become conscious that in real life we have known scarcely any one resembling them. Some, like Hamlet and Cleopatra, have genius. Others, like Othello, Lear, Macbeth, Coriolanus, are built on the grand scale; and desire, passion, or will attains in them a terrible force. In almost all we observe a marked one-sidedness, a predisposition in some particular direction; a total incapacity, in certain circumstances, of resisting the force which draws in this direction; a fatal tendency to identify the whole being with one interest, object, passion, or habit of mind. This, it would seem, is, for Shakespeare, the fundamental tragic trait. It is present in his early heroes, Romeo and Richard II., infatuated men, who otherwise rise comparatively little above the ordinary level. It is a fatal gift, but it carries with it a touch of greatness; and when there is joined to it nobility of mind, or genius, or immense force, we realise the full power and reach of the soul, and the conflict in which it engages acquires that magnitude which stirs not only sympathy and pity, but admiration, terror, and awe.

"The Substance of Shakespearean Tragedy" is from A. C. Bradley, *Shakespearean Tragedy*. Reprinted with permission of Macmillan & Company Ltd., St. Martin's Press Inc., and the Macmillan Company of Canada Ltd.

The easiest way to bring home to oneself the nature of the tragic character is to compare it with a character of another kind. Dramas like *Cymbeline* and the *Winter's Tale,* which might seem destined to end tragically, but actually end otherwise, owe their happy ending largely to the fact that the principal characters fail to reach tragic dimensions. And, conversely, if these persons were put in the place of the tragic heroes, the dramas in which they appeared would cease to be tragedies. Posthumus would never have acted as Othello did; Othello, on his side, would have met Iachimo's challenge with something more than words. If, like Posthumus, he had remained convinced of his wife's infidelity, he would not have repented her execution; if, like Leontes, he had come to believe that by an unjust accusation he had caused her death, he would never have lived on, like Leontes. In the same way the villain Iachimo has no touch of tragic greatness. But Iago comes nearer to it, and if Iago had slandered Imogen and had supposed his slanders to have led to her death, he certainly would not have turned melancholy and wished to die. One reason why the end of the *Merchant of Venice* fails to satisfy us is that Shylock is a tragic character, and that we cannot believe in his accepting his defeat and the conditions imposed on him. This was a case where Shakespeare's imagination ran away with him, so that he drew a figure with which the destined pleasant ending would not harmonise.

In the circumstances where we see the hero placed, his tragic trait, which is also his greatness, is fatal to him. To meet these circumstances something is required which a smaller man might have given, but which the hero cannot give. He errs, by action or omission; and his error, joining with other causes, brings on him ruin. This is always so with Shakespeare. As we have seen, the idea of the tragic hero as a being destroyed simply and solely by external forces is quite alien to him; and not less so is the idea of the hero as contributing to his destruction only by acts in which we see no flaw. But the fatal imperfection or error, which is never absent, is of different kinds and degrees. At one extreme stands the excess and precipitancy of Romeo, which scarcely, if at all, diminish our regard for him; at the other the murderous ambition of Richard III. In most cases the tragic error involves no conscious breach of right; in some (*e.g.* that of Brutus or Othello) it is accompanied by a full conviction of right. In Hamlet there is a painful consciousness that duty is being neglected; in Antony a clear knowledge that the worse of two courses is being pursued; but Richard and Macbeth are the only heroes who do what they themselves recognise to be villainous. It is important to observe that Shakespeare does admit such heroes, and also that he appears to feel, and exerts himself to meet, the difficulty that arises from their admission. The difficulty is that the spectator must desire their defeat and even their destruction; and yet this desire, and the satisfaction of it, are not tragic feelings. Shakespeare gives to Richard therefore a power which excites astonishment, and a courage which extorts admiration. He gives to Macbeth a similar, though less extraordinary, greatness, and adds to it a conscience so terrifying in its warnings and so maddening in its reproaches that the spectacle of inward torment compels a horrified sympathy and awe which balance, at the least, the desire for the hero's ruin.

The tragic hero with Shakespeare, then, need not be 'good,' though generally he is 'good' and therefore at once wins sympathy in his error. But it is necessary that he should have so much of greatness that in his error and fall we may be vividly conscious of the possibilities of human nature.[1] Hence, in the first place, a Shakespearean tragedy is never, like some miscalled tragedies, depressing. No one ever closes the book with the feeling that man is a poor mean creature. He may be wretched and he may be awful, but he is not small. His lot may be heartrending and mysterious, but it is not contemptible. The most confirmed of cynics ceases to be a cynic while he reads these plays. And with this greatness of the tragic hero (which is not always confined to him) is connected, secondly, what I venture to describe as the centre of the tragic impression. This central feeling is the impression of waste. With Shakespeare, at any rate, the pity and fear which are stirred by the tragic story seem to unite with, and even to merge in, a profound sense of sadness and mystery, which is due to this impression of waste. 'What a piece of work is man,' we cry; 'so much more beautiful and so much more terrible than we knew! Why should he be so if this beauty and greatness only tortures itself and throws itself away?' We seem to have before us a type of the

[1] Richard II. is perhaps an exception, and I must confess that to me he is scarcely a tragic character, and that, if he is nevertheless a tragic figure, he is so only because his fall from prosperity to adversity is so great.

mystery of the whole world, the tragic fact which extends far beyond the limits of tragedy. Everywhere, from the crushed rocks beneath our feet to the soul of man, we see power, intelligence, life and glory, which astound us and seem to call for our worship. And everywhere we see them perishing, devouring one another and destroying themselves, often with dreadful pain, as though they came into being for no other end. Tragedy is the typical form of this mystery, because that greatness of soul which it exhibits oppressed, conflicting and destroyed, is the highest existence in our view. It forces the mystery upon us, and it makes us realise so vividly the worth of that which is wasted that we cannot possibly seek comfort in the reflection that all is vanity.

In this tragic world, then, where individuals, however great they may be and however decisive their actions may appear, are so evidently not the ultimate power, what is this power? What account can we give of it which will correspond with the imaginative impressions we receive? This will be our final question.

The variety of the answers given to this question shows how difficult it is. And the difficulty has many sources. Most people, even among those who know Shakespeare well and come into real contact with his mind, are inclined to isolate and exaggerate some one aspect of the tragic fact. Some are so much influenced by their own habitual beliefs that they import them more or less into their interpretation of every author who is 'sympathetic' to them. And even where neither of these causes of error appears to operate, another is present from which it is probably impossible wholly to escape. What I mean is this. Any answer we give to the question proposed ought to correspond with, or to represent in terms of the understanding, our imaginative and emotional experience in reading the tragedies. We have, of course, to do our best by study and effort to make this experience true to Shakespeare; but, that done to the best of our ability, the experience is the matter to be interpreted, and the test by which the interpretation must be tried. But it is extremely hard to make out exactly what this experience is because, in the very effort to make it out, our reflecting mind, full of everyday ideas, is always tending to transform it by the application of these ideas, and so to elicit a result which, instead of representing the fact, conventionalises it. And the consequence is not only mistaken theories; it is that many a man will declare that he feels in reading a tragedy what he never really felt, while he fails to recognise what he actually did feel. It is not likely that we shall escape all these dangers in our effort to find an answer to the question regarding the tragic world and the ultimate power in it.

It will be agreed, however, first, that this question must not be answered in 'religious' language. For although this or that *dramatis persona* may speak of gods or of God, of evil spirits or of Satan, of heaven and of hell, and although the poet may show us ghosts from another world, these ideas do not materially influence his representation of life, nor are they used to throw light on the mystery of its tragedy. The Elizabethan drama was almost wholly secular; and while Shakespeare was writing he practically confined his view to the world of non-theological observation and thought, so that he represents it substantially in one and the same way whether the period of the story is pre-Christian or Christian.[2] He looked at this 'secular' world most intently and seriously; and he painted it, we cannot but conclude, with entire fidelity, without the wish to enforce an opinion of his own, and, in essentials, without regard to anyone's hopes, fears, or beliefs. His greatness is largely due to this fidelity in a mind of extraordinary power; and if, as a private person, he had a religious faith, his tragic view can hardly have been in contradiction with this faith, but must have been included in it, and supplemented, not abolished, by additional ideas.

Two statements, next, may at once be made regarding the tragic fact as he represents it: one, that it is and remains to us something piteous, fearful and mysterious; the other, that the representation of it does not leave us crushed, rebellious or desperate. These statements will be accepted, I believe, by any reader who is in touch with Shakespeare's mind and can observe his own. Indeed such a reader is rather likely to complain that they are painfully obvious. But if they are true as well as obvious, something follows from them in regard to our present question.

From the first it follows that the ultimate power in the tragic world is not adequately described as a law or order which we can see to be just and benevolent,—as, in that sense, a 'moral order': for in that case the spectacle of suffering and waste could not seem to us so fearful and mysterious as it does. And from the second it follows that this ultimate power is not adequately described as a fate, whether malicious

---

[2] I say substantially; but the concluding remarks on *Hamlet* will modify a little the statements above.

and cruel, or blind and indifferent to human happiness and goodness: for in that case the spectacle would leave us desperate or rebellious. Yet one or other of these two ideas will be found to govern most accounts of Shakespeare's tragic view or world. These accounts isolate and exaggerate single aspects, either the aspect of action or that of suffering; either the close and unbroken connection of character, will, deed and catastrophe, which, taken alone, shows the individual simply as sinning against, or failing to conform to, the moral order and drawing his just doom on his own head; or else that pressure of outward forces, that sway of accident, and those blind and agonised struggles, which, taken alone, show him as the mere victim of some power which cares neither for his sins nor for his pain. Such views contradict one another, and no third view can unite them; but the several aspects from whose isolation and exaggeration they spring are both present in the fact, and a view which would be true to the fact and to the whole of our imaginative experience must in some way combine these aspects.

Let us begin, then, with the idea of fatality and glance at some of the impressions which give rise to it, without asking at present whether this idea is their natural or fitting expression. There can be no doubt that they do arise and that they ought to arise. If we do not feel at times that the hero is, in some sense, a doomed man; that he and others drift struggling to destruction like helpless creatures borne on an irresistible flood towards a cataract; that, faulty as they may be, their fault is far from being the sole or sufficient cause of all they suffer; and that the power from which they cannot escape is relentless and immovable, we have failed to receive an essential part of the full tragic effect.

The sources of these impressions are various, and I will refer only to a few. One of them is put into words by Shakespeare himself when he makes the player-king in *Hamlet* say:

Our thoughts are ours, their ends none of our own;

'their ends' are the issues or outcomes of our thoughts, and these, says the speaker, are not our own. The tragic world is a world of action, and action is the translation of thought into reality. We see men and women confidently attempting it. They strike into the existing order of things in pursuance of their ideas. But what they achieve is not what they intended: it is terribly unlike it. They understand nothing, we say to ourselves, of the world on which they operate. They fight blindly in the dark, and the power that works through them makes them the instrument of a design which is not theirs. They act freely, and yet their action binds them hand and foot. And it makes no difference whether they meant well or ill. No one could mean better than Brutus, but he contrives misery for his country and death for himself. No one could mean worse than Iago, and he too is caught in the web he spins for others. Hamlet, recoiling from the rough duty of revenge, is pushed into blood-guiltiness he never dreamed of, and forced at last on the revenge he could not will. His adversary's murders, and no less his adversary's remorse, bring about the opposite of what they sought. Lear follows an old man's whim, half generous, half selfish; and in a moment it looses all the powers of darkness upon him. Othello agonises over an empty fiction, and, meaning to execute solemn justice, butchers innocence and strangles love. They understand themselves no better than the world about them. Coriolanus thinks that his heart is iron, and it melts like snow before a fire. Lady Macbeth, who thought she could dash out her own child's brains, finds herself hounded to death by the smell of a stranger's blood. Her husband thinks that to gain a crown he would jump the life to come, and finds that the crown has brought him all the horrors of that life. Everywhere, in this tragic world, man's thought, translated into act, is transformed into the opposite of itself. His act, the movement of a few ounces of matter in a moment of time, becomes a monstrous flood which spreads over a kingdom. And whatsoever he dreams of doing, he achieves that which he least dreamed of, his own destruction.

All this makes us feel the blindness and helplessness of man. Yet by itself it would hardly suggest the idea of fate, because it shows man as in some degree, however slight, the cause of his own undoing. But other impressions come to aid it. It is aided by everything which makes us feel that a man is, as we say, terribly unlucky; and of this there is, even in Shakespeare, not a little. Here come in some of the accidents already considered, Juliet's waking from her trance a minute too late, Desdemona's loss of her handkerchief at the only moment when the loss would have mattered, that insignificant delay which cost Cordelia's life. Again, men act, no doubt, in accordance with their characters; but what is it that brings them just the one problem which is fatal to them and would be easy to another, and sometimes brings it to them just when they are least fitted to face it? How is it that Othello comes to be the companion of the one man in the world who is at once able enough, brave enough, and vile enough to ensnare him? By what strange fatality does it happen that Lear has such daughters and Cordelia such sisters? Even character itself contributes to these feelings of fatality. How could men escape, we cry, such vehement propensities as drive Romeo, Antony, Coriolanus, to their doom? And why is it that a man's virtues help to destroy him, and that his weakness or defect is so intertwined with everything that is admirable in him that we can hardly separate them even in imagination?

If we find in Shakespeare's tragedies the source of impressions like these, it is important, on the other hand, to notice what we do *not* find there. We find practically no trace of fatalism in its more primitive, crude and obvious forms. Nothing, again, makes us think of the actions and sufferings of the persons as somewhat arbitrarily fixed beforehand without regard to their feelings, thoughts and resolutions. Nor, I believe, are the facts ever so presented that it seems to us as if the supreme power, whatever it may be, had a special spite against a family or an individual. Neither, lastly, do we receive the impression (which, it must be observed, is not purely fatalistic) that a family, owing to some hideous crime or impiety in early days, is doomed in later days to continue a career of portentous calamities and sins. Shakespeare, indeed, does not appear to have taken much interest in heredity, or to have attached much importance to it.

What, then, is this 'fate' which the impressions already considered lead us to describe as the ultimate power in the tragic world? It appears to be a mythological expression for the whole system or order, of which the individual characters form an inconsiderable and feeble part; which seems to determine, far more than they, their native dispositions and their circumstances, and, through these, their action; which is so vast and complex that they can scarcely at all understand it or control its workings; and which has a nature so definite and fixed that whatever changes take place in it produce other changes inevitably and without regard to men's desires and regrets. And whether this system or order is best called by the name of fate or no,[3] it can hardly be denied that it does appear as the ultimate power in the tragic world, and that it has such characteristics as these. But the name 'fate' may be intended to imply something more—to imply that this order is a blank necessity, totally regardless alike of human weal and of the difference between good and evil or right and wrong. And such an implication many readers would at once reject. They would maintain, on the contrary, that this order shows characteristics of quite another kind from those which made us give it the name of fate, characteristics which certainly should not induce us to forget those others, but which would lead us to describe it as a moral order and its necessity as a moral necessity.

Let us turn, then, to this idea. It brings into the light those aspects of the tragic fact which the idea of fate throws into the shade. And the argument which leads to it in its simplest form may be stated briefly thus: 'Whatever may be said of accidents, circumstances and the like, human action is, after all, presented to us as the central fact in tragedy, and also as the main cause of the catastrophe. That necessity which so much impresses us is, after all, chiefly the necessary connection of actions and consequences. For these actions we, without even raising a question on the subject, hold the agents responsible; and the tragedy would disappear for us if we did not. The critical action is, in greater or less degree, wrong or bad. The catastrophe is, in the main, the return of this action on the head of the agent. It is an example of justice; and that order which, present alike within the agents and outside them, infallibly brings it about, is therefore just. The rigour of its justice is terrible, no doubt, for a tragedy is a terrible story; but, in spite of fear and pity, we acquiesce, because our sense of justice is satisfied.'

Now, if this view is to hold good, the 'justice' of which it speaks must be at once distinguished from what is called 'poetic justice.'

---

[3] I have raised no objection to the use of the idea of fate, because it occurs so often both in conversation and in books about Shakespeare's tragedies that I must suppose it to be natural to many readers. Yet I doubt whether it would be so if Greek tragedy had never been written; and I must in candour confess that to me it does not often occur while I am reading, or when I have just read, a tragedy of Shakespeare. Wordsworth's lines, for example, about

poor humanity's afflicted will
Struggling in vain with ruthless destiny

do not represent the impression I receive; much less do images which compare man to a puny creature helpless in the claws of a bird of prey. The reader should examine himself closely on this matter.

'Poetic justice' means that prosperity and adversity are distributed in proportion to the merits of the agents. Such 'poetic justice' is in flagrant contradiction with the facts of life, and it is absent from Shakespeare's tragic picture of life; indeed, this very absence is a ground of constant complaint on the part of Dr. Johnson. Δράσαντι παθεῖν, 'the doer must suffer'—this we find in Shakespeare. We also find that villainy never remains victorious and prosperous at the last. But an assignment of amounts of happiness and misery, and assignment even of life and death, in proportion to merit, we do not find. No one who thinks of Desdemona and Cordelia; or who remembers that one end awaits Richard III. and Brutus, Macbeth and Hamlet; or who asks himself which suffered most, Othello or Iago; will ever accuse Shakespeare of representing the ultimate power as 'poetically' just.

And we must go further. I venture to say that it is a mistake to use at all these terms of justice and merit or desert. And this for two reasons. In the first place, essential as it is to recognise the connection between act and consequence, and natural as it may seem in some cases (e.g. Macbeth's) to say that the doer only gets what he deserves, yet in very many cases to say this would be quite unnatural. We might not object to the statement that Lear deserved to suffer for his folly, selfishness and tyranny; but to assert that he deserved to suffer what he did suffer is to do violence not merely to language but to any healthy moral sense. It is, moreover, to obscure the tragic fact that the consequences of action cannot be limited to that which would appear to us to follow 'justly' from them. And, this being so, when we call the order of the tragic world just, we are either using the word in some vague and unexplained sense, or we are going beyond what is shown us of this order, and are appealing to faith.

But, in the second place, the ideas of justice and desert are, it seems to me, in *all* cases—even those of Richard III. and of Macbeth and Lady Macbeth—untrue to our imaginative experience. When we are immersed in a tragedy, we feel towards dispositions, actions, and persons such emotions as attraction and repulsion, pity, wonder, fear, horror, perhaps hatred; but we do not *judge*. This is a point of view which emerges only when, in reading a play, we slip, by our own fault or the dramatist's, from the tragic position, or when, in thinking about the play afterwards, we fall back on our everyday legal and moral notions. But tragedy does not belong, any more than religion belongs, to the sphere of these notions; neither does the imaginative attitude in presence of it. While we are in its world we watch what is, seeing that so it happened and must have happened, feeling that it is piteous, dreadful, awful, mysterious, but neither passing sentence on the agents, nor asking whether the behaviour of the ultimate power towards them is just. And, therefore, the use of such language in attempts to render our imaginative experience in terms of the understanding is, to say the least, full of danger.

Let us attempt then to re-state the idea that the ultimate power in the tragic world is a moral order. Let us put aside the ideas of justice and merit, and speak simply of good and evil. Let us understand by these words, primarily, moral good and evil, but also everything else in human beings which we take to be excellent or the reverse. Let us understand the statement that the ultimate power or order is 'moral' to mean that it does not show itself indifferent to good and evil, or equally favourable or unfavourable to both, but shows itself akin to good and alien from evil. And, understanding the statement thus, let us ask what grounds it has in the tragic fact as presented by Shakespeare.

Here, as in dealing with the grounds on which the idea of fate rests, I choose only two or three out of many. And the most important is this. In Shakespearean tragedy the main source of the convulsion which produces suffering and death is never good: good contributes to this convulsion only from its tragic implication with its opposite in one and the same character. The main source, on the contrary, is in every case evil; and, what is more (though this seems to have been little noticed), it is in almost every case evil in the fullest sense, not mere imperfection but plain moral evil. The love of Romeo and Juliet conducts them to death only because of the senseless hatred of their houses. Guilty ambition, seconded by diabolic malice and issuing in murder, opens the action in *Macbeth*. Iago is the main source of the convulsion in *Othello;* Goneril, Regan and Edmund in *King Lear*. Even when this plain moral evil is not the obviously prime source within the play, it lies behind it: the situation with which Hamlet has to deal has been formed by adultery and murder. *Julius Caesar* is the only tragedy in which one is even tempted to find an exception to this rule. And the inference is obvious. If it is chiefly evil that violently disturbs the order of the world, this order cannot be friendly to evil or indifferent between evil and good, any more than a body which is convulsed by poison is friendly to it or indifferent to the distinction between poison and food.

Again, if we confine our attention to the hero, and to those cases where the gross and palpable evil is not in him but elsewhere, we find that the comparatively innocent hero still shows some marked imperfection or defect,—irresolution, precipitancy, pride, credulousness, excessive simplicity, excessive susceptibility to sexual emotions, and the like. These defects or imperfections are certainly, in the wide sense of the word, evil, and they contribute decisively to the conflict and catastrophe. And the inference is again obvious. The ultimate power which shows itself disturbed by this evil and reacts against it, must have a nature alien to it. Indeed its reaction is so vehement and 'relentless' that it would seem to be bent on nothing short of good in perfection, and to be ruthless in its demand for it.

To this must be added another fact, or another aspect of the same fact. Evil exhibits itself everywhere as something negative, barren, weakening, destructive, a principle of death. It isolates, disunites, and tends to annihilate not only its opposite but itself. That which keeps the evil man prosperous, makes him succeed, even permits him to exist, is the good in him (I do not mean only the obviously 'moral' good). When the evil in him masters the good and has its way, it destroys other people through him, but it also destroys him. At the close of the struggle he has vanished, and has left behind him nothing that can stand. What remains is a family, a city, a country, exhausted, pale and feeble, but alive through the principle of good which animates it; and, within it, individuals who, if they have not the brilliance or greatness of the tragic character, still have won our respect and confidence. And the inference would seem clear. If existence in an order depends on good, and if the presence of evil is hostile to such existence, the inner being or soul of this order must be akin to good.

These are aspects of the tragic world at least as clearly marked as those which, taken alone, suggest the idea of fate. And the idea which they in their turn, when taken alone, may suggest, is that of an order which does not indeed award 'poetic justice,' but which reacts through the necessity of its own 'moral' nature both against attacks made upon it and against failure to conform to it. Tragedy, in this view, is the exhibition of that convulsive reaction; and the fact that the spectacle does not leave us rebellious or desperate is due to a more or less distinct perception that the tragic suffering and death arise from collision, not with a fate or blank power, but with a moral power, a power akin to all that we admire and revere in the characters themselves. This perception produces something like a feeling of acquiescence in the catastrophe, though it neither leads us to pass judgment on the characters nor diminishes the pity, the fear, and the sense of waste, which their struggle, suffering and fall evoke. And, finally, this view seems quite able to do justice to those aspects of the tragic fact which give rise to the idea of fate. They would appear as various expressions of the fact that the moral order acts not capriciously or like a human being, but from the necessity of its nature, or, if we prefer the phrase, by general laws,—a necessity or law which of course knows no exception and is as 'ruthless' as fate.

It is impossible to deny to this view a large measure of truth. And yet without some amendment it can hardly satisfy. For it does not include the whole of the facts, and therefore does not wholly correspond with the impressions they produce. Let it be granted that the system or order which shows itself omnipotent against individuals is, in the sense explained, moral. Still—at any rate for the eye of sight—the evil against which it asserts itself, and the persons whom this evil inhabits, are not really something outside the order, so that they can attack it or fail to conform to it; they are within it and a part of it. It itself produces them,—produces Iago as well as Desdemona, Iago's cruelty as well as Iago's courage. It is not poisoned, it poisons itself. Doubtless it shows by its violent reaction that the poison *is* poison, and that its health lies in good. But one significant fact cannot remove another, and the spectacle we witness scarcely warrants the assertion that the order is responsible for the good in Desdemona, but Iago for the evil in Iago. If we make this assertion we make it on grounds other than the facts as presented in Shakespeare's tragedies.

Nor does the idea of a moral order asserting itself against attack or want of conformity answer in full to our feelings regarding the tragic character. We do not think of Hamlet merely as failing to meet its demand, of Antony as merely sinning against it, or even of Macbeth as simply attacking it. What we feel corresponds quite as much to the idea that they are *its* parts, expressions, products; that in their defect or evil *it* is untrue to its soul of goodness, and falls into conflict and collision with itself; that, in making them suffer and waste themselves, *it* suffers and wastes itself; and that when, to save its life and regain peace from this intestinal struggle, it casts them out, it has lost a part of its own substance,—a part more dangerous and unquiet, but far more valuable and nearer to its heart, than that which remains,—a Fortinbras, a Malcolm, an Octavius. There is no tragedy in its expulsion of evil: the tragedy is that this involves the waste of good.

Thus we are left at last with an idea showing two sides or aspects which we can neither separate nor reconcile. The whole or order against which the individual part shows itself powerless seems to be animated by a passion for perfection: we cannot otherwise explain its behaviour towards evil. Yet it appears to engender this evil within itself, and in its effort to overcome and expel it it is agonised with pain, and driven to mutilate its own substance and to lose not only evil but priceless good. That this idea, though very different from the idea of a blank fate, is no solution of the riddle of life is obvious; but why should we expect it to be such a solution? Shakespeare was not attempting to justify the ways of God to men, or to show the universe as a Divine Comedy. He was writing tragedy, and tragedy would not be tragedy if it were not a painful mystery. Nor can he be said even to point distinctly, like some writers of tragedy, in any direction where a solution might lie. We find a few references to gods or God, to the influence of the stars, to another life: some of them certainly, all of them perhaps, merely dramatic—appropriate to the person from whose lips they fall. A ghost comes from Purgatory to impart a secret out of the reach of its hearer—who presently meditates on the question whether the sleep of death is dreamless. Accidents once or twice remind us strangely of the words, 'There's a divinity that shapes our ends.' More important are other impressions. Sometimes from the very furnace of affliction a conviction seems borne to us that somehow, if we could see it, this agony counts as nothing against the heroism and love which appear in it and thrill our hearts. Sometimes we are driven to cry out that these mighty or heavenly spirits who perish are too great for the little space in which they move, and that they vanish not into nothingness but into freedom. Sometimes from these sources and from others comes a presentiment, formless but haunting and even profound, that all the fury of conflict, with its waste and woe, is less than half the truth, even an illusion, 'such stuff as dreams are made on.' But these faint and scattered intimations that the tragic world, being but a fragment of a whole beyond our vision, must needs be a contradiction and no ultimate truth, avail nothing to interpret the mystery. We remain confronted with the inexplicable fact, or the no less inexplicable appearance, of a world travailing for perfection, but bringing to birth, together with glorious good, an evil which it is able to overcome only by self-torture and self-waste. And this fact or appearance is tragedy.[4]

CAROLINE SPURGEON
1869-1942

CAROLINE SPURGEON'S *Shakespeare's Imagery and What It Tells Us* (1935) was anticipated by Walter Whiter's study of Shakespearean image clusters in *A Specimen of a Commentary* (1794) and, among other criticism, by Dowden's remarks on the blood imagery in *Macbeth* and by Bradley's discussion of the animal imagery in *King Lear*. Her work has been carried forward in new directions by Wolfgang Clemen, who has studied the development of Shakespeare's imagery in relation to his total development as an artist, and by G. Wilson Knight and Robert B. Heilman, who have discussed the imagery of individual plays in relation to other elements in them. However, despite predecessors, Miss Spurgeon stands as an important pioneer—a pioneer whose work, despite the valuable work of her successors, retains its own abiding value.

The study of Shakespeare's imagery can be as easily abused as the study of his characters. It can be mechanical, counting the images within each category without seeing which are conventional and which come strikingly alive. It can be short-sighted, not per-

[4] Partly in order not to anticipate later passages, I abstained from treating fully here the question why we feel, at the death of the tragic hero, not only pain but also reconciliation and sometimes even exultation.

ceiving that images classified in one way could just as well be classified in another way. Above all, it can abstract a number of images and by artificially interweaving them impose a factitious pattern upon the play. Without an ever-present sense of the total experience of the play, concentration upon the imagery, as is true of concentration upon any other element of the play, will result in distortion. But Miss Spurgeon's sensitive study of the dominating images of the plays (although her statement about her card-indexing may give a false impression of an unimaginative scholar) enriches our appreciation of them. Her book, however, is at its weakest in its attempt to make inferences concerning Shakespeare the man from the images which he employed.

In the selection which follows, a portion of a lecture she delivered to the English Association in 1930, Miss Spurgeon discusses the running images of the tragedies. Her discussion enables us to see how essential the poetry is to Shakespeare's poetic drama.

It may be worth pointing out that Paul A. Jorgenson has found that the image of the hidden ulcer, which Miss Spurgeon found to be "descriptive of the unwholesome condition of Denmark morally" in *Hamlet,* was used by Elizabethan writers to symbolize the effete condition of a seemingly healthy society enervated by prolonged peace. Here again scholarship and criticism reinforce each other.

LEADING MOTIVES IN THE IMAGERY OF SHAKESPEARE'S TRAGEDIES

IT HAS NOT, so far as I know, ever yet been noticed that recurrent images play a part in raising, developing, sustaining, and repeating emotion in the tragedies, which is somewhat analogous to the action

"Leading Motives in the Imagery of Shakespeare's Tragedies" is from Shakespeare Association Lecture (1930). By permission of R. S. Ingram and Mrs. M. I. Crofts, Trustees of Will of the late Caroline Spurgeon.

of a recurrent theme or 'motif' in a musical fugue or sonata, or in one of Wagner's operas.

Perhaps, however, a more exact analogy to the function of Shakespeare's images in this respect is the unique work of another great artist, of the peculiar quality of which they constantly remind one, that is, Blake's illustrations to his prophetic books. These are not, for the most part, illustrations in the ordinary sense of the term, the translation by the artist of some incident in the narrative into a visual picture; they are rather a running accompaniment to the words in another medium, sometimes symbolically emphasizing or interpreting certain aspects of the thought, sometimes supplying frankly only decoration or atmosphere, sometimes grotesque and even repellent, vivid, strange, arresting, sometimes drawn with an almost unearthly beauty of form and colour. Thus, as the leaping tongues of flame which illuminate the pages of *The Marriage of Heaven and Hell* show the visual form which Blake's thought evoked in his mind, and symbolize for us the purity, the beauty, and the two-edged quality of life and danger in his words, so the recurrent images in *Macbeth* or *Hamlet* reveal the dominant picture or sensation—and for Shakespeare the two are identical—in terms of which he sees and feels the main problem or theme of the play, thus giving us an unerring clue to the way he looked at it, as well as a direct glimpse into the working of his mind and imagination.

These dominating images are a characteristic of Shakespeare's work throughout, but whereas in the earlier plays they are often rather obvious and of set design, taken over in some cases with the story itself from a hint in the original narrative; in the later plays, and especially in the great tragedies, they are born of the emotions of the theme, and are, as in *Macbeth,* subtle, complex, varied, but intensely vivid and revealing; or as in *Lear,* so constant and all-pervading as to be reiterated, not only in the word-pictures, but also in the single words themselves.

Any reader, of course, must be aware of certain recurrent symbolic imagery in Shakespeare, such as that of a tree and its branches, and of planting, lopping, or rooting up, which runs through the English historical plays; they are conscious of the imaginative effect of the animal imagery in *Lear,* or of the flash of explosives in *Romeo and Juliet,* but it was not until the last few years, when in the course of an intensive study of Shakespeare's imagery I had listed and classified and card-indexed and counted every image in every play thrice over, that the actual facts as to these dominating pictures stared me in the face.

I found that there is a certain range of images, and roughly a certain proportion of these, to be expected in every play, and that certain familiar categories, of nature, animals, and what one may call 'everyday' or 'domestic,' easily come first. But in addition to this normal grouping, I have found, especially in the tragedies, certain groups of images which, as it were, stick out in each particular play and immediately attract attention because they are peculiar either in subject or quantity, or both.

These seem to form the floating image or images in Shakespeare's mind called forth by that particular play, and I propose now, as briefly as possible, just to look at the tragedies from the point of view of these groups of images only.

In *Romeo and Juliet* the beauty and ardour of young love is seen by Shakespeare as the irradiating glory of sunlight and starlight in a dark world. The dominating image is *light,* every form and manifestation of it; the sun, moon, stars, fire, lightning, the flash of gunpowder, and the reflected light of beauty and of love; while by contrast we have night, darkness, clouds, rain, mist, and smoke.

Each of the lovers thinks of the other as light; Romeo's overpowering impression when he first catches sight of Juliet on the fateful evening at the Capulets' ball is seen in his exclamation,

> O, she doth teach the torches to burn bright!

To Juliet, Romeo is 'day in night'; to Romeo, Juliet is the sun rising from the east, and when they soar to love's ecstasy, each alike pictures the other as stars in heaven, shedding such brightness as puts to shame the heavenly bodies themselves.

The intensity of feeling in both lovers purges even the most highly affected and euphuistic conceits of their artificiality, and transforms them into the exquisite and passionate expression of love's rhapsody.

Thus Romeo plays with the old conceit that two of the fairest stars in heaven, having some business on earth, have entreated Juliet's eyes to take their place till they return, and he conjectures,

> What if her eyes were there, they in her head?

If so,

> The brightness of her cheek would shame those stars,
> As day-light doth a lamp:

and then comes the rush of feeling, the overpowering realization and immortal expression of the transforming glory of love,

> her eyes in heaven
> Would through the airy region stream so bright
> That birds would sing and think it were not night.

And Juliet, in her invocation to night, using an even more extravagant conceit such as Cowley or Cleveland at his wildest never exceeded, transmutes it into the perfect and natural expression of a girl whose lover to her not only radiates light but is, indeed, very light itself:

> Give me my Romeo; and, when he shall die,
> Take him and cut him out in little stars,
> And he will make the face of heaven so fine,
> That all the world will be in love with night,
> And pay no worship to the garish sun.

Love is described by Romeo, before he knows what it really is, as

> a smoke raised with the fume of sighs;
> Being purged, a fire sparkling in lovers' eyes;

and the messengers of love are seen by Juliet, when she is chafing under the nurse's delay, as one of the most exquisite effects in nature, especially on the English hills in spring, of the swift, magical, transforming power of light; 'love's heralds,' she cries, 'should be thoughts,

> Which ten times faster glide than the sun's beams,
> Driving back shadows over louring hills.'

The irradiating quality of the beauty of love is noticed by both lovers; by Juliet in her first ecstasy, when she declares that lovers' 'own beauties' are sufficient light for them to see by, and at the end by Romeo, when, thinking her dead, he gazes on her and cries

> her beauty makes
> This vault a feasting presence full of light.

There can be no question, I think, that Shakespeare saw the story, in its swift and tragic beauty, as an almost blinding flash of light, suddenly ignited and as swiftly quenched. He quite deliberately compresses the action from over nine months to the almost incredibly short period of five days; so that the lovers meet on Sunday, are wedded on Monday, part at dawn on Tuesday, and are reunited in death on the night of Thursday. The sensation of swiftness and

brilliance, accompanied by danger and destruction, is accentuated
again and again; by Juliet when she avows their betrothal

> is too rash, too unadvised, too sudden,
> Too like the lightning, which doth cease to be
> Ere one can say 'It lightens';

and by Romeo and the Friar, who instinctively make repeated use of
the image of the quick destructive flash of gunpowder (III. iii. 103,
132; v. i. 63). Indeed the Friar, in his well-known answer to Romeo's
prayer for instant marriage, succinctly, in the last nine words, sums up
the whole movement of the play,

> These violent delights have violent ends,
> And in their triumph die; like fire and powder
> Which as they kiss consume.

Even old Capulet, whom one does not think of as a poetical person,
though he uses many images—some of great beauty—carries on the
idea of light to represent love and youth and beauty, and of the cloud-
ing of the sun for grief and sorrow. He promises Paris that on the
evening of the ball he shall see at his house

> Earth-treading stars that make dark heaven light,

and when he encounters Juliet weeping, as he thinks for her cousin
Tybalt's death, he clothes his comment in similar nature-imagery of
light quenched in darkness,

> When the sun sets, the air doth drizzle dew;
> But for the sunset of my brother's son
> It rains downright.

In addition to this more definite symbolic imagery we find that
radiant light, sunshine, starlight, moonbeams, sunrise and sunset, the
sparkle of fire, a meteor, candles, torches, quick-coming darkness,
clouds, mist, rain, and night, form a pictorial background or running
accompaniment to the play, which augments unconsciously in us this
same sensation.

We meet it at once in the Prince's description of the attitude of the
rival houses

> That quench the fire of your pernicious rage
> With purple fountains issuing from your veins;

and later, in the talk of Benvolio and Montagu about the rising sun, the dew, and clouds (I. i. 117–18, 130–6), followed by Romeo's definition of love (I. i. 189–90), Capulet's words just quoted, Benvolio's riming proverb about fire (I. ii. 46), the talk of Romeo and Mercutio about torches, candles, lights, and lamps (I. iv. 35–45), the flashing lights and torches of the ball, four times accentuated (I. v. 28, 45, 88, 126), Romeo's conception of Juliet as a 'bright angel,' 'as glorious to this night'

> As is a winged messenger of heaven;

the moonlight in the orchard, the sunrise Friar Lawrence watches from his cell, the sun clearing from heaven Romeo's sighs (II. iii. 73), the exquisite light and shadow swiftly chasing over Juliet's words in the orchard (II. v. 4–11), the 'black fate' of the day on which Mercutio was killed, the 'fire-eyed fury' which leads Romeo to challenge Tybalt, their fight, to which they go 'like lightning,' the sunset which Juliet so ardently desires to be swift 'and bring in cloudy night immediately,' the exquisite play of quivering light from darkness through dawn, till

> jocund day
> Stands tip-toe on the misty mountain tops,

which forms the theme of the lovers' parting song; and at the last, Romeo's anguished reply to Juliet, pointing the contrast between the coming day and their own great sorrow,

> More light and light: more dark and dark our woes!

And then at the end we see the darkness of the churchyard, lit by the glittering torch of Paris, quickly quenched; Romeo's arrival with his torch, the swift fight and death, the dark vault, which is not a grave but a lantern irradiated by Juliet's beauty, Romeo's grim jest on the 'lightning before death,' followed immediately by the self-slaughter of the 'star-crossed' lovers, the gathering together of the stricken mourners as the day breaks, and the 'glooming' peace of the overcast morning when

> The sun for sorrow will not show his head. . . .

In *Hamlet,* naturally, we find ourselves in an entirely different atmosphere, and if we look closely we see this is partly due to the number of images of sickness, disease, or blemish of the body in the play, and we discover that the idea of an ulcer or tumour, as descriptive of the unwholesome condition of Denmark morally, is, on the whole, the dominating one.

Hamlet speaks of his mother's sin as a blister on the 'fair forehead of an innocent love,' and as in *Lear,* the emotion is so strong and the picture so vivid, that the metaphor overflows into the verbs and adjectives; heaven's face, he tells her, is *thought-sick* at the act; her husband is a *mildew'd ear, blasting* his *wholesome* brother, and to have married him her sense must be not only *sickly* but *apoplex'd,* and at the end of that terrific scene (iii. 4) he implores her not to soothe herself with the belief that his father's apparition is due to her son's madness and not to her own guilt, for that

> will but skin and film the ulcerous place
> Whiles rank corruption, mining all within,
> Infects unseen.

So also, later, he compares the unnecessary fighting between Norway and Poland to a kind of tumour which grows out of too much prosperity. He sees the country and the people in it alike in terms of a sick body needing medicine or the surgeon's knife. When he surprises Claudius at his prayers, he exclaims

> This physic but prolongs thy sickly days,

and he describes the action of conscience in the unforgettable picture of the healthy, ruddy countenance turning pale with sickness (III. i. 84). A mote in the eye, a 'vicious mole,' a galled chilblain, a probed wound and purgation, are also among Hamlet's images; and the mind of Claudius runs equally on the same theme.

When he hears of the murder of Polonius he declares that his weakness in not sooner having had Hamlet shut up was comparable to the cowardly action of a man with a 'foul disease' who

> To keep it from divulging, let it feed
> Even on the pith of life;

and later, when arranging to send Hamlet to England and to his death, he justifies it by the proverbial tag:

> diseases desperate grown
> By desperate appliance are relieved,
> Or not at all;

and adjures the English king to carry out his behest, in the words of
a fever patient seeking a sedative,

> For like the hectic in my blood he rages,
> And thou must cure me.

When working on Laertes so that he will easily fall in with the
design for the fencing match, his speech is full of the same underlying
thought of a body sick or ill at ease,

> goodness, growing to a plurisy,
> Dies in his own too much,

and finally, he sums up the essence of the position and its urgency
with lightning vividness in a short medical phrase,

> But, to the quick o' the ulcer:
> Hamlet comes back.

In marked contrast to *Lear,* though bodily disease is emphasized,
bodily action and strain are little drawn upon; indeed, only in Hamlet's great speech is it brought before us at all (*to be shot at* with
slings and arrows, *to take arms against* troubles and *oppose* them, *to
suffer* shocks, *to bear* the lash of whips, and *endure* pangs, to *grunt*
and *sweat* under burdens, and so on), and here, as in *Lear,* it serves
to intensify the feeling of mental anguish. In *Hamlet,* however,
anguish is not the dominating thought, but *rottenness,* disease, corruption, the result of *dirt;* the people are 'muddied,'

> Thick and unwholesome in their thoughts and whispers,

and this corruption is, in the words of Claudius, 'rank' and 'smells to
heaven,' so that the state of things in Denmark which shocks, para-
lyses, and finally overwhelms Hamlet, is as the foul tumour breaking
inwardly and poisoning the whole body, while showing

> no cause without
> Why the man dies.

Thus, to Shakespeare's pictorial imagination, the problem in Hamlet
is not predominantly that of will and reason, of a mind too philo-
sophic or a nature temperamentally unfitted to act quickly; he sees it
pictorially, *not as the problem of an individual at all,* but as something
greater and even more mysterious, as a *condition* for which the individual himself is apparently not responsible, any more than the sick
man is to blame for the cancer which strikes and devours him, but

which, nevertheless, in its course and development impartially and relentlessly annihilates him and others, innocent and guilty alike. That is the tragedy of Hamlet, as it is, perhaps, the chief tragic mystery of life.

It is hardly necessary to point out, in a play so well known and of such rich imaginative quality, how the ugliness of the dominating image (disease, ulcer) is counteracted, and the whole lighted up by flashes of sheer beauty in the imagery; beauty of picture, of sound and association, more particularly in the classical group and in the personifications. Thus the tragic, murky atmosphere of Hamlet's interview with his mother, with its ever-repeated insistence on physical sickness and revolting disease, is illumined by the glow of his description of his father's portrait, the associations of beauty called up by Hyperion, Jove, and Mars, or the exquisite picture evoked by the contemplation of the grace of his father's poise,

> like the herald Mercury
> New-lighted on a heaven-kissing hill.

These beauties are specially noticeable in the many personifications, as when, with Horatio, we see 'the morn in russet mantle clad,' as she 'walks o'er the dew of yon high eastward hill,' or with Hamlet watch Laertes leaping into Ophelia's grave and ask

> whose phrase of sorrow
> Conjures the wandering stars and makes them stand
> Like wonder-wounded hearers?

Peace, with her wheaten garland, Niobe all tears, Ophelia's garments 'heavy with their drink,' who pull her from her 'melodious lay' to muddy death, or the magnificent picture of the two sides of the Queen's nature at war, as seen by the elder Hamlet,

> But look, amazement on thy mother sits:
> O, step between her and her fighting soul:

these, and many more, are the unforgettable and radiant touches of beauty in a play which has, as images, much that is sombre and unpleasant. . . .

The imagery in *Macbeth* appears to me to be more rich and varied, more highly imaginative, more unapproachable by any other writer, than that of any other single play. It is particularly so, I think, in the continuous use made of the simplest, humblest, everyday things, drawn from the daily life in a cottage, as a vehicle for sublime poetry. But that is beside our point here.

The ideas in the imagery are in themselves more imaginative, more subtle and complex than in other plays, and there are a greater number of them, interwoven the one with the other, recurring and repeating. There are at least four of these main ideas and many subsidiary ones.

One is the picture of Macbeth himself.

Few simple things—harmless in themselves—have such a curiously humiliating and degrading effect as the spectacle of a small, ignoble man enveloped in a coat far too big for him. Comic actors know this well—Charlie Chaplin, for instance—and it is by means of this homely picture that Shakespeare shows us his imaginative view of the hero, and expresses the fact that the honours for which the murders were committed are, after all, of very little worth to him.

The idea constantly recurs that Macbeth's new honours sit ill upon him, like a loose and badly fitting garment belonging to some one else. Macbeth himself first expresses it, quite early in the play, when, immediately following the first appearance of the witches and their prophecies, Ross arrives from the King and greets him as thane of Cawdor, to which Macbeth quickly replies,

> The thane of Cawdor lives: why do you dress me
> In borrow'd robes?

And a few minutes later, when he is rapt in ambitious thoughts suggested by the confirmation of two out of the three 'prophetic greetings,' Banquo, watching him, murmurs,

> New honours come upon him,
> Like our strange garments, cleave not to their mould
> But with the aid of use.

When Duncan is safely in the castle, Macbeth's better nature for a moment asserts itself and, in debate with himself, he revolts from the contemplated deed for a threefold reason: because of its incalculable results, the treachery of such action from one who is both kinsman and host, and Duncan's own virtues and greatness as king. When his wife joins him his repugnance to the deed is as great, but it is significant that he gives three quite different reasons for not going ahead with it, reasons which he hopes may appeal to her, for he knows the others would not.

So he urges that he has been lately honoured by the king, people think well of him, and therefore he should reap the reward of these things at once, and not upset everything by this murder which they have planned.

There is irony in the fact that to express the position he uses the same metaphor of clothes:

> I have bought
> Golden opinions from all sorts of people,
> Which would be worn now in their newest gloss,
> Not cast aside so soon.

To which Lady Macbeth retorts contemptuously, and quite unmoved:

> Was the hope drunk
> Wherein you dress'd yourself?

After the murder, when Ross says he is going to Scone for Macbeth's coronation, Macduff uses the same simile:

> Well, may you see things well done there: adieu!
> Lest our old robes sit easier than our new!

And, at the end, when the tyrant is at bay at Dunsinane and the English troops are advancing, the Scottish lords still have this image in their minds. Caithness sees him as a man vainly trying to fasten a large garment on him with too small a belt:

> He cannot buckle his distemper'd cause
> Within the belt of rule;

while Angus, in a similar image, vividly sums up the essence of what they all have been thinking ever since Macbeth's accession to power,

> now does he feel his title
> Hang loose about him, like a giant's robe
> Upon a dwarfish thief.

This imaginative picture of a small, ignoble man encumbered and degraded by garments unsuited to him, should be put against the view emphasized by some critics (notably Coleridge and Bradley) of the likeness between Macbeth and Milton's Satan in grandeur and sublimity.

Undoubtedly Macbeth is built on great lines and in heroic proportions, with great possibilities—there could be no tragedy else. He is great, magnificently great, in courage, in passionate, indomitable ambition, in imagination and capacity to feel. But he could never be put beside, say Hamlet or Othello, in nobility of nature; and there *is* an aspect in which he is but a poor, vain, cruel, treacherous creature, snatching ruthlessly over the dead bodies of kinsman and friend at place and power he is utterly unfitted to possess. It is worth remembering that it is thus that Shakespeare, with his unshrinking clarity of vision, repeatedly *sees* him.

Another image or idea which runs through *Macbeth* is the reverberation of sound echoing over vast regions, even into the limitless spaces beyond the confines of the world. Echoing sound, as also reflected light, always interested Shakespeare; he is very quick to notice it, and in the earlier plays he records it often, quite simply and directly, as in the reverberating roll of drums in *King John,* the smack of Petruchio's kiss resounding through the church, Juliet's delicate picture of Echo with her airy tongue repeating 'Romeo,' Viola's assertion that if she were Orsino she would make the

> babbling gossip of the air
> Cry out 'Olivia!'

or her more fanciful remark to the Duke that the tune he likes

> gives a very echo to the seat
> Where love is throned.

He specially loves and describes repeatedly (in the *Dream, Titus,* and the *Shrew*) the re-echoing sound of hounds and horn,

> the musical confusion
> Of hounds and echo in conjunction;

its doubling and mocking quality attracts him,

> the babbling echo mocks the hounds
> Replying shrilly to the well-tuned horns,
> As if a double hunt were heard at once,

and it is this quality which Warwick applies most appositely, when having been roused in the small hours to soothe the sleepless and fretful king he finally loses patience with Henry's fears that the revolutionaries must be fifty thousand strong, and retorts, somewhat tartly,

> It cannot be, my lord;
> Rumour doth double, like the voice and echo,
> The numbers of the fear'd. Please it your grace
> To go to bed.

It is not until after 1600, and most noticeably in *Troilus,* that Shakespeare uses this same idea of reverberation and reflection to illustrate subtle and philosophic thought. Ulysses' mind is full of it, and he applies it constantly; Kent, in *Lear,* seizes on an analogous natural fact to point the truth that noise and protestation do not necessarily indicate deep feeling, while in *Macbeth* the peculiar quality of echoing and re-echoing sound is used to emphasize in the most highly imaginative and impressive way a thought constantly present with Shakespeare in his middle years, the incalculable and boundless effects of evil in the nature of one man.

Macbeth himself, like Hamlet, is fully conscious of how impossible it is to 'trammel up the consequence' of his deed, and by his magnificent images of angels pleading trumpet-tongued, pity, like a naked new-born babe striding the blast,

> or heaven's cherubin horsed
> Upon the sightless couriers of the air,

who

> Shall blow the horrid deed in every eye,
> That tears shall drown the wind,

he fills our imagination with the picture of its being broadcast through great spaces with reverberating sound.

This is taken up again by Macduff, when he cries,

> each new morn
> New widows howl, new orphans cry, new sorrows
> Strike heaven on the face, that it resounds
> As if it felt with Scotland and yell'd out
> Like syllable of dolour,

and again by Ross, when he is trying to break the terrible news of Macbeth's latest murders to Macduff—the destruction of his own wife and children—

> I have words
> That would be howl'd out in the desert air,
> Where hearing should not latch them.

One can scarcely conceive a more vivid picture of the vastnesses of space than this, and of the overwhelming and unending nature of the consequences or reverberations of the evil deed.

Another constant idea in the play arises out of the symbolism that light stands for life, virtue, goodness; and darkness for evil and death. 'Angels are bright,' the witches are 'secret, black and mid-night hags,' and, as Dowden says, the movement of the whole play might be summed up in the words, 'good things of day begin to droop and drowse.'

This is, of course, very obvious, but out of it develops the further thought which is assumed throughout, that the evil which is being done is so horrible that it would blast the sight to look on it, so darkness or partial blinding is necessary to carry it out.

Like so much in the play it is ironic that it should be Duncan who first starts this simile, the idea of which turns into a leading motive in the tragedy. When he is conferring the new honour on his son, he is careful to say that others, kinsmen and thanes, will also be rewarded:

> *Signs of nobleness, like stars, shall shine*
> On all deservers.

No sooner has the king spoken than Macbeth realizes that Malcolm, now a Prince of the realm, is an added obstacle in his path, and suddenly, shrinking from the blazing horror of the murderous thought which follows, he cries to himself,

> Stars, hide your fires;
> Let not light see my black and deep desires.

And from now on, the idea that only in darkness can such evil deeds be done is ever present with both Macbeth and his wife, as is seen in their two different and most characteristic invocations to darkness; her blood-curdling cry

> Come thick night,
> And pall thee in the dunnest smoke of hell,

which takes added force when we hear later the poignant words, 'She has light by her continually'; and his more gentle appeal in the language of falconry,

> Come, seeling night,
> Scarf up the tender eye of pitiful day.

And when Banquo, sleepless, uneasy, with heart heavy as lead, crosses the courtyard on the fateful night, with Fleance holding the flaring torch before him, and, looking up to the dark sky, mutters,

> There's husbandry in heaven,
> Their candles are all out,

we know the scene is set for treachery and murder.

So it is fitting that on the day following 'dark night strangles the travelling lamp', and

> darkness does the face of earth entomb
> When living light should kiss it.

The idea of deeds which are too terrible for human eyes to look on is also constant; Lady Macbeth scoffs at it, 'the sleeping and the dead,' she argues, 'are but as pictures':

> 'tis the eye of childhood
> That fears a painted devil;

but Macduff, having seen the slain king, rushes out, and cries to Lennox,

> Approach the chamber, and destroy your sight
> With a new Gorgon.

Macbeth boldly asserts he dare look on that 'which might appal the devil,' and the horror and fear he feels on seeing one 'too like the spirit of Banquo' in the procession of kings is expressed in his agonized cry,

> Thy crown does sear mine eye-balls;

while in his bitter and beautiful words at the close, the dominant thoughts and images are the quenching of light and the empty reverberation of sound and fury, 'signifying nothing.'

The fourth of the chief symbolic ideas in the play is one which is very constant with Shakespeare and is to be found all through his work, that sin is a disease—Scotland is sick.

So Macbeth, while repudiating physic for himself, turns to the doctor and says if he could by analysis find Scotland's disease

> And purge it to a sound and pristine health,
> I would applaud thee to the very echo,

> That should applaud again . . .
> What rhubarb, senna, or what purgative drug,
> Would scour these English hence?

Malcolm speaks of his country as weeping, bleeding, and wounded, and later urges Macduff to

> make us medicines of our great revenge,
> To cure this deadly grief,

while Caithness calls Malcolm himself the 'medicine of the sickly weal,' 'the country's purge.'

It is worth noting that all Macbeth's images of sickness are remedial or soothing in character; balm for a sore, sleep after fever, a purge, physic for pain, a 'sweet oblivious antidote,' thus intensifying to the reader or audience his passionate and constant longing for well-being, rest, and, above all, peace of mind.

Other subsidiary motives in the imagery, which work in and out through the play, insensibly but deeply affect the reader's imagination.

One of these is the idea of the *unnaturalness* of Macbeth's crime, that it is a convulsion of nature. This is brought out repeatedly and emphasized by imagery, as are also the terrible results of going against nature.

Macbeth himself says that Duncan's wounds 'look'd like a breach in nature'

> For ruin's wasteful entrance,

and Macduff compares his murder to the sacrilege of breaking open the Lord's anointed temple.

The events which accompany and follow it are terrible because unnatural; an owl kills a falcon, horses eat each other, the earth was feverous and did shake, day becomes night; all this, says the old man, is unnatural,

> Even like the deed that's done.

Macbeth's greatest trouble is the unnatural one that he has 'murdered sleep,' and the whole feeling of dislocation is increased by such images as 'let this frame of things disjoint,' or by Macbeth's conjuration to the witches with the terrible list of the convulsions of nature which may result from their answering him. Indeed, if from one angle the movement of the play may be summed up in Macbeth's words,

Good things of day begin to droop and drowse,

from another it is completely described by the doctor in his diagnosis of the doomed Queen's malady as 'a great perturbation of nature.'

In addition to these running images symbolizing or expressing an idea, there are groups of others which might be called atmospheric in their effect, that is, they raise or increase certain feelings and emotions.

Such is the action of rapid riding which contributes and emphasizes a certain sense of rushing, relentless, and goaded motion, of which we are very conscious in the play. This is symbolized externally by the rapid ride of the messenger to Lady Macbeth arriving 'almost dead for breath,' ahead of Macbeth, who himself has outridden Duncan, who remarks in unconscious irony,

he rides well,
And his great love, sharp as his spur, hath holp him
To his home before us.

It is noticeable what a large part riding plays in the images which crowd on Macbeth's heated brain when he is weighing the *pros* and *cons* of his plan; the new-born babe 'striding the blast,' heaven's cherubin horsed

Upon the sightless couriers of the air,

and finally, the vision of his 'intent,' his aim, as a horse lacking sufficient spur to action, which melts into the picture of himself as a rider vaulting into the saddle with such energy that it 'o'er-leaps itself,' and he falls on the farther side.

The feeling of fear, horror, and pain is increased by the constant and recurring images of blood; these are very marked and have been noticed by others, especially by Bradley, the most terrible being Macbeth's description of himself wading in a river of blood, while the most stirring to the imagination, perhaps in the whole of Shakespeare, is the picture of him gazing, rigid with horror, at his own bloodstained hand and watching it dye the whole green ocean red.

The images of animals also, nearly all predatory, unpleasant, or fierce, add to this same feeling; such are a nest of scorpions, a venomous serpent and a snake, a 'hell-kite' eating chickens, a devouring vulture, a swarm of insects, a tiger, rhinoceros, and bear, the tiny wren fighting the owl for the life of her young, small birds with the fear of the net, lime, pitfall, or gin, used with such bitter ironic effect by Lady Macduff and her boy just before they are murdered, the shrieking owl, and the bear tied to a stake fighting savagely to the end.

Enough has been said, I think, to indicate how complex and varied is the symbolism in the imagery of *Macbeth,* and to make it clear that an appreciable part of the emotions we feel throughout of pity, fear, and horror are due to the subtle but definite and repeated action of this imagery upon our minds, of which, in our preoccupation with the main theme, we remain often largely unconscious.

The main image in *Othello* is that of animals in action, preying upon one another, mischievous, lascivious, cruel, or suffering, and through these, the general sense of pain and unpleasantness is much increased and kept constantly before us.

More than half the animal images in the play are Iago's, and all these are contemptuous or repellent, a plague of flies, a quarrelsome dog, the recurrent image of bird-snaring, leading asses by the nose, a spider catching a fly, beating an offenceless dog, wild cats, wolves, goats, and monkeys.

To this Othello adds his pictures of foul toads breeding in a cistern, summer flies in the shambles, the ill-boding raven over the infected house, a toad in a dungeon, the monster 'too hideous to be shown,' bird-snaring again, aspics' tongues, crocodiles' tears, and his reiteration of 'goats and monkeys.' In addition Ludovico very suitably calls Iago 'that viper,' and the green-eyed monster 'begot upon itself, born on itself,' is described or referred to by Iago, Emilia, and Desdemona.

It is interesting to compare the animal imagery in *Othello* with that in *Lear*. The plays have certain likenesses; they were written near together (*Othello* probably in 1604, *King Lear* about 1605), they are the most painful of the great tragedies, and they are both studies of torture.

But the torture in *Lear* is on so vast and so inhuman a scale, the cruelty of child to parent in the doubly repeated plot is so relentless and ferocious, that the jealous and petty malignity of Iago shrinks beside it.

This difference in scale is expressed in the animal imagery. In *Othello* we see a low type of life, insects and reptiles swarming and preying on each other, not out of special ferocity but just in accordance with their natural instincts, mischievous and irresponsible wild cats, goats, and monkeys, or the harmless, innocent animal trapped or beaten. This reflects and repeats the spectacle of the wanton torture of one human being by another which we witness in the tragedy, the human spider and his fly; whereas in *Lear* our imagination is filled with the accumulated pictures of active ferocity, of wolf, tiger, wild boar, vulture, serpent, and sea-monster, all animals of a certain dignity and grandeur, though seen here only when

> their desires
> Are wolfish, bloody, starved and ravenous.

This represents the terrific scale of the suffering in *Lear,* which makes us feel—as we never do in *Othello*—that the vileness of humanity is so great, so unchecked and universal, that if the gods do not intervene, the end of such horrors must come and

> Humanity must perforce prey on itself,
> Like monsters of the deep.

But the gods, who 'keep this dreadful pother,' do not intervene, and the most terrible lines in Shakespeare are those breathed by Gloucester in his agony, when he attributes to the gods themselves in their dealings with men, not only indifference and callousness, but the sheer wanton delight in torture, which in *Othello* we see exercised only by one human being on another.

If animals in action symbolize the main motive in *Othello,* there is another recurrent image which gives atmosphere and background. As is fitting, with a setting of two famous seaports, the sea, its images and language, play an important part throughout.

Iago, who possibly may have been seaman before he was soldier, uses it easily and very early; when complaining that Othello had passed him over for Cassio, he describes himself as 'be-lee'd and calm'd,' he knows the state has not another of Othello's 'fathom,' he says he must 'show out a flag and sign of love,' that Brabantio will take action against Othello to whatever extent the law 'will give him cable'; later he coarsely describes his general's marriage in the terms of a pirate taking a prize galleon, he declares to Roderigo he is knit to his deserving 'with cables of perdurable toughness,' and when he sees his plots shaping well, he murmurs with satisfaction,

> My boat sails freely, both with wind and stream.

The opening of Act II, when those in Cyprus are anxiously awaiting the arrival of Desdemona and of Othello, is full of sea-pictures and personifications, the ruffian wind upon the sea, the 'chidden billow' and the 'wind-shaked surge,' so that it is well in keeping with the setting and atmosphere when Cassio, in high rhetorical terms, pictures the seas and rocks as traitors concealed to waylay the ship, who, on catching sight of the beauty of Desdemona, 'do omit their mortal natures' and let her go safely by.

Othello's use of sea-images is noteworthy; they come to him naturally, for on each occasion it marks a moment of intense emotion. The first, at the height of his happiness when he rejoins Desdemona, is an exclamation which to us, who know what lies before them, is in its opening one of the most poignant and moving in the play:

> O my soul's joy!
> If after every tempest comes such calms,
> May the winds blow till they have waken'd death!

The next is at the height of his torture when, having been shown the handkerchief, suspicion becomes certainty and he vows vengeance. To clinch this Iago urges patience, and suggests that perhaps his mind may change; to which Othello instantly reacts as his torturer intends and affirms the unalterable quality of his resolve by comparing it to the 'icy current and compulsive course' of the ebbless Pontic Sea.

And at the end, when he has carried out his resolve and has suffered and realized all, again it is in sea-language that he expresses his equally set determination to follow Desdemona:

> Here is my journey's end, here is my butt
> And very sea-mark of my utmost sail.

The intensity of feeling and emotion in *Lear,* and the sharpness of its focus is revealed by the fact that in Shakespeare's imagination there runs throughout only one overpowering and dominating continuous image. So compelling is this that even well-marked different and subsidiary images are pressed into its service and used to augment and emphasize it.

In the play we are conscious all through of the atmosphere of buffeting, strain and strife, and, at moments, of bodily tension to the point of agony. So naturally does this flow from the circumstances of the drama and the mental sufferings of Lear, that we scarcely realize how greatly this sensation in us is increased by the general 'floating' image, kept constantly before us, chiefly by means of the verbs used but also in metaphor, of a human body in anguished movement, tugged, wrenched, beaten, pierced, stung, scourged, dislocated, flayed, gashed, scalded, tortured, and finally broken on the rack.

One can scarcely open a page of the play without being struck by these images and verbs, for every kind of bodily movement, generally involving pain, is used to express mental and abstract as well as physical facts. To name only a few of them. Lear, in his agonized remorse, pictures himself as a man *wrenched* and tortured by an 'engine,' beating at the gate (his head) that let his folly in. Goneril has power to *shake* his manhood; he complains that she has *struck* him with her tongue; the hot tears *break* from him; his heart, he says, *will break into a hundred thousand flaws*. Albany wonders how far Goneril's eyes may *pierce,* Gloucester's '*flaw'd heart*' is cracked, and finally it '*burst* smilingly.' Kent longs *to tread* Oswald into mortar, and in his heated description of the steward's character he evokes images of rats *biting* cords, weathercocks *turning,* dogs *following,* and geese being *driven.* '*Tis worse than murder,* cries Lear, this *violent outrage* of putting Kent in the stocks, and his emotion on witnessing it *swells* and *climbs,* while the fool adds the picture of a man being dragged along by *holding on* when a great wheel *runs down hill,* and *letting go* only in time to save his *neck being broken.*

So also in scenes not directly concerned with Lear, such as Gloucester's conversations with Edmund, we find the same characteristic.

When Edmund, having roused his father's anger against the unwitting Edgar, desires to restrain him from immediate action until he has furnished further proof of his wickedness, he words his argument thus: If you will suspend your indignation until you have 'better testimony of his intent, you should *run a certain course*; where, if you *violently proceed against* him, mistaking his purpose, it would *make a great gap* in your own honour and *shake in pieces the heart* of his obedience.' And a little later, Gloucester being indeed shaken to the heart by Edmund's revelations, in the course of ten lines uses these verbs and nouns, *scourged, cools, falls off, divide, cracked, falls from bias, follow disquietly, mutinies, discord, machinations, hollowness, ruinous disorders.*

This use of verbs and images of bodily and generally anguished motion is almost continuous, and it is reinforced by similar words used in direct description, as in the treatment of Gloucester; he is *bound* to a chair, *plucked* by the beard, his hairs are *ravished* from his chin, he is *tied to a stake,* like a bear to *stand the course,* and with his eyes blinded and bleeding, he is *thrust out* of the gates to *smell his way* to Dover.

All through the play the simplest abstract things, such as Cornwall's well-known obstinacy, are described in similar terms; the duke's disposition, says Gloucester, will not be *rubb'd* nor *stopp'd.* Even in a scene, pleasant in itself, such as the gentleman's ornate but delightful description of Cordelia's reception of his news (IV. iii), this sense of bodily movement and strain is constant. The letters *pierced* her to a demonstration of grief, her passion

> most rebel-like
> Sought to be king o'er her;

it *moved* her, patience and sorrow *strove,* she *heaved* the name of 'father' *pantingly forth* as if it *press'd her heart*; she *shook* the tears from her eyes, and away she *started*

> To deal with grief alone.

Look at the six lines which follow, in which Kent, having declared that Lear will not *yield* to see his daughter, describes his master's mental and emotional suffering in a series of pictures of physical buffeting, pain, and opposition, which, in addition to the two images of brutal dogs and poisonous serpents, have a cumulative and almost overwhelming effect on the mind:

> A sovereign shame so *elbows him:* his own unkindness

stripped Cordelia from his benediction, *turn'd* her to foreign casualties,

> these things *sting*
> *His mind so venomously,* that *burning* shame
> *Detains him* from Cordelia.

The idea of unnatural horrors, of human beings *preying on themselves* 'like monsters of the deep,' or like wolves and tigers tearing one another's flesh, is also constantly before us. Lear is sure that Regan, when she hears how he has been mistreated, with 'her nails' will *flay* Goneril's *wolfish visage*; filial ingratitude is as if *the mouth should tear the hand*

> For lifting food to't.

Gloucester boldly avows to Regan he has sent Lear to Dover because

> I would not see *thy cruel nails*
> *Pluck out* his *poor old eyes,* nor thy *fierce sister*
> *In his anointed flesh stick boarish fangs;*

and Albany, crying to Goneril that she and Regan are 'tigers,' not daughters, declares if he followed his inclination he would *dislocate* and *tear her flesh and bones.*

The large number of animal images, and their effect in the play, has often been noticed (notably by Bradley, *Shakespearean Tragedy,* pp. 266 and following). I would only point out here that in addition to the feeling they give us that 'humanity' is 'reeling back into the beast,' they also, because portrayed chiefly in angry or anguished action, very distinctly augment the sensation of horror and bodily pain. In addition to savage wolves, tigers, and other animals there are *darting* serpents, the *sharp-toothed* vulture and *detested* kite, *stinging* adders and insects, *gnawing* rats, the *baited* bear, as well as *whipped, whining, barking, mad* and *biting* dogs. All this helps to create and increase an unparalleled atmosphere of rapine, cruelty, and bodily pain.

To this is added as an overtone running through the crisis of the tragedy, the fury of the elements, described, be it remarked, wholly in terms of the human body. They are *wild, fretful, unique;* the wind and rain are *to and fro conflicting;* with these, the old king, with his *heart-struck injuries is contending, tearing* his white hair.

> Which the *impetuous* blasts, with *eyeless rage,*
> *Catch* in their *fury;*

and bidding the winds to blow and *crack their cheeks,* until at the height of his half-demented passion he commands the *all-shaking* thunder to '*smite flat* the thick rotundity o' the world.' This last amazing image is one of several in Shakespeare, notably in *Antony and Cleopatra,* which evoke the spectacle of devastating bodily action on so stupendous a scale that the emotions which give rise to it are lifted to a similar terrific and vast intensity. So the picture which follows here of the great gods, through the bursts of thunder and groans of roaring wind and rain, remorselessly seeking and finding out their enemies, while 'close *pent-up* guilts' *rive* their concealing continents, and *cry*

> These dreadful summoners grace,

seems natural and only in keeping with the feeling aroused in the imagination of a Being or a Force mighty enough to remould the shape of the globe with one resounding blow.

The sense of bodily torture continues to the end. Gloucester catches the recurrent theme of the tragedy and crystallizes it for ever in the terrible picture of men being torn limb from limb by the gods in sport, to whom they are but 'as flies to wanton boys.' Lear tells Cordelia he is bound

> Upon a wheel of fire, that mine own tears
> Do scald like molten lead;

Edgar sees the gods making instruments of torture with which to plague men; and, at the close, when Kent, who loved him, breathes the only valediction possible over his dead master's body, it is still the same metaphor which rises to his lips,

> O, let him pass! he hates him
> That would upon the rack of this tough world
> Stretch him out longer. . . .

The group of images in *Antony* which, on analysis, immediately attracts attention as peculiar to this play, are images of the world, the firmament, the ocean, and vastness generally.

That is the dominating note in the play, magnificence and grandeur, expressed in many ways and pictured by continually stimulating our imaginations to see the colossal figure of Antony, 'demi-Atlas of this earth,' 'triple pillar of the world,' built on so vast a scale that the whole habitable globe is but a toy to him, as it were a ball or apple which he quarters with his sword, playing with 'half the bulk of it' as he pleases, 'making and marring fortunes.'

Antony himself touches this note at once in his royal love-making, when he tells Cleopatra that if she would put a bourne to the measure of his love, she must 'needs find out new heaven, new earth.'

Indeed, nothing short of the whole universe suffices for comparison with Antony, and in Cleopatra's lyrical elegies, wherein is concentrated all the passion and poetry of the most passionate and poetical of the plays, she likens him to one whose face was as the heavens,

> and therein stuck
> A sun and moon, which kept their course and lighted
> The little O, the earth.

In these soaring love-laments she sees him and makes us see him as a stupendous super-being, the 'crown o' the earth,' whose 'legs bestrid the ocean,' whose 'rear'd arm crested the world,' and whose qualities can be compared only to the vast elemental forces of nature; his voice, to friends,

> was propertied
> As all the tuned spheres, . . .
> But when he meant to quail and shake the orb
> He was as rattling thunder.

Even the verbs used of his aspect are such as are applicable to the sun and planets; when he smiles, he would *shine* on those

> That make their looks by his,

and Alexas, lately come from him, is *gilded* with his *tinct*.

The perennial seasons themselves, with their wealth of association, become as mere adjectives to express the magnificence and scale of his bounty,

> There was no winter in't; an autumn 'twas
> That grew the more by reaping.

When, mortally wounded, he is borne aloft to her, Cleopatra calls on the sun to burn up the sphere in which it is fixed and so plunge the earth in darkness, and, when he dies, she knows there is

> nothing left remarkable
> Beneath the visiting moon.

Not only Cleopatra thinks of him thus; by a natural instinct all who know him compare him to great natural phenomena: he is a 'mine of bounty,' says Enobarbus; in temper, reports Alexas,

> Like to the time o' the year between the extremes
> Of hot and cold, he was nor sad nor merry;

his faults in him, cries Lepidus,

> seem as the spots of heaven,
> More fiery by night's blackness;

and his messenger, Euphronius, is so conscious of his inferiority to his master, that he avows he was

> of late as petty to his ends
> As is the morn-dew on the myrtle-leaf
> To his grand sea.

When the battle goes against him, Scarus remarks 'the greater cantle of the world is lost,'

> we have kissed away
> Kingdoms and provinces;

and when he dies, so great a convulsion of nature is it that Caesar declares

> the round world
> Should have shook lions into civil streets,
> And citizens to their dens. The death of Antony
> Is not a single doom; in the name lay
> A moiety of the world.

This vastness of scale is kept constantly before us by the use of the word 'world,'[1] which occurs forty-two times, nearly double or more than double as often as in most other plays, and it is continually employed in a way which increases the sense of grandeur, power, and space, which fills the imagination with the conception of beings so great that physical size is annihilated and the whole habitable globe shrinks in comparison with them. Caesar, lamenting his differences with Antony, cries,

> if I knew
> What hoop should hold us staunch, from edge to edge
> O' the world I would pursue it;

and Octavia declares that wars between these two mighty ones, her husband and her brother, would be

> As if the world should cleave, and that slain men
> Should solder up the rift.

The emotional effect of such a simile as this is incalculable, with its amazing picture of the gigantic gaping fissures in the round globe packed tight with the bodies of the dead. Were the feeling in it not so intense it would verge on the grotesque, as do some others among these vast world-images. Such, for instance, is the kind of huge gar-

[1] In *Julius Caesar* 'world' occurs 17 times; in *Lear,* 18; in *Coriolanus,* 19; in *Othello,* 23; in *Hamlet,* 29.

goyle depicted by the saturnine Enobarbus when he hears that Caesar
has deposed Lepidus, thus leaving only Antony and himself in power.
He imagines them as the two mighty jaws in the world's face, grinding
and destroying everything that comes between them, and exclaims,

> Then, world, thou hast a pair of chaps, no more;
> And throw between them all the food thou hast,
> They'll grind the one the other.

Antony's imagination moves on this same vast plane, and the pictures
that he draws stimulate our vision and keep us ever conscious of the
puny size of even the greatest of worldly princes, powers, and spaces
compared to his stupendous force. Especially is this so when power is
slipping from him, when the old lion is dying, and the tragedy is thus
increased by contrast. With what a sublime sweep of simple words he
sums up his earlier activities,

> . . . I, that with my sword
> Quarter'd the world, and o'er green Neptune's back
> With ships made cities;

and how vivid is the picture of the kings of the earth starting forth at
his call, like small boys in a scramble, crying out to know what is his
will. When he is angry, the insolent magnificence of his images surpasses all others in Shakespeare. Thus, after his defeat at sea, when,
furious with Caesar's messenger, he has him soundly whipped and
bids him get back to his master, he gives a characteristic picture in
style and scale of the reason why it is particularly easy just then to
anger him, for his 'good stars' that were his 'former guides'

> Have empty left their orbs and shot their fires
> Into the abysm of hell;

and when earlier, Cleopatra mischievously suggests that Caesar has
sent for him, the thunder of his reply in majestic sweep and cadence
still comes echoing down the centuries:

> Let Rome in Tiber melt, and the wide arch
> Of the ranged empire fall! Here is my space.

It has only been possible to sketch the merest outline of this particular point in the imagery of the tragedies, but this is perhaps
sufficient to show how definite and how potent are these images within
images.

No other writer, so far as I know, certainly no other dramatist, makes such continual use of the running and recurrent symbol as does Shakespeare.

Shelley, in his *Prometheus Unbound,* perhaps comes nearest to it when he brings out and emphasizes by means of his nature-imagery, certain philosophical and ethical thoughts; but the *Prometheus,* though nominally a drama, is really a lyrical poem in a single mood, which lends itself far more readily to such continuity of symbolism than do Shakespeare's varied and tremendous dramas.

This method of working by way of suggestion, springing from a succession of vivid pictures and concrete details, is, of course, of the very essence of 'romantic' art; and, in the case of Shakespeare, the poet's mind, unlike the dyer's hand, subdues to itself what it works in, and colours with its dominating emotion all the varied material which comes his way, colours it so subtly and so delicately that for the most part we are unconscious of what is happening, and know only the total result of the effect on our imaginative sensibility.

Hence it seems to me that a study of his imagery from the angle from which we have just been looking at it helps us to realize a little more fully and accurately one of the many ways by which he so magically stirs our emotions and excites our imagination, and I believe it not only does this, but that it sometimes even throws a fresh ray of light on the significance of the play concerned, and—most important of all—on the way Shakespeare himself saw it.

PAUL N. SIEGEL
1916-

IT HAS BECOME customary for the editor of an anthology to include blandly and without comment a selection from his own work. I find myself, however, like Browning's Fra Lippo Lippi, who put himself, blushing and ill at ease amidst the august company, in his painting of heaven. My apology must be that even a man of ordinary stature can, by standing on the top of a pyramid of giants, obtain a clearer vision—or think he obtains such a vision—of a great and marvelously complex expanse.

In my book I sought to study the relation between Shakespearean tragedy and the society in which it was born. "Literature," wrote E. E. Stoll, "reflects the taste of the time rather than the time itself." But that taste, and with it the ideas of the audience, is in turn formed by the intellectual and emotional environment created by social changes. If literature does not reflect life, it, in the words of Harry Levin, "refracts it." I have attempted to "determine the angle of refraction."

The thesis of my book I summarized in my preface as follows:

> The Elizabethan social order was based on a social, political, and religious compromise dependent on the fact that the old pre-Tudor aristocracy, the new Tudor aristocracy, and the bourgeoisie balanced one another in strength and that the continuation of this compromise was rendered impossible when the bourgeoisie grew in power after the defeat of the Spanish Armada. The destruction of the Elizabethan compromise brought with it questionings of the Christian humanist world view, a rationalization of the social position of the new aristocracy that dominated the thought of the time. Shakespearean tragedy expresses this world view and the philosophical and emotional reverberations caused by the breaking up of its material basis.

The general view taken in the chapter here reprinted, that the tragedies are expressive of the Christianity of Shakespeare's time in a way that has not been hitherto realized, is one that is widely held today. On the other hand, it has been fiercely contested by many. In fact, the question of the Christian implications of Shakespearean tragedy is probably the chief controversy in Shakespearean criticism today. This controversy is really a carrying over into the Shakespearean arena of the larger controversy concerning the medievalism of the Renaissance. In general, those who find Shake-

spearean tragedy to have as its basis Christian humanism, not secular humanism or scholastic philosophy,
and who find it to be profoundly affected by the allegorical tradition, although not allegorical itself, are in
the position of the Renaissance scholars who reject the
older concept of the Renaissance as a dawn coming up
like thunder but who deny also that it cannot be dif-
ferentiated from the Middle Ages, holding it to be an
age of transition with more medieval strands of
thought than the earlier scholars had realized. The
controversy as far as Shakespeare is concerned is complicated by the continuing desire of many to appropriate Shakespeare for their own philosophy, whether
religious or secular, so that frequently Shakespearean
criticism becomes something like an essay in the discovery of one's own belief and, on the other hand,
what is intended to be historical scholarship is often
mistakenly assumed to be such an essay.

THE SUBSTANCE OF SHAKESPEAREAN TRAGEDY AND THE ELIZABETHAN COMPROMISE

1

"A TRAGIC WRITER," says Joseph Wood Krutch, "does not have to
believe in God, but he must believe in man."[1] This is well said and,
I believe, correct: Christian humanism is not the only kind of humanism capable of producing tragedy. So in the appreciation of
Shakespearean tragedy it is most important that we rise to Shakepeare's perception of the greatness of man. But in order to gain
this perception most fully we have to understand the Christian

"The Substance of Shakespearean Tragedy and the Elizabethan Compromise"
is from Paul N. Siegel, *Shakespearean Tragedy and the Elizabethan Compromise* (New York University Press, 1957), pp. 81–98. By permission of the
publisher.
[1] Joseph Wood Krutch, *The Modern Temper* (New York, 1929), p. 127.

humanist basis of Shakespearean tragedy, for it happens that his exalted view of man springs from his acceptance of this particular
form of humanism. We must look at the plays as perceptive Elizabethans looked at them if we are to apprehend most fully the
Shakespearean vision of the potentialities and weaknesses of man
and of the possibilities of chaos, with all of the significance this vision
has for us today.

In this chapter I shall seek to present in summary form the essential characteristics of Shakespeare's tragic universe, using A. C.
Bradley's remarkable analysis as a convenient point of departure,
and to indicate in so doing how this universe is composed of the
intellectual and emotional materials given to Shakespeare by his
time. I shall, for the most part, reserve the illustrative detail of my
analysis for my discussions of the individual tragedies, referring the
reader to the passages bearing out my general statements.

Bradley found that Shakespeare's tragic universe conveys the impression of being a moral order that casts out evil by the laws of its
own nature but that mysteriously continues to engender it and expels
it only through a fearsome struggle in which good as well as evil is
destroyed. There are four major alterations that have to be made in
his picture of Shakespearean tragedy: (1) Shakespearean tragedy
conveys a sense of divine providence; (2) this divine providence
visits a poetically appropriate retribution upon the guilty; (3) characters and action suggest analogies with the Bible story; (4) there
are intimations of the heaven and hell of Christian religion. In short,
Bradley's analysis of the Shakespearean tragic universe must be
altered to make the order manifested in the course of the tragedies
explicitly Christian, its laws the laws ordained by God, the evil
within it the consequences of man's fall constantly threatening to
overthrow the entire hierarchy of nature. Written when the challenge
to Christian humanist values was felt most keenly, the tragedies
present most vividly the imperilment of the universal order by man's
evil passions, the legacy of his fall, reflecting in doing so the dissolution of the Elizabethan compromise.

2

"A ghost comes from Purgatory," Bradley comments, "to impart
a secret out of the reach of its hearer—who presently meditates on
the question whether the sleep of death is dreamless. Accidents once

or twice remind us strangely of the words, 'There's a divinity that shapes our ends.' . . . But these faint and scattered intimations . . . avail nothing to interpret the mystery."[2] But what he does not see is that, while ghosts, prophecies, premonitory dreams, and portents are often doubted or disregarded, they are always vindicated.[3] Thus in *Richard III* the prophecies of divine vengeance of Margaret and of Richard's mother, the Duchess of York, are disregarded by the ironically skeptical, mocking Richard, only for him to find out that God is not to be mocked; in the destiny-haunted *Julius Caesar,* Caesar, Calpurnia, and Cassius give up their skepticism under the pressure of the supernatural; in *Hamlet,* Horatio's doubts concerning the existence of ghosts are resolved.

The fact that they do not at first recognize the indications of the supernatural only contributes to the sense of man's blindness to the world of heavenly powers about him. Observing their ironic unawareness of the significance of prophecies and portents, the Elizabethan spectator would have had a certain godlike feeling of superiority, but he himself would have remained in the dark as to precisely how the prophecies and portents are to be realized. He would not have wondered whether a deity guides men's destinies but how it was to manifest itself.

Shakespeare, in keeping with the Christian humanist world view, shows man as part of a divine scheme of things the details of whose workings are beyond human ken but on whose general laws human beings may rely. The indications of divine providence used by Shakespeare would have been readily recognized by his audience, for they were commonly accepted as such. "One of the notions most useful to pamphleteers, writers of homiletic treatises, and playwrights," says Henry Hitch Adams,

was that Divine Providence intervened in the lives of men to assure the operation of divine justice. Divine Providence is a specific power of God which employs signs, portents, coincidences, seeming accidents, plagues, natural or unnatural phenomena, or minor miracles to dispense rewards and punishments according to His laws, either through His direct action or through His agents. The phrase "Divine Providence" was common

[2] *Shakespearean Tragedy* (London, 1949), pp. 38–39.

[3] For disregarded premonitory dreams in Elizabethan drama, see Bain Tate Stewart, "The Misunderstood Dreams in the Plays of Shakespeare and His Contemporaries," *Essays in Honor of Walter Clyde Curry* (Vanderbilt University Press, 1954), pp. 197–206.

enough in nondramatic literature, but was seldom employed by the play-wrights. For this reason, providential operations have commonly gone unrecognized in investigations of the drama of the period.[4]

To find that Shakespeare, like the writers of bourgeois domestic "tragedy," uses the doctrine of divine providence without explicit reference to it is not, as has been contended,[5] to reduce his tragedy to homiletic drama. If one were to argue only on the basis of the use of the doctrine and not on how it is used, one could speak of Chaucer's "Pardoner's Tale" as just another homily on the text "Greed is the root of all evil." What matters is the depth and intensity of the writer's vision, whether he is reciting trite commonplaces or has made familiar doctrine come alive, whether he has shrunk life to fit a pattern or has presented the pattern as emerging from the contemplation of a work of art that seems to render the complexity of life.

Shakespearean tragedy, then, conveys an impression of an omnipotent power that is in command of the universe while somehow allowing man's will to be free to choose good or evil, a power whose operations, however, are shrouded in darkness, holding more things in itself than are dreamed of in the philosophy of Renaissance skeptics or in the metaphysical speculation of medieval scholastics. Even in *Romeo and Juliet* and the Roman tragedies, where Shakespeare relies upon his audience to free itself from conventional religious attitudes and regard the suicide of his heroes and heroines sympathetically as the noblest action that those guided by the attitudes and emotions of romantic love and by the philosophy of stoicism could take, there is a sense of providence at work. In *Romeo and*

---

[4] *English Domestic or Homiletic Tragedy* (New York, 1943), p. 18.

[5] Cf. Sylvan Barnet, "Some Limitations of a Christian Approach to Shakespeare," *ELH*, XXII (1955), 85. For other objections to the reading of Shakespearean tragedy as having Christian implications, see H. B. Charlton, *Shakespearian Tragedy* (Cambridge University Press, 1948), pp. 10–11; Clifford Leech, *Shakespeare's Tragedies and Other Studies in Seventeenth Century Drama* (London, 1950), p. 18; J. A. K. Thomson, *Shakespeare and the Classics* (London, 1952), pp. 253–54. These critics have based themselves on some well-known theories of tragedy. Compare Leech, p. 18, and Barnet, 82 and 84, with W. MacNeile Dixon, *Tragedy* (London, 1924), pp. 37–38; Charlton, pp. 10–11, Leech, pp. 10–11, and Barnet, 92 with I. A. Richards, *Principles of Literary Criticism* (New York, 1948), p. 246; Thomson, pp. 253–54 and Barnet, 87, with F. L. Lucas, *Tragedy* (London, 1949), p. 108. I trust that in the course of this chapter I have answered their objections in passing.

Juliet the adverse destiny of the lovers, pitiful and grievous as it is, is presented as part of the larger plan of divine providence. It is the means, the necessary means, by which their parents are punished in a manner that brings an end to the feud which had endangered the peace of the state. Throughout the Roman plays there is implicit a view of Roman history in which Rome was destined to become a great empire, only, having become decadent and disunited, its plebeians ungrateful, its aristocracy arrogant, its emperors degenerate, to succumb at the height of its pride to barbarism, a view of history which invests the lives of the heroes with their country's grandeur and tragedy.

3

Although the ways of divine providence are dark, once its dictates have been achieved, they are seen to have been inevitable. The consequences of man's actions, which can only imperfectly be foreseen, seem in retrospect to follow so inexorably from their causes that a sense of natural law is conveyed, a natural law which the intimations of the supernatural indicate, however, is only part of a universal order. Retribution, in particular, appears in a form poetically appropriate to the crime. Bradley observed (p. 32) that in Shakespeare "villainy never remains victorious and prosperous at the last." What he did not notice—and it has been little noticed[6] is the poetic fitness of the retribution that overtakes villainy. Such retribution is in accord with how Shakespeare's contemporaries thought God manifests Himself in this world.

It is to be observed that the poetic justice of which I have been speaking is not the same as the poetic justice of the neo-classical critics. Sidney claimed that poetry is superior as a teacher to history, since history must frequently show the good dying in misfortune and the evil triumphing, while poetry can always—and should—show the good, having demonstrated their virtue in misfortune, come to prosperity, with the evil being punished. This became the credo of neo-classical criticism, a credo which, pressed to its logical conclusion, as was not generally done in practice, would make tragedy impossible, for only a villain, whose fall could excite neither pity nor fear, could

[6] See, however, for poetically fitting retribution in *King Lear* Robert B. Heilman, *This Great Stage* (Louisiana State University Press, 1948), pp. 41–51, 53–57 and 150–51.

come to misfortune. Samuel Johnson thus found Shakespeare's gravest defect to be his lack of a narrowly didactic poetic justice: "He makes no just distribution of good or evil."[7] There is indeed in Shakespeare no distribution of rewards and punishments so mathematical that all suffering is either shown to be warranted or made up for by subsequent happiness. A poetically appropriate retribution is, however, visited upon each of his villains.

4

Shakespeare's villains, whose reason, while skillfully employed, has been perverted to serve their individualistic desires, blow themselves up in the explosion they themselves cause by their disregard of the law of nature. These desires, like the foibles and idiosyncrasies of the "humors" characters in the comedies, they make the be-all and end-all of their lives. In *Twelfth Night* the gracious living at Olivia's Tudor country seat would be destroyed if either the grim spirit of the "humorous" Malvolio, the aspiring puritanical steward of her estate, or the loose conduct of the old feudal retainer Sir Toby Belch were the rule, just as the Elizabethan compromise was maintained only by bourgeois independent enterprise and feudal decentralization being held in check. In the tragedies it is ruthless individualism which threatens the natural order, whether the individualism is that of the feudal lords Richard and Macbeth striking at the rightful kings or that of the mercenary Iago, speaking the language of mercantile calculation, and of the adventurer Edmund, whose words "Let me, if not by birth, have lands by wit" (*King Lear,* I, ii, 199) might have served as a motto for the acquisitive bourgeoisie.

Shakespeare's villains, then, embody values destructive to the ideal of Christian humanism. The conflict between different "passions, tendencies, ideas, principles, forces" animating opposing persons or groups that Bradley finds in the tragedies (p. 17) may be generalized as a conflict between Christian humanist values and anti-Christian humanist values. And, as Bradley says (p. 18), the hero does not oppose "to a hostile force an undivided soul." In *Hamlet* the center of the struggle between these two conflicting values is within the prince; in *Othello* they are embodied in Desdemona and Iago, between whom Othello has to choose; in *Macbeth* the hero

---

[7] "Preface to Shakespeare," *Shakespeare Criticism,* ed. D. Nichol Smith (Oxford University Press, 1946), p. 89.

chooses values opposed to Christian humanism early in the play, but only at the end does he realize himself by the standard he has selected; in *King Lear* Edmund and the two sisters are arrayed on one side as against Edgar and Cordelia on the other, while Lear, in rejecting life before he is reclaimed by Cordelia, is opposing the values of Christian humanism in another way than do Edmund and the sisters.

It may be added that Shakespeare gave this clash of values universal significance by placing the tragedies in the remote past or in distant countries while using contemporary character types and topical references. Each tragedy, as H. B. Charlton has pointed out, has a lightly suggested cultural setting, just as, contemporary illustrations indicate, the costumes of the actors, while predominantly Elizabethan, contained touches hinting of the historical period presented in the play, and this cultural setting contributes to giving each tragedy its own distinctive atmosphere. At the same time, however, each tragedy has features reminiscent of Elizabethan England, thus inviting the audience to think of the events of its own day as illustrating the eternal nature of man.

5

The eternally tragic fact is that evil, in destroying itself, also destroys good. Yet it is important to note, as Bradley did (pp. 34–35), that the tragic hero also contributes to his own downfall. He is not merely the victim of evil, potent though it may be in this world, or of blind fortune, uncertain as this life is.[8] He has, Bradley found (p. 20), a "fatal tendency to identify the whole being with one interest, object, passion, or habit of mind." In doing so, it may be added, he becomes, to use the subtitle of Lily B. Campbell's *Shake-*

[8] The Elizabethans followed Boethius and the Middle Ages in emphasizing the mutability of the things of this world, over which fortune prevails, while maintaining that the uncertainties of life, beyond human foresight, are in reality part of the divine scheme of things. Spenser's "Cantoes of Mutabilitie" is the *locus classicus*. The humanist treatises of moral philosophy and religious consolation account for the misfortunes of the good by the doctrine that adversity teaches them to rise above worldly things and to grow in love for their fellow men and God. Thus Hamlet and Lear learn from their ordeals. This contributes to a sense of reconciliation on our part, although it does not wipe away our memory of their pain. Desdemona and Cordelia, unlike the heroes of Shakespearean tragedy, suffer through no fault of their own, but they are Christ-like figures who exemplify the Christian virtue of accepting entirely unmerited calamities with unshrinking fortitude and undiminished love.

speare's Tragic Heroes, a "slave of passion." The downfall of the
Shakespearean tragic hero is brought about through some fatal defect
in the armor of "solid virtue" with which he faces the "shot of
accident" and the "dart of chance" (*Othello,* IV, i, 277–78), which
can hurt his unconquerable mind only by using the opening provided
by some passion. This is true not only of the guilty heroes Othello
and Macbeth but of the comparatively innocent heroes Hamlet and
Lear.

Concerned though Shakepeare's humanist drama is with the passions and struggles of human individuals rather than with the oppositions of allegorical figures, his characters, following the old patterns
of temptation, sin, and retribution and of sin, repentance, and salvation, often are implicitly or explicitly compared with the biblical
archetypes of erring humanity, diabolical evil, and divine goodness.
In the Elizabethan homilies Adam's disobedience of God, Lucifer's
rebellion against Him, and Christ's sacrifice for the sake of mankind
were repeatedly presented as basic patterns which men followed in
their conduct. Writing for an audience accustomed to think in such
terms of biblical analogy, Shakespeare was able through figurative
language and allusions to suggest analogies in the course of his
tragedies of human passion that gave them a deeper significance.
The tragedies do not, however, contain within themselves elaborate
and consistent systems of equivalences; Shakespeare's method, as
in the history plays, was like that of the Christian humanists in using
the analogies between the various hierarchies of nature rather than
allegorizing nature in detail.

The presence and significance of biblical analogies in Shakespearean drama are only just now being realized. Theobald, for instance, stumbled upon one of them in his observation that Othello's
statement that Desdemona's death should have been accompanied
by earthquakes and eclipses cannot but make us recall the earthquakes and eclipses at the time of the crucifixion, but he was shocked
by what seemed to him a blasphemous comparison whose purpose he
could not fathom. By his time the Elizabethan audience's habit of
thinking in terms of biblical analogy had been lost. Today, however,
we understand that an allusion to the Christ story implying a comparison between a character and Christ would not at all have been
regarded as blasphemous by the Elizabethans but would rather have

been regarded as illustrating the idea that the best conduct is that which is most closely imitative of the conduct of Christ.

A character thus compared to Christ does not have to be inhumanly perfect or without any touch of earthiness. Desdemona, beguiling her anxiety for Othello by pretending to be merry, listens smilingly to Iago's double entendres and, frightened by Othello's violence, tells him a lie; she is, however, as we shall see, a Christ figure. A character can even take on the aspect of a Christ figure for a moment although his conduct at other times is quite blameworthy. Thus Richard II, who has been a profligate and irresponsible monarch, in comparing himself to Christ is not merely engaged in self-dramatization but makes the audience regard him as one who through his deposition has become a martyr king.[9] Similarly, although Timon becomes an embittered misanthrope, there are allusions in the early part of the play, too clear and distinct to be merely fortuitous, which invite comparison between Timon's boundless generosity and Christ's overflowing love and between the duplicity of those who feed at Timon's expense and the duplicity of Judas at the Last Supper.[10] The analogies suggested in such scenes would have been recognized by the perceptive theatergoer of Shakespeare's day, just as the audience of Arthur Miller's *The Crucible* was able to recognize

[9] IV, i, 169–71, 239–42. The Bishop of Carlisle immediately before Richard's entrance in this scene had linked him with Christ, saying (IV, i, 125, 126, 144) that if Richard, "the figure of God's majesty" and His "deputy-elect," is deposed, England will be called "the field of Golgotha and dead men's skulls." But, although England must suffer for the deposition, York indicates that Richard, in bearing with gentle fortitude the indignities inflicted upon him by the masses as, stripped of his crown, he rides through the streets, is a Christlike figure whose passion serves God's ultimately beneficent purpose:

> But dust was thrown upon his sacred head;
> Which with such gentle sorrow he shook off,
> His face still combating with tears and smiles,
> The badges of his grief and patience,
> That had not God, for some strong purpose, steel'd
> The hearts of men, they must perforce have melted,
> And barbarism itself have pitied him.
> But heaven hath a hand in these events,
> To whose high will we bound our calm contents.
> (V, ii, 30–38)

The description of Richard's "tears and smiles" in his "grief and patience" resembles that of the "smiles and tears" of Cordelia, another Christlike figure . . . in her "patience and sorrow." (*King Lear*, IV, iii, 18–21.)

[10] G. Wilson Knight, *The Wheel of Fire* (London, 1949), p. 235 and n.

in it parallels to the stifling of intellectual freedom in its own day even though not a sentence explicitly related the Salem witch hunts to the happenings of the time. Such analogies are most prevalent in *Othello, Macbeth,* and *King Lear.*

6

However, what most distinguishes these three tragedies and *Hamlet* —the four great tragedies which Bradley selected for extended discussion as having "one and the same substance" (p. 3)—is that the afterlife of Christian religion acts in them as an imposing but faintly painted and unobtrusive backdrop for the action. It is this backdrop which gives them what Bradley calls (p. 185) "the power of dilating the imagination by vague suggestions of huge universal powers working in the world of individual fate and passion." But, although there is suggested to the audience's imagination a heaven and a hell awaiting the outcome of the struggles of the characters, its attention is focused on this world, in which these struggles take place.

Christian humanism, ethical rather than theological in its emphasis, made possible Shakespearean tragedy, for tragedy must be concerned with this world, as the medieval moralities were not. I. A. Richards overstated what is essentially true when he wrote: "The least touch of any theology which has a compensating Heaven to offer the tragic hero is fatal [to the tragic effect]."[11] We can correct this overstatement by referring to Bradley, who, although misled by the mistaken notion of his time that Elizabethan thought and Elizabethan drama were "almost wholly secular" (p. 25), hovered on the brink of understanding the Christian implications of Shakespearean tragedy (p. 324):[12]

[11] Richards, p. 246.

[12] He noted Shakespeare's use of "current religious ideas" in *Macbeth* and *Hamlet* (pp. 172–73): "The horror in Macbeth's soul is more than once represented as desperation at the thought that he is eternally 'lost'; the same idea appears in the attempt of Claudius at repentance; and as *Hamlet* nears its close the 'religious' tone of the tragedy is deepened. . . ." Bradley's use of quotation marks with "lost" and "religious" is an attempt to save his concept of Shakespearean tragedy as essentially secular. If we listen, however, with our ears open to the implications of words that for the Elizabethans would have had a profoundly religious significance, the plays take on new overtones. When Richard III, for instance, concludes his speech of bravado to his troops with (V, iv, 312–13), "March on, join bravely, let us to 't pell-mell;/If not to heaven, then hand in hand to hell," the ringing couplet becomes more than a rhetorical flourish; it is seen to be dramatically ironic: Richard really is going to his eternal damnation, as Margaret had prophesied.

The feeling I mean is the impression that the heroic being . . . is rather set free from life than deprived of it. . . . It accompanies the more prominent tragic impressions, and regarded alone, could hardly be called tragic. It implies that the tragic world . . . is no final reality, but only a part of reality taken for the whole, and, when so taken, illusive; and that if we could see the whole, and the tragic facts in their true place in it, we should find them, not abolished, of course, but so transmuted that they had ceased to be strictly tragic. . . .

He adds in a footnote (p. 325): "It follows from the above that, if this idea were made explicit and accompanied our reading of a tragedy throughout, it would confuse or even destroy the tragic impression. So would the constant presence of Christian belief."

The intimation of an afterlife in Shakespearean tragedy does not become so dominant that the suffering of the good is made to seem unimportant in the light of eternity. There is no triumphant ascent to heaven, only a glimpse beyond the veil that contributes to the reconciliation essential to tragedy but does not nullify the suffering we have witnessed. We are left not amid the glories of heaven but with the survivors in this harsh world—a world, however, that, after doubts and perplexities, we have come to understand is ruled by a natural law through which is manifested its Creator. This understanding is no easy reassurance but a dearly acquired perception which has been attained only after we have been forced to look unblinkingly at man's situation here on earth and to accept it with all of its misery.

A resemblance with a difference between the ending of *Everyman* and that of *Hamlet* is significant. After Everyman has descended into his grave, Knowledge stands over it and says (ll. 892–94): "Methinketh that I hear angels sing, / And make great joy and melody, / Where Everyman's soul shall received be!" An angel's voice is then heard saying, in the final speech of the play, "Come, excellent elect spouse to Jesu! / . . . Now shalt thou in to the heavenly sphere." No angel's voice is heard after Horatio utters his farewell and prayerful wish (V, ii, 370–71), "Good night, sweet prince; / And flights of angels sing thee to thy rest!" Instead, there is a moment's silence, during which the audience may think back upon Hamlet's regeneration in the last act and may fancy that it hears what it will—and then its thoughts are brought back to this earth by the sound of Fortinbras's drum.

So, too, while Lear is accompanied and sustained at the end of his pilgrimage by the Cordelia whom he has shunted, as Everyman is accompanied and sustained by the Good Deeds whom he has neglected, there is only a shadowy intimation at the end of Shakespeare's play that Lear, in joining Cordelia in death, is following "the one companion who is willing to go with him through Death up to the throne of the Everlasting Judge,"[13] but at the end of *Everyman* Knowledge proclaims (l. 980), "The Good Deeds shall make all sure." Both plays use Christian doctrine, but they use it differently. *King Lear,* with its tempest and its stormy human passions, its omnipresent animal imagery, and its vision of humanity finally devouring itself "like monsters of the deep" (IV, ii, 48–50), may be said to be a dramatization of the words of God in *Everyman,* which, since the play is concerned with the next world rather than with this one, remain undramatized in *Everyman* itself:

> For and I leave the people thus alone
> In their way of life and wicked tempests,
> Verily they will become much worse than beasts;
> For now one would by envy another up eat;
> Charity they all do clean forget. (lines 47–51)

And after the *Lear* storm has worked its havoc, if order has been restored, it is an order that can be maintained only by the unremitting care of those to whom has been assigned the task to bear "the weight of this sad time" and "the gored state sustain" (V, iii, 322, 320) and that, we feel, must always be precarious as long as there remain in man the evil passions we have witnessed.

Just as the intimation of heaven does not obliterate the sense of tragic waste we feel in witnessing the suffering of the comparatively innocent heroes Hamlet and Lear, so the intimation of hell does not destroy our sympathy for the guilty heroes Othello and Macbeth. Dante's artistic breadth of sympathy made it possible for him to describe himself as fainting with pity for Paolo and Francesca when he saw in the second circle of Hell these two noble souls who had been overcome with passion. So, too, what makes *Othello* so painful is the fact that the audience is made to sympathize with the hero even as it is made to recognize that he has transgressed divine law and incurred damnation. That he acts in accordance with his character, with its fierce passion lying deep beneath superb self-command,

[13] Oscar James Campbell, "The Salvation of Lear," *ELH,* XV (1948), 107.

gives a sense of dramatic inevitability, but this sense of dramatic inevitability only strengthens the feeling of "he is proceeding to his damnation; the pity of it!" Similarly, the audience shudderingly accepts the justice of Macduff's epithet "hellhound" (V, viii, 3) for Macbeth, and yet underneath this response it retains some sympathy for him, a sympathy which has more of awed admiration intermingled with fear and less of pity than its sympathy for Othello.

Such bravery and skill in war as win the enthusiasm of everyone about him; such an imagination as few but poets possess; a conscience so vivid that his deed is to him beforehand a thing of terror, and, once done, condemns him to that torture of the mind on which he lies in restless ecstasy; a determination so tremendous and a courage so appalling that, for all this torment, he never dreams of turning back, but, even when he has found that life is a tale full of sound and fury, signifying nothing, will tell it out to the end though earth and heaven and hell are leagued against him; are not these things, in themselves, good, and gloriously good? Do they not make you, for all your horror, admire Macbeth, sympathize with his agony, pity him, and see in him the waste of forces on which you place a spiritual value?[14]

Bradley's discussion of the admiration and sympathy we feel for the guilty hero brings us to the central paradox of Shakespearean tragedy. That paradox is expressed in his statement that the hero's tragic trait is also his greatness. The passion which brings about his downfall springs from a force of character that raises him above persons of ordinary clay. That force, that intensity, that Promethean fire, although it enlarges his capacity for suffering and brings it upon him, reveals the possibilities of existence, which we, dozing in our day-by-day routinism, forget. His vitality, the vitality of a Raleigh, of an Essex, and of all those other striking personalities of the new aristocracy who have made the word "Elizabethan" have such vibrant connotations, has potentialities for both good and bad, and the fact that it brings about his downfall does not destroy our awareness of this.

In giving his tragic hero the stature of a titan Shakespeare was making use of the Elizabethan concept of the king. A king, regarded as greater in every way than other men, was considered to have more occasion and capacity for intense feeling than they. "This jealousy,"

14 A. C. Bradley, *Oxford Lectures on Poetry* (London, 1909), pp. 87–88.

says Polixenes of Leontes (*The Winter's Tale,* I, ii, 451–54), "Is for a precious creature. As she's rare, / Must it be great; and as his person's mighty, / Must it be violent." The king was, in effect, a magnification of ordinary humanity, for, if his powers of reason were superior, his judgment was threatened by his greater intensity of emotion. Thus, while the members of the audience regarded the king or other great person who was the tragic hero with respectful awe, they were also able to regard him as representative of themselves, to feel that

> the death of Antony
> Is not a single doom; in the name lay
> A moiety of the world. (*Antony and Cleopatra,* V, i, 1709)

The tragedy of the hero was their tragedy, his transgressions their transgressions, his suffering and death the payment every man has to make for them.

The Elizabethan audience's feeling toward the tragic hero would also have been influenced by the folk ceremonies in which its members participated, ceremonies that were survivals of pagan fertility cults in which a divine king or a god was presented as dying and being reborn in order to bring about through sympathetic magic the awakening of spring after the death of winter. The Londoner going to Paris Garden for his May games and mummers' plays may not have had the anthropologist's full knowledge of their significance (although the Puritan attacks show an awareness of their pagan origin), but, surrounded by the rural England from which he was often transplanted, he retained something of the peasant's sense of taking part in a vitally meaningful act. His feeling of everyone's fate being tied up with everyone else's, of communal life being renewed through the death of a powerful superhuman being, affected his response to tragedy. "Though the audience might not consciously equate the tragic hero and the god or king who suffers and dies for his people, the prevalence of the beliefs and habits of thought described must have served to increase the hero's dignity and to have gathered around him many associations of mystery and awe. . . ."[15]

Much more important in affecting the audience's response, how-

---

[15] Douglas Hewitt, "The Very Pompes of the Divell—Popular and Folk Elements in Elizabethan and Jacobean Drama," *Review of English Studies,* XXV (1949), 21.

ever, must have been the Christian adaptation of the ancient myth and ritual pattern of which the folk ceremonies of the Elizabethans were remnants, the idea of the blessing wrought for mankind through the suffering and death of a man greater than other men. "Orthodox Christianity," writes Herbert Weisinger, "had at its disposal two versions of the paradox of the fortunate fall: the death and resurrection of Christ and the theme of Adam's fall and its subsequent benefits for mankind."[16] Each of these versions of the paradox of the fortunate fall was associated with the idea of tragedy. "To call the Passion tragic," points out William Empson, "was a commonplace."[17] Christ's agony was conventionally presented to call forth pity as a supreme example of undeserved suffering. So, too, it was a commonplace to refer to the fall of Adam as the first tragedy and the origin of all the rest. Adam's transgression was conventionally presented to call forth terror as a momentous act resulting in the greatest misfortune and performed in ironic ignorance of its consequences. Neither a divinely perfect Christ nor a more than human Adam could become the subject of genuine tragedy, but the association of each with the idea of tragedy must have influenced powerfully the way in which the audience regarded the tragic hero. The suffering and death of such comparatively innocent Shakespearean heroes as Richard II, Timon, Hamlet, and Lear bear some general resemblance to the passion of Christ: the heroes seem to take on the burden of the world's suffering, and at the conclusion of their ordeal there is a sense of the renewal of life. The transgressions of such guilty Shakespearean heroes as Othello and Macbeth bear some general resemblance to the fall of Adam: the heroes, noble men succumbing to temptation, bring to every man a new, deeper knowledge of the nature of evil that is harrowing and terrifying, but they bring also the inner paradise of a more profound faith in the order of things which has been disturbed by their actions. We need not suppose awareness of these general resemblances on the part of either the dramatist or the audience, except at the moments of biblical allusion, when unconscious associations were crystallized into conscious awareness, to say that they entered into the effect of the tragedy.

[16] Herbert Weisinger, *Tragedy and the Paradox of the Fortunate Fall* (Michigan State College Press, 1953), p. 225n.
[17] William Empson, *Some Versions of Pastoral* (Norfolk, Conn., n.d.), pp. 84–85.

If the Shakespearean tragic hero, however, carried with him associations of the suffering and dying god or god king of the pagan fertility cults surviving in semi-feudal Elizabethan England and of the Adam and Christ of Christianity, he also carried with him associations of the scapegoat who embodied the forces of barrenness and evil and was, as Sir James Frazer has shown, identified with or substituted for the divine victim.[18] It is noteworthy that the comparatively innocent heroes Hamlet and Lear are malcontents, persons whose destructive cynicism good Elizabethans regarded with fear and shuddering. Hamlet, clothed in gloomy black, brooding morbidly, obsessed with thoughts of the body's decay and the foulness of sex, is a figure of death. Lear in his madness, seeing humanity as wholly evil, calls for the thunder to destroy all the seeds that produce men. Probing deeply into life and exposing that which the "normal" man would prefer to forget, they, like the guilty heroes, challenge the order of things. It is this challenge to the order of things which makes the Shakespearean tragedies not merely dramatic exempla that comfortably reassured their spectators concerning the rightness of their views but imaginative experiences that shook them up only to renew their basic faith and render it richer and deeper by having been forced to assimilate what Hamlet and Lear saw.

[18] The situation of Hamlet, Lear, and Richard II is not unlike that of the scapegoat in the Elizabethan folk ceremonies who was accorded regal honors and then derisively expelled, a custom related to that of having a fool preside over revels and giving him the honors of a king. Hamlet, isolated amidst the sycophantic court of Claudius, who has deprived him of the throne, is in a sense a prince in name only and is, as he says (III, ii, 401), fooled to the top of his bent—that is, treated as a fool, a deranged person, to the limits of his endurance. Lear, with only a nominal kingship, flouted by his daughters, driven out into the storm, and wandering about crowned with nettles and weeds, also endures the utmost of humiliation. The Fool suggests more than once that they could exchange places. So, too, Richard II speaks of himself (IV, i, 260) as "a mockery king." The derisive treatment of Hamlet, Lear, and Richard II as mock kings parallels not only the Elizabethan folk ceremonies but the passion of Christ, who was crowned with thorns, given a reed for a scepter, and mockingly hailed as the king of the Jews.

EDWARD DOWDEN
1843-1913

DOWDEN HERE CARRIES on the work of the romantics, which he makes use of and at the same time corrects. He is primarily concerned with character analysis in the manner of Hazlitt, but he is aware, as Hazlitt was, of what Coleridge called "the unity of feeling" and sees the characters in relation to the atmosphere of the play. This atmosphere he finds to be limned in the comic first scene, which suggests the disaster to come, as Coleridge had already indicated in discoursing on the significance of Shakespeare's opening scenes. Moreover, Dowden sees the characters not in isolation but acting as foils to each other, as Schlegel had observed Shakespeare's characters do. Dowden, however, is not a mere docile pupil. His corrections of Schlegel and Hazlitt in their description of the atmosphere of the play and of Coleridge in his statement of the frame of mind in which Juliet drinks the potion are well taken.

Dowden is respectful of Schlegel, whom Wordsworth and Hazlitt had spoken of as the fountain-head of Shakespearean criticism, but he is contemptuous of the later German critics. Writing with a good deal of nationalistic feeling and intent on proving that Shakespeare, in spite of all temptation to belong spiritually to nineteenth-century Germany, was a true-blue Englishman, he continually condemns the Germans as mystical, narrowly moralistic, and pedantic. Although Dowden is almost always right, his ardor may sometimes lead him to react too sharply. If Romeo's words are, as he says in answering Gervinus's statement that Friar Laurence has a choric function, "at least as true as the Friar's," then the Friar's words also contain a truth which Dowden slights, thereby reducing the complexity of the play.

ATMOSPHERE AND CHARACTER IN ROMEO AND JULIET

THE EXTERNAL ATMOSPHERE of the tragedy of Romeo and Juliet, its Italian colour and warmth, have been so finely felt by M. Philarète Chasles that his words deserve to be a portion of every criticism of that play.—"Who does not recall those lovely summer nights, in which the forces of nature seem eager for development, and constrained to remain in drowsy languor—a mingling of intense heat, superabundant energy, impetuous power, and silent freshness?

"The nightingale sings in the depths of the woods. The flower-cups are half-closed. A pale lustre is shed over the foliage of the forests, and upon the brow of the hills. The deep repose conceals, we are aware, a procreant force; the melancholy reserve of nature is the mask of a passionate emotion. Under the paleness and the coolness of the night you divine restrained ardours, and flowers which brood in silence, impatient to shine forth.

"Such is the peculiar atmosphere with which Shakspere has enveloped one of his most wonderful creations—Romeo and Juliet.

"Not only the substance, but the forms of the language come from the South. Italy was the inventor of the tale: she drew it from her national memorials, her old family-feuds, her annals filled with amorous and bloody intrigues. In its lyric accent, its blindness of passion, its blossoming and abundant vitality, in the brilliant imagery, in the bold composition, no one can fail to recognise Italy. Romeo utters himself like a sonnet of Petrarch, with the same refined choice, and the same antitheses; there is the same grace and the same pleasure in versifying passion in allegorical stanzas. Juliet, too, is wholly the woman of Italy; with small gift of forethought, and absolutely ingenuous in her *abandon,* she is at once vehement and pure."[1]

The season is midsummer. It wants a fortnight and odd days of Lammastide (August 1st). Wilhelm Schlegel, and after him Hazlitt, have spoken as if the atmosphere of the play were that of a southern spring. Such a criticism indicates a want of sensibility to the tone and colouring of the piece. The mid-July heat broods over the five tragic

"Atmosphere and Character in *Romeo and Juliet*" is from *Shakspere: His Mind and Art.*

[1] Études sur W. Shakspeare, Marie Stuart et L'Arétin, pp. 141–42.

days of the story. The mad blood is stirring in men's veins during these hot summer days.[2] There is a thunderous feeling in the moral element. The summer was needed also that the nights and mornings might quickly meet. The nights are those luminous nights from which the daylight seems never wholly to depart, nights through which the warmth of day still hangs over the trees and flowers. . . .

Romeo is not the determiner of events in the play. He does not stand prominently forward, a single figure in the first scene, as does Marlowe's Barabas, and Shakspere's Richard III., soliloquising about his own persons and his plans. The first scene of the play prepares a place for Romeo, it presents the moral environment of the hero, it exhibits the feud of the houses which determines the lovers' fate, although they for a brief space forget these grim realities in the rapture of their joy. The strife of the houses Capulet and Montague appears in this first scene in its trivial, ludicrous aspect; threatening, however, in a moment to become earnest and formidable. The serving men Gregory and Samson biting thumbs at the serving-men Abraham and Balthasar,—this is the obverse of the tragic show. Turn to the other side, and what do we see? The dead bodies of young and beautiful human creatures, of Tybalt and Paris, of Juliet and Romeo, the bloody harvest of the strife. This first scene, half ludicrous, but wholly grave, was written not without a reference to the final scene. The bandying of vulgar wit between the servants must not hide from us a certain grim irony which underlies the opening of the play. Here the two old rivals meet; they will meet again. And the prince appears in the last scene as in the first. Then old Capulet and Montague will be pacified; then they will consent to let their desolated lives decline to the grave in quietness. Meanwhile serving-men with a sense of personal dignity must bite their thumbs, and other incidents may happen.

Few critics of the play have omitted to call attention to the fact that Shakspere represents Romeo as already in love before he gives his heart to Juliet, in love with the pale-cheeked, dark-eyed, disdainful Rosaline. "If we are right," Coleridge wrote, ". . . in pronouncing this one of Shakspere's early dramas, it affords a strong instance of the fineness of his insight into the nature of the passions, that Romeo is introduced already love-bewildered." The circumstance is not of

---

[2] *Benvolio.*—"For now these hot days is the mad blood stirring." See the extract from Dr Theodor Sträter in H. H. Furness's Variorum Edition of Romeo and Juliet, pp. 461–62.

Shakspere's invention. He has retained it from Brooke's poem; but that he thought fit to retain the circumstance, fearlessly declaring that Romeo's supreme love is not his first love, is noteworthy. The contrast in the mind of the earlier poet between Rosaline, who

> From her youth was fostered evermore
> With vertues foode, and taught in schole, of wisdomes skilfull lore,

and Juliet, who yields to her passion, and by it is destroyed, was a contrast which Shakspere rejected as a piece of formal and barren morality. Of what character is the love of Romeo for Rosaline? Romeo's is not an active practical nature like Henry V.; neither is he great by intellect, a thinker in any high sense of the word. But if he lives and moves and has his being neither heroically in the objective world of action, like Henry V., nor in the world of the mind like Hamlet, all the more he lives, moves, and has his being in the world of mere emotion. To him emotion which enriches and exalts itself with the imagination, emotion apart from thought, and apart from action, is an end in itself. Therefore it delights him to hover over his own sentiment, to brood upon it, to feed upon it richly. Romeo must needs steep his whole nature in feeling, and, if Juliet does not appear, he must love Rosaline.

Nevertheless the love of Rosaline cannot be to Romeo as is the love of Juliet. It is a law in moral dynamics, too little recognised, that the breadth, and height, and permanence of a feeling depend in a certain degree at least upon the actual force of its external cause. No ardour of self-protection, no abandonment prepense, no self-sustained energy, can create and shape a passion of equal volume, and possessing a like certainty and directness of advance with a passion shaped, determined, and for ever re-invigorated by positive, objective fact. Shakspere had become assured that the facts of the world are worthy to command our highest ardour, our most resolute action, our most solemn awe; and that the more we penetrate into fact the more will our nature be quickened, enriched, and exalted. The play of Romeo and Juliet exhibits to us the deliverance of a man from dream into reality. In Romeo's love of Rosaline we find represented the dream-life as yet undisturbed, the abandonment to emotion for emotion's sake. Romeo nurses his love; he sheds tears; he cultivates solitude; he utters his groans in the hearing of the comfortable friar; he stimulates his fancy with the sought-out phrases, the curious antitheses of the amorous dialect of the period.

> Why, then, O brawling love! O loving hate!
> O anything, of nothing first create!
> O heavy lightness! Serious vanity!
> Mis-shapen chaos of well-seeming forms!
> Feather of lead, bright smoke, cold fire, sick health!

He broods upon the luxury of his sorrow. And then Romeo meets Juliet. Juliet is an actual force beyond and above himself, a veritable fact of the world. Nevertheless there remains a certain clinging self-consciousness, an absence of perfect simplicity and directness even in Romeo's very real love of Juliet. This is placed by Shakspere in designed contrast with the singleness of Juliet's nature, her direct unerroneous passion which goes straight to its object, and never broods upon itself. It is Romeo who says in the garden scene,—

> How silver-sweet sound lovers' tongues by night,
> Like softest music to attending ears.

He has overheard the voice of Juliet, and he cannot answer her call until he has drained the sweetness of the sound. He is one of those men to whom the emotional atmosphere which is given out by the real object, and which surrounds it like a luminous mist, is more important than the reality itself. As he turns slowly away, loath to leave, Romeo exclaims,—

> Love goes toward love, as school-boys from their books,
> But love from love, towards school with heavy looks.

But Juliet's first thought is of the danger to which Romeo is exposed in her father's grounds. It is Juliet who will not allow the utterance of any oath because the whole reality of that night's event, terrible in its joy, has flashed upon her, and she, who lives in no golden haze of luxurious feeling, is aroused and alarmed by the sudden shock of too much happiness. It is Juliet who uses direct and simple words—

> Farewell compliment!
> Dost thou love me? I know thou wilt say "Ay,"
> And I will take thy word.

She has declared that her bounty is measureless, that her love is infinite, when a sudden prosaic interruption occurs; the nurse calls within, Juliet leaves the window, and Romeo is left alone. Is this new joy a dream?

> O blessed, blessed night! I am afeard,
> Being in night, all this is but a dream,
> Too flattering-sweet to be substantial.

But Juliet hastily reappears with words upon her lips which make it evident that it is no dream of joy in which she lives.

> Three words, dear Romeo, and good night indeed.
> If that thy bent of love be honourable,
> Thy purpose marriage, send me word to-morrow,
> By one that I'll procure to come to thee,
> Where, and what time thou wilt perform the rite,
> And all my fortunes at thy foot I'll lay,
> And follow thee, my lord, throughout the world.

The wholeness and crystalline purity of Juliet's passion is flawed by no double self. She is all and entire in each act of her soul. While Romeo, on the contrary, is as yet but half delivered from self-consciousness. . . .

Juliet at once takes the lead. It is she who proposes and urges on the sudden marriage. She is impatient for complete self-surrender, eager that the deed should become perfect and irreversible. When, after the death of Tybalt, Romeo learns from the lips of the Friar that he has been condemned to banishment he is utterly unmanned. He abandons himself to helpless and hopeless despair. He turns the tender emotion upon himself, and extracts all the misery which is contained in that one word "banished." He throws himself upon the ground and grovels pitifully in the abjectness of his dismay. His will is unable to deal with his own emotions so as to subdue or control them. Upon the next day, after her casting away of her own kindred, after her parting with her husband, Juliet comes to the same cell of Friar Laurence, her face pale and traces of tears upon it which she cannot hide. Paris, the lover whom her father and mother have designed for Juliet, is there. She meets him with gay words, gallantly concealing the heart which is eager and trembling, and upheld from desperation only by a high-strung fortitude. Then when the door is shut her heart relieves itself, and she urges the Friar, with passionate energy, to devise forthwith a remedy for the evil that has befallen.

In her home Juliet is now without adviser or sustainer; a girl of fourteen years, she stands the centre of a circle of power which is tyrannous, and pledged to crush her resistance; old Capulet (the Capulets are a fiery self-willed race, unlike the milder Montagues) has vehemently urged upon her the marriage with Count Paris. She turns her pale face upon her father, and addresses him appealingly.[3]

> Good father, I beseech you on my knees
> Hear me with patience but to speak a word.

She turns to her mother,—the proud Italian matron, still young, who had not married for love, whose hatred is cold and deadly, and whose relation with the child, who is dear to her, is pathetically imperfect.

> Is there no pity sitting in the clouds,
> That sees into the bottom of my grief?
> O sweet my mother, cast me not away!
> Delay this marriage for a month, a week.

Last she looks for support to her Nurse, turning in that dreadful moment with the instinct of childhood to the woman on whose breast she had lain, and uttering words of desperate and simple earnestness:—

> O God! O nurse! how shall this be prevented?
> . . . .
> Some comfort, nurse.

The same unfaltering severity with which a surgeon operates is shown by Shakspere in his fidelity here to the nurse's character. The gross and wanton heart, while the sun of prosperity is full, blossoms into broad vulgarity; and the raillery of Mercutio deals with it sufficiently. Now in the hour of trial her grossness rises to the dignity of a crime. "The Count is a lovely gentleman; Romeo's a dishclout to him; the second match excels the first; or if it does not, Juliet's first is dead, or as good as dead, being away from her." "This moment," Mrs. Jameson has finely said, "reveals Juliet to herself. She does not break into upbraidings; it is no moment for anger; it is incredulous amazement, succeeded by the extremity of scorn and abhorrence, which

---

[3] Shakspere, as Mr Clark notices, contrives to bring before us the paleness of Juliet's face in this great crisis of her life, dramatically, by means of old Capulet's vituperative terms:—
> Out you green-sickness carrion! out you baggage!
> You tallow face!

takes possession of her mind. She assumes at once and asserts all her own superiority, and rises to majesty in the strength of her despair." Here Juliet enters into her solitude.

The Friar has given Juliet a phial containing a strange, untried mixture, and she is alone in her chamber. Juliet's soliloquy ends with one of those triumphant touches by which Shakspere glorified that which he appropriated from his originals. In Brooke's poem, Juliet swallows the sleeping-potion hastily lest her courage should fail. "Shakspere," Coleridge wrote, "provides for the finest decencies. It would have been too bold a thing for a girl of fifteen;—but she swallows the draught in a fit of fright." This deprives Juliet of all that is most characteristic in the act. In the night and the solitude, with a desperate deed to do, her imagination is intensely and morbidly excited. All the hideous secrets of the tomb appear before her. Suddenly in her disordered vision the figure of the murdered Tybalt rises, and is manifestly in pursuit of some one. Of whom? Not of Juliet, but of her lover who had slain him. A moment before Juliet had shrunk with horror from the thought of confronting Tybalt in the vault of the Capulets. But now Romeo is in danger. All fear deserts her. To stand by Romeo's side is her one necessity. With a confused sense that this draught will somehow place her close to the murderous Tybalt, and close to Romeo whom she would save, calling aloud to Tybalt to delay one moment,—"Stay, Tybalt, stay!"—she drains the phial, not "in a fit of fright," but with the words "Romeo! I come; this do I drink to thee."

The brooding nature of Romeo, which cherishes emotion, and lives in it, is made salient by contrast with Mercutio, who is all wit, and intellect, and vivacity, an uncontrollable play of gleaming and glancing life. Upon the morning after the betrothal with Juliet, a meeting happens between Romeo and Mercutio. Previously, while lover of Rosaline, Romeo had cultivated a lover-like melancholy. But now, partly because his blood runs gladly, partly because the union of soul with Juliet has made the whole world more real and substantial, and things have grown too solid and lasting to be disturbed by a laugh, Romeo can contend in jest with Mercutio himself, and stretch his wit of cheveril "from an inch narrow to an ell broad." Mercutio and the nurse are Shakspere's creations in this play. For the character of the former he had but a slight hint in the poem of Arthur Brooke. There we read of Mercutio as a courtier who was bold among the bashful maidens as a lion among lambs, and we are told that he had an "ice-cold hand." Putting together these two suggestions, discovering a significance in them, and animating them with the breath of his own life, Shakspere created the brilliant figure which lights up the first half of Romeo and Juliet, and disappears when the colours become all too grave and sombre.

Romeo has accepted the great bond of love. Mercutio, with his ice-cold hand, the lion among maidens, chooses above all things a defiant liberty, a liberty of speech, gaily at war with the proprieties, an airy freedom of fancy, a careless and masterful courage in dealing with life, as though it were a matter of slight importance. He will not attach himself to either of the houses. He is invited by Capulet to the banquet; but he goes to the banquet in company with Romeo and the Montagues. He can do generous and disinterested things; but he will not submit to the trammels of being recognised as generous. He dies maintaining his freedom, and defying death with a jest. To be made worm's meat of so stupidly, by a villain that fights by the book of arithmetic, and through Romeo's awkwardness, is enough to make a man impatient. "A plague o' both your houses!" The death of Mercutio is like the removal of a shifting breadth of sunlight, which sparkles on the sea; now the clouds close in upon one another, and the stress of the gale begins.[4]

The moment that Romeo receives the false tidings of Juliet's death, is the moment of his assuming full manhood. Now, for the first time, he is completely delivered from the life of dream, completely adult, and able to act with an initiative in his own will, and with manly determination. Accordingly, he now speaks with masculine directness and energy:—

> Is it even so? Then I defy you, stars!

Yes; he is now master of events; the stars cannot alter his course;

> Thou know'st my lodgings: get me ink and paper,
> And hire post-horses; I will hence to-night.
>   *Bal.* I do beseech you, sir, have patience.
> Your looks are pale and wild, and do import
> Some misadventure.

---

[4] The German Professor sometimes does not quite keep pace with Shakspere, and is heard stumbling heavily behind him. Gervinus thus describes Mercutio: "A man without culture, coarse and rude, ugly, a scornful ridiculer of all sensibility and love."

> *Rom.*   Tush! thou art deceiv'd.
> Leave me, and do the thing I bid thee do.
> Hast thou no letters to me from the Friar?
> *Bal.* No, my good lord.
> *Rom.*   No matter; get thee gone,
> And hire those horses; I'll be with thee straight.

"Nothing," as Maginn has observed, "can be more quiet than his final determination,

> Well, Juliet, I will lie with thee to-night.

It is plain Juliet. . . . There is nothing about 'Cupid's arrow,' or 'Dian's wit'; no honeyed word escapes his lips, nor again does any accent of despair. His mind is so made up; the whole course of the short remainder of his life so unalterably fixed that it is perfectly useless to think more about it."[5] These words because they are the simplest are amongst the most memorable that Romeo utters. Is this indeed the same Romeo who sighed, and wept, and spoke sonnet-wise, and penned himself in his chamber, shutting the daylight out for love of Rosaline? Now passion, imagination, and will, are fused together, and Romeo who was weak has at length become strong.

In two noteworthy particulars Shakspere has varied from his original. He has compressed the action from some months into four or five days. Thus precipitancy is added to the course of events and passions. Shakspere has also made the catastrophe more calamitous than it is in Brooke's poem. It was his invention to bring Paris across Romeo in the church-yard. Paris comes to strew his flowers, uttering in a rhymed sextain (such as might have fallen from Romeo's lips in the first Act), his pretty lamentation. Romeo goes resolutely forward to death. He is no longer "young Romeo," but adult, and Paris is the boy. He speaks with the gentleness, and with the authority of one who knows what life and death are, of one who has gained the superior position of those who are about to die over those who still may live:

> Good, gentle youth, tempt not a desperate man.
> Fly hence and leave me; think upon these gone;
> Let them affright thee. I beseech thee, youth,
> Put not another sin upon my head,
> By urging me to fury.

5 Shakespeare Papers, p. 99.

He would save Paris if that might be. But Paris still crosses Romeo, and he must needs be dealt with:

> Wilt thou provoke me? then have at thee, boy!

Romeo has now a definite object; he has a deed to do, and he will not brook obstacles.

Friar Laurence remains to furnish the Prince with an explanation of the events. It is impossible to agree with those critics, among others Gervinus, who represent the Friar as a kind of chorus expressing Shakspere's own ethical ideas, and his opinions respecting the characters and action. It is not Shakspere's practice to expound the moralities of his artistic creations; nor does he ever by means of a chorus stand above and outside the men and women of his plays, who are bone of his bone and flesh of his flesh. The nearest approach perhaps to a chorus, is to be found in the person of Enobarbus in Antony and Cleopatra. Hamlet commissions Horatio to report him and his cause aright to the unsatisfied; and Horatio placing the bodies of the dead upon a stage is about, in judicial manner, to declare the causes of things; but Shakspere declines to put on record for us the explanations made by Horatio. No! Friar Laurence also is moving in the cloud, and misled by error as well as the rest. Shakspere has never made the moderate, self-possessed, sedate person, a final or absolute judge of the impulsive and the passionate; the one sees a side of truth which is unseen by the other; but to neither is the whole truth visible. The Friar had supposed that by virtue of his prudence, his moderation, his sage counsels, his amiable sophistries, he could guide these two young, passionate lives, and do away the old tradition of enmity between the houses. There in the tomb of the Capulets is the return brought in by his investment of kindly scheming. Shakspere did not believe that the highest wisdom of human life was acquirable by mild, monastic meditation, and by gathering of simples in the coolness of the dawn. Friar Laurence too, old man, has his lesson to learn.

In accordance with his view that the Friar represents the chorus in this tragedy, Gervinus discovers as the leading idea of the piece a lesson of moderation; the poet makes his confession that "excess in any enjoyment, however pure in itself, transforms its sweet into bitterness, that devotion to any single feeling, however noble, bespeaks its ascendancy; that this ascendancy moves the man and woman out of their natural spheres."[6] It is somewhat hard upon Shakspere to suppose that he secreted in each of his dramas a central idea for a German critic to discover. But if there be a central idea in Romeo and Juliet can this be it? What! did Shakspere then mean that Romeo and Juliet loved too well? That all would have been better if they had surrendered their lives each to the other less rapturously, less absolutely? At what precise point ought a discreet regard for another human soul to check itself and say, "Thus far towards complete union will I advance, but here it is prudent to stop"? Or are not Romeo's words at least as true as the Friar's?

> Come what sorrow can,
> It cannot countervail the exchange of joy
> That one short minute gives me in her sight.
> Do thou but close our hands with holy words,
> Then love-devouring Death do what he dare,
> It is enough I may but call her mine.

Doubtless, also, Cordelia misunderstood the true nature of the filial relation; upon perceiving a possibility of defeat, she ought to have retreated to the safe coast of France. Portia upon hearing that the enemies of Brutus were making head, weakly "fell distract," and swallowed fire, not having learned that a well-balanced heart bestows upon a husband only a regulated moderation of love; Shakspere, by the example of Portia, would teach us that a penalty is paid for excess of wifely loyalty! No; this method of judging characters and actions by gross awards of pleasure and pain as measured by the senses does not interpret the ethics or the art of Shakspere, or of any great poet. Shakspere was aware that every strong emotion which exalts and quickens the inner life of man at the same time exposes the outer life of accident and circumstance to increased risk. But the theme of tragedy, as conceived by the poet, is not material prosperity or failure; it is spiritual; fulfilment or failure of a destiny higher than that which is related to the art of getting on in life. To die under certain conditions may be a higher rapture than to live.

Shakspere did not intend that the feeling evoked by the last scene of this tragedy of Romeo and Juliet should be one of hopeless sorrow or despair in presence of failure, ruin, and miserable collapse. Juliet and Romeo, to whom Verona has been a harsh step-mother,

[6] Shakespeare Commentaries, by Gervinus, translated by F. E. Bunnett. 1863. Vol. i. p. 293.

have accomplished their lives. They loved perfectly. Romeo had attained to manhood. Juliet had suddenly blossomed into heroic womanhood. Through her, and through anguish and joy, her lover had emerged from the life of dream into the waking life of truth. Juliet had saved his soul; she had rescued him from abandonment to spurious feeling, from abandonment to morbid self-consciousness, and the enervating luxury of emotion for emotion's sake. What more was needed? And as secondary to all this, the enmity of the houses is appeased. Montague will raise in pure gold the statue of true and faithful Juliet; Capulet will place Romeo by her side. Their lives are accomplished; they go to take up their place in the large history of the world, which contains many such things. Shakspere in this last scene carries forward our imagination from the horror of the tomb to the better life of man, when such love as that of Juliet and Romeo will be publicly honoured, and remembered by a memorial all gold.

HARLEY GRANVILLE-BARKER
1877-1946

A PRODUCER, ACTOR, and playwright with a scholar's knowledge of the Elizabethan theatre and a fine literary sensitivity, Harley Granville-Barker contributed notably to analyzing the stage-craft of Shakespeare's plays in the prefaces to the plays published at various times from 1927 and issued in two volumes in 1946 and 1947. In doing so, he took issue with the romantic view that Shakespeare's plays are imaginative creations which transcend the stage. Perhaps it can be said that each experience—the reading experience, in which one ponders over the subtleties of Shakespeare, and the theatrical experience, in which one joins in a communal response to a work whose art is directed toward its presentation on a stage—gives something that the other cannot give. To each kind of experience

Granville-Barker's criticism has contributed, for his work has not only helped to improve modern productions of Shakespeare but has enhanced the enjoyment of readers of Shakespeare.

In this excerpt from his preface to *Romeo and Juliet,* Granville-Barker shows how the Elizabethan unlocalized stage, that shifting scene to which the neoclassical critics had objected, made possible effects of tragic irony of which Shakespeare made rich use. The rapidity of action and the dramatic contrasts which Dowden had found in the play assume greater significance as distinguishing characteristics.

TRAGIC IRONY IN ROMEO AND JULIET

To APPRAISE THE value of the next effect he makes we must again visualize the Elizabethan stage.[1] Below

Enter Capulet, Lady Capulet and Paris.

With Tybalt hardly buried, Juliet weeping for him, it has been no time for urging Paris' suit.

'Tis very late [says Capulet], she'll not come down to-night:
I promise you, but for your company,
I should have been a-bed an hour ago.

Paris takes his leave, asks Lady Capulet to commend him to her daughter. She answers him:

I will, and know her mind early to-morrow;
To-night she's mewed up to her heaviness.

But *we* know that, at this very moment, Romeo and Juliet, bride and bridegroom, are in each other's arms.

"Tragic Irony in *Romeo and Juliet*" is from Harley Granville-Barker, *Prefaces to Shakespeare* (Princeton University Press, 1947), II, 315–317, 318–319. By permission of the publisher.
[1] But we must do this throughout.

Paris is actually at the door, when, with a sudden impulse, Capulet recalls him.[2]

> Sir Paris, I will make a desperate tender
> Of my child's love. I think she will be ruled
> In all respects by me; nay, more, I doubt it not.
> Wife, go you to her ere you go to bed;
> Acquaint her here of my son Paris' love,
> And bid her, mark you me, on Wednesday next . . .

And by that sudden impulse, so lightly obeyed, the tragedy is precipitated. Capulet, bitten by an idea, is in a ferment.

> Well, Wednesday is too soon;
> O' Thursday let it be:—o' Thursday, tell her,
> She shall be married to this noble earl.
> Will you be ready? Do you like this haste? . . .

(In a trice he has shaken off the mourning uncle and turned jovial, roguish father-in-law.)

> Well, get you gone! O' Thursday be it then.—
> Go you to Juliet ere you go to bed,
> Prepare her, wife, against this wedding day. . . .

(What, we are asking, will Lady Capulet find if she does go?)

> Farewell, my lord.—Light to my chamber, ho!
> Afore me, it's so very late
> That we may call it early by and by:—
> Good-night.

Now comes the well-prepared effect. Hardly have the three vanished below, bustling and happy; when with

> Wilt thou begone? It is not yet near day. . . .

Juliet and Romeo appear at the window above, clinging together, agonized in the very joy of their union, but all ignorant of this new and deadly blow which (again) *we* know is to fall on them.

Only the unlocalized stage is capable of just such an effect as this. Delay in the shifting of scenery may be overcome by the simple lift-

[2] And we may rely on this as one of the very few authenticated pieces of Shakespearean "business." For Q1 says,
Paris offers to goe in and Capolet calls him againe.
If the presumed reporter watching the performance thought it important and had the time to note this down, it must have been markedly done.

ing of a front scene to discover Romeo and Juliet in her chamber behind it; but Shakespeare's audience had not even to shift their imaginations from one place to another. The lower stage was anywhere downstairs in Capulet's house. The upper stage was associated with Juliet; it had served for her balcony and had been put to no other use.[3] So while Capulet is planning the marriage with Paris not only will our thoughts have been traveling to her, but our eyes may have rested speculatively, too, on those closed curtains above. . . .

We come now to another and still more important effect, that is (yet again) only to be realized in the theater for which it was designed. The curtains of the inner stage are drawn back to show us Juliet's bed. Her nurse and her mother leave her; she drinks the potion, and—says that note-taker at the performance, whose business it was, presumably, to let his employers know exactly how all the doubtful bits were done—

She falls upon the bed within the curtains.

There has been argument upon argument whether this means the curtains of the bed or of the inner stage—which would then close on her. The difference in dramatic effect will be of degree and not kind. What Shakespeare aims at in the episodes that follow is to keep us conscious of the bed and its burden; while in front of it, Capulet and the servants, Lady Capulet and the Nurse pass hither and thither, laughing and joking over the preparation for the wedding, till the bridal music is playing, till, to the very sound of this, the Nurse bustles up to draw back the curtains and disclose the girl there stark and still.[4]

This is one of the chief dramatic effects of the play; and it can only be gained by preserving the continuity of the action, with its agonies and absurdities cheek by jowl, with that bridal music sharpening the

[3] The musicians at Capulet's supper would probably have sat in it; but this is hardly a dramatic use. Nor does the mere association with Juliet *localize* it. There is no such scientific precision in the matter.

[4] To Shakespeare's audience it would make little matter which sort of curtains they were. A closed bed standing shadowed on the inner stage is at once to be ignored and recognized. We also, with a little practice, can ignore it, with Capulet; though to our more privileged gaze there it significantly is, in suspended animation, as it were, till the Nurse, fingering its curtains, brings it back to dramatic life, as we have known she must, as we have been waiting breathlessly for her to do. Whether they should be bed curtains or stage curtains is a matter of convention, a question of more imagination or less.

irony at the last. It is a comprehensive effect, extending from the drinking of the potion to the Nurse's parrot scream when she finds Juliet stiff and cold; and even beyond, to the coming of the bridegroom and his train, through the long-spoken threnody, to the farce of the ending—which helps to remind us that, after all, Juliet is not dead. It is one scene, one integral stretch of action; and its common mutilation by *Scene iv. Hall in Capulet's house . . . Scene v. Juliet's chamber. Enter Nurse . . .* , with the consequences involved, is sheer editorial murder.

SAMUEL TAYLOR COLERIDGE
1772-1834

NEO-CLASSICAL CRITICISM had been enthusiastic about the first scene of *Hamlet,* but it had not examined it in relation to the rest of the play. Coleridge, regarding the plays as organic unities, looked at the opening scenes as the embryos from which the rest of the plays developed. His suggestive discussion of the opening scene of *Hamlet* pays tribute to Shakespeare's truth to general human nature, comparing the psychological state of the sentries with that of historical persons in similar situations, but it does more than that. It is closely analytic, paying attention to diction and imagery as well as to character analysis and stage effects. It is aware of *Hamlet* as poetic drama both conventionalistic and naturalistic ("the language of nature," says Coleridge, is present in parts but not in "the whole composition"). But in analyzing the details it sees the scene as part of a whole.

THE FIRST SCENE OF HAMLET

BUT AS OF more importance, so more striking, is the judgment displayed by our truly dramatic poet, as well as poet of the drama, in the management of his first scenes. With the single exception of *Cymbeline,* they either place before us at one glance both the past and the future in some effect, which implies the continuance and full agency of its cause, as in the feuds and party-spirit of the servants of the two houses in the first scene of *Romeo and Juliet;* or in the degrading passion for shews and public spectacles, and the overwhelming attachment for the newest successful war-chief in the Roman people, already become a populace, contrasted with the jealousy of the nobles in *Julius Cæsar;*—or they at once commence the action so as to excite a curiosity for the explanation in the following scenes, as in the storm of wind and waves, and the boatswain in the *Tempest,* instead of anticipating our curiosity, as in most other first scenes, and in too many other first acts;—or they act, by contrast of diction suited to the characters, at once to heighten the effect, and yet to give a naturalness to the language and rhythm of the principal personages, either as that of Prospero and Miranda by the appropriate lowness of the style,—or as in *King John,* by the equally appropriate stateliness of official harangues or narratives, so that the after blank verse seems to belong to the rank and quality of the speakers, and not to the poet;—or they strike at once the key-note, and give the predominant spirit of the play, as in the *Twelfth Night* and in *Macbeth;*—or finally, the first scene comprises all these advantages at once, as in *Hamlet.*

Compare the easy language of common life, in which this drama commences, with the direful music and wild wayward rhythm and abrupt lyrics of the opening of *Macbeth.* The tone is quite familiar;—there is no poetic description of night, no elaborate information conveyed by one speaker to another of what both had immediately before their senses—(such as the first distich in Addison's *Cato,* which is a translation into poetry of 'Past four o'clock and a dark morning!');—and yet nothing bordering on the comic on the one hand, nor any striving of the intellect on the other. It is precisely the language of sensation among men who feared no charge of effeminacy

"The First Scene of *Hamlet*" is from Coleridge's *Lectures.*

for feeling, what they had no want of resolution to bear. Yet the armour, the dead silence, the watchfulness that first interrupts it, the welcome relief of the guard, the cold, the broken expressions of compelled attention to bodily feelings still under control—all excellently accord with, and prepare for, the after gradual rise into tragedy;—but, above all, into a tragedy, the interest of which is as eminently *ad et apud intra,* as that of *Macbeth* is directly *ad extra.*

In all the best attested stories of ghosts and visions, as in that of Brutus, of Archbishop Cranmer, that of Benvenuto Cellini recorded by himself, and the vision of Galileo communicated by him to his favourite pupil Torricelli, the ghost-seers were in a state of cold or chilling damp from without, and of anxiety inwardly. It has been with all of them as with Francisco on his guard,—alone, in the depth and silence of the night;—' 'twas bitter cold, and they were sick at heart, and *not a mouse stirring.*' The attention to minute sounds,—naturally associated with the recollection of minute objects, and the more familiar and trifling, the more impressive from the unusualness of their producing any impression at all—gives a philosophic pertinency to this last image; but it has likewise its dramatic use and purpose. For its commonness in ordinary conversation tends to produce the sense of reality, and at once hides the poet, and yet approximates the reader or spectator to that state in which the highest poetry will appear, and in its component parts, though not in the whole composition, really is, the language of nature. If I should not speak it, I feel that I should be thinking it;—the voice only is the poet's,—the words are my own. That Shakspeare meant to put an effect in the actor's power in the very first words—'Who's there?'—is evident from the impatience expressed by the startled Francisco in the words that follow—'Nay, answer me: stand and unfold yourself.' A brave man is never so peremptory, as when he fears that he is afraid. Observe the gradual transition from the silence and the still recent habit of listening in Francisco's—'I think I hear them'—to the more cheerful call out, which a good actor would observe, in the—'Stand ho! Who is there?' Bernardo's inquiry after Horatio, and the repetition of his name and in his own presence indicate a respect or an eagerness that implies him as one of the persons who are in the foreground; and the scepticism attributed to him,—

> Horatio says, 'tis but our fantasy;
> And will not let belief take hold of him—

prepares us for Hamlet's after eulogy on him as one whose blood
and judgment were happily commingled. The actor should also be
careful to distinguish the expectation of gladness of Bernardo's 'Welcome, Horatio!' from the mere courtesy of his 'Welcome, good
Marcellus!'

Now observe the admirable indefiniteness of the first opening out
of the occasion of all this anxiety. The preparation informative of
the audience is just as much as was precisely necessary, and no more;
—it begins with the uncertainty appertaining to a question:—

> *Mar.* What, has *this thing* appear'd again to-night?—

Even the word 'again' has its *credibilizing* effect. Then Horatio, the
representative of the ignorance of the audience, not himself, but by
Marcellus to Bernardo, anticipates the common solution—' 'tis but
our fantasy!' upon which Marcellus rises into

> This dreaded sight, twice seen of us—

which immediately afterwards becomes 'this apparition,' and that,
too, an intelligent spirit, that is, to be spoken to! Then comes the
confirmation of Horatio's disbelief;—

> Tush! tush! 'twill not appear!—

and the silence, with which the scene opened, is again restored in
the shivering feeling of Horatio sitting down, at such a time, and with
the two eye-witnesses, to hear a story of a ghost, and that, too, of a
ghost which had appeared twice before at the very same hour. In the
deep feeling which Bernardo has of the solemn nature of what he is
about to relate, he makes an effort to master his own imaginative
terrors by an elevation of style,—itself a continuation of the effort,—
and by turning off from the apparition, as from something which
would force him too deeply into himself, to the outward objects, the
realities of nature, which had accompanied it:—

> *Ber.* Last night of all,
> When yon same star, that's westward from the pole
> Had made his course to illume that part of heaven
> Where now it burns, Marcellus and myself,
> The bell then beating one—

This passage seems to contradict the critical law that what is told,
makes a faint impression compared with what is beholden; for it

does indeed convey to the mind more than the eye can see; whilst the interruption of the narrative at the very moment, when we are most intensely listening for the sequel, and have our thoughts diverted from the dreaded sight in expectation of the desired, yet almost dreaded, tale—this gives all the suddenness and surprise of the original appearance;—

> *Mar.* Peace, break thee off; look, where it comes again!—

Note the judgment displayed in having the two persons present, who, as having seen the Ghost before, are naturally eager in confirming their former opinions,—whilst the sceptic is silent, and after having been twice addressed by his friends, answers with two hasty syllables —'Most like,'—and a confession of horror:

> —It harrows me with fear and wonder.

O heaven! words are wasted on those who feel, and to those who do not feel the exquisite judgment of Shakspeare in this scene, what can be said?—Hume himself could not but have had faith in this Ghost dramatically, let his anti-ghostism have been as strong as Sampson against other ghosts less powerfully raised. . . .

G. WILSON KNIGHT
1897-

G. WILSON KNIGHT is the author of a series of books on Shakespeare: *Myth and Miracle* (1929), *The Wheel of Fire* (1930), *The Imperial Theme* (1932), *The Shakespearian Tempest* (1932), *Principles of Shakespearian Production* (1936), *The Crown of Life* (1947), *The Mutual Flame* (1955) and *The Sovereign Flower* (1958). These have had a more profound influence than the work of any other critic of our generation. A neo-romantic, Knight resembles Coleridge, whose flow of rhetoric intoxicated (and stupified) his hearers, except that Knight has devoted the energy which Coleridge expended in talk to writing. As with Coleridge, the reaction of his audience has not been uniform. He has provoked some sharp comments from historical critics. But as he himself once complained, commentators will often warn their readers to be wary of his subjective interpretations at the same time that they borrow freely from him what suits them. The commentators are right in their warnings, and he is right in his complaint. Knight is a critic of unusual suggestiveness who has enabled us to see Shakespeare differently, but the visionary flashes which shoot forth like lightning from his frequently cloudy prose may distort as well as illuminate. Such a vision, however, is preferable to poking about in the darkness with a pocket flashlight.

Revolutionary as he is, Knight is, as he himself has claimed, in the tradition of Shakespearean criticism. In demanding interpretative rather than judicial criticism and in regarding the plays as obeying self-imposed laws, he is clearly following the romantics. His animadversions on the psychological analysis of character as being based on an analogy with real life that disregards the "peculiar atmosphere" of each play and his dictum that "the commentator must be true to his artistic, not his normal, ethic" in discussing character are in agreement with Bradley's view and go back to Lamb, who said, "While we are reading any of his great criminal characters—Macbeth, Richard, even Iago—we think not so much of the crimes which they commit, as of the ambition, the aspiring spirit, the intellectual activity, which prompts them to overleap those moral fences." For the great romantic critics and their followers, if not for their epigones, Shakespeare's characters are not the ordinary human beings of the real world but supermen moving in a poetic world created by Shakespeare. Hence the romantic imagination, tending to think symbolically and not merely in terms of art as mirroring nature, anticipated Knight's symbolistic criticism in such statements as Coleridge's that *King Lear* is a picture "more terrific than any which a Michel Angelo, inspired by a Dante, could have conceived."

Although Knight is not in sympathy with the work of the historical scholars, his own criticism has anticipated and corroborated much of what students of Elizabethan intellectual history have had to say, and their work in turn has reinforced a good many of his interpretations. His description of Shakespeare's use throughout his drama of certain images (raging tempests, oceans swallowing up land, rivers in angry flood overflowing their banks, unrestrained weeping) to suggest disturbances in the natural order of the universe, of the state, and of man, and other images (harmonious music, gentle breezes, rivers flowing gently to the ocean) to suggest the smooth operation of natural law on the universal scale, social concord, the well-integrated personality, and love is in keeping with Tillyard's scholarly re-discovery of the Elizabethan world-picture, with its concepts of interrelated cosmic, social and psychological orders, of creation as held together by God's love, of which human love is an expression, and of the universe and the state as constituting musical harmonies. The analogies with Christ and the biblical echoes which he has found are also in keeping with the Elizabethan analogical habit of thinking pointed out by Tillyard, L. A. Cormican, and others. The "hate-theme" (cynicism toward love, disgust at the physical, revulsion from life and dismay at death) which he has found to be significant in the plays from 1599 to 1611 can be understood as an expression of that current of thought and feeling which Theodore Spencer has called the "Counter-Renaissance."

In the extract from an essay on *Hamlet* which follows, Knight discusses "that unique mental or spiritual experience of the hero which is at the heart of the play." In doing so, he succeeds in saying something startling (if not entirely new) about the character most discussed in the world's literature. Bradley, after reviewing the different types of interpretation of Hamlet's character (the delicate, gentle youth of Goethe, the irresolute philosopher of Schlegel-Coleridge-Dowden, the energetic hero deterred by external obstacles of Werder) had presented his own interpretation of Hamlet as an idealistic young man of high moral sensibility who in the play is disabled, despite his strength of character, by the profound depression attendant upon disillusionment. Knight, without really contradicting Bradley, changes the focus. He dwells on Hamlet's nihilistic cynicism, seeing him as a figure of death. In a later essay in the revised edition of *The Wheel of Fire* he qualifies what he says in "The Embassy of Death":

> I challenged the obvious reading of Hamlet as wholly— or almost wholly—sympathetic and Claudius as a thorough stage villain. To that challenge I still, in general, adhere, with this reservation; that the obvious reading is, as it were, assumed and supposed to be modified, not dispelled, by the new remarks.

Knight's change of emphasis from Bradley, his dwelling upon what Lamb called the "harsh and unpleasant . . . temporary deformities in the character" of Hamlet which we "explain by the whole of his character" (although certainly exaggerated in portions of the essay not here reprinted) is not merely arbitrary. It brings out more sharply the complexity of a play in which the frame of mind of the hero is opposed to life almost until its conclusion. It might be noted that Knight's interpretation of *Hamlet* is in keeping with the findings of Lawrence Babb, in *The Elizabethan Malady* (1951), on the Elizabethan idea of the melancholiac and with those of Fredson Bowers, in *Elizabethan Revenge Tragedy* (1940), on the Elizabethan attitude toward the malcontent revenger.

THE EMBASSY OF DEATH:
AN ESSAY ON HAMLET

IN THIS FIRST section I shall indicate the nature of Hamlet's mental suffering. It will then be clear that many of the scenes and incidents which have proved difficult in the past may be considered as expressions of that unique mental or spiritual experience of the hero which is at the heart of the play. In thus isolating this element for analysis I shall attempt to simplify at least one theme—and that the most important one—in a play baffling and difficult in its totality. My purpose will therefore be first limited strictly to a discussion, not of the play as a whole, nor even of Hamlet's mind as a whole, but of this central reality of pain, which, though it be necessarily related, either as effect or cause, to the events of the plot and to the other persons, is itself ultimate, and should be the primary object of our search.

Our attention is early drawn to the figure of Hamlet. Alone in the gay glitter of the court, silhouetted against brilliance, robustness, health, and happiness, is the pale, black-robed Hamlet, mourning. When first we meet him, his words point the essential inwardness of his suffering:

> But I have that within which passeth show;
> These but the trappings and the suits of woe.   (I. ii. 85)

When he is alone he reveals his misery more clearly:

> O, that this too too solid flesh would melt,
> Thaw and resolve itself into a dew!
> Or that the Everlasting had not fix'd
> His canon 'gainst self-slaughter! O God! O God!
> How weary, stale, flat, and unprofitable
> Seem to me all the uses of this world!
> Fie on't! ah fie! 'tis an unweeded garden,
> That grows to seed; things rank and gross in nature
> Possess it merely.   (I. ii. 129)

"The Embassy of Death: An Essay on *Hamlet*" is from G. Wilson Knight, *The Wheel of Fire* (Methuen, London, 1949), pp. 17–30. By permission of the publisher.

The mood expressed by these lines is patent. To Hamlet the light has been extinguished from the things of earth. He has lost all sense of purpose. We already know one reason for Hamlet's state: his father's death. Claudius and his mother have already urged him to

> throw to earth
> This unprevailing woe . . .   (I. ii. 106)

Now, during Hamlet's soliloquy, we see another reason: disgust at his mother's second marriage:

> . . . within a month:
> Ere yet the salt of most unrighteous tears
> Had left the flushing in her galled eyes,
> She married. O, most wicked speed, to post
> With such dexterity to incestuous sheets!   (I. ii. 153)

These two concrete embodiments of Hamlet's misery are closely related. He suffers from misery at his father's death and agony at his mother's quick forgetfulness: such callousness is infidelity, and so impurity, and, since Claudius is the brother of the King, incest. It is reasonable to suppose that Hamlet's state of mind, if not wholly caused by these events, is at least definitely related to them. Of his two loved parents, one has been taken for ever by death, the other dishonoured for ever by her act of marriage. To Hamlet the world is now an 'unweeded garden.'

Hamlet hears of his father's Ghost, sees it, and speaks to it. His original pain is intensified by knowledge of the unrestful spirit, by the terrible secrets of death hinted by the Ghost's words:

> I could a tale unfold whose lightest word
> Would harrow up thy soul, freeze thy young blood . . .
>   (I. v. 15)

This is added to Hamlet's sense of loss: this knowledge of the father he loved suffering in death:

> Doom'd for a certain term to walk the night,
> And for the day confin'd to fast in fires . . .   (I. v. 10)

Nor is this all. He next learns that his father's murderer now wears the crown, is married to his faithless mother. Both elements in his original pain are thus horribly intensified. His hope of recovery to the normal state of healthy mental life depended largely on his ability to forget his father, to forgive his mother. Claudius advised him well. Now his mother's honour is more foully smirched than ever; and the living cause and symbol of his father's death is firmly placed on Denmark's throne. Forgetfulness is impossible, forgetfulness that might have brought peace. The irony of the Ghost's parting word is terrible:

> Adieu, adieu! Hamlet, remember me.   (I. v. 91)

If the spirit had been kind, it would have prayed that Hamlet might forget. This is the Ghost's last injunction, the one most indelibly printed in Hamlet's mind:

> Remember thee!
> Ay, thou poor ghost, while memory hold a seat
> In this distracted globe. Remember thee!
> Yea, from the table of my memory
> I'll wipe away all trivial fond records . . .   (I. v. 95)

Confronted by his irrevocable fate Hamlet repeats the words:

> Now to my word,
> It is 'Adieu, Adieu! remember me.'
> I have sworn't.   (I. v. 110)

And he keeps his oath throughout the play.

When Horatio and Marcellus join him he relieves the unnatural tension of his mind by joking and laughter. As in *King Lear,* extreme mental agony tends towards expression in the region of the essentially comic. He makes his friends swear secrecy, thereby ensuring his future loneliness in the knowledge of the King's crime. He suggests that he may 'put an antic disposition on' (I. v. 172) to deceive the court. He cries out against the cruel fate that has laid on him, whose own soul is in chaos, the command of righting the evil in the state:

> O cursed spite,
> That ever I was born to set it right!   (I. v. 188)

Hamlet, when we first meet him, has lost all sense of life's significance. To a man bereft of the sense of purpose there is no possibility of creative action, it has no meaning. No act but suicide is rational. Yet to Hamlet comes the command of a great act—revenge: therein lies the unique quality of the play—a sick soul is commanded to heal, to cleanse, to create harmony. But good cannot come of evil: it is seen that the sickness of his soul only further infects the state—his dis-integration spreads out, disintegrating.

Hamlet's soul is sick to death—and yet there was one thing left that might have saved him. In the deserts of his mind, void with the utter vacuity of the knowledge of death—death of his father, death of his mother's faith—was yet one flower, his love of Ophelia.

> He hath, my lord, of late made many tenders
> Of his affection to me.   (I. iii. 99)

So speaks Ophelia to Polonius. Again:

> *Ophelia.* My lord, he hath importuned me with love
> In honourable fashion.
> *Polonius.* Ay, fashion you may call it; go to, go to.
> *Ophelia.* And hath given countenance to his speech, my lord,
> With almost all the holy vows of Heaven.   (I. iii. 110)

This was before Hamlet saw the Ghost: perhaps before his father's death. Now there is one supreme enemy to the demon of neurotic despair, its antithesis and bright antagonist: romantic love. For this has assured power, it can recreate the sense of purpose, it inspires to heroism and action. And it is self-creative. The lonely flower can soon overspread the desert with a multiplicity of colour and delight. The love of Ophelia is thus Hamlet's last hope. This, too, is taken from him. Her repelling of his letters and refusing to see him, in obedience to Polonius' command, synchronizes unmercifully with the terrible burden of knowledge laid on Hamlet by the revelation of the Ghost. The result is given to us indirectly—but with excruciating vividness:

> *Ophelia.* My lord, as I was sewing in my closet,
> Lord Hamlet, with his doublet all unbraced;
> No hat upon his head; his stockings foul'd,
> Ungarter'd, and down-gyved to his ankle;
> Pale as his shirt; his knees knocking each other;
> And with a look so piteous in purport
> As if he had been loosed out of Hell
> To speak of horrors—he comes before me.   (II. i. 77)

This is no mock-madness. To see it as such is to miss the power of the central theme of the play. Hamlet would not first try the practical joke of pretended madness on Ophelia whom he loved. That pallor was no cosmetic. Hamlet, indeed, was in truth 'loosed out of Hell to speak of horrors': on top of the Ghost's revelation has come Ophelia's unreasonable repulsion of that his last contact with life, his love for her. Therefore

> He took me by the wrist and held me hard;
> Then goes he to the length of all his arm;
> And, with his other hand thus o'er his brow,
> He falls to such perusal of my face
> As he would draw it. Long stay'd he so;
> At last, a little shaking of mine arm,
> And thrice his head thus waving up and down,
> He raised a sigh so piteous and profound
> As it did seem to shatter all his bulk
> And end his being . . .   (II. i. 87)

From henceforth he must walk alone within the prison of mental death. There is surely no more pitiful thing in literature than this description. Polonius sees the truth. 'This is the very ecstasy of love . . . ' he says. And he is right. If we remember that Hamlet loves Ophelia; that he has just seen his father's ghost; and that now Ophelia has refused to admit him—we need search no further for an explanation of Hamlet's behaviour. The suggestion that in these circumstances, at this moment in his history, he has the presence of mind to pretend madness to Ophelia is, indeed, a perversion of commentary.

It is, however, certain that Hamlet does simulate madness before the court, and the King and Queen are both rightly unwilling to relate this madness to Hamlet's love of Ophelia. Says the Queen, when she hears that Polonius thinks he has traced the true cause:

> I doubt it is no other but the main;
> His father's death, and our o'erhasty marriage.
>
>   (II. i. 56)

The King later decides that love is not the cause of Hamlet's trouble:

> Love! his affections do not that way tend.   (III. i. 171)

This is after Hamlet's meeting with Ophelia. Here the King is partly wrong, and again there is truth in Polonius' words:

>   . . . but yet do I believe
> The origin and commencement of his grief
> Sprung from neglected love . . .   (III. i. 185)

It is not the whole truth. Hamlet's pain is a complex of different themes of grief. But absolute loss of control is apparent only in his dealings with Ophelia. Three times after the Ghost scene he utterly loses mental control: first, in the incident narrated by Ophelia; second, in his meeting with her in III. i.; and third, in the Graveyard scene, with Laertes over Ophelia's body. On all other occasions his abnormal behaviour, though it certainly tends towards, and might even be called, madness in relation to his environment, is yet rather the abnormality of extreme melancholia and cynicism.

Throughout the middle scenes of the play we become more closely acquainted with Hamlet's peculiar disease. He is bitterly cynical:

. . . to be honest, as this world goes, is to be one man picked out of ten thousand.   (II. ii. 179)

And

Use every man after his desert, and who should 'scape whipping?
                                                   (II. ii. 561)

To Hamlet the world is a 'goodly' prison

in which there are many confines, wards, and dungeons, Denmark being one o' the worst.   (II. ii. 255)

His mind is drawn to images in themselves repellent, and he dwells on the thought of foulness as the basis of life:

For if the sun breed maggots in a dead dog . . .   (II. ii. 183)

Hamlet reads, or says he is reading, a satirical book, which observes that

. . . old men have grey beards, that their faces are wrinkled, their eyes purging thick amber and plum-tree gum, and that they have a plentiful lack of wit, together with most weak hams.   (II. ii. 202)

The body of an old man is shown as something stupid, unpleasant: and Hamlet means it. Now all this is integral to Hamlet's state of mind. He is well described in a passage by William James in another connexion:

. . . you see how the entire consciousness of the poor man is so choked with the feeling of evil that the sense of there being any good in the world is lost for him altogether. His attention excludes it, cannot admit it: the sun has left his heaven.

(*The Varieties of Religious Experience*, p. 149)

Hamlet's soul is sick. The symptoms are, horror at the fact of death and an equal detestation of life, a sense of uncleanliness and evil in the things of nature; a disgust at the physical body of man; bitterness, cynicism, hate. It tends towards insanity. All these elements are insistent in Hamlet. He can describe the glories of heaven and earth—but for him those glories are gone. And he knows not why. The disease is deeper than his loss of Ophelia, deeper than his mother's sexual impurity and his father's death. These are, like his mourning dress, the 'trappings and the suits of woe.' They are the outward symbols of it, the 'causes' of it: but the thing itself is ultimate, beyond causality. That is why the theme is here related to the supernatural, to the Ghost. He describes it thus:

I have of late—but wherefore I know not—lost all my mirth, foregone all custom of exercises; and indeed it goes so heavily with my disposition that this goodly frame, the earth, seems to me a sterile promontory; this most excellent canopy, the air, look you, this brave o'erhanging firmament, this majestical roof fretted with golden fire, why, it appears no other thing to me than a foul and pestilent congregation of vapours.   (II. ii. 313)

It will be clear that Hamlet's outstanding peculiarity in the action of this play may be regarded as a symptom of this sickness in his soul. He does not avenge his father's death, not because he dare not, not because he hates the thought of bloodshed, but because his 'wit's diseased' (III. ii. 341); his will is snapped and useless, like a broken leg. Nothing is worth while. After the player has worked himself into a tragic passion in the recitation of 'Aeneas' Tale to Dido,' Hamlet looks inward and curses and hates himself for his lack of passion, and then again he hates himself the more for his futile self-hatred. He cannot understand himself:

> . . . it cannot be
> But I am pigeon-liver'd and lack gall
> To make oppression bitter.   (II. ii. 612)

Aware of his own disease, he wonders if the spirit he has seen may be an evil spirit:

> The spirit that I have seen
> May be the Devil: and the Devil hath power
> To assume a pleasing shape; yea, and perhaps
> Out of my weakness and my melancholy,
> As he is very potent with such spirits,
> Abuses me to damn me.   (II. ii. 635)

This fear strikes nearer the truth than the comments of many Shakespearian scholars.

In Hamlet's interview with Ophelia we are again brought up against obvious symptoms of his spiritual atrophy. At first sight of her his love wells up instinctively:

> Nymph, in thy orisons
> Be all my sins remember'd.   (III. i. 89)

But he quickly recovers. The stupidity of love can have no place in his mind. Ophelia offers him back some old gifts. The voice of cynicism answers:

> No, not I;
> I never gave you aught.   (III. i. 95)

This is true. The Hamlet that gave those 'remembrances' is dead— dead as his father. The ghost of him alone hovers pathetically over this dialogue. His past love seems now to Hamlet a childish and absurd thing: he cannot admit he was ever so puerile as to be cheated by it. Between the sick soul and the knowledge of love there are all the interstellar spaces that divide Hell from Heaven: for Hell and Heaven are but spatial embodiments of these two modes of the spirit. Therefore:

Hamlet. Ha, ha! are you honest?
Ophelia. My lord?
Hamlet. Are you fair?
Ophelia. What means your lordship?
Hamlet. That if you be honest and fair, your honesty should admit no discourse to your beauty.
Ophelia. Could beauty, my lord, have better commerce than with honesty?
Hamlet. Ay, truly; for the power of beauty will sooner transform honesty from what it is to a bawd than the force of honesty can translate beauty into his likeness: this was sometime a paradox, but now the time gives it proof. I did love you once.
Ophelia. Indeed, my lord, you made me believe so.
Hamlet. You should not have believed me; for virtue cannot so inoculate our old stock but we shall relish of it: I loved you not.

(III. i. 103)

Hamlet denies the existence of romantic values. Love, in his mind, has become synonymous with sex, and sex with uncleanness. Therefore beauty is dangerous and unclean. Sick of the world, of man, of love, Hamlet denies the reality of his past romance: 'I loved you not.' This statement alone fits coherently into his diseased mind, and so it is, to him, the truth. He cannot have loved, since love is unreal: if it were real, there would be meaning, passion, purpose in existence. These things are gone and love must go too.

Next he curses himself, accuses himself of all the crimes he can think of. This, too, is what we expect. He has seen through all things, including himself, to the foulness within. In self-hatred he cries:

What should such fellows as I do crawling between earth and heaven?
(III. i. 132)

Therefore why should Ophelia be a 'breeder of sinners?' Why should anyone carry on the stupid act of procreation? Hamlet denies the significance of humanity. There is only one course for Ophelia whose beauty perhaps yet echoes in Hamlet's mind some faint rhythm, as from a different existence, of his old love—to cut herself off from contact with an unclean and aimless world:

. . . Go thy ways to a nunnery.
(III. i. 134)

At this point it seems that Hamlet becomes aware of the spies behind the arras. He realizes that Ophelia is a decoy. He breaks out into uncontrollable hatred and fury. He cries:

Go to, I'll no more on't; it hath made me mad.
(III. i. 155)

His words at the end of this scene are indeed 'wild and whirling.' He loses control and gives voice to the loathing that is in him, the cynicism that borders on madness. He has seen through love. Ophelia —once a goddess—is a stupid doll who 'lisps,' 'ambles,' and paints her face. Unjust, no doubt. It is truth to Hamlet's mind.

Hamlet in this scene is cruel to Ophelia: so too he is cruel to his mother later. He tortures both of them, because he once loved them. They agonize him with the remembrance of what they once were to him, of what he himself is now. There are often moments when reincarnations of what must have been his former courteous and kindly nature—of which we hear, but which we only see by fits and starts—break through the bitterness of Hamlet as he appears in the play, but they do not last: cynicism and consequent cruelty, born of the burden of pain within him, blight the spontaneous gentleness that occasionally shows itself, strangle it. There is a continual process of self-murder at work in Hamlet's mind. He is cruel to Ophelia and his mother. He exults in tormenting the King by the murder of Gonzago, and when he finds him conscience-stricken, at prayer, takes a demoniac pleasure in the thought of preserving his life for a more damning death:

> Up, sword; and know thou a more horrid hent:
> When he is drunk asleep, or in his rage,
> Or in the incestuous pleasure of his bed;
> At gaming, swearing, or about some act
> That has no relish of salvation in't;
> Then trip him, that his heels may kick at Heaven,
> And that his soul may be as damn'd and black
> As Hell, whereto it goes.   (III. iii. 88)

With a callousness and a most evident delight that shocks Horatio he sends his former school-friends to an undeserved death, 'not shriving time allowed,' again hoping to compass the eternal damnation of his enemy (v. ii. 47):

> *Horatio.* So Guildenstern and Rosencrantz go to't.
> *Hamlet.* Why, man, they did make love to this employment;
>   They are not near my conscience; their defeat
>   Does by their own insinuation grow:
>   'Tis dangerous when the baser nature comes
>   Between the pass and fell incensed points
>   Of mighty opposites.   (v. ii. 56)

Hamlet thus takes a devilish joy in cruelty towards the end of the play: he is like Iago. It is difficult to see the conventional courtly Prince of Denmark in these incidents. We have done ill to sentimentalize his personality. We have paid for it—by failing to understand him; and, failing to understand, we have been unable to sympathize with the demon of cynicism, and its logical result of callous cruelty, that has Hamlet's soul in its remorseless grip. Sentiment is an easy road to an unprofitable and unreal sympathy. Hamlet is cruel. He murders Polonius in error:

> Thou wretched, rash, intruding fool, farewell!
> I took thee for thy better: take thy fortune;
> Thou find'st to be too busy is some danger.   (III. iv. 31)

He proceeds from this to vile abuse of his own mother:

> Hamlet.   Nay, but to live
> In the rank sweat of an enseamed bed,
> Stew'd in corruption, honeying and making love
> Over the nasty sty—
> Queen.   O, speak to me no more;
> These words, like daggers, enter in mine ears;
> No more, sweet Hamlet!   (III. iv. 91)

At the end of his scene with his mother there is one beautiful moment
when Hamlet gains possession of his soul:

> For this same lord,
> I do repent: but Heaven hath pleased it so,
> To punish me with this, and this with me.   (III. iv. 172)

And his filial love wells up in:

> So, again, good-night.
> I must be cruel only to be kind:
> Thus bad begins and worse remains behind.   (III. iv. 177)

But it is short-lived. Next comes a long speech of the most withering,
brutal, and unnecessary sarcasm:

> Let the bloat king tempt you again to bed;
> Pinch wanton on your cheek; call you his mouse . . .
>   (III. iv. 182)

Even more horrible are his disgusting words about Polonius, whom
he has unjustly killed, to the King:

King. Now, Hamlet, where's Polonius?

Hamlet. At supper.

King. At supper! where?

Hamlet. Not where he eats, but where he is eaten: a certain convocation
of politic worms are e'en at him. Your worm is your only emperor for
diet: we fat all creatures else to fat us, and we fat ourselves for maggots:
your fat king and your lean beggar is but variable service, two dishes, but
to one table: that's the end.

King. Alas, alas!

Hamlet. A man may fish with the worm that hath eat of a king, and eat
of the fish that hath fed of that worm.

King. What dost thou mean by this?

Hamlet. Nothing but to show you how a king may go a progress
through the guts of a beggar.

King. Where is Polonius?

Hamlet. In Heaven; send thither to see: if your messenger find him not there, seek him i' the other place yourself. But indeed, if you find him not within this month, you shall nose him as you go up the stairs into the lobby.   (iv. iii. 17)

A long and unpleasant quotation, I know. But it is necessary. The horror of humanity doomed to death and decay has disintegrated Hamlet's mind. From the first scene to the last the shadow of death broods over this play. In the exquisite prose threnody of the Grave-yard scene the thought of physical death is again given utterance. There its pathos, its inevitability, its moral, are emphasized: but also its hideousness. Death is indeed the theme of this play, for Hamlet's disease is mental and spiritual death. So Hamlet, in his most famous soliloquy, concentrates on the terrors of an after life. The uninspired, devitalized intellect of a Hamlet thinks pre-eminently in terms of time. To him, the body disintegrates in time; the soul persists in time too; and both are horrible. His consciousness, functioning in terms of evil and negation, sees Hell but not Heaven. But the intuitive faith, or love, or purpose, by which we must live if we are to remain sane, of these things, which are drawn from a timeless reality within the soul, Hamlet is unmercifully bereft. Therefore he dwells on the foul appearances of sex, the hideous decay of flesh, the deceit of beauty either of the spirit or of the body, the torments of eternity if eternity exist. The universe is an 'unweeded garden,' or a 'prison,' the canopy of the sky but a 'pestilent congregation of vapours,' and man but a 'quintessence of dust,' waiting for the worms of death.

It might be objected that I have concentrated unduly on the un-pleasant parts of the play. It has been my intention to concentrate. They are the most significant parts. I have tried by various quotations and by suggestive phrases to indicate this sickness which eats into Hamlet's soul. Its nature is pointed further in the chapter entitled 'The Sick Soul' in *The Varieties of Religious Experience.* Now by empha-sizing these elements in the figure of Hamlet I have essayed to pluck out the heart of his mystery. And it will be clear that the elements which I have emphasized, the matter of Hamlet's madness, his patent cruelty, his coarse humour, his strange dialogue with Ophelia, his inability to avenge his father's death, are all equally related to the same sickness within. The coherence of these elements in the play must be evident. Creative action; love; passion—all these can find none but a momentary home in Hamlet's paralysed mind. Before the action of the play, Hamlet was, no doubt

> The glass of fashion and the mould of form.   (III. i. 162)

But that is over—or nearly over—when Ophelia speaks her lovely words. When we first meet Hamlet the poison has started its disintegrating work. During the rest of the play the outstanding peculiarities of him are his bitterness, his disillusionment, his utter loss of purpose: and many of his humorous speeches which are often performed as pleasant witticisms, or as playful mock-madness, would be more truly rendered with the scornful stare and grating voice of cynicism.

The impression of the play, as a whole, is not so gloomy as the main theme: if it were, it would not have been so popular. There are many individual scenes of action, passion, humour, and beauty, that take our thoughts from the essentially morbid impact of Hamlet's melancholia. Hamlet himself at times recovers his old instinctive friendliness, humour, and gentleness. We can guess what he was like before. That side of his nature which never quite dies, appearing intermittently until the end, is important: it lends point and pathos to the inroads of his cynicism and disgust. His mind wavers between the principle of good, which is love, and that of evil, which is loathing and cruelty. But too much emphasis has been laid on this element of Hamlet. The popularity of the play is not innocent of misunderstanding. To ignore the unpleasant aspects of Hamlet blurs our vision of the protagonist, the play as a whole, and its place in Shakespeare's work. The matter of the disease-theme in relation to the rest of the play is difficult. The total impression, the imaginative impact of the whole, leaves us with a sense of gaiety, health, superficiality, and colour, against which is silhouetted the pale black-robed figure of Hamlet who has seen what lies behind the smiles of benevolence, who has broken free of the folly of love because he has found its inward tawdriness and deceit, who knows that king and beggar alike are bound for the same disgusting 'convocation of worms,' and that even an 'indifferent honest' man is too vile to be 'crawling between heaven and earth.'

There is no fallacy in Hamlet's reasoning. We cannot pick on this or that of his most bitter words, and prove them false. The solitary and inactive figure of Hamlet is contrasted with the bustle and the

glitter of the court, the cancer of cynicism in his mind, himself a
discordant and destructive thing whose very presence is a poison
and a menace to the happiness and health of Denmark, fulfilling to
the letter the devilish command of the Ghost:

> Adieu, Adieu, Hamlet, remember me.   (I. v. 91)

Hamlet does not neglect his father's final behest—he obeys it, not
wisely but only too well. Hamlet remembers—not alone his father's
ghost, but all the death of which it is a symbol. What would have
been the use of killing Claudius? Would that have saved his mother's
honour, have brought life to his father's mouldering body, have
enabled Hamlet himself, who had so long lived in death, to have
found again childish joy in kisses of Ophelia? Would that have altered
the universal scheme? To Hamlet, the universe smells of mortality;
and his soul is sick to death.

SAMUEL TAYLOR COLERIDGE
1772-1834

COLERIDGE'S FAMOUS PHRASE, "the motive-hunting of
a motiveless malignity," in his discussion of Iago has
echoed through Shakespearean criticism. Hazlitt comments: "Some persons, more nice than wise, have
thought this whole character unnatural, because his
villainy is *without a sufficient motive*." This is not directed at Coleridge, for Coleridge was extolling rather
than finding fault with the characterization, but Hazlitt
is concerned with defending the psychological credi-
bility of Iago denied in the word "motiveless." He finds
Iago true to the general laws of human nature—Shakespeare "knew that the love of power, which is another
name for the love of mischief, is natural to man"—
although, expanding upon Coleridge's hint about Iago's
intellectuality and passionlessness, he also finds him to

be a remarkable character. Bradley holds that those who believe that Iago's action "springs from a 'motiveless malignity' " are "much nearer to Shakespeare's Iago" than most critics, who reduce him to "an ordinary villain"; nevertheless, Iago as a "motiveless malignity . . . is, if not a psychological impossibility, at any rate, not a *human* being. He might be in place, therefore, in a symbolical poem like *Faust,* but in a purely human drama like *Othello* he would be a ruinous blunder." Bradley's own interpretation of Iago, built upon Hazlitt and Swinburne, is that he is an extraordinary man, supremely wicked, but a man with "traces of conscience, shame and humanity," not an inhuman being. Stoll, however, finds that the conscience of which Bradley speaks is really the knowledge of the difference between good and evil of the stage Machiavel who, leagued with hell, is guided only by evil. This incarnate devil, to be sure, exists in Iago together with a character possessing the traits found by Hazlitt and his followers. There is the "rampant devil" of the soliloquies and the asides and there is the "Iago out in the world—and out of the limelight, as it were, of the Judgment Day." The whole, however, while psychologically impossible, is "alive and immortal" through "the individual tone and manner, the expression, the life-giving touch." Thus, while Stoll is not a symbolist critic, his interpretation of Iago leaves *Othello* open to being at once a human drama, if not a "purely human" one, and a "symbolical poem."

The wheel has, it would seem, come full circle, for these seem also to be implications of Coleridge's pregnant sentences. "Whilst he is still allowed to bear the divine image, it is too fiendish for his own steady view." The "still" indicates that Iago's "divine image," his human form, is only temporary and hints that after his death he will assume in hell the diabolic visage of the inner Iago revealed in his soliloquy. There is some difference between Coleridge and Stoll in that Coleridge holds that Iago shrinks from the contemplation of his own absolute wickedness, while Stoll finds that "the very accumulation of his motives and the uncertainty and flimsiness of his suspicions but show the hellishness of his purpose." But in each we have an Iago whose diabolical evil is inexplicable in terms of human psychology, a "motiveless malignity," co-existing with an Iago whose sentiments are "the true Iagoism of, alas! how many!" Coleridge's Iago, in conjunction with his reference to Desdemona as Othello's "angel," his allusion to Lucifer in the statement that Othello believes she has "fallen from the heaven of her native innocence" and his perception of the moral stature of Othello, prepares the way for the twentieth-century criticism of those who regard the play, at least on one level, as being, in the words of G. Wilson Knight, an "expanded metaphor."

THE MOTIVELESS MALIGNITY OF IAGO

ACT I. sc. 5. Iago's speech:—
Virtue? a fig! 'tis in ourselves, that we are thus, or thus, &c.
This speech comprises the passionless character of Iago. It is all will in intellect; and therefore he is here a bold partizan of a truth, but yet of a truth converted into a falsehood by the absence of all the necessary modifications caused by the frail nature of man. And then comes the last sentiment,—

Our raging motions, our carnal stings, our unbitted lusts, whereof I take this, that you call—love, to be a sect or scion!

Here is the true Iagoism of, alas! how many! Note Iago's pride of mastery in the repetition of 'Go, make money!' to his anticipated dupe, even stronger than his love of lucre: and when Roderigo is completely won—

I am chang'd. I'll go sell all my land—

"The Motiveless Malignity of Iago" is from Coleridge's *Lectures*.

when the effect has been fully produced, the repetition of triumph—

> Go to; farewell; put money enough in your purse!

The remainder—Iago's soliloquy—the motive-hunting of a motiveless malignity—how awful it is! Yea, whilst he is still allowed to bear the divine image, it is too fiendish for his own steady view,—for the lonely gaze of a being next to devil, and only not quite devil,—and yet a character which Shakspeare has attempted and executed, without disgust and without scandal! . . .

Finally, let me repeat that Othello does not kill Desdemona in jealousy, but in a conviction forced upon him by the almost superhuman art of Iago, such a conviction as any man would and must have entertained who had believed Iago's honesty as Othello did. We, the audience, know that Iago is a villain from the beginning; but in considering the essence of the Shakespearian Othello, we must perseveringly place ourselves in his situation, and under his circumstances. Then we shall immediately feel the fundamental difference between the solemn agony of the noble Moor, and the wretched fishing jealousies of Leontes, and the morbid suspiciousness of Leonatus, who is, in other respects, a fine character. Othello had no life but in Desdemona:—the belief that she, his angel, had fallen from the heaven of her native innocence, wrought a civil war in his heart. She is his counterpart; and, like him, is almost sanctified in our eyes by her absolute unsuspiciousness, and holy entireness of love. As the curtain drops, which do we pity the most?

PAUL N. SIEGEL
1916-

WHILE READING THIS excerpt the reader should remember my words in the previous selection: "Although there is suggested to the audience's imagination a heaven and a hell awaiting the outcome of the struggles of the characters, its attention is focused on this world, in which these struggles take place." In calling attention to what had been unduly neglected, the "afterlife of Christian religion" acting as "an imposing but faintly painted and unobtrusive backdrop for the action," I have concerned myself more with the backdrop than with the characters participating in that action, which have been analyzed at great length in previous criticism. But, in affirming against Bradley that *Othello* is indeed a "symbolical poem," I have not been unaware that it is also a "human drama."

The backdrop, however, is part of the presentation. To speak of the intimations of an afterlife contained in the play is not to leave the dramatic universe. Othello's words, "When we shall meet at compt, This look of thine will hurl my soul from heaven, And fiends will snatch at it," are similar in effect to the words of Eugene O'Neill's Lavinia Mannon: "I'll live alone with the dead, and keep their secrets, and let them hound me, until the curse is paid out and the last Mannon is let die! I know they will see to it I live for a long time!" To say that Lavinia cannot know that she will live long, that she may die tomorrow, is to confuse literature and life. To say that the play ends with the banging sound of the closing shutters, that Lavinia does not live at all after the curtain goes down, is to confuse literature and life in a different way. The Lavinia on the stage does not live either—except in our imagination, where lives the Lavinia seen in the closing words of the stage-Lavinia. The picture of Lavinia continuing on into the indefinite future in the darkened house with the Mannon dead is part of the imaginative effect of the play. The same holds true of the picture of Othello in hell. The difficulty for the modern reader is that he finds it hard to realize that Othello means his words literally. Hence the reader does not realize that he is being called upon to give them dramatic credence.

In addition to the anticipations by Granville-Barker and Bethell pointed out in my footnote, I find that I have been anticipated in my reading of *Othello* as concerned with the damnation of a noble soul by W. H. Auden in his discussion of the tragic hero in his *Portable Greek Reader* (1948), by Virgil K. Whitaker in *Shakespeare's Use of Learning* (1951), and by Herbert Barrows in his discussion of symbolism in *British Literature,* vol. 2 (1952).

CHRISTIAN OVERTONES IN ORTHELLO

JUST AS BRABANTIO has been made to see the marriage in a false light and Cassio has been robbed of his senses, Othello is "unwitted" and made to see Desdemona as a "fair devil" (III, iii, 478). In a deception worthy of Satan, "the father of lies," Iago contrives for him a drama of a wicked, deceitful Italy, in which Desdemona plays the part to be played by Vittoria Corombona, "the white devil," in Webster's drama of a world dominated by evil. She, who appears "like one of heaven" (IV, ii, 36), has a "young and sweating devil" (III, iv, 42) in her moist palm, the sign of her sensuality. "Devil!" he exclaims as he strikes her (IV, i, 251). Emilia, whom he treats as the madam of the house where Desdemona prostitutes herself, he addresses (IV, ii, 90–92), "You, mistress, / That have the office opposite to Saint Peter, / And keep the gate of hell!"

In seeing the heavenly Desdemona as a fair devil, Othello gives himself over to the devil of cynicism. He accepts Iago as an authority on human nature, one who is able to anatomize humanity and who speaks forthrightly about his findings (III, iii, 258–60): "This fellow's of exceeding honesty, / And knows all qualities, with a learned spirit, / Of human dealings." "Good sir, be a man," Iago adjures him (IV, i, 66). Manhood consists of the knowledge and the cynical acceptance that married men are bound to be cuckolded: "No, let me know; / And knowing what I am, I know what she shall be." "O, thou art wise; 'tis certain," responds Othello (IV, i, 73–75). He accepts the

"Christian Overtones in *Othello*" is from Paul N. Siegel, *Shakespearean Tragedy and the Elizabethan Compromise* (New York University Press, 1957), pp. 368–383. By permission of the publisher.

picture of Desdemona as a "super-subtle Venetian," one of the Venetian ladies who had acquired a reputation for marital deceptions, and, in doing so, takes the role of the Italian husband, who was notorious for avenging himself by such means as the hiring of bravoes to kill the gallant and by secret wife murder. He does not realize that when Iago says, "O, 'tis the spite of hell, the fiend's arch-mock, / To lip a wanton in a secure couch, / And to suppose her chaste" (IV, i, 71–73), the reverse is true, that it is his fiend's mocking way of stating that hell laughs at the murder of an innocent woman in her marriage bed by a husband who believes her false.

In giving himself over to the devil of cynicism, Othello, like Adam, who was made to question the justice of God's injunction, is made to question Desdemona, who is "heavenly true" (V, ii, 135), and, like Adam, he loses an earthly paradise. After a storm at sea he had come to the island of Cyprus to find Desdemona miraculously waiting for him. The island citadel of which he was to be governor with Desdemona at his side was his harbor, the blissful end of his life's voyage as the soldier of a maritime state. But there was a serpent in his Eden.[1] There was truly need for the "grace of heaven" (II, i, 85) which Cassio had called upon to encircle Desdemona when she landed on Cyprus. Even as Othello and Desdemona are voicing the exquisite harmony of their ecstatic love, Iago is expressing with satanic malice at the sight of the happy pair his intention of destroying that harmony (II, ii, 202–4): "O, you are well tuned now! / But I'll set down the pegs that make this music, / As honest as I am."[2]

The loss of his paradise makes Othello, like Adam, the prey of his passion. He had been a commanding personage, grand, self-contained, dignified, "the noble Moor whom our full senate / Call all in all sufficient . . . the nature / Whom passion could not shake" (IV, i, 275–77). His acceptance of Iago's view wrenches him apart and looses the passions which gush forth from within him. A man from a southern nation, whose inhabitants, wrote John Davies of Hereford, are "if good, most good, if bad exceeding bad,"[3] Othello contained within

[1] "If any wretch have put this in your head," says Emilia to Othello (IV, ii, 15–16), speaking of her husband without knowing it, "Let heaven requite it with the serpent's curse!" The words remind us of the Genesis account.

[2] One Christian tradition, later made use of by Milton, was that Satan's envy of Adam in his bliss impelled him to tempt him. . . .

[3] *Microcosmus* (London, 1603), p. 62.

himself the utmost potentialities for good and evil. In his greatness and
his weakness he showed the possibilities of human nature. That a man
of his nobility could fall as he did was a terrifying reminder of the
fall of Adam, the noblest of men, and of man's subsequent proneness
to soul-destroying sin.

The moment of his kneeling to vow revenge is the moment of
Othello's giving himself over to Iago. "Do not rise yet," commands
Iago (III, iii, 461). He kneels side by side with Othello and vows to
be at his service in "what bloody business ever." The oaths that the
two exchange are horrifying in their solemnity: it is a pact with the
devil that Othello has made. "Now art thou my lieutenant," says
Othello. "I am your own for ever," replies Iago in the last words of
the scene. Iago becomes Othello's Mephistopheles, and in making the
devil his servant Othello gives himself up into his power.

Like Faustus, however, Othello cannot rest easily in his pact. As
he thinks of Desdemona's sweetness, his vengefulness gives way to
poignant regret. Each time he voices this regret, however, Iago reminds him of his dedication to revenge—"Nay, you must forget that,"
"Nay, that's not your way" (IV, i, 190, 197)—and each time Othello
is called back to his purpose, only to lapse once more into tender
reminiscence. "O! she will sing the savageness out of a bear," he
exclaims, and for a moment it seems that Desdemona's divine virtues
will triumph, that the sweet harmony of her nature will quell the storm
within Othello. But Iago overcomes the influence of Desdemona, as
the bad angel overcomes the influence of the good angel in the moralities; he rouses Othello's jealousy and sense of outraged honor so that,
accepting the drama of Iago's contriving as reality, he goes through
with his assigned role as the Italian husband. His promise to abide by
his vow, "Ay, let her rot, and perish, and be damned tonight; for she
shall not live," is a reaffirmation of his pact with the devil which
brings him closer to his doom: he himself will be damned that night
in the murder of Desdemona.

When Othello comes to kill Desdemona, he does so in the exalted
mood of being about to render divine justice, not to perform revenge.[4]

[4] Kittredge glosses "This sorrow's heavenly;/It strikes where it doth love"
(*Sixteen Plays of Shakespeare*, New York, 1946, p. 1307): "My sorrow is like
that which God feels when he punishes the guilty; he loves the sinner, yet
punishes the guilty: Cf. Hebrews, xii, 6; 'Whom the Lord loveth he chasteneth.'"
There is profound irony in Othello's comparing himself to God as he makes
ready to do that which is forbidden by God.

And this justice is to include clemency. Desdemona is to be given the opportunity to pray and ask for heaven's forgiveness (V, ii, 31–32): "I would not kill thy unprepared spirit; / No; heaven forfend! I would not kill thy soul." But the soul that he is about to kill, the divine light that he is about to quench, is his own. The mercy that he offers Desdemona and the mood of elevated pity in which he offers it are Othello's last hope of escaping damnation. When he says "amen" in reply to Desdemona's "Then Lord have mercy on me!" Desdemona exclaims, "And have you mercy too!" (57–58) But Othello cannot call up from within him the forgiveness of Christ and, forgetting the Lord's Prayer, loses his own claim to God's mercy. When Desdemona denies having been unfaithful to him, Othello's rage is rekindled: "O perjured woman! thou dost stone my heart, / And makest me call what I intend to do / A murder, which I thought a sacrifice" (63–65). In his oscillation of feeling he is back to the vengeful spirit in which he had told Iago (IV, i, 193–94), "My heart is turned to stone; / I strike it, and it hurts my hand." No more does he speak of "justice" but of his "great revenge" (17, 74). Desdemona is now not "sweet soul" but "strumpet" (50, 77). When Desdemona entreats, "But while I say one prayer," he refuses her the opportunity for salvation which he had previously offered her and stifles her, saying, "It is too late" (83). At this moment Emilia pounds on the locked door to tell Othello of the attempted assassination of Cassio, who, escaped from death, can help the truth to be revealed, but it is indeed too late: the noise only makes him hurry the killing of Desdemona.

An old tradition of the stage has it that at this point he stabs her, a form of death which would make Desdemona's regaining of consciousness more plausible than death by strangling. This would further dramatize the contrast between the reverential mood in which he entered and the revengeful manner in which he commits the murder, for he had said (V, ii, 3–5), "Yet I'll not shed her blood; / Nor scar that whiter skin of hers than snow, / And smooth as monumental alabaster." His cry (III, iii, 451), "O, blood, blood, blood," made when he had given himself over to revenge, and his statement after he thinks Cassio has been killed (V, i, 34–36), "Strumpet, I come. . . . Thy bed, lust-stain'd, shall with lust's blood be spotted," would then be fulfilled.

Othello kills Desdemona, as Granville-Barker says, with a "cold deliberate anger" so that "the abrupt knocking at the door and Emilia's insistent voice can set his wits alertly on the defensive even while the fully sentient man barely yet comprehends what he has done."[5] His mind continues to work with swift defensiveness, concerned with whether or not the murder has been truly completed and, if it has, whether it is safest to admit Emilia—"Shall she come in? Were't good? / I think she stirs again. No" (V, ii, 94–95)—as Emilia's pounding resounds with the reverberations of Macduff's on the gates of Macbeth's castle, for his thinking is undisturbed by any flow of normal feeling. His heart made "stone," it is only with the utterance of the word "wife" (V, ii, 96) that his frozen, blocked-up emotion is pierced, and a torrent of agonized grief is released. His earlier "I that am cruel am yet merciful; / I would not have thee linger in thy pain" Granville-Barker rightly characterizes (p. 80) as "hangman humanity." The paradox of the mercifulness of his cruelty in slaying her forthwith, voiced with a kind of grim irony as he proceeds to dispatch her, is the expression of his benumbed feeling, which causes him to regard the struggling Desdemona with the detachedly "humanitarian" consideration of an executioner who seeks to kill with but one stroke of his ax.

The moment he gets his revenge it turns sour. Emilia enters to inform him that Cassio is alive, and Othello exclaims (115–16): "Not Cassio kill'd! then murder's out of tune, / And sweet revenge turns harsh." As if to emphasize his words comes Desdemona's cry: "O, falsely, falsely murder'd!" (117) When she takes upon herself, however, the guilt for her death, Othello, in his bitterness at what he believes to be her final lie, asserts that he killed her and, defending himself against Emilia's charge that Desdemona was "heavenly true" and that he is "a devil" (135, 133), affirms his certitude in terms that

[5] Harley Granville-Barker, *Prefaces to Shakespeare* (Princeton University Press, 1947), II, 80. Granville-Barker anticipated my thesis that Othello is to be regarded as damned (p. 114): "Othello wakes as from a nightmare only to kill himself, his prospect hell." Cf. also S. L. Bethell, "Shakespeare's Imagery: The Diabolic Images in *Othello*," *Shakespeare Survey,* ed. Allardyce Nicoll, V (1952), 78–79. Before Bradley cast his potent spell it was not considered to be obvious to all that Othello remains spiritually innocent in spite of his murder. The question was, in fact, so long debated in earlier Shakespearean criticism that the *Edinburgh Review* of July 1840 could say: "The character of the Moor, in which the explication must be sought [i.e., an explication of the play that would provide a 'moral justification of its horror'], has been interpreted more contradictorily than any other in the range of the poet's works, *Hamlet* itself not excepted." Cf. the Furness Variorum edition of *Othello,* p. 419. For examples of the view that Othello, despite his goodness, is overcome and destroyed by the evil within him, see Furness, pp. 419–20, 420, 421–22, 422–23, 425–28, 431–32, 444–45, 452–53.

confirm his damnation (137–39): "O, I were damn'd beneath all depth in hell, / But that I did proceed upon just grounds / To this extremity." And when the truth is finally revealed to him, he is overwhelmed by the feeling that he is indeed damned. "Will you, I pray, demand that demi-devil / Why he hath thus ensnared my soul and body?" he asks (301–2).

Crushed by the sight of her lying pale on the white marriage sheets, the symbol of her purity, he calls to be transported to hell at once. His words are expressive of what the "Homily of Repentance" calls "Judas' repentance," that is, the overwhelming sense of guilt without faith in the mercy of God which is the heinous sin of despair. The sight of his victim blasts any hope of salvation in him (V, ii, 273–75): "When we shall meet at compt, / This look of thine will hurl my soul from heaven, / And fiends will snatch at it." When he continues, "Whip me, ye devils, / From the possession of this heavenly sight," he is not only expressing his despair but is already entering upon the punishments of hell in this life.

In committing self-murder at the conclusion he is continuing to follow Judas' example. His behavior in his last moments, therefore, would have confirmed Elizabethans in the impression that his soul is lost which they gained from observing the dramatic irony of his offering Desdemona an opportunity, as he supposes, for salvation and then withdrawing it in a rage, not realizing that his own salvation is at issue and forgetting that those who do not forgive will not be forgiven.

In killing Desdemona he had rejected her divine goodness and cast away, he says in his final speech, a pearl worth more than all the world, losing his soul.[6] His last words, however, are not those of heartbreak or of self-torture. They are spoken with the resolution of one who

---

[6] Modern editors generally follow the Quarto reading of the lines (V, ii, 346–48) in which Othello speaks of himself as "one whose hand,/Like the base Indian, threw a pearl away/Richer than all his tribe." Richmond Noble (*Shakespeare's Biblical Knowledge* [New York, 1935], pp. 91–93) argues convincingly, however, for the Folio reading "base Iudean." "Iudean" would refer to Judas Iscariot, who, like Othello, killed himself in despair at his guilt and whose kiss of betrayal, bringing death to Christ, is recalled by Othello's words (V, ii, 358) "I kiss'd thee ere I kill'd thee." "Just as Judas threw away his Saviour, the most precious possession of his Tribe, so he (Othello) destroyed what had been his most precious blessing." "Pearl" not only refers to Christ but alludes to the "pearl of great price" (Matthew, xiii, 46), the kingdom of heaven and the soul whose abode it is. Cf. *Macbeth*, III, i, 68–69: "And mine eternal jewel/Given to the common enemy of man," i.e., his immortal soul given to the devil, who (Rev., xii, 9) "deceiveth all the world."

knows his irrevocable fate and the regret of one who knows the preciousness of what he has lost and act as a valediction summing up for us the pathos of the ensnarement of this noble nature.

The painfulness of this conclusion is mitigated by the fact that, although Iago triumphs over Othello, it is at the same time demonstrated that his values cannot triumph over Othello's. His view of reality is false: Desdemona is pure. She remains heavenly true to Othello, although the worldly cynical Emilia lightheartedly suggests that she avenge herself by cuckolding her husband, as the devilishly cynical Iago had counseled revenge to Othello. "Wouldst thou do such a deed for all the world?" asks Desdemona (IV, iii, 67). We are reminded of Christ's rejection of the temptation to possess the world. "Marry, I would not do such a thing for a joint-ring," Emilia replies (73–79), "nor for measures of lawn, nor for gowns, petticoats, nor caps, nor any petty exhibition; but, for the whole world,—why, who would not make her husband a cuckold to make him a monarch? I should venture purgatory for 't." Although she is speaking jestingly to divert her mistress, it is clear that Christ's words (Mark, viii, 36) "What shall it profit a man to gain the whole world and lose his soul?" have no great significance for her.

This is Desdemona's temptation scene, the counterpart of Othello's temptation scene, as Bradley calls it. Of course, Desdemona's scene does not have the long-drawn-out dramatic intensity of Othello's, as the Christlike Desdemona is immune to the temptation offered her. It does, however, parallel it and contrast with it significantly. Unlike Othello, she does not follow her preceptor's ethic of revenge; she obeys the vow she had made, kneeling in the presence of Iago as Othello had kneeled to vow hatred and revenge, that she would continue in her love and devotion for Othello no matter what he does to her. In doing so she follows the Christian ethic of returning good for evil, accepting ill-treatment as a discipline enabling her to grow in virtue: "Good night, good night: heaven me such uses send, / Not to pick bad from bad, but by bad mend!" (107–8) What makes her deeply painful suffering tolerable is that as a result of this suffering she is able to reach heights of love and sacrifice that enable her to transcend it. The words in which she accepts her misfortune echo the centuries-long praise of adversity as a teacher of Christian patience and as a means by which we attain the "felicity or perfect good which is God" and are guided by "the love of God," which "keepeth the world in due order and good accord" and "knitteth together the sacrament of wedlock with chaste love between man and wife."[7] They help to reconcile the audience to her suffering and death, as through her Griselda-like patience and devotion she becomes a saint and a martyr in her love, dying with a divine lie upon her lips, ironically committing the deathbed perjury against which Othello had warned her, but a perjury which makes her, as Emilia says (V, ii, 130), "the more angel."

Although Emilia attends Desdemona as Iago does Othello, instead of her corrupting Desdemona as Iago corrupts Othello, Desdemona summons forth the best in Emilia's nature. In her easy-going tolerance of her husband, the depths of whose iniquity she does not realize, in her theft of the handkerchief at his behest, she plays a part in her mistress's calamity, but she redeems herself by her loyalty. "I durst, my lord, to wager she is honest," she tells Othello (IV, ii, 12–13), "Lay down my soul at stake." She does indeed stake her soul on the

---

[7] *Boethius' Consolation of Philosophy,* tr. George Colville (1556), ed. Ernest Belfort Bax (London, 1897), pp. 51–52. Desdemona's words of resignation (IV, ii, 128), "It is my wretched fortune," express Christian endurance of adversity as God's will. She is, as "A Sermon of Christian Love and Charity" recommended (*Certain Sermons,* p. 65), following the example of Christ in taking his "cup of death" with the words "Thy will be done." In the next line, in answer to Iago's question "How comes this trick upon him [Othello]?" she replies, "Nay, heaven doth know." Men are in the dark, but heaven knows all things, permits the suffering of the good for its own purposes, and will perform justice—this is the feeling communicated to the audience, as it observes Iago's malevolently ironic pretense of ignorance met by Desdemona's faith in an all-seeing providence. Although Desdemona does not speak in the theological terms of the good angel of the moralities, she is a Christian figure. To Othello's question "Are not you a strumpet?" she replies (IV, ii, 82–85):

> No, as I am a Christian:
> If to preserve this vessel for my lord
> From any other foul unlawful touch
> Be not to be a strumpet, I am none.

She is here, as she continues to be in her cry (IV, ii. 88), "O, heaven forgive us" in response to Othello's unjust accusation and in her hope (IV, ii, 135) "heaven pardon him" for the unknown villain who has calumniated her, "made one with Christ," in the words of "A Sermon against Whoredom and Uncleanness" (*Certain Sermons,* p. 122): "And a little before he [St. Paul] saith, *Do ye not know, that your bodies are the members of Christ? Shall I then take the members of Christ and make them the members of a whore?* . . . How unseemly a thing is it then to cease to be incorporate or embodied and made one with Christ. . . ."

purity of Desdemona. "Moor, she was chaste," she says (V, ii, 249–50) as she lies dying, "she loved thee, cruel Moor; / So come my soul to bliss, as I speak true." These words, at the supreme moment of death, carry the assurance that in losing her life by heroically defying Iago and revealing the truth she has won her soul. They also carry the assurance that there are virtues in ordinary humanity unsuspected by a cynical Iago.

Desdemona raises and redeems such earthly souls as Emilia. Belief in her, the symbolic equivalent in the play of belief in Christ, is a means of salvation for Cassio as well as for Emilia. Cassio, like Othello, is deceived by Iago, but he makes no pact with him, as Othello does, and his worship of Desdemona, expressed in his rapturous description of the storm miraculously permitting "the divine Desdemona" to come to Cyprus (II, i, 68–73), is constant. He rejects Iago's insinuating "What an eye she has! methinks it sounds a parley of provocation" with "an inviting eye; and yet methinks right modest" (II, iii, 22–25). If in Othello Shakespeare's audience had a terrifying reminder of the possibility of even the noblest of men succumbing to the wiles of the devil, in Cassio it had a hopeful reminder of the possibility of the ordinary man—one who, like each of them, was subject to mortal frailty—achieving salvation through faith and repentance.

Cassio has the conventional weaknesses of the gentleman just as Emilia has the conventional weaknesses of the servant-confidante, and Iago makes use of these weaknesses, just as he makes use of the weaknesses of Emilia in having her steal the handkerchief. One of Cassio's vulnerable points is his false sense of honor, which Iago uses to get him drunk by inviting "a brace of Cyprus gallants that would fain have a measure to the health of black Othello" (II, iii, 31–33). His courtliness then becomes a narrowly constricting social code that obligates him to drink with them: "I have very poor and unhappy brains for drinking: I could well wish courtesy would invent some other custom of entertainment." The gallants, moreover, swaggering, quarrelsome in their cups, sensitive about points of honor, "noble swelling spirits, / That hold their honours in a wary distance, / The very elements of this warlike isle," have also been befuddled with drink by Iago. Cassio, in consorting with them, disregards the words of "A Sermon against Contention and Brawling" in denouncing the extreme touchiness of spirit demanded by the feudalistic code (*Certain Sermons*, p. 145): "And the wise King Solomon saith, *Honour is due*

*to a man that keepeth himself from contention; and all that mingle
themselves therewith be fools."* In following the forms of courtesy, in
obeying the punctilios of the code of honor, by which "a cross word is
ground enough for a challenge, . . . not to pledge a health is cause
enough to lose health and life too,"[8] Cassio, driven by "the devil
drunkenness" (II, iii, 297) and forgetting "Christian shame," engages
in a "barbarous brawl" (II, iii, 172), losing, ironically, his honorable
reputation as a trustworthy officer.[9]

Iago also makes use of Cassio's sexual laxity, guying him about
Bianca while Othello goes mad thinking that Cassio's lighthearted contemptuous laughter is directed at Desdemona. "Did you perceive how
he laughed at his vice?" Iago asks Othello (IV, i, 181). It is a laughter
for which all pay dear. Cassio himself is set upon and wounded as he
comes home from Bianca's house in a night scene of fighting in the
streets, of calls for help, and of lights making the darkness visible that
acts as the final peal of thunder and flash of lightning, the culmination
of the ominous reverberations of the previous street-fighting scenes,
before the awful quietness in which Othello looks upon Desdemona
lying asleep in her bedchamber. "This is the fruit of whoring," says
Iago over the wounded Cassio (V, i, 116). He is trying to attach the
blame for the attempted assassination to Bianca, but there is a sense
in which the words are true. Cassio's dalliance with Bianca was one
point around which Iago spun his web, and in order to assure himself
that the web would not be broken Iago had to try to kill him. From
our weaknesses the devil derives his strength; from our blind spots
comes his attack upon us.

But Cassio's sins are venial, not mortal. Having atoned for his
weaknesses with his shame and his blood, he is worthy of the position
that Othello, a greater man than he, has lost. "I hold him to be unworthy of his place that does those things," he says (II, iii, 102-3),

[8] Thomas Adams, *The Devil's Banquet* (London, 1614), pp. 58–59. Quoted
by Fredson Bowers, *Elizabethan Revenge Tragedy, 1587–1642* (Princeton University Press, 1940), pp. 30–34.

[9] So, too, adherence to the Italian aristocratic code of honor makes Othello
lose his virtue, the only true source of honor. When, broken by his sense of
guilt, he is disarmed, he says (V, ii, 245–46), "But why should honour out-
live honesty? /Let it go all." "Honour" here means "reputation for valor,"
and "honesty" means "honorable character." Why keep one's escutcheon un-
blemished when one's soul is black with guilt? Elsewhere (V, ii, 294) he
speaks of himself with bitter irony as an "honourable murderer." He had
thought that he was acting in honor and had proved to be a base murderer.

attempting to regain his dignity when he has got drunk on his watch. Unworthy indeed, but repentance wipes out the stains of misdoing. In his realization that he has done wrong he exclaims, albeit with drunken piety, "Forgive us our sins!" His contrition when he comes to himself is deep. "Confess yourself freely to [Desdemona]," Iago advises him (II, ii, 323–28). "Importune her help to put you in your place again: she is of so free, so kind, so apt, so blessed a disposition, she holds it a vice in her goodness not to do more than she is requested." The blessed Desdemona, to whom Cassio dedicates himself as her "true servant" (III, iii, 9), in a feeling of gratitude for her bounteous goodness akin to the Mariolatry which affected the language of chivalric devotion in which he speaks, does intercede for him after he has confessed himself to her. Her intercession brings martyrdom for herself, a martyrdom prefigured by her words "thy solicitor shall rather die / Than give thy cause away" (III, iii, 27–28), which remind us of the steadfastness of Christ in sacrificing Himself for mankind. At the conclusion, however, Cassio gains an even higher place than the one he had lost, as all sons of Adam who repent their sins gain a higher place than they lost when they sinned in Adam. "I hope to be saved," he had said in his drunken religiousness, which, though ludicrous, had serious overtones. He was.

Roderigo, on the other hand, is the ordinary weak man led on by his sensual desires to damnation. He at first regards Desdemona as highly as does Cassio, speaking of her as "blessed" (II, ii, 255) in a scene that immediately precedes and contrasts with the one in which Cassio rejects Iago's cynical insinuations. His damnation parallels that of Othello in a subplot which has something of the flavor of Jonsonian comedy. Roderigo is the degenerate gentleman gulled by a knave. Effeminate, shallow, stupid, weak, at the mercy of his sensual desires, he is controlled by a contemptuous wave of the hand by the boldly clever, coldly emotionless Iago, who uses him for his "sport and profit" (I, iii, 392). "I will incontinently drown myself," he whimpers when Othello's marriage has been ratified (I, iii, 306), but after Iago has forcefully told him that if he does not foolishly do away with himself in his passion but pursues Desdemona with bribes he will get his desires, he agrees to talk no more of drowning (I, iii, 388): "I am changed: I'll go sell all my land." Sell his ancestral land he does, bit by bit, making himself bankrupt to buy jewels which supposedly go to Desdemona. Each time he weakly protests that Iago has not delivered the goods, Iago convinces him that he should wait or sends him on a new enterprise, hustling him off before he has time to think. In this way, goaded by his passion, propelled by Iago, he engages, even though he has no stomach for fighting, in a brawl with Cassio, in which he is soundly thrashed.

But Roderigo is being gulled by no ordinary parasite who merely swindles him of his money and tricks him into being beaten but by a devil. It is his soul that is at stake. "If thou wilt needs damn thyself," Iago had told him (I, iii, 359–61), "do it a more delicate way than drowning." The words are spoken in the lightly jesting manner of the man of the world, but they are the temptation of the fiend. Damned Roderigo is, but he is cheated even of the luxurious manner of damning himself in Desdemona's arms that has been promised. For a moment he has a chance to save himself. Complaining petulantly that Iago has given him false promises, he announces his readiness to give up a fruitless chase (IV, ii, 199–202): "I will make myself known to Desdemona: if she will return me my jewels, I will give over my suit and repent my unlawful solicitation." In his expressed intention to repent lies his hope for salvation. But, flattered by Iago, who commends his dim-witted suspicion of him as perspicacity and his petulance as spirit, and urged by him to show his courage and determination in a valiant action that will prevent Desdemona from leaving Cyprus, he permits himself to be persuaded to participate in the assassination attempt on Cassio. " 'Tis but a man gone," he says to himself (V, i, 10), as he stands concealed behind a building, ready to fall upon his intended victim. The words seal his own doom: Iago attacks him in the confusion created by his assault upon Cassio and kills him. "Kill men i' the dark!" Iago cries in self-righteous incredulity. It is ironic that these words be spoken by this Machiavellian arch-intriguer, but they indicate, nevertheless, the retribution that overtakes Roderigo in dying in the manner in which he had planned to kill Cassio: the devil has his part to play in bringing punishment to vicious men.

This element of dramatic justice helps to make the conclusion of *Othello* tolerable. Iago himself, who has put Othello "on the rack" (III, iii, 335), is sentenced to torture. "If thou the next night following enjoy not Desdemona," he had told Roderigo, knowing this was not to be, "take me from this world with treachery and devise engines for my life." He is indeed betrayed by the treachery of Emilia, who had been devoted to him, a treachery that is in reality a higher loyalty —as she says (V, ii, 196), " 'Tis proper I obey him, but not now"— and has "engines," instruments of torture, ingeniously contrived "cunning cruelty / That can torment him much and hold him long," (V, ii, 333–34) devised for him. These torments are merely the temporal prelude to the eternal torments of hell, to which he returns. "I hate him," he had said of Othello early in the play (I, i, 155), "as I do hell-pains," speaking as if of something with which he is familiar. They are also merely the extreme continuation of the torments he had suffered in life, where his thoughts did "like a poisonous mineral, gnaw [his] inwards," as hell in Emilia's imprecation upon the unknown villain who is her husband is to "gnaw his bones" (IV, ii, 136). Iago, the spirit of negation, is self-consuming and self-destructive.

And Othello himself, having voiced the pathos of his loss, in killing himself as he had killed "a malignant and a turban'd Turk" who "beat a Venetian and traduced the state" (V, ii, 353–54), visits justice upon himself. The Turk is symbolic in *Othello* of the evil in human nature destructive of order. "Are we turn'd Turks, and to ourselves do that / Which heaven hath forbid the Ottomites?" exclaims Othello at the sight of the fighting which has disturbed Cyprus (II, iii, 170–72). "For Christian shame, put by this barbarous brawl." The threat of the Turks to Cyprus had been dispelled by the destruction of their fleet by a storm. But this was merely the visible threat from without; the invisible threat from within the island, the evil passions within men which leads to civil strife, still remained. Even as Othello is being waited for on the quay after the destruction of the Turkish fleet, Iago laughingly affirming the validity of his cynical statements about women (II, i, 115), says, "Nay, it is true, or else I am a Turk." It is not true: his statements are the inventions of the Turk inciting to chaos, of Satan seeking to extend the domain of negation. When Othello thrusts his sword into his breast, he is stabbing the Turk, the evil, within himself which Iago, evil incarnate, had aroused. "Good, good: the justice of it pleases: very good," he had said when Iago had suggested, "Do it not with poison, strangle her in her bed, even the bed she hath contaminated" (IV, i, 220–23). He had sought to execute poetic justice in avenging himself and in doing so had laid himself open to such justice at the hands of God. "Going about to revenge evil, we show ourselves to be evil" (*Certain*

Sermons, p. 138). He falls upon the bed upon which he himself has done foul murder. To him, if we take "lust" in the general sense of "passion," apply his words, "Thy bed, lust-stain'd, shall with lust's blood be spotted" (V, i, 36). His fate is the inevitable consequence of his action. "Perdition catch my soul," he had said (III, iii, 90–92), "But I do love thee! and when I love thee not, / Chaos is come again." He has indeed brought chaos to his moral being and perdition to his soul, having traduced divine goodness and violated the law of God.

THOMAS DE QUINCEY
1785-1859

IN ADDITION TO his famous essay on the knocking on the gate in *Macbeth,* Thomas De Quincey wrote an article on Shakespeare, heavily indebted to Schlegel and Coleridge, for the seventh edition of the *Encyclopedia Britannica* in 1838. His chief contribution to Shakespearean criticism, however, is the *Macbeth* essay, with its fervent concluding statement of the need for surrendering oneself to the imaginative effect of a Shakespearean drama, secure in the faith of its perfection. We may not be able to regard Shakespeare as a god, but at least the initial assumption of order and purpose in his created dramatic universe is a useful one.

De Quincey brilliantly exemplifies his point by his analysis of a remarkable piece of stage business, whose imaginative effect he apprehended before he could account for it. Noteworthy is his view of Macbeth and Lady Macbeth as murderers "a poet will condescend to," characters of such passion that they become greater than human, are "conformed to the image of devils" and "taken out of the region of human things" into a poetically realized hell. They are in contrast with the Mr. Williams of real life, the wholesale murderer whose artistry De Quincey, as a connoisseur of murder, ironically extols.

In connection with De Quincey's statement that Macbeth's passion creates a hell within him, it is worth noting that it was an Elizabethan religious commonplace that the passions tormenting sinners on earth are an antechamber to the punishments of hell. His recalling of Lady Macbeth's soliloquy in which she summons evil spirits to unsex her and his statement that a "fiendish heart" has indeed entered her body should be read in conjunction with W. C. Curry's discussion of this scene in his *Shakespeare's Philosophical Patterns* (1937) as a dramatization of the Elizabethans' belief in literal demonic possession.

It is interesting that De Quincey has nothing to say about the effect of the words of the Porter, which accompany the knocking at the gate after Macbeth and Lady Macbeth have left the stage. Was he too much under the influence of Coleridge to challenge his opinion about the spuriousness of the passage?

ON THE KNOCKING AT THE GATE IN MACBETH

FROM MY BOYISH days I had always felt a great perplexity on one point in *Macbeth*. It was this: the knocking at the gate, which succeeds to the murder of Duncan, produced to my feelings an effect for which I never could account. The effect was, that it reflected back upon the murderer a peculiar awfulness and a depth of solemnity; yet, however obstinately I endeavoured with my understanding to comprehend this, for many years I never could see *why* it should produce such an effect.

"On the Knocking at the Gate in *Macbeth*" was first published in *The London Magazine,* October 1823.

Here I pause for one moment, to exhort the reader never to pay any attention to his understanding, when it stands in opposition to any other faculty of his mind. The mere understanding, however useful and indispensable, is the meanest faculty in the human mind, and the most to be distrusted; and yet the great majority of people trust to nothing else, which may do for ordinary life, but not for philosophical purposes. Of this out of ten thousand instances that I might produce, I will cite one. Ask of any person whatsoever, who is not previously prepared for the demand by a knowledge of the perspective, to draw in the rudest way the commonest appearance which depends upon the laws of that science; as, for instance, to represent the effect of two walls standing at right angles to each other, or the appearance of the houses on each side of a street, as seen by a person looking down the street from one extremity. Now in all cases, unless the person has happened to observe in pictures how it is that artists produce these effects, he will be utterly unable to make the smallest approximation to it. Yet why? For he has actually seen the effect every day of his life. The reason is—that he allows his understanding to overrule his eyes. His understanding, which includes no intuitive knowledge of the laws of vision, can furnish him with no reason why a line which is known and can be proved to be a horizontal line, should not *appear* a horizontal line; a line that made any angle with the perpendicular, less than a right angle, would seem to him to indicate that his houses were all tumbling down together. Accordingly, he makes the line of his houses a horizontal line, and fails, of course, to produce the effect demanded. Here, then, is one instance out of many, in which not only the understanding is allowed to overrule the eyes, but where the understanding is positively allowed to obliterate the eyes, as it were; for not only does the man believe the evidence of his understanding in opposition to that of his eyes, but (what is monstrous!) the idiot is not aware that his eyes ever gave such evidence. He does not know that he has seen (and therefore *quoad* his consciousness has *not* seen) that which he *has* seen every day of his life.

But to return from this digression, my understanding could furnish no reason why the knocking at the gate in *Macbeth* should produce any effect, direct or reflected. In fact, my understanding said positively that it could *not* produce any effect. But I knew better; I felt that it did; and I waited and clung to the problem until further knowledge should enable me to solve it. At length, in 1812, Mr. Williams made his *début* on the stage of Ratcliffe Highway, and executed those unparalleled murders which have procured for him such a brilliant and undying reputation. On which murders, by the way, I must observe, that in one respect they have had an ill effect, by making the connoisseur in murder very fastidious in his taste, and dissatisfied by anything that has been since done in that line. All other murders look pale by the deep crimson of his; and, as an amateur once said to me in a querulous tone, 'There has been absolutely nothing *doing* since his time, or nothing that's worth speaking of.' But this is wrong; for it is unreasonable to expect all men to be great artists, and born with the genius of Mr. Williams. Now it will be remembered, that in the first of these murders (that of the Marrs), the same incident (of a knocking at the door) soon after the work of extermination was complete, did actually occur, which the genius of Shakespeare has invented; and all good judges, and the most eminent dilettanti, acknowledged the felicity of Shakespeare's suggestion, as soon as it was actually realized. Here, then, was a fresh proof that I was right in relying on my own feeling, in opposition to my understanding; and I again set myself to study the problem; at length I solved it to my own satisfaction, and my solution is this. Murder, in ordinary cases, where the sympathy is wholly directed to the case of the murdered person, is an incident of coarse and vulgar horror; and for this reason, that it flings the interest exclusively upon the natural but ignoble instinct by which we cleave to life; an instinct which, as being indispensable to the primal law of self-preservation, is the same in kind (though different in degree) amongst all living creatures: this instinct, therefore, because it annihilates all distinctions, and degrades the greatest of men to the level of 'the poor beetle that we tread on,' exhibits human nature in its most abject and humiliating attitude. Such an attitude would little suit the purposes of the poet. What then must he do? He must throw the interest on the murderer. Our sympathy must be with *him* (of course I mean a sympathy of comprehension, a sympathy by which we enter into his feelings, and are made to understand them,—not a sympathy of pity or approbation). In the murdered person, all strife of thought, all flux and reflux of passion and of purpose, are crushed by one overwhelming panic; the fear of instant death smites him 'with its petrific mace.' But in the murderer, such a murderer as a poet will condescend to, there must be raging some great storm of passion—jealousy, ambition, vengeance, hatred —which will create a hell within him; and into this hell we are to look.

In *Macbeth,* for the sake of gratifying his own enormous and teeming faculty of creation, Shakespeare has introduced two murderers: and, as usual in his hands, they are remarkably discriminated: but, though in Macbeth the strife of mind is greater than in his wife, the tiger spirit not so awake, and his feelings caught chiefly by contagion from her,—yet, as both were finally involved in the guilt of murder, the murderous mind of necessity is finally to be presumed in both. This was to be expressed; and on its own account, as well as to make it a more proportionable antagonist to the unoffending nature of their victim, 'the gracious Duncan,' and adequately to expound 'the deep damnation of his taking off,' this was to be expressed with peculiar energy. We were to be made to feel that the human nature, i.e. the divine nature of love and mercy, spread through the hearts of all creatures, and seldom utterly withdrawn from man—was gone, vanished, extinct, and that the fiendish nature had taken its place. And, as this effect is marvellously accomplished in the *dialogues* and *soliloquies* themselves, so it is finally consummated by the expedient under consideration; and it is to this that I now solicit the reader's attention. If the reader has ever witnessed a wife, daughter, or sister in a fainting fit, he may chance to have observed that the most affecting moment in such a spectacle is *that* in which a sigh and a stirring announce the recommencement of suspended life. Or, if the reader has ever been present in a vast metropolis, on the day when some great national idol was carried in funeral pomp to his grave, and chancing to walk near the course through which it passed, has felt powerfully in the silence and desertion of the streets, and in the stagnation of ordinary business, the deep interest which at that moment was possessing the heart of man—if all at once he should hear the death-like stillness broken up by the sound of wheels rattling away from the scene, and making known that the transitory vision was dissolved, he will be aware that at no moment was his sense of the complete suspension and pause in ordinary human concerns so full and affecting, as at that moment when the suspension ceases, and the goings-on of human life are suddenly resumed. All action in any direction is best expounded, measured, and made apprehensible, by reaction. Now apply this to the case in *Macbeth*. Here, as I have said, the retiring of the human heart, and the entrance of the fiendish heart was to be expressed and made sensible. Another world has stept in; and the murderers are taken out of the region of human things, human purposes, human desires. They are transfigured: Lady Macbeth is 'unsexed;' Macbeth has forgot that he was born of woman; both are conformed to the image of devils; and the world of devils is suddenly revealed. But how shall this be conveyed and made palpable? In order that a new world may step in, this world must for a time disappear. The murderers, and the murder must be insulated— cut off by an immeasurable gulf from the ordinary tide and succession of human affairs—locked up and sequestered in some deep recess; we must be made sensible that the world of ordinary life is suddenly arrested—laid asleep—tranced—racked into a dread armistice; time must be annihilated; relation to things without abolished; and all must pass self-withdrawn into a deep syncope and suspension of earthly passion. Hence it is, that when the deed is done, when the work of darkness is perfect, then the world of darkness passes away like a pageantry in the clouds: the knocking at the gate is heard; and it makes known audibly that the reaction has commenced; the human has made its reflux upon the fiendish; the pulses of life are beginning to beat again; and the re-establishment of the goings-on of the world in which we live, first makes us profoundly sensible of the awful parenthesis that had suspended them.

O mighty poet! Thy works are not as those of other men, simply and merely great works of art; but are also like the phenomena of nature, like the sun and sea, the stars and the flowers; like frost and snow, rain and dew, hail-storm and thunder, which are to be studied with entire submission of our own faculties, and in the perfect faith that in them there can be no too much or too little, nothing useless or inert—but that, the farther we press in our discoveries, the more we shall see proofs of design and self-supporting arrangement where the careless eye had seen nothing but accident!

A. C. BRADLEY
1851-1935

IN THIS DESCRIPTION of the atmosphere of *Macbeth*
Bradley anticipates the study of imagery of later writers. It might be noted too that in it, illustrated with
concrete detail, may be found a presentation of the
three themes of L. C. Knights's exposition (in "How
Many Children Had Lady Macbeth?") of the pattern
of *Macbeth,* which he believed Bradley distorted in
dwelling on character:

> *Macbeth* is a statement of evil. . . . Two main themes,
> which can only be separated for the purpose of analysis,
> are blended in the play,—the themes of the reversal of
> values and of unnatural disorder. And closely related to
> each is a third theme, that of deceitful appearance, and
> consequent doubt, uncertainty and confusion.

The difference is that Bradley presents them not in the
language of anatomical analysis but of evocative description, showing the living body moving in response
to the flexing of muscles.

THE ATMOSPHERE OF MACBETH

A SHAKESPEAREAN TRAGEDY, as a rule, has a special tone or atmosphere of its own, quite perceptible, however difficult to describe. The
effect of this atmosphere is marked with unusual strength in *Macbeth.*
It is due to a variety of influences which combine with those just
noticed, so that, acting and reacting, they form a whole; and the desolation of the blasted heath, the design of the Witches, the guilt in the
hero's soul, the darkness of the night, seem to emanate from one and
the same source. This effect is strengthened by a multitude of small

"The Atmosphere of *Macbeth*" is from A. C. Bradley, *Shakespearean
Tragedy,* pp. 333–340. Reprinted with permission of Macmillan & Company
Ltd., St. Martin's Press Inc., and the Macmillan Company of Canada Ltd.

touches, which at the moment may be little noticed but still leave their mark on the imagination. We may approach the consideration of the characters and the action by distinguishing some of the ingredients of this general effect.

Darkness, we may even say blackness, broods over this tragedy. It is remarkable that almost all the scenes which at once recur to memory take place either at night or in some dark spot. The vision of the dagger, the murder of Duncan, the murder of Banquo, the sleep-walking of Lady Macbeth, all come in night-scenes. The Witches dance in the thick air of a storm, or, 'black and midnight hags,' receive Macbeth in a cavern. The blackness of night is to the hero a thing of fear, even of horror; and that which he feels becomes the spirit of the play. The faint glimmerings of the western sky at twilight are here menacing: it is the hour when the traveller hastens to reach safety in his inn, and when Banquo rides homeward to meet his assassins; the hour when 'light thickens,' when 'night's black agents to their prey do rouse,' when the wolf begins to howl, and the owl to scream, and withered murder steals forth to his work. Macbeth bids the stars hide their fires that his 'black' desires may be concealed; Lady Macbeth calls on thick night to come, palled in the dunnest smoke of hell. The moon is down and no stars shine when Banquo, dreading the dreams of the coming night, goes unwillingly to bed, and leaves Macbeth to wait for the summons of the little bell. When the next day should dawn, its light is 'strangled,' and 'darkness does the face of earth entomb.' In the whole drama the sun seems to shine only twice; first, in the beautiful but ironical passage where Duncan sees the swallows flitting round the castle of death; and, afterwards, when at the close the avenging army gathers to rid the earth of its shame. Of the many slighter touches which deepen this effect I notice only one. The failure of nature in Lady Macbeth is marked by her fear of darkness; 'she has light by her continually.' And in the one phrase of fear that escapes her lips even in sleep, it is of the darkness of the place of torment that she speaks.

The atmosphere of *Macbeth*, however, is not that of unrelieved blackness. On the contrary, as compared with *King Lear* and its cold dim gloom, *Macbeth* leaves a decided impression of colour; it is really the impression of a black night broken by flashes of light and colour, sometimes vivid and even glaring. They are the lights and colours of the thunder-storm in the first scene; of the dagger hanging before

Macbeth's eyes and glittering alone in the midnight air; of the torch
borne by the servant when he and his lord come upon Banquo crossing the castle-court to his room; of the torch, again, which Fleance
carried to light his father to death, and which was dashed out by one
of the murderers; of the torches that flared in the hall on the face of
the Ghost and the blanched cheeks of Macbeth; of the flames beneath
the boiling caldron from which the apparitions in the cavern rose; of
the taper which showed to the Doctor and Gentlewoman the wasted
face and blank eyes of Lady Macbeth. And, above all, the colour is
the colour of blood. It cannot be an accident that the image of blood
is forced upon us continually, not merely by the events themselves,
but by full descriptions, and even by reiteration of the word in unlikely parts of the dialogue. The Witches, after their first wild appearance, have hardly quitted the stage when there staggers onto it a
'bloody man,' gashed with wounds. His tale is of a hero whose
'brandished steel smoked with bloody execution,' 'carved out a passage' to his enemy, and 'unseam'd him from the nave to the chaps.'
And then he tells of a second battle so bloody that the combatants
seemed as if they 'meant to bathe in reeking wounds.' What metaphors! What a dreadful image is that with which Lady Macbeth greets
us almost as she enters, when she prays the spirits of cruelty so to
thicken her blood that pity cannot flow along her veins! What pictures
are those of the murderer appearing at the door of the banquet-room
with Banquo's 'blood upon his face'; of Banquo himself 'with twenty
trenched gashes on his head,' or 'blood-bolter'd' and smiling in derision at his murderer; of Macbeth, gazing at his hand, and watching
it dye the whole green ocean red; of Lady Macbeth, gazing at hers,
and stretching it away from her face to escape the smell of blood that
all the perfumes of Arabia will not subdue! The most horrible lines
in the whole tragedy are those of her shuddering cry, 'Yet who would
have thought the old man to have had so much blood in him?' And it
is not only at such moments that these images occur. Even in the
quiet conversation of Malcolm and Macduff, Macbeth is imagined as
holding a bloody sceptre, and Scotland as a country bleeding and
receiving every day a new gash added to her wounds. It is as if the
poet saw the whole story through an ensanguined mist, and as if it
stained the very blackness of the night. When Macbeth, before Banquo's murder, invokes night to scarf up the tender eye of pitiful day,
and to tear in pieces the great bond that keeps him pale, even the

invisible hand that is to tear the bond is imagined as covered with blood.

Let us observe another point. The vividness, magnitude, and violence of the imagery in some of these passages are characteristic of *Macbeth* almost throughout; and their influence contributes to form its atmosphere. Images like those of the babe torn smiling from the breast and dashed to death; of pouring the sweet milk of concord into hell; of the earth shaking in fever; of the frame of things disjointed; of sorrows striking heaven on the face, so that it resounds and yells out like syllables of dolour; of the mind lying in restless ecstasy on a rack; of the mind full of scorpions; of the tale told by an idiot, full of sound and fury;—all keep the imagination moving on a 'wild and violent sea,' while it is scarcely for a moment permitted to dwell on thoughts of peace and beauty. In its language, as in its action, the drama is full of tumult and storm. Whenever the Witches are present we see and hear a thunder-storm: when they are absent we hear of ship-wrecking storms and direful thunders; of tempests that blow down trees and churches, castles, palaces and pyramids; of the frightful hurricane of the night when Duncan was murdered; of the blast on which pity rides like a new-born babe, or on which Heaven's cherubim are horsed. There is thus something magnificently appropriate in the cry 'Blow, wind! Come, wrack!' with which Macbeth, turning from the sight of the moving wood of Birnam, bursts from his castle. He was borne to his throne on a whirlwind, and the fate he goes to meet comes on the wings of storm.

Now all these agencies—darkness, the lights and colours that illuminate it, the storm that rushes through it, the violent and gigantic images—conspire with the appearances of the Witches and the Ghost to awaken horror, and in some degree also a supernatural dread. And to this effect other influences contribute. The pictures called up by the mere words of the Witches stir the same feelings,—those, for example, of the spell-bound sailor driven tempest-tost for nine times nine weary weeks, and never visited by sleep night or day; of the drop of poisonous foam that forms on the moon, and, falling to earth, is collected for pernicious ends; of the sweltering venom of the toad, the finger of the babe killed at its birth by its own mother, the tricklings from the murderer's gibbet. In Nature, again, something is felt to be at work, sympathetic with human guilt and supernatural malice. She labours with portents.

Lamentings heard in the air, strange screams of death,
And prophesying with accents terrible,

burst from her. The owl clamours all through the night; Duncan's
horses devour each other in frenzy; the dawn comes, but no light with
it. Common sights and sounds, the crying of crickets, the croak of the
raven, the light thickening after sunset, the home-coming of the rooks,
are all ominous. Then, as if to deepen these impressions, Shakespeare
has concentrated attention on the obscurer regions of man's being, on
phenomena which make it seem that he is in the power of secret
forces lurking below, and independent of his consciousness and will:
such as the relapse of Macbeth from conversation into a reverie, during
which he gazes fascinated at the image of murder drawing closer and
closer; the writing on his face of strange things he never meant to
show; the pressure of imagination heightening into illusion, like the
vision of a dagger in the air, at first bright, then suddenly splashed
with blood, or the sound of a voice that cried 'Sleep no more' and
would not be silenced. To these are added other, and constant, allusions to sleep, man's strange half-conscious life; to the misery of its
withholding; to the terrible dreams of remorse; to the cursed thoughts
from which Banquo is free by day, but which tempt him in his sleep:
and again to abnormal disturbances of sleep; in the two men, of whom
one during the murder of Duncan laughed in his sleep, and the other
raised a cry of murder; and in Lady Macbeth, who rises to re-enact
in somnambulism those scenes the memory of which is pushing her
on to madness or suicide. All this has one effect, to excite supernatural alarm and, even more, a dread of the presence of evil not only
in its recognised seat but all through and around our mysterious
nature. Perhaps there is no other work equal to *Macbeth* in the production of this effect.

It is enhanced—to take a last point—by the use of a literary expedient. Not even in *Richard III.,* which in this, as in other respects, has
resemblances to *Macbeth,* is there so much of Irony. I do not refer
to irony in the ordinary sense; to speeches, for example, where the
speaker is intentionally ironical, like that of Lennox in III. VI. I refer
to irony on the part of the author himself, to ironical juxtapositions
of persons and events, and especially to the 'Sophoclean irony' by
which a speaker is made to use words bearing to the audience, in
addition to his own meaning, a further and ominous sense, hidden

from himself and, usually, from the other persons on the stage. The very first words uttered by Macbeth,

> So foul and fair a day I have not seen,

are an example to which attention has often been drawn; for they startle the reader by recalling the words of the Witches in the first scene,

> Fair is foul, and foul is fair.

When Macbeth, emerging from his murderous reverie, turns to the nobles saying, 'Let us toward the King,' his words are innocent, but to the reader have a double meaning. Duncan's comment on the treachery of Cawdor,

> There's no art
> To find the mind's construction in the face:
> He was a gentleman on whom I built
> An absolute trust,

is interrupted by the entrance of the traitor Macbeth, who is greeted with effusive gratitude and a like 'absolute trust.' I have already referred to the ironical effect of the beautiful lines in which Duncan and Banquo describe the castle they are about to enter. To the reader Lady Macbeth's light words,

> A little water clears us of this deed:
> How easy is it then,

summon up the picture of the sleep-walking scene. The idea of the Porter's speech, in which he imagines himself the keeper of hell-gate, shows the same irony. So does the contrast between the obvious and the hidden meanings of the apparitions of the armed head, the bloody child, and the child with the tree in his hand. It would be easy to add further examples. Perhaps the most striking is the answer which Banquo, as he rides away, never to return alive, gives to Macbeth's reminder, 'Fail not our feast.' 'My lord, I will not,' he replies, and he keeps his promise. It cannot be by accident that Shakespeare so frequently in this play uses a device which contributes to excite the vague fear of hidden forces operating on minds unconscious of their influence.

GEORGE LYMAN KITTREDGE
1860-1941

GEORGE LYMAN KITTREDGE did not write much on Shakespeare, but he was a great Shakespearean. He made his influence felt through generations of students who, under the impress of his commanding personality and immense erudition, left his graduate classes at Harvard to become college teachers and spread the gospel according to "Kitty." He did publish, however, annotated editions of sixteen of the plays which are invaluable by reason of his knowledge of Elizabethan language and literature and the perspicacity of his comments.

In his solid common sense and his "no nonsense" approach and manner, Kittredge is like another Samuel Johnson, to whom he paid tribute as the "most sensible and serviceable" of Shakespeareans at the opening of the lecture of which a portion follows. In this selection he demolishes the romantic critics on the Porter's scene, as Johnson had demolished the extreme neo-classical critics on the three unities, pointing out that *Macbeth* is a drama and that the Porter's scene serves a dramatic function. Yet at the conclusion of his discussion he pays his respects to the great romantics and calls attention to the perceptiveness displayed in a romantic critic's appreciation of the dramatic irony of the Porter's pretense that he is keeper of hell-gate. He does not expand, however, on the further irony of the contrast between the Porter's bleary-eyed, grumbling return to his normal workaday routine after a night of carousing and the pretense of Macbeth and Lady Macbeth, after their unknown night of horror, of awakening to ordinary, everyday reality. The relief which the audience experiences in the Porter scene is combined, as De Quincey pointed out in discussing the effect of the knocking, with a fuller realization of the horror of the previous scene. We might say that both Kittredge's Johnsonian comment on comic relief and on theatrical necessities and the romantic perception of ironic juxtapositions in Shakespeare's art contribute to the appreciation of this scene.

THE DRAMATIC FUNCTION OF THE PORTER'S SCENE

HIS WORKS WERE regarded [by the romantic critics and their succcessors], not as plays written for immediate performance, with an eye to contemporary spectators and their tastes and conventions and preconceived ideas, but rather as dark oracles, pronounced with eternity alone in mind; not as dramas constructed with more or less artistic skill, but as revelations, or mere sermons, cast into dramatic form, either because that form came easiest (as being the most generally cultivated in Shakspere's age) or because it gave best opportunity for impressing the lesson or driving home the moral.

Let us study the disease in a symptom. Take the soliloquy of the drunken porter in Macbeth. Here there is no mystery at all, nor much chance for moralizing, provided the play is looked upon as a play. Shakspere needed a short scene to fill an interval between the exit of Macbeth and his wife immediately after the murder, and Macbeth's re-entrance with the blood washed off his hands, and the air of one called up from bed by an early knock at the portal. Obviously he could not utilize any of the principal characters for the purpose. Obviously, too, the scene could not be allowed to advance the action. Obviously, again, the spectators needed relief. Their emotions had just been strung to the highest tension. Yet another moment was soon to come of tension equally terrific, when the deed should be discovered, and the murderers should have to face their crime. For Shakspere—profoundly and practically versed in stagecraft, and intimately acquainted with the audience from the actor's point of view

"The Dramatic Function of the Porter's Scene" is from George Lyman Kittredge, *Shakspere* (Harvard University Press, 1916), pp. 28–33. By permission of the publisher.

—there was but one method of filling such a gap: by comic relief. And the comedy had to be low, so that the laughter might be full-throated. A drunken porter, philosophizing on human society as he rubbed the sleep from his eyes—cataloguing the stock of traditional sinners when he ought to have been opening the door—and coming at last to be broad awake, as his body realized that the place was "too cold for hell" and his mind reasserted itself sufficiently to ask for his tip ("I pray you remember the porter")! What lay readier at hand, particularly since the whole thing would be a realistic touch? For there was a porter, of course, and of course he had been carousing with his fellows until the second cock. For had not the gracious Duncan sent forth great largess to the servants? A simple passage, assuredly! safe, one might suppose, in its strict conformity to method, its manifest adaptation to the emergencies of the curtainless Elizabethan stage!

But how was it dealt with? Why, variously, variously—on the *quot homines* principle. Some demanded its excision. Away with it! it is mere foolery, and not good foolery either. Argal, it is spurious and out it should go. This dictum was, after all, but an idolatrous variant of the eighteenth-century manner. Instead of censuring Shakspere for mixing drollery with tragedy (a stricture which, be it right or wrong, was at least intelligible and regular), this idolatrous variant, though condemning the passage equally and on much the same grounds, absolved the author by assuming an interpolation. Yet, after all, one phrase was too Shaksperean to reject: "the primrose way to the everlasting bonfire." That could not be the coinage of any clownish player, or jog-trot fabricator of counterfeit speeches. What then? Why, we must save that phrase and delete the residue. The passage, we are told, was "written for the mob by some other hand, perhaps with Shakspere's consent; and, finding it take, he, with the remaining ink of a pen otherwise employed, just interpolated the words" in question. "Of the rest, not one syllable has the ever-present being of Shakspere." Now this subjective and impressionistic tinkering with the text is not, as one might fancy, the toilsome trifling of some academic pedant, one of those humble scholiasts whose lives are spent in piling up junk-heaps for a Variorum to sort and sift. By no means. It is the handiwork of a noble poet and a profound, if somewhat misty, thinker—of no less a man than Coleridge. Yet what could be more futile? Not a word of the real pertinency of the passage! Not a hint of the place it occupies in the structural economy of the drama as a drama—as a play to be performed, that is, on an actual stage, by human beings, who have their exits and their entrances, for which it is the business of the playwright to provide in a workmanlike manner.

Still, a worse thing was possible; and of course it was duly perpetrated—this time by a constructive reviser. Schiller transforms the character of the rough porter completely. Under his refining hand he becomes a lyric personage, who might be singing an aubade to Romeo:—"The gloomy night has departed; the lark is carolling; the day awakes; the sun is rising in splendor; he shines alike on the palace and the cottage. Praise be to God, who watches over this house!" O most gentle pulpiter! what a tedious homily have you wearied your parishioners withal, and never cried "Have patience, good people!"

I am anxious not to be misunderstood. Mere scholarship should not be arrogant. The reaction of a mind like Coleridge's, or of a mind like Schiller's, under the Shaksperean goad is by no means negligible. For it is a fact in and for itself, one of the phenomena to be accounted for, a part of the *res gestae* of the case. And now and then there emerges, even from the chaos and welter of sheer impressionism, a created and symmetrical judgment. Such, for instance, is the remark of Bodenstedt about our low comedian: "He never dreams, while imagining himself a porter of hell-gate, how near he comes to the truth!" That is fine; that is indeed illuminating. That is enough to rehabilitate the passage, to make us ashamed that we have ever presumed to cast suspicion on its paternity.

A. C. BRADLEY
1851-1935

NOTABLE IN THIS description of the dramatic universe of *King Lear* is its statement of the humanism underlying *King Lear,* its sense of the dignity of man despite his suffering and wretchedness. For Bradley the final impression left by *King Lear* is not, as it is with Swin-

burne and with T. S. Eliot (in his "Shakespeare and
the Stoicism of Seneca") represented by Gloucester's
words "As flies to wanton boys are we to the gods;
They kill us for their sport."

Bradley's description of Britain as a timeless and
vast world, in which we see not so much ancient
Britons as man, has been expanded upon by G. Wilson Knight in one of his best essays, "The *Lear* Universe," in *The Wheel of Fire,* which indeed is heavily
indebted to Bradley in a number of respects. His statement that *King Lear* discloses a mode of imagination
not very far removed from the mode which produced
the morality plays and *The Faerie Queene* anticipates
modern ideas about Shakespeare's drama generally.
His discussion of "the explosion of Lear's passion" and
"the bursts of rain and thunder" as "manifestations of
one thing" point the way to the scholarly explications
of the Elizabethan ideas concerning interrelated hierarchical orders and the disorder wrought in all of nature by man's choice of evil.

THE WORLD OF KING LEAR

How is it, now, that this defective drama so overpowers us that we
are either unconscious of its blemishes or regard them as almost irrelevant? As soon as we turn to this question we recognize, not
merely that *King Lear* possesses purely dramatic qualities which far
outweigh its defects, but that its greatness consists partly in imaginative
effects of a wider kind. And, looking for the sources of these effects,
we find among them some of those very things which appeared to us
dramatically faulty or injurious. Thus, to take at once two of the
simplest examples of this, that very vagueness in the sense of locality
which we have just considered, and again that excess in the bulk of
the material and the number of figures, events and movements, while

"The World of *King Lear*" is from A. C. Bradley, *Shakespearean Tragedy,*
pp. 261–279, 303–305. Reprinted with permission of Macmillan & Company
Ltd., St. Martin's Press Inc., and the Macmillan Company of Canada Ltd.

they interfere with the clearness of vision, have at the same time a positive value for imagination. They give the feeling of vastness, the feeling not of a scene or particular place, but of a world; or, to speak more accurately, of a particular place which is also a world. This world is dim to us, partly from its immensity, and partly because it is filled with gloom; and in the gloom shapes approach and recede, whose half-seen faces and motions touch us with dread, horror, or the most painful pity,—sympathies and antipathies which we seem to be feeling not only for them but for the whole race. This world, we are told, is called Britain; but we should no more look for it in an atlas than for the place, called Caucasus, where Prometheus was chained by Strength and Force and comforted by the daughters of Ocean, or the place where Farinata stands erect in his glowing tomb, "Come avesse lo Inferno in gran dispitto."

Consider next the double action. It has certain strictly dramatic advantages, and may well have had its origin in purely dramatic considerations. To go no further, the secondary plot fills out a story which would by itself have been somewhat thin, and it provides a most effective contrast between its personages and those of the main plot, the tragic strength and stature of the latter being heightened by comparison with the slighter build of the former. But its chief value lies elsewhere, and is not merely dramatic. It lies in the fact—in Shakespeare without a parallel—that the sub-plot simply repeats the theme of the main story. Here, as there, we see an old man "with a white beard." He, like Lear, is affectionate, unsuspicious, foolish, and self-willed. He, too, wrongs deeply a child who loves him not less for the wrong. He, too, meets with monstrous ingratitude from the child whom he favours, and is tortured and driven to death. This repetition does not simply double the pain with which the tragedy is witnessed: it startles and terrifies by suggesting that the folly of Lear and the ingratitude of his daughters are no accidents or merely individual aberrations, but that in that dark cold world some fateful malignant influence is abroad, turning the hearts of the fathers against their children and of the children against their fathers, smiting the earth with a curse, so that the brother gives the brother to death and the father the son, blinding the eyes, maddening the brain, freezing the springs of pity, numbing all powers except the nerves of anguish and the dull lust of life.[1]

---

[1] This effect of the double action seems to have been pointed out first by Schlegel.

Hence too, as well as from other sources, comes that feeling which haunts us in *King Lear,* as though we were witnessing something universal,—a conflict not so much of particular persons as of the powers of good and evil in the world. And the treatment of many of the characters confirms this feeling. Considered simply as psychological studies few of them, surely, are of the highest interest. Fine and subtle touches could not be absent from a work of Shakespeare's maturity; but, with the possible exception of Lear himself, no one of the characters strikes us as psychologically a *wonderful* creation, like Hamlet or Iago, or even Macbeth; one or two seem even to be somewhat faint and thin. And, what is more significant, it is not quite natural to us to regard them from this point of view at all. Rather we observe a most unusual circumstance. If Lear, Gloster and Albany are set apart, the rest fall into two distinct groups, which are strongly, even violently, contrasted: Cordelia, Kent, Edgar, the Fool on one side, Goneril, Regan, Edmund, Cornwall, Oswald on the other. These characters are in various degrees individualised, most of them completely so; but still in each group there is a quality common to all the members, or one spirit breathing through them all. Here we have unselfish and devoted love, there hard self-seeking. On both sides, further, the common quality takes an extreme form; the love is incapable of being chilled by injury, the selfishness of being softened by pity; and, it may be added, this tendency to extremes is found again in the characters of Lear and Gloster, and is the main source of the accusations of improbability directed against their conduct at certain points. Hence the members of each group tend to appear, at least in part, as varieties of one species; the radical differences of the two species are emphasized in broad hard strokes; and the two are set in conflict, almost as if Shakespeare, like Empedocles, were regarding Love and Hate as the two ultimate forces of the universe.

The presence in *King Lear* of so large a number of characters in whom love or self-seeking is so extreme, has another effect. They do not merely inspire in us emotions of unusual strength, but they also stir the intellect to wonder and speculation. How can there be such men and women? we ask ourselves. How comes it that humanity can take such absolutely opposite forms? And, in particular, to what omission of elements which should be present in human nature, or, if there is no omission, to what distortion of these elements is it due that such beings as some of these come to exist? This is a question which Iago (and perhaps no previous creation of Shakespeare's) forces us to ask, but in *King Lear* it is provoked again and again. And more, it seems to us that the author himself is asking this question. "Then let them anatomise Regan, see what breeds about her heart. Is there any cause in nature that makes these hard hearts?"—the strain of thought which appears here seems to be present in some degree throughout the play. We seem to trace the tendency which, a few years later, produced Ariel and Caliban, the tendency of imagination to analyse and abstract, to decompose human nature into its constituent factors, and then to construct beings in whom one or more of these factors is absent or atrophied or only incipient. This, of course, is a tendency which produces symbols, allegories, personifications of qualities and abstract ideas; and we are accustomed to think it quite foreign to Shakespeare's genius, which was in the highest degree concrete. No doubt in the main we are right here; but it is hazardous to set limits to that genius. The Sonnets, if nothing else, may show us how easy it was to Shakespeare's mind to move in a world of "Platonic" ideas, and, while it would be going too far to suggest that he was employing conscious symbolism or allegory in *King Lear,* it does appear to disclose a mode of imagination not so very far removed from the mode with which, we must remember, Shakespeare was perfectly familiar in Morality plays and in the *Fairy Queen.*

This same tendency shows itself in *King Lear* in other forms. To it is due the idea of monstrosity—of beings, actions, states of mind, which appear not only abnormal but absolutely contrary to nature; an idea, which, of course, is common enough in Shakespeare, but appears with unusual frequency in *King Lear,* for instance in the lines:

> *Ingratitude, thou marble-hearted fiend,*
> *More hideous when thou show'st thee in a child*
> *Than the sea-monster!*

or in the exclamation,

> *Filial ingratitude!*
> *Is it not as this mouth should tear this hand*
> *For lifting food to't?*

It appears in another shape in that most vivid passage where Albany, as he looks at the face which had bewitched him, now distorted with dreadful passions, suddenly sees it in a new light and exclaims in horror:

> *Thou changed and self-cover'd thing, for shame,*
> *Bemonster not thy feature. Were't my fitness*
> *To let these hands obey my blood,*
> *They are apt enough to dislocate and tear*
> *Thy flesh and bones: howe'er thou art a fiend,*
> *A woman's shape doth shield thee.*[2]

It appears once more in that exclamation of Kent's, as he listens to the description of Cordelia's grief:

> *It is the stars,*
> *The stars above us, govern our conditions;*
> *Else one self mate and mate could not beget*
> *Such different issues.*

(This is not the only sign that Shakespeare had been musing over heredity, and wondering how it comes about that the composition of two strains of blood or two parent souls can produce such astonishingly different products.)

This mode of thought is responsible, lastly, for a very striking characteristic of *King Lear*—one in which it has no parallel except *Timon*—the incessant references to the lower animals and man's likeness to them. These references are scattered broadcast through the whole play as though Shakespeare's mind were so busy with the subject that he could hardly write a page without some allusion to it. The dog, the horse, the cow, the sheep, the hog, the lion, the bear, the wolf, the fox, the monkey, the pole-cat, the civet-cat, the pelican, the owl, the crow, the chough, the wren, the fly, the butterfly, the rat, the mouse, the frog, the tadpole, the wall-newt, the water-newt, the worm—I am sure I cannot have completed the list, and some of them are mentioned again and again. Often, of course, and especially in the talk of Edgar as the Bedlam, they have no symbolical meaning; but not seldom, even in his talk, they are expressly referred to for their typical qualities—"hog in sloth, fox in stealth, wolf in greediness, dog in madness, lion in prey," "The fitchew nor the soiled horse goes to't With a more riotous appetite." Sometimes a person in the drama is compared, openly or implicitly, with one of them. Goneril is a kite:

[2] The monstrosity here is a being with a woman's body and a fiend's soul. . . .

her ingratitude has a serpent's tooth: she has struck her father most serpent-like upon the very heart: her visage is wolvish: she has tied sharp-toothed unkindness like a vulture on her father's breast: for her husband she is a gilded serpent: to Gloster her cruelty seems to have the fangs of a boar. She and Regan are dog-hearted: they are tigers, not daughters: each is an adder to the other: the flesh of each is covered with the fell of a beast. Oswald is a mongrel, and the son and heir of a mongrel: ducking to everyone in power, he is a wag-tail: white with fear, he is a goose. Gloster, for Regan, is an in-grateful fox: Albany, for his wife, has a cowish spirit and is milk-liver'd: when Edgar as the Bedlam first appeared to Lear he made him think a man a worm. As we read, the souls of all the beasts in turn seem to us to have entered the bodies of these mortals; horrible in their venom, savagery, lust, deceitfulness, sloth, cruelty, filthiness; miserable in their feebleness, nakedness, defencelessness, blindness; and man, "consider him well," is even what they are. Shakespeare, to whom the idea of the transmigration of souls was familiar and had once been material for jest, seems to have been brooding on humanity in the light of it. It is remarkable, and somewhat sad, that he seems to find none of man's better qualities in the world of the brutes (though he might well have found the prototype of the selfless love of Kent and Cordelia in the dog whom he so habitually maligns); but he seems to have been asking himself whether that which he loathes in man may not be due to some strange wrenching of this frame of things, through which the lower animal souls have found a lodgment in human forms, and there found—to the horror and confusion of the thinking mind—brains to forge, tongues to speak, and hands to act, enormities which no mere brute can conceive or execute. He shows us in *King Lear* these terrible forces bursting into monstrous life and flinging themselves upon those human beings who are weak and de-fenceless, partly from old age, but partly because they *are* human and lack the dreadful undivided energy of the beast. And the only com-fort he might seem to hold out to us is the prospect that at least this bestial race, strong only where it is vile, cannot endure: though stars and gods are powerless, or careless, or empty dreams, yet there must be an end of this horrible world:

> *It will come;*
> *Humanity must perforce prey on itself*
> *Like monsters of the deep.*

The influence of all this on imagination as we read *King Lear* is very great; and it combines with other influences to convey to us, not in the form of distinct ideas but in the manner proper to poetry, the wider or universal significance of the spectacle presented to the inward eye. But the effect of theatrical exhibition is precisely the reverse. There the poetic atmosphere is dissipated; the meaning of the very words which create it passes half-realised; in obedience to the tyranny of the eye we conceive the characters are mere particular men and women; and all that mass of vague suggestion, if it enters the mind at all, appears in the shape of an allegory which we immediately reject. A similar conflict between imagination and sense will be found if we consider the dramatic centre of the whole tragedy, the Storm-scenes. The temptation of Othello and the scene of Duncan's murder may lose upon the stage, but they do not lose their essence, and they gain as well as lose. The Storm-scenes in *King Lear* gain nothing and their very essence is destroyed. It is comparatively a small thing that the theatrical storm, not to drown the dialogue, must be silent whenever a human being wishes to speak, and is wretchedly inferior to many a storm we have witnessed. Nor is it simply that, as Lamb observed, the corporal presence of Lear, "an old man tottering about the stage with a walking-stick," disturbs and depresses that sense of the greatness of his mind which fills the imagination. There is a further reason, which is not expressed, but still emerges, in these words of Lamb's: "the explosions of his passion are terrible as a volcano: they are storms turning up and disclosing to the bottom that sea, his mind, with all its vast riches." Yes, "they are *storms*." For imagination, that is to say, the explosions of Lear's passion, and the bursts of rain and thunder, are not, what for the senses they must be, two things, but manifestations of one thing. It is the powers of the tormented soul that we hear and see in the "groans of roaring wind and rain" and the "sheets of fire"; and they that, at intervals almost more overwhelming, sink back into darkness and silence. Nor yet is even this all; but, as those incessant references to wolf and tiger made us see humanity "reeling back into the beast" and ravening against itself, so in the storm we seem to see Nature herself convulsed by the same horrible passions; the "common mother,"

> *Whose womb immeasurable and infinite breast*
> *Teems and feeds all,*

turning on her children, to complete the ruin they have wrought upon themselves. Surely something not less, but much more, than these helpless words convey, is what comes to us in these astounding scenes; and if, translated thus into the language of prose, it becomes confused and inconsistent, the reason is simply that it itself is poetry, and such poetry as cannot be transferred to the space behind the footlights, but has its being only in imagination. Here then is Shakespeare at his very greatest, but not the mere dramatist Shakespeare.

And now we may say this also of the catastrophe, which we found questionable from the strictly dramatic point of view. Its purpose is not merely dramatic. This sudden blow out of the darkness, which seems so far from inevitable, and which strikes down our reviving hopes for the victims of so much cruelty, seems now only what we might have expected in a world so wild and monstrous. It is as if Shakespeare said to us: "Did you think weakness and innocence have any chance here? Were you beginning to dream that? I will show you it is not so."

I come to a last point. As we contemplate this world, the question presses on us What can be the ultimate power that moves it, that excites this gigantic war and waste, or, perhaps, that suffers them and overrules them? And in *King Lear* this question is not left to *us* to ask, it is raised by the characters themselves. References to religious or irreligious beliefs and feelings are more frequent than is usual in Shakespeare's tragedies, as frequent perhaps as in his final plays. He introduces characteristic differences in the language of the different persons about fortune or the stars or the gods, and shows how the question What rules the world? is forced upon their minds. They answer it in their turn: Kent, for instance:

> *It is the stars,*
> *The stars above us, govern our condition:*

Edmund:

> *Thou, nature, art my goddess; to thy law*
> *My services are bound:*

and again,

> *This is the excellent foppery of the world, that, when we are sick in*
> *fortune—often the surfeit of our own behaviour—we make guilty of our*
> *disasters the sun, the moon and the stars; as if we were villains by*

*necessity, fools by heavenly compulsion, . . . and all that we are evil
in by a divine thrusting on:*

Gloster:

> As flies to wanton boys are we to the gods;
> They kill us for their sport;

Edgar:

> Think that the clearest gods, who make them honours
> Of men's impossibilities, have preserved thee.

Here we have four distinct theories of the nature of the ruling power.
And besides this, in such of the characters as have any belief in gods
who love good and hate evil, the spectacle of triumphant injustice or
cruelty provokes questionings like those of Job, or else the thought,
often repeated, of divine retribution. To Lear at one moment the
storm seems the messenger of heaven:

> Let the great gods,
> That keep this dreadful pother o'er our heads,
> Find out their enemies now. Tremble, thou wretch,
> That hast within thee undivulged crimes. . . .

At another moment those habitual miseries of the poor, of which he
has taken too little account, seem to him to accuse the gods of injustice:

> Take physic, pomp;
> Expose thyself to feel what wretches feel,
> That thou mayst shake the superflux to them
> And show the heavens more just;

and Gloster has almost the same thought (IV. i. 67 ff.). Gloster again,
thinking of the cruelty of Lear's daughters, breaks out,

> but I shall see
> The winged vengeance overtake such children.

The servants who have witnessed the blinding of Gloster by Cornwall
and Regan, cannot believe that cruelty so atrocious will pass un-
punished. One cries,

> I'll never care what wickedness I do,
> If this man come to good;

and another,

> *if she live long,*
> *And in the end meet the old course of death,*
> *Women will all turn monsters.*

Albany greets the news of Cornwall's death with the exclamation,

> *This shows you are above,*
> *You justicers, that these our nether crimes*
> *So speedily can venge;*

and the news of the deaths of the sisters with the words,

> *This judgment of the heavens, that makes us tremble,*
> *Touches us not with pity.*

Edgar, speaking to Edmund of their father, declares

> *The gods are just, and of our pleasant vices*
> *Make instruments to plague us,*

and Edmund himself assents. Almost throughout the latter half of the drama we note in most of the better characters a preoccupation with the question of the ultimate power, and a passionate need to explain by reference to it what otherwise would drive them to despair. And the influence of this preoccupation and need joins with other influences in affecting the imagination, and in causing it to receive from *King Lear* an impression which is at least as near of kin to the *Divine Comedy* as to *Othello*.

For Dante that which is recorded in the *Divine Comedy* was the justice and love of God. What did *King Lear* record for Shakespeare? Something, it would seem, very different. This is certainly the most terrible picture that Shakespeare painted of the world. In no other of his tragedies does humanity appear more pitiably infirm or more hopelessly bad. What is Iago's malignity against an envied stranger compared with the cruelty of the son of Gloster and the daughters of Lear? What are the sufferings of a strong man like Othello to those of helpless age? Much too that we have already observed—the repetition of the main theme in that of the under-plot, the comparisons of man with the most wretched and the most horrible of the beasts, the impression of Nature's hostility to him, the irony of the unexpected catastrophe—these, with much else, seem even to indicate an intention to show things at their worst, and to return the sternest of replies to that question of the ultimate power and those appeals for retribution. Is it an accident, for example, that Lear's first appeal to something beyond the earth,

> *O heavens,*
> *If you do love old men, if your sweet sway*
> *Allow obedience, if yourselves are old,*
> *Make it your cause:*

is immediately answered by the iron voices of his daughters, raising by turns the conditions on which they will give him a humiliating harbourage; or that his second appeal, heart-rending in its piteousness,

> *You see me here, you gods, a poor old man,*
> *As full of grief as age; wretched in both:*

is immediately answered from the heavens by the sound of the breaking storm? Albany and Edgar may moralise on the divine justice as they will, but how, in the face of all that we see, shall we believe that they speak Shakespeare's mind? Is not his mind rather expressed in the bitter contrast between their faith and the events we witness, or in the scornful rebuke of those who take upon them the mystery of things as if they were God's spies? Is it not Shakespeare's judgment on his kind that we hear in Lear's appeal,

> *And thou, all-shaking thunder,*
> *Smite flat the thick rotundity o' the world!*
> *Crack nature's moulds, all germens spill at once,*
> *That make ingrateful man!*

and Shakespeare's judgment on the worth of existence that we hear in Lear's agonised cry, "No, no, no life!"?

Beyond doubt, I think, some such feelings as these possess us, and, if we follow Shakespeare, ought to possess us, from time to time as we read *King Lear*. And some readers will go further and maintain that this is also the ultimate and total impression left by the tragedy. *King Lear* has been held to be profoundly "pessimistic" in the full meaning of that word,—the record of a time when contempt and loathing for his kind had overmastered the poet's soul, and in despair he pronounced man's life to be simply hateful and hideous. And if we exclude the biographical part of this view, the rest may claim some support even from the greatest of Shakespearean critics since the days of Coleridge, Hazlitt and Lamb. Mr. Swinburne, after observing that

King Lear is "by far the most Aeschylean" of Shakespeare's works, proceeds thus:

"But in one main point it differs radically from the work and the spirit of Aeschylus. Its fatalism is of a darker and harder nature. To Prometheus the fetters of the lord and enemy of mankind were bitter; upon Orestes the hand of heaven was laid too heavily to bear; yet in the not utterly infinite or everlasting distance we see beyond them the promise of the morning on which mystery and justice shall be made one; when righteousness and omnipotence at last shall kiss each other. But on the horizon of Shakespeare's tragic fatalism we see no such twilight of atonement, such pledge of reconciliation as this. Requital, redemption, amends, equity, explanation, pity and mercy, are words without a meaning here.

> *As flies to wanton boys are we to the gods;*
> *They kill us for their sport.*

Here is no need of the Eumenides, children of Night everlasting; for here is very Night herself.

"The words just cited are not casual or episodical; they strike the keynote of the whole poem, lay the keystone of the whole arch of thought. There is no contest of conflicting forces, no judgment so much as by casting of lots: far less is there any light of heavenly harmony or of heavenly wisdom, of Apollo or Athene from above. We have heard much and often from theologians of the light of revelation: and some such thing indeed we find in Aeschylus; but the darkness of revelation is here."[3]

It is hard to refuse assent to these eloquent words, for they express in the language of a poet what we feel at times in reading *King Lear* but cannot express. But do they represent the total and final impression produced by the play? If they do, this impression, so far as the substance of the drama is concerned (and nothing else is in question here), must, it would seem, be one composed almost wholly of painful feelings,—utter depression, or indignant rebellion, or appalled despair. And that would surely be strange. For *King Lear* is admittedly one of the world's greatest poems, and yet there is surely no other of these poems which produces on the whole this effect, and we regard it as a very serious flaw in any considerable work of art

[3] *A Study of Shakespeare*, pp. 171, 172.

that this should be its ultimate effect.[4] So that Mr. Swinburne's description, if taken as final, and any description of *King Lear* as "pessimistic" in the proper sense of that word, would imply a criticism which is not intended, and which would make it difficult to leave the work in the position almost universally assigned to it.

But in fact these descriptions, like most of the remarks made on *King Lear* in the present lecture, emphasise only certain aspects of the play and certain elements in the total impression; and that impression of the effect of these aspects, though far from being lost, is modified by that of others. I do not mean that the final effect resembles that of the *Divine Comedy* or the *Oresteia:* how should it, when the first of these can be called by its author a "Comedy," and when the second, ending (as doubtless the *Prometheus* trilogy also ended) with a solution, is not in the Shakespearean sense a tragedy at all? Nor do I mean that *King Lear* contains a revelation of righteous omnipotence or heavenly harmony, or even a promise of the reconciliation of mystery and justice. But then, as we saw, neither do Shakespeare's other tragedies contain these things. Any theological interpretation of the world on the author's part is excluded from them, and their effect would be disordered or destroyed equally by the ideas of righteous or of unrighteous omnipotence. Nor, in reading them, do we think of "justice" or "equity" in the sense of a strict requital or such an adjustment of merit and prosperity as our moral sense is said to demand; and there never was vainer labour than that of critics who try to make out that the persons in these dramas meet with "justice" or their "deserts." But, on the other hand, man is not represented in these tragedies as the mere plaything of a blind or capricious power, suffering woes which have no relation to his character and actions; nor is the world represented as given over to darkness. And in these respects *King Lear,* though the most terrible of these works, does not differ in essence from the rest. Its keynote is surely to be heard neither in the words wrung from Gloster in his anguish, nor in Edgar's words "the gods are just." Its final and total result is one in which pity and terror, carried perhaps to the extreme limits of art, are so blended with a sense of law and beauty that we feel at last, not

---

[4] A flaw, I mean, in a work of art considered not as a moral or theological document but as a work of art,—an aesthetic flaw. I add the word "considerable" because we do not regard the effect in question as a flaw in a work like a lyric or a short piece of music, which may naturally be taken as expressions merely of a mood or a subordinate aspect of things.

depression and much less despair, but a consciousness of greatness in pain, and of solemnity in the mystery we cannot fathom. . . .

What are we to say of the world which contains these five beings, Goneril, Regan, Edmund, Cornwall, Oswald? I have tried to answer this question in our first lecture; for in its representation of evil *King Lear* differs from the other tragedies only in degree and manner. It is the tragedy in which evil is shown in the greatest abundance; and the evil characters are peculiarly repellent from their hard savagery, and because so little good is mingled with their evil. The effect is therefore more startling than elsewhere; it is even appalling. But in substance it is the same as elsewhere; and accordingly, although it may be useful to recall here our previous discussion, I will do so only by the briefest statement.

On the one hand we see a world which generates terrible evil in profusion. Further, the beings in whom this evil appears at its strongest are able, to a certain extent, to thrive. They are not unhappy, and they have power to spread misery and destruction around them. All this is undeniable fact.

On the other hand this evil is *merely* destructive: it founds nothing, and seems capable of existing only on foundations laid by its opposite. It is also self-destructive: it sets those beings at enmity; they can scarcely unite against a common and pressing danger; if it were averted they would be at each other's throats in a moment; the sisters do not even wait till it is past. Finally, these beings, all five of them, are dead a few weeks after we see them first; three at least die young; the outburst of their evil is fatal to them. These also are undeniable facts; and, in face of them, it seems odd to describe *King Lear* as "a play in which the wicked prosper" (Johnson).

Thus the world in which evil appears seems to be at heart unfriendly to it. And this impression is confirmed by the fact that the convulsion of this world is due to evil, mainly in the worst forms here considered, partly in the milder forms which we call the errors or defects of the better characters. Good, in the widest sense, seems thus to be the principle of life and health in the world; evil, at least in these worst forms, to be a poison. The world reacts against it violently, and, in the struggle to expel it, is driven to devastate itself.

If we ask why the world should generate that which convulses and wastes it, the tragedy gives no answer, and we are trying to go beyond tragedy in seeking one. But the world, in this tragic picture, *is* convulsed by evil, and rejects it.

And if here there is 'very night herself,' she comes "with stars in her raiment." Cordelia, Kent, Edgar, the Fool—these form a group not less remarkable than that which we have just left. There is in the world of *King Lear* the same abundance of extreme good as of extreme evil. It generates in profusion self-less devotion and unconquerable love. And the strange thing is that neither Shakespeare nor we are surprised. We approve these characters, admire them, love them; but we feel no mystery. We do not ask in bewilderment, Is there any cause in nature that makes these kind hearts? Such hardened optimists are we, and Shakespeare,—and those who find the darkness of revelation in a tragedy which reveals Cordelia. Yet surely, if we condemn the universe for Cordelia's death, we ought also to remember that it gave her birth. The fact that Socrates was executed does not remove the fact that he lived, and the inference thence to be drawn about the world that produced him.

R. W. CHAMBERS
1874-1942

CHAMBERS'S LECTURE ON KING LEAR, published by the University of Glasgow in 1940 and not since reprinted, does not seem to be as well known as it should be. Through a study of Shakespeare's sources, often regarded as unimaginative drudgery, as indeed it all too often is, Chambers shows how the elimination by Shakespeare of Cordelia's despair is of key significance and brilliantly corroborates Bradley's brilliant perception that Lear dies in ecstasy. He finds, however, in Lear's belief that Cordelia is alive a symbolic truth which Bradley does not. In this he anticipates Oscar James Campbell, who in his 1948 article "The Salvation of Lear" finds that the play derives from the homily, frequently dramatized in the moralities, of man following his one true companion, variously represented as faith, hope, charity or good works, through death to everlasting life.

Such an interpretation has been objected to as giving an optimistic ending to the darkest of Shakespeare's tragedies. However, it might be argued that tragedy, as Richard B. Sewall has said, in "The Tragic Form" (1954), cannot be contained in the categories "pessimism" and "optimism."

> Tragedy could . . . be called pessimistic in its view of the evil in the universe as . . . the necessary condition of existence. It is pessimistic, also, in its view of the overwhelming proportion of evil to good and in its awareness of the mystery of why this should be . . . But it is optimistic in what might be called its vitalism, which is in some sense mystical, not earth-bound; in its faith in a cosmic good; in its vision, however fleeting, of a world in which all questions could be answered.

The emphasis of Chambers may be too much on the similarity of *King Lear* and *The Divine Comedy* and not enough on the difference, but his interpretation (like Bradley's) is not in opposition to the view that tragedy transcends both "pessimism" and "optimism."

KING LEAR

THE ESSENCE OF Cordelia's sorrowful story in the chronicles is her utter dereliction. She is left with none to comfort her in prison, or to mourn her when dead. Her story is very like another tale which Geoffrey cannot have known, that of Antigone who, after comforting her father and burying her brother, is punished by being immured alive in a rocky tomb, where she hangs herself. Antigone complains that no one laments her lot, that it receives no tear. Yet divine vengeance intervenes in the end, not indeed to save the life of Antigone, but to vindicate the righteousness of her cause. It is not so

"King Lear" is from R. W. Chambers, *"King Lear,"* *Glasgow University Publications,* LIV (1940), 20–52.

with the Cordelia of the chronicles. She has no one to lament or to vindicate her.

Critics who speak of the text of the chronicles seem strangely ignorant of the story which that text tells. Still stranger is the habit of ignoring all Tudor versions of the story except the old play. That comes from the indefensible modern habit of thinking of literature in water-tight compartments—history of the drama, history of the novel, and so on.

John Addington Symonds, in his *Shakspere's Predecessors,* tells us that the author of the old play adhered to the letter of his text when he left Cordelia happy. Symonds then continues:

We shall never know what moved Shakspere to drop that pall of darkness upon the mystery of inscrutable woe at the very moment when there dawned a brighter day for Lear united to his blameless daughter. For once, it would appear, he chose to sound the deepest depths of the world's suffering, a depth deeper than that of Æschylean or Sophoclean tragedy, deeper than the tragedy of 'Othello,' deeper than Malebolge or Caïna, a stony black despairing depth of voiceless and inexplicable agony.

All this is very strange; and equally strange is Dr. Johnson's statement, that to suffer 'the virtue of Cordelia to perish in a just cause' is 'contrary to the faith of chronicles.'

Shakespeare probably felt it permissible to treat his authorities more freely than he would have done in a more authentic period of history. But, broadly, he follows the practice, usual in his history plays, of preserving the essential facts of his original, but dealing as he chooses with chronology. In Act V of his *King Lear* Shakespeare telescopes, as it were, two battles into one. The battle begins as the battle fought by Cordelia to restore her father to the throne: it ends as the battle in which Cordelia is captured by her foes. By thus combining the two battles, Shakespeare is able to give to Cordelia one who will comfort her distress and mourn her death. Her comforter is the father whom she herself has saved from despair.

Thus Shakespeare's manipulation of the plot humanizes it, by removing the cruel feature which Geoffrey's story shares with the Greek tale of Antigone as Sophocles tells it, in which the faithful girl, after all her pious care for her kinsfolk, is herself left lonely in her own despair. Cordelia is slain. *But not by herself*; there Shakespeare *does* depart from historic fact, as he had received it. For it is extremely unlikely that Shakespeare could have known any of the

Fifteenth Century versions in which Cordelia is saved from suicide by being murdered. Nor would many of his audience have known them, except perhaps stray antiquarian students. There was, in Shakespeare's day, no living tradition of Cordelia's death, save by her own hand. She was the most illustrious, most innocent, and most pitiful suicide in British or English story.

I can imagine that some of Shakespeare's audience, as they watched the play drawing to its end, may have asked themselves: How will the poet finish this? Will he break off Cordelia's story in the middle, and refuse to follow her to the end? Or will he make this brave gentle girl slay herself in despair? If he chooses to do this, then, in the words of the *Mirror for Magistrates*: 'Who ever saw such cruelty before?'

Shakespeare does neither of these unbearable things. For suicide would be unbearable in the case of Shakespeare's Cordelia. Shakespeare does indeed allow Othello or Brutus, Antony and Cleopatra to slay themselves in order to avoid intolerable dishonour. And even Christian casuists have disputed whether, to save their honour, men and women may not in some cases choose death. But the feeling of Christendom, and often of the pagan world also, has been that men and women may not kill themselves to avoid the torture or the tedium of imprisonment or sickness.

In our days the message has been smuggled out of Concentration Camps: 'You will be told that I committed suicide: it will not be true.' The sender of the message has wished to save his reputation from what he feels would be a slur upon it. And, as in the case of many a medieval writer before him, whose work he did not know, Shakespeare feels this about Cordelia. When Cordelia is brought on the stage a prisoner, Shakespeare's audience, as I have said, may have feared that the story would end (as in the versions they knew) by her despair and suicide. Shakespeare makes it clear at once that he is not conceiving the story so. Cordelia turns to Lear:

> For thee, oppressed king, am I cast down;
> Myself could else outfrown false Fortune's frown.

This, Professor Raleigh complains, is a rhyming tag, which might have been addressed by a chorus to the audience:

> For the oppressed king is she cast down;
> Herself could else outfrown false Fortune's frown.

To Raleigh it seemed hardly in character that Cordelia, who cannot heave her heart into her mouth even to tell of her love to her father, should tell of her courage to all and sundry in this way. Raleigh felt that Shakespeare is 'making one of his most cherished characters do the menial explanatory work of a chorus.'[1] But (even if this be so) a study of the sources shows us (what Raleigh did not see) that there is a reason for this 'menial, explanatory work.' The Attic dramatists sometimes did the same. They, too, retold stories familiar to their audience in other forms: and they sometimes put words into the mouth of a speaker, expressly to show that the poet's conception is different from that of some predecessor.

Then Shakespeare makes his point still clearer. The dying Edmund confesses that his writ 'is on the life of Lear and on Cordelia.' The Captain, he continues, has commission from Goneril and him

> To hang Cordelia in the prison and
> To lay the blame upon her own despair
> That she fordid herself.

But, since Lear is also to be slain, *his* death has also to be accounted for. Logically the words should surely therefore be '*their* own despair, that *they* fordid themselves.' Why only Cordelia's despair? Because Shakespeare's mind is going back to the current story in which (after Lear has died a natural death) a lonely Cordelia slays herself. That, he says, is not true of the Cordelia of my play: it is the kind of libel an Edmund or a Goneril might have invented. So intent is he on contradicting this current story that he allows Lear (for the moment) to slip out of the memory of his audience.

If anyone still doubts that Shakespeare remodels the story to save Cordelia from despair, let him consider this fact. Shakespeare has provided in *King Lear* a sub-plot which simply repeats the theme of the main story. And, as critic after critic has pointed out, this is done that we may feel that we are witnessing something universal—a conflict not so much of particular persons as of the powers of good and evil in the world. Shakespeare, accordingly, looked round for some second story which should support his main theme, and his choice is significant. He chose, from Sidney's *Arcadia*, the story of the Blind Paphlagonian King who was saved from despair by his son. And here again we see the use of reading Shakespeare's sources. We

---

[1] *Shakespeare*, p. 170.

are told by Sir Edmund Chambers that Shakespeare's design was to make his play bear the burden of the final victory of evil. Sir Edmund also tells us that Shakespeare added this sub-plot so that the theme of his play should be of universal significance.[2] Yet the theme of the sub-plot which Shakespeare deliberately chose from the *Arcadia* is the final victory of good.

My argument, then, is that Shakespeare, by taking his usual liberties with time, has remodelled the story of Cordelia: that he makes it end, not in the final victory of evil, as it does in the chronicles, but in the final victory of good: that he saves Cordelia from despair, and gives her to console her, in her captivity, the father whom she has herself consoled.

Such, I admit, is not the view usually held about Shakespeare's treatment of his sources in *King Lear*. The key, I think, will be found in this sub-plot which Shakespeare has added from the *Arcadia*. And that is naturally so, because the sub-plot, we all agree, was added to drive home the meaning of the main plot.

The Blind Paphlagonian King, with his kind and unkind son, is renamed by Shakespeare Gloucester, with his loyal son Edgar and his wicked son Edmund. And it is in the words of Gloucester in his despair that 'many, perhaps most,'[3] have found the meaning of the whole of Shakespeare's *King Lear:*

> As flies to wanton boys are we to the gods;
> They kill us for their sport.

Mr. Granville-Barker, to whom we are all of us under such a heavy debt, tells us that it was to the tune of these words that Shakespeare's dramatic mind was working when he wrote *King Lear*.[4] Nor need I quote more than one of the innumerable other critics who have said the same. Swinburne says it with Swinburnian emphasis:

The words are not casual or episodical: they strike the keynote of the whole poem, lay the keystone of the whole arch of thought. There is no contest of conflicting forces . . . far less is there any light of heavenly harmony or of heavenly wisdom, of Apollo or Athene from above. We have heard much and often from theologians of the light of revelation:

[2] *Shakespeare, A Survey,* 1925, pp. 246–7.
[3] Dover Wilson, *The Essential Shakespeare,* p. 125.
[4] *Prefaces to Shakespeare, First Series,* 1933, p. 183.

and some such thing indeed we find in Æschylus; but the darkness of revelation is here. . . .

Requital, redemption, amends, equity, explanation, pity and mercy, are words without a meaning here.

> As flies to wanton boys are we to the gods;
> They kill us for their sport.

'It is hard to refuse assent to these eloquent words,'[5] says A. C. Bradley, though in the end he does refuse assent.

I am sometimes reminded of an elementary examination paper I once read in which, in answer to the question, 'What do you know about Shakespeare?' the poor child had replied, 'Shakespeare wrote the Calendar.' She had seen a 'Shakespeare Calendar' in the shops. So I gave her high marks for original observation. She was, of course, mistaken. But do we not all sometimes make the same mistake of thinking of the great dramatists as if they were gnomic poets— purveyors of snippets of wisdom a line and a half long? A verse of extraordinary vigour sticks in our memories: we forget the context, and the verse assumes an importance quite unjustified by, or even quite contrary to, the part it plays in the drama.

A glaring instance of this comes in the *Hippolytus* of Euripides. The hero is tricked into taking a certain oath. When he realizes what his oath really involves, he exclaims, 'My tongue swore, but my mind took no oath.' And, through the ages, thoughtless people have said that Euripides was immoral in providing so convenient an excuse for perjury. Yet Hippolytus, on reflection, feels that his oath is binding, and does not, in fact, break it.

Now I submit that, in any great drama, however vigorous a sentence may be, we should ask:

First, *Who* speaks it: a wise man or a rash one?

Secondly, *How* does he speak it: in haste, like Hippolytus at first, or deliberately, like Hippolytus later? And

Thirdly, above all, What light does the sequel throw upon it?

Professor Walter Raleigh has instanced,[6] as proof of Shakespeare's 'width of sympathy,' his 'utter freedom of thought,' that, whilst he is 'at one with' Isabella when she gives utterance to the central truth of Christianity:

[5] *Shakespearean Tragedy*, p. 277.
[6] *Shakespeare*, p. 19.

> all the souls that were, were forfeit once,
> And he that might the vantage best have took
> Found out the remedy;

he is also 'at one with' Gloucester when, from the depths of his despair, he impugns the mercy of Heaven:

> As flies to wanton boys are we to the gods;
> They kill us for their sport.

But what do we mean when we say that Shakespeare is 'at one with' his characters? Shakespeare is a dramatist who allows even the characters with whom he least agrees to put their case shrewdly. He does so with Caliban, and with persons whom he liked much less than Caliban, such as the Tribunes in *Coriolanus*. There is even a horrible plausibility in the complaints of Goneril and Regan against Lear. And Shakespeare allows Angelo to state effectively his case against the pleading of Isabella. Yet Shakespeare is entirely on the side of the distressed sister pleading for pity and mercy before a pedantic disciplinarian. The sequel shows it. Angelo rejects Isabel's plea, and the result is that he falls from depth to depth, till he longs for death to cover his shame. Shakespeare believed in pity and mercy.

Now apply this test to Gloucester's words. What sort of a man is Gloucester? In what circumstances does he speak? Above all, what is the sequel?

Gloucester opens the play, introducing his bastard son Edmund. I remember, with some horror, a father introducing his daughter. She was a most beautiful girl, but clearly with a strain of blood which was not European. The father introduced her as 'my illegitimate daughter.' He was afraid of being suspected of having *married* a coloured woman. It is with a similar recklessness of his child's feelings and of the rights of human personality that Gloucester gloats in retrospect over his sin. Kent seeks to save the situation by the most soothing and tactful comment ever made: 'I cannot wish the fault undone, the issue of it being so proper.' But such compliments are lost upon Edmund, as Shakespeare conceives him. The iron has entered too deeply into his soul.

The character of Gloucester has been sketched with much skill by Mr. Granville-Barker. He is 'the average sensual man': 'The civilized world is full of Gloucesters': 'An egoist, knowing least of what he should know most, of his own two sons': 'With his pother about "these late eclipses of the sun and moon," the sort of man who might at any moment be taken in by any sort of tale.' His son Edmund ridicules his superstition. He is a cheap commonplace type, but (despite Bradley) he is very much alive. It is easy to despise such a man; yet there may be in him possibilities which we did not suspect. But, even so, he is hardly the man from whose mouth we should expect Shakespeare's deepest thoughts on the ways of God to man.

And though Gloucester is foolish, timid, unheroic, unwilling to take sides, nevertheless, when compelled, he defies the tyrants with a resolution which surprises us. Such men often do surprise us. Blinded, he learns that it is his bastard son Edmund, on whom he has relied, who has betrayed him. Then he surprises us still more. He leaps at once to the truth, that the bastard Edmund, who has thus wronged his father, must have been likewise wronging his brother Edgar, when he accused him to his father.

Yet Gloucester never utters one word of reproach against the 'unkind' son who has betrayed him to blindness, and who would betray him to death. He only blames himself. His whole being goes out in love for his loyal son, for whom he has been pining even whilst seeking to inflict death on him for his supposed attempt at parricide:

> Ah, dear son Edgar,
> The food of thy abused father's wrath!
> Might I but live to see thee in my touch,
> I'd say I had eyes again.

Edgar, disguised as Poor Tom, is watching Gloucester as he says these words. It is here, just before Edgar links his arm with him to guide his body and his soul, that Gloucester utters those despairing lines about the gods killing us for their sport. Yet the gods *are* giving Gloucester his wish, and, if he can but be saved from despair, he will live to know it. Shakespeare's irony runs deep: too deep, indeed, for some of his critics to perceive.

So much for the circumstances under which Gloucester speaks these words. Let us turn then to the sequel, which is the change that comes over Gloucester through the love which is between him and Edgar. Such a change of character marks one of the differences between Shakespearian tragedy and Attic tragedy, where it is less evident. Euripides does indeed make Iphigeneia at Aulis grow from a timid girl to a fearless, self-less, enthusiastic heroine. But so little was this appreciated, that Aristotle censures it as an inconsistency.

Gloucester's growth in patience under Edgar's guidance is shown in his prayer, 'You mighty gods.' Edgar tells him that his life is a miracle (as, indeed, the life of every one of us is). Edgar persuades Gloucester that 'the clearest gods' have preserved him: that he must 'bear free and patient thoughts,' till to Gloucester the gods become 'You ever-gentle gods.' Then comes the final catastrophe; at the news of Lear's defeat Gloucester would remain on the battlefield to die:

<blockquote>

A man may rot even here.

Edgar.   What, in ill thoughts again? Men must endure
Their going hence, even as their coming hither;
Ripeness is all.   Come on.

Gloucester   And that's true too.

</blockquote>

Those are his last words in the play. But we are told what happens when he knows that it has been his son Edgar who

<blockquote>

became his guide
Led him, begg'd for him, sav'd him from despair.

</blockquote>

Gloucester, whom we first met as a commonplace, sensual egoist, dies from a love too great to sustain.

Edgar shows himself becoming gradually 'in this pagan play, a very Christian gentleman.' (The words are those of Mr. Granville-Barker.) And it is Edgar who, by the discovery of the plot against Albany, frustrates the villains. Few characters carry, so obviously as does Edgar, the marks of their author's approval. And Edgar's strength lies in his optimism, and his optimism in the conviction that 'The gods are just.' Edgar never gets cold feet. It is in such men that Shakespeare sees the salvation of the state. And Albany, who begins as a neutral character, comes to share Edgar's belief in the 'justicers above,' and to share his task of saving the state.

Shakespeare thoroughly likes Edgar's optimism—but it does not follow that he always agrees with it. When Edgar starts forward to recover the dying Lear, Shakespeare makes the older Kent stop him: 'Vex not his ghost.'[7]

Doubtless, 'by and large,' men *do* get what they sow; to that

---

[7] Granville-Barker, *op. cit.*, p. 213.

extent the gods *are* just. Even pessimists admit so much. W. P. Ker and I were once listening together to the first academic discourse of a professor destined to prove a very great scholar and a very great poet. The lecturer, incidentally, assured us that 'Fortitude and continence and honesty on the whole *do* conduce to material success.' And A. E. Housman was assuredly no easy optimist. Yet such justice is only 'on the whole': 'by and large.' 'We may perhaps "justify the ways of God to man"; but we cannot justify in detail His ways to this or that man.'[8] Can it justly be said that Gloucester, for all his weaknesses, deserved such a fate as he suffered? Or Lear, for all his hideous rashness? Are we to say that Desdemona deserved death, for her lie about the handkerchief? People who say such things, it has been truly remarked, should be forbidden to read Shakespeare. Yet said such things have been, and that by most illustrious critics. The late Dr. John S. Smart, of this University, once dealt faithfully with those critics in an essay[9] which, like all of the little that he has left us, should be known to every student of English literature. I leave those critics in his able hands.

'The gods are just,' says Edgar. How far can man be a judge of the justice of the gods? On the one hand, we must obviously take our own highest standards of justice as valid, as a sacred revelation. 'We could not carry and hand on the torch if we doubted its light.' Nevertheless, we must be very careful how we measure the gods by the yardstick of our fallible human justice. Human justice has persistently imprisoned and put to death the noblest men and women, from the Hebrew prophets or Socrates, through the long roll of apostles and martyrs to Joan of Arc or Thomas More or William Tyndall, and so to the tens of thousands who are suffering martyrdom to-day.

Lear, in his madness (or rather his illumination), said of human justice:

> Plate sin with gold,
> And the strong lance of justice hurtless breaks;
> Arm it in rags, a pygmy's straw does pierce it.

Edgar, a young man, speaks of the justice of the gods: Lear, of fourscore and upward, speaks of the injustice of man. Conscious of his

[8] Matthews, *Essays in Construction,* p. 163. Cf. also p. 218.
[9] 'Tragedy' in *Essays and Studies by members of the English Association,* vol. viii, 1922.

own injustice, Lear comes to think of the sufferings of others, not of his own, and to see that what we call the 'injustice' of the gods is often in fact the injustice of men to each other. Regan and Goneril thrust Lear out into the storm, and he prays:

> Poor naked wretches, wheresoe'er you are,
> That bide the pelting of this pitiless storm,
> How shall your houseless heads and unfed sides,
> Your loop'd and window'd raggedness, defend you
> From seasons such as these? O, I have ta'en
> Too little care of this!   Take physic, pomp:
> Expose thyself to feel what wretches feel,
> That thou mayst shake the superflux to them
> And show the heavens more just.

And, lest we should not fully grasp his drift, Shakespeare has repeated this. Gloucester, whom we first met as an easy-going, superficial sensualist, and then as one who thinks of the gods as killing men in their sport, this selfish Gloucester comes to rejoice that his own misfortunes make others happier:

> Heavens, deal so still!
> Let the superfluous and lust-dieted man,
> That slaves your ordinance, that will not see
> Because he doth not feel, feel your power quickly;
> So distribution should undo excess,
> And each man have enough.

And Edgar speaks of himself as:

> A most poor man, made tame to fortune's blows;
> Who, by the art of known and feeling sorrows,
> Am pregnant to good pity.

It is a commonplace that in *King Lear* Shakespeare reminds us of Æschylus. In fact, he reminds us not only of Æschylus, but also of some of the Old Testament prophets and of the 'Wisdom' books of the Apocrypha. Our modern critics do not remark this Biblical parallel quite so frequently. That is because it is well for the critic to show that he knows his Æschylus, whilst it is fashionable to pretend that Shakespeare did not know his Bible. Yet, as an intelligent church-going Elizabethan, Shakespeare must have known his Bible better than most of us do to-day.[10]

---

[10] See the excellent study of 'Shakespeare's Biblical Knowledge' by Richmond Noble (1935).

We are reminded in *King Lear* of Æschylus, or of the *Apology of Socrates*, or of the Prophets, or the Psalms, or Job, or the 'Wisdom' Books, because of the underlying problem which they all face: How can we reconcile the suffering of man with the justice and mercy of God?

In primitive times religion and magic are often not separate things. By incantation, by prayer, by sacrifice, man thinks that he can place an obligation upon the gods to reward him. He finds that the gods do not. The gods, he says, are unjust. Then he goes deeper. At least by righteous dealing he can place an obligation on God to reward him: 'According to the cleanness of my hands shall he recompense me.' He finds that God does not. God, he says, is unjust. But by the Fifth Century B.C.,

> The shiftings of the mighty winds that blow
> Hither and thither all the changing thoughts
> Of man

were working among Hebrews and Greeks alike towards a new interpretation: that the gods force wisdom on man by man's suffering. Æschylus gave this answer in the first chorus of the *Agamemnon*. Æschylus had shared in the victory of Marathon, had seen Athens evacuated, occupied by the Persian host, and utterly destroyed. He had seen the enemy in turn miserably slaughtered, and with a lifetime of crowded experience behind him and with the wisdom of old age he wrote how

Zeus leads mortals in the way of understanding, and has established it as a law that wisdom comes by suffering. As trouble, and memory of pain, drops o'er the mind of men in sleep, so wisdom comes to men in their own despite. The favour of the gods, enthroned upon their awful seats, is, I ween, forced upon men.

By suffering, wisdom has come to the aged Lear and to Gloucester, to young Edgar too, and to Albany. Kent realizes how suffering opens men's eyes. 'Nothing almost sees miracles but misery.' Yet there is a mystery beyond this. The miracle which has been revealed to Kent in his misery is the depth of the love which Cordelia bears to Lear. Why, then, should Cordelia be killed? Why should Socrates be killed? Socrates had spent his life in the search for wisdom. He told his judges that this was a task which had been laid upon him by the oracle of Delphi. The God had given him a station which he could not desert, any more than he could have left his place in the ranks of battle at Potidaea and Amphipolis and Delium. He obeyed the command of the God, as he understood it: and therefore his fellow-citizens condemned him to death. Yet he did not think his life-work thereby stultified. He did not expect the God to intervene to save him. But neither did he think that the God had deserted him. No doubt in his place I should have argued—I have obeyed the gods: I am to be put to death: death is an evil: the gods are unjust. Not so Socrates. He argues—the gods are just: I have obeyed the gods: I am to be put to death: therefore, for me, at this time, death cannot be an evil. He told his friends that they must hold to this one truth: that to a good man evil cannot come, in life or after death, and that the gods do not neglect his affairs. And this has influenced human thought ever since. It was the same conviction which came, about the same time, upon the Hebrew exile of the dispersion. The city, the place of his fathers' sepulchres, was waste, and the gates thereof were consumed with fire. The daily sacrifice was not offered. Humiliation and suffering were his lot, as they are to-day the lot of millions of his race. He realized that this suffering *was* the daily sacrifice. And so we have the picture in the *Second Isaiah* which has influenced human thought ever since: the picture of the man of sorrows, the righteous servant, who by his knowledge justifies many. Or we have the words of the *Book of Wisdom,*

> In the sight of the unwise they seemed to die, and their departure is taken for misery. . . . But . . . as gold in the furnace has he tried them, and received them as a burnt offering.

'He has received them.' That is Lear's comfort to Cordelia, before they pass from our sight to the prison where Cordelia is to die:

> Upon such sacrifices, my Cordelia,
> The gods themselves throw incense.

That is the wisdom of 'fourscore and upward.' Tragedy, as Dr. John S. Smart said, is a mystery. But man, too, is a mystery. We cannot explain the mystery, 'as if we were God's spies.'

Socrates, on the day of his death, surprised and shocked his friend Simmias by saying that the right study of philosophy was about nothing but dying and being dead. And surely that is the right study of tragedy. Why then be surprised and shocked at Cordelia's death? It is the nature of tragedy to lead up to the death of hero or heroine. The question is, *how* they die. Shakespeare found in the chronicles a grim story of a noble girl who comforted her father's old age and then, separated from him by death, was left to despair and suicide. Instead of this, he shows us an ancient sage and his greathearted daughter led to prison together, the father consoling his child by the words which, in one form or another, have consoled all the noble army of martyrs, from the time of Socrates; and which will continue to console them so long as there are martyrs, which seems likely, by all present indications, to be long enough: The gods are not unmindful; they have received our sacrifice. The gods do indeed give their rewards, but it is 'not as the world giveth.'

I cannot agree with Bradley that this speech of Lear to Cordelia is meant to depict 'a mind greatly enfeebled,' and that this is shown by the fact that it never crosses Lear's mind that he and Cordelia 'have anything more than imprisonment to fear.' It would be insolent for me to pit my intuition against that of Bradley. But in this case we have the sources of the play, to make clear to us what was Shakespeare's intention. According to the current story, as known to contemporaries, it *was* precisely lifelong imprisonment which Cordelia *had* to fear when she fell into the hands of her foes. True, it is Shakespeare's intention to alter that current story. But Shakespeare cannot have expected his audience to draw the conclusion that Lear's mind is enfeebled, from the fact that Lear anticipates for Cordelia exactly what current story represented as her fate. How could any audience have put such an interpretation upon Lear's words? Since Cordelia's story was that she was

kept in prison long
Till wearie of that wretched life her selfe she hong,

the comforting words of Lear cannot have seemed so inappropriate as to betoken an enfeebled mind.

Brave men and women may face death without flinching: but to live to see heroic effort tumble to disgraceful ruin whilst foes triumph and deride—is not that the uttermost sacrifice which the gods can demand from proud souls like Lear and his daughter? Yet such sacrifices are demanded; and often. 'We are not the first,' says Cordelia. No: nor the last. 'Upon such sacrifices the gods themselves throw incense,' Lear replies. Cordelia makes no answer: as before, she loves and is silent. (We must not misinterpret the silences of a Cordelia or an Isabel. The boy, upon whom was placed the responsibility of presenting their 'prone and speechless dialect' before the assembled chivalry and wisdom of England's court, had William Shakespeare to guide his demeanour through silences which are to us a mere blank.)

Lear had prayed: 'You heavens, give me that patience, patience I need.' The heavens have indeed given him patience. But his patience is not the mark of an enfeebled mind. Lear's deep words, at the moment of his greatest humiliation, when with Cordelia he is led captive behind Edmund 'in conquest,' are no more an expression of weakness than are the words of Kent, at the moment of *his* greatest humiliation, in the stocks: 'Nothing almost sees miracles but misery.' Lear is heroic to the end; he will live to avenge his daughter single-handed, as he now lives to console her.

In the old play of *King Leir* the pitiful bourgeois king is shoved back by his benevolent daughter and son-in-law upon a throne which he is ludicrously incapable of occupying. That is what is called 'a happy ending.' Shakespeare's play shows us a mighty old warrior-king suffering intolerable wrong, learning thereby to blame himself because he has allowed others to go hungry and naked, learning to pity the victims of the arrogant 'justice' of the rich ('Robes and furr'd gowns hide all'); learning to think rather of the sufferings of his poor jester than of his own:

> Poor fool and knave, I have one part in my heart
> That's sorry yet for thee. . . . In, boy; go first.

The old King finds that the love of Cordelia, which he has renounced, has never renounced him.

And such is the power of this love that it matters nothing to Lear, when a sudden change of fortune makes him the prisoner of those who have most wronged him. He is still the old proud warrior-king. He forbids Cordelia to weep in the presence of her foes:

> The goodyears shall devour 'em, flesh and fell,
> Ere they shall make us weep.

But what do the battle and his crown matter? We are moving in the same plane of thought as was that stout soldier Socrates, when he judged the judges who had condemned him, and comforted those who had voted for his acquittal by showing them the meaning of what had happened to him. Lear does not blame the gods because he has again lost his crown, or because the succour which Cordelia has sought to bring to him has brought nothing but disaster on her. He shows her the meaning of what has happened, as Socrates showed his friends that his fate was not the terrible thing they thought—they must grasp this one truth, that the gods are not disregardful:

> Upon such sacrifices, my Cordelia,
> The gods themselves throw incense.

And that, Mr. Chairman, is what illustrious critics call 'the final victory of evil,' 'a stony black despairing depth of voiceless and inexplicable agony.'

For a century and a half this final scene was thought too horrible to be acted on the stage. Yet Shakespeare has been careful to mitigate the horror, to dismiss us 'with calm of mind, all passion spent.' Let us see how.

I can imagine a critic replying to all that I have urged: 'Yes, I grant that Shakespeare has saved Cordelia from the horror of despair which the chronicles depicted as her fate: but he has done this only by heaping horror and despair on Lear himself, though the chronicles allowed Lear to die a king, with Cordelia watching over his death-bed, and burying him when dead.'

But Shakespeare gives us as much of this as is consistent with Cordelia being preserved from further danger and distress. It is true that the chronicles represented Lear as restored to his throne and dying 'every inch a king.' Well: Shakespeare also gives us this consolation. That is the explanation of Albany's words, uttered over the dying Lear:

> We will resign,
> During the life of this old Majesty,
> To him our absolute power.

Shakespeare's Lear, then, dies a king. But he could not have continued to live a king. After what he has suffered, and still more after what he has learnt, it would be, as Charles Lamb has said, 'a childish pleasure' to 'get his gilt robes and sceptre again.'

Bradley asks that Shakespeare should at least have given Lear 'peace and happiness by Cordelia's fireside.' And it is never safe to differ from Bradley. Nevertheless, I submit that what really matters in the play is neither gilt robes or sceptre, nor yet a peaceful fireside, but the thought that is passing in the soul of Lear under the influence of Cordelia—and likewise in the soul of Gloucester, under the guidance of his pious son.

In the first scene,

> By all the operation of the orbs
> From whom we do exist and cease to be

Lear had challenged the power of Love. He had renounced Cordelia:

> So be my grave my peace, as here I give
> Her father's heart from her. . . .
> > We
> Have no such daughter, nor shall ever see
> That face of hers again.

In the last scene this is answered by Lear's cry of desolation: 'Thou'lt come no more,' followed by the five times repeated 'never.' Nothing else could express the length and breadth and depth and height of the victory of Cordelia and of Love. To anyone who doubts this, I would put the question: Would we sacrifice those lines which Lear, dying, utters after he has entered with the dead Cordelia in his arms? Would we barter them for any picture of Lear, peaceful and happy, by Cordelia's fireside?

The thing that matters, I repeat, is what is happening in the soul of Lear. In the chronicle story, Cordelia was there to watch over Lear's last years, and to bury him when dead. In accordance with the chronicle story, then, a dramatist might have depicted Lear seeing (the last thing he sees as the world fades from him) the lips of Cordelia moving, speaking to him.

Well: that is how Shakespeare's Lear *does* pass. Shakespeare's text is perfectly clear. Lear dies, as Gloucester dies, from the unbearable joy, after all his sufferings, of thinking that his beloved child lives.

Bradley pointed out, thirty-five years ago, that the agony in which Lear actually dies is one, not of pain, but of ecstasy:

Suddenly, with a cry represented in the oldest text by a four-times repeated 'O,' he exclaims:

> Do you see this? Look on her, look, her lips,
> Look there, look there!

These are the last words of Lear. He is sure, at last, that she *lives;* . . . It seems almost beyond question that any actor is false to the text who does not attempt to express, in Lear's last accents and gestures and look, an unbearable *joy*.[11]

Bradley expressed a fear that this interpretation might be condemned as fantastic. It has been praised as 'a fine piece of perception' by Mr. Granville-Barker,[12] whose praise carries weight indeed. But elsewhere it has not always received due attention. That Bradley's interpretation is *not* fantastic, but a true perception of Shakespeare's meaning, can be proved, I think, when we examine Shakespeare's sources. We can then see the stages by which Shakespeare reached this culmination of his tragedy. We have seen how, wishing to duplicate and reinforce the story of Lear, he chose the parallel story of the blind king for Sidney's *Arcadia.* And it is precisely such an ecstasy of joy, succeeding affliction, which Sidney depicts as killing his old king. The blind king set the crown upon his son's head with many tears both of joy and sorrow and

even in a moment died; as it should seem, his heart broken with unkindness and affliction, stretched so far beyond his limits with this excess of comfort, as it was able no longer to keep safe his royal spirits.[13]

Shakespeare reproduces this in the death of Gloucester:

> his flaw'd heart . . .
> 'Twixt two extremes of passion, joy and grief,
> Burst smilingly.

Shakespeare then gives the same death to Lear. And, with the extraordinary parallelism which runs through the whole play, both Gloucester and Lear have said that this would be recompense for all their sufferings:

> *Gloucester.*   Might I but live to see thee in my touch,
> I'd say I had eyes again. . . .

[11] *Shakespearean Tragedy,* p. 291.
[12] *Op. cit.,* p. 185.
[13] *Arcadia,* ed. Feuillerat, I. 212.

Lear. It is a chance which does redeem all sorrows
That ever I have felt.

It is an interesting fact that, twenty years after the death which his reckless chivalry brought upon him, Philip Sidney, that 'inheritor of unfulfilled renown,' should have suggested to our greatest poet the consummation of his greatest work.

But, it will be retorted, Gloucester's reunion with Edgar was real; Lear's vision of Cordelia as still living is not real: he is deceived.

But what do we mean by this distinction?

Bradley says, I admit, that 'To us, perhaps, the knowledge that [Lear] is deceived may bring a culmination of pain.' But he also indicates that there is something other than pain; and what that something is, seems to me to be given by another sentence of Bradley's:

While it would be going too far to suggest that Shakespeare was employing conscious symbolism or allegory in *King Lear,* it does appear to disclose a mode of imagination not so very far removed from the mode with which, we must remember, Shakespeare was perfectly familiar in Morality plays and in the *Fairy Queen.*

As W. P. Ker puts it:

All poetry has something of a representative character in it, and often it matters little for the result whether the composer has any definite symbolical intention or not.[14]

To Shakespeare, certainly, the transitoriness of the stage play was symbolical of the transitoriness of all earthly things. 'The best in this kind are but shadows.' So Shakespeare, when a very young man, had made Theseus say. But the most passionate assertion of this truth comes, as we all know, at the end of Shakespeare's work. The masque in *The Tempest* vanishes 'to a strange hollow and confused noise': and this symbolizes to Prospero that

the great globe itself,
Yea, all which it inherit, shall dissolve,
And like this insubstantial pageant faded,
Leave not a rack behind.

But the same thought is running through *King Lear.* Gloucester recognizes the mad Lear by his voice, and says, as he stoops to kiss his hand,

---

[14] *English Literature: Medieval,* p. 187.

> O ruin'd piece of nature! This great world
> Shall so wear out to nought.

And also to Kent and to Edgar the dying Lear, with the dead Cordelia in his arms, is an image of the end of the world.

Now, so far as reality goes, the tradition which Shakespeare's audience (and probably Shakespeare himself) regarded as real and true history allowed a living Cordelia to tend Lear's last hours and to bury and mourn him when dead. Shakespeare deliberately altered this historic tradition; because Lear's desolation over Cordelia dead gave him the symbolic truth he wanted. Yet the moving of Cordelia's lips is the last thing seen by Lear's dying eyes. That also gave Shakespeare the symbolic truth he wanted. And it may have corresponded (more closely than his own altered story did) to what Shakespeare believed to be historic fact. For Shakespeare probably thought of these tales from British history much as Milton did: their historic truth was 'defended by many, denied utterly by few.' But in *King Lear* we are in a world like that of the *Divine Comedy,* where symbolic truth matters, not historic truth.

Bradley contrasts *King Lear* with the *Divine Comedy,* emphasizing the difference between them. Yet is the difference as deep as Bradley thought? In both we are at once taken down into Hell. Gloucester's sin of incontinence belongs to the uppermost circle, but we are plunged deeper and deeper. In Edmund's plot to cause his brother's death, we reach Caïna, which 'hath the primal eldest curse upon it, a brother's murder.' We go lower yet. At last we reach the one unpardonable sin, the sin of Judas—despair. For Judas might have been pardoned, if he would have asked for pardon, and so, some held, might the Devil himself. The lowest pit is reached, in Dante, with Judas and Satan; in Shakespeare with the despairing cry that the gods kill us for their sport.

And there, if we like it, we may stay. But if we follow Dante and Shakespeare we ascend: because, from that abyss, all movement, in whatever direction, is ascent. We issue, and again see the stars. The moment of despair is the moment when help arrives. Lear and Gloucester, guided by Kent and Cordelia and Edgar, climb the mountain of Purgatory. And, like the souls in the *Purgatorio* (xi, 31–3), in the midst of their own crushing sorrows, Lear and Gloucester, Kent and Edgar and Cordelia are praying and thinking for others.

> Poor naked wretches, wheresoe'er you are. . . .

We begin to see the world as Keats saw it—not so much a Vale of Tears as a Vale of Soul Making, till Lear, consoled, ends by teaching patience to Gloucester and to Cordelia.

'Shakespeare draws no morals': he draws life as he sees it. Did he then see life as a Mountain of Purgatory? It has been said that we should be near the truth 'if we called the poem *The Redemption of King Lear.*' At the end, it has been said, 'Lear's education is complete, his regeneration accomplished.' But that is not the whole truth. Has Lear been 'bound upon a wheel of fire' only that he may be educated? Are gods who kill us that they may improve our characters really more lovable than gods who kill us for their sport? The choruses in which Æschylus speaks of the omnipotence of Zeus, and of how he teaches man by suffering, are austerely magnificent. But Æschylus also shows us Zeus as Prometheus sees him: a strangely unlovable God. The world may be depicted as a 'vale of soul-making' in a way which repels us.

God is represented too often as a kind of experimental psychologist Who examines with curiosity the reactions of His creatures to varied stimuli. Or sometimes He is thought of as the Governor of a vast Borstal institution, in which depraved persons are submitted to a salutary and well-thought-out discipline.[15]

If there were no more in *King Lear* than a tale of redemption through suffering, it would be as unbearable as the *Purgatorio* would be without the *Paradiso*. But *King Lear* is, like the *Paradiso,* a vast poem on the victory of true love. The 'hot-blooded France' tells us at the outset

> Love's not love
> When it is mingled with regards that stand
> Aloof from the entire point.

Years before, Shakespeare had written

> Love is not love
> Which alters when it alteration finds
> Or bends with the remover to remove.
> O, no! it is an ever-fixed mark
> That looks on tempests and is never shaken.

[15] Matthews, *Essays in Construction,* pp. 173–4.

In order 'that the theme of the play should be of universal significance,' the same motive is repeated in *King Lear* three times. A young
girl, an old man, and a young man are all alike cast off by the
being whom they most love. The young girl and the young man win
back the utter love of the father who has cast them off. The 'strings
of life begin to crack' in Kent, as he witnesses the death of Gloucester
between joy and grief. He enters, 'to bid his king and master aye
good night,' begging, like a dog, for one moment's recognition of his
faithfulness: 'Where is your servant Caius?' But Kent's pleading
rouses no recollection in Lear's mind, for Lear has no thought save
for Cordelia; and Kent, still unrecognized as Caius, sees how Lear
falls in an ecstasy of joy. Therefore, when Edgar seeks to recover
Lear, Kent interposes:

> O, let him pass!   He hates him
> That would upon the rack of this tough world
> Stretch him out longer.

Kent's wish is that Lear should not return to a world in which,
indeed, Lear might realize who it was who had served him as Caius,
but in which he would find Cordelia dead. Lear will not come to him,
but he will go to Lear:

> I have a journey, sir, shortly to go;
> My master calls me, I must not say no.

There is, I think no idea in the mind of Kent of any recognition by
Lear in some future life: recognized or unrecognized, Kent must be
with his master in death as in life. This is assuredly the 'ecstasy of
charity and infinite feeling of communion.' Of such love it is not
right to say much.

A thing is known by its contraries, and it is the absence of love
which makes a Regan or a Goneril. What they say about Lear is very
largely true—he *was* irritable and unreasonable. That man must be
curiously wanting in self-criticism who does not ask himself: Have I
never (and that when I most thought myself in the right) said the
sort of thing which Regan and Goneril say? Their wickedness has
its root in entire absence of 'charity and the feeling of communion.'
In them we see what Augustine meant—'Evil has no positive
existence: but the loss of good has received the name of evil.'[16] So far

16 *City of God*, xi. 9.

is *King Lear* from being a play (as Dr. Johnson said) in which the wicked prosper, that by the end of the play the wicked not only are dead but have already ceased to concern us. The bodies of Regan and Goneril are lying there: Lear does not see them nor heed the news of their death. Edmund's death is announced. 'That's but a trifle here,' says Albany—though it is not a trifle that before Edmund died he had forgiven his slayer and Edgar had forgiven him. Love alone matters, as Edgar tells the story of his reunion with his father, and Lear bends over Cordelia dead. Gloucester had seen in Lear an image of the great world wearing itself out to nought, and as the world vanishes from Gloucester and Lear and Kent, their 'strings of life crack' in a passion of love which, after all they have suffered, they cannot sustain. This world passes away, and the fashion of it, and we are left, as at the end of the *Divine Comedy,* with

> The love that moves the sun and all the stars.
> Love bears it out even to the edge of doom.

'If this be error,' Shakespeare had said, 'I never writ': and for those who think it error, for them he has written in vain.

ON SHAKESPEARE'S TRAGI-COMIC ROMANCES

FOR THE VICTORIANS Shakespeare's last plays—*Cymbeline, The Winter's Tale* and *The Tempest*—were expressive of the serenity, tolerance and detachment which he attained after the tragedies. For Lytton Strachey and later critics, they were the slack, undramatic products of a Shakespeare grown careless and bored and succumbing to the self-hypnosis of his poetic fancy. Others saw them as shaped to meet the new demands of the theatrical audience. A large group of modern critics sees them as having mythic qualities, romances with legendary significance in their vision of regeneration and renewal. As such, they are now regarded more highly than ever before.

EDWARD DOWDEN
1843-1913

DOWDEN FOUND SHAKESPEARE'S last plays to reflect a personal mood of serenity and detachment. We may reject this biographical inference but accept his description of the mood projected by the plays. He does not, as has often been alleged, disregard the existence of evil in the last plays, the goblins, as Lytton Strachey phrased it, in the land of fairy (they show, he says, "wrongs of man to man as cruel as those of the great tragedies"). But he finds the dissonance resolved into harmony, a reconciliation differing in kind from the tragic reconciliation. Dowden is aware, although he does not expatiate upon it, that the last plays contain the surprises and improbabilities of romance and the scenic spectacle which Ashley H. Thorndike, J. Q. Adams, and Gerald E. Bentley have explained by reference to changes in the theatre for which Shakespeare was writing. But he finds them to be bound to each other not so much by these common elements as by theme and atmosphere. In pointing to the recurring motif of lost royal children brought up in the midst of nature, he shows how it contributes to the "strange, pathetic, ideal light" in which these plays are bathed. He does not, however, mention the renewal and the regeneration, the sense of spring succeeding winter, which later critics have shown is affected by the recovery of lost royalty.

THE MOOD OF SHAKSPERE'S LAST PLAYS

THE PLAYS BELONGING to Shakspere's final period of authorship, which I shall consider, are three: Cymbeline, The Winter's Tale, and The Tempest. . . . Characteristics of versification and style, and the enlarged place given to scenic spectacle, indicate that these plays were produced much about the same time. But the ties of deepest kinship between them are spiritual. There is a certain romantic element in each.[1] They receive contributions from every portion of Shak-

"The Mood of Shakspere's Last Plays" is from Dowden's *Shakspere: His Mind and Art.*

[1] The same remark applies to Shakspere's part of Pericles, which belongs to this period.

spere's genius, but all are mellowed, refined, made exquisite; they avoid the extremes of broad humour and of tragic intensity; they were written with less of passionate concentration than the plays which immediately precede them, but with more of a spirit of deep or exquisite recreation.

There are moments when Shakspere was not wholly absorbed in his work as artist at this period; it is as if he were thinking of his own life, or of the fields and streams of Stratford, and still wrote on; it is as if the ties which bound him to his art were not severing with thrills of strong emotion, but were quietly growing slack. The soliloquy of Belarius, at the end of the third scene of the third act of Cymbeline, and that of Imogen when she discovers the headless body of Cloten, were written as if Shakspere were now only moderately interested in certain portions of his dramatic work. Such lines as the following, purporting to be part of a soliloquy, but being in fact an explanation addressed to the audience, could only have been written when the poet did not care to energize over the less interesting, but still necessary passages of his drama:—

Belarius.   O Cymbeline! heaven and my conscience knows
Thou didst unjustly banish me: whereon,
At three and two years old, I stole these babes;
Thinking to bar thee of succession, as
Thou reft'st me of my lands. Euriphile,
Thou wast their nurse; they took thee for their mother,
And every day do honour to her grave :
Myself, Belarius, that am Morgan call'd,
They take for natural father.

The impression that Shakspere's interest in his art was less intense than previously it had been is confirmed by the circumstance that he now contributes portions to plays which are completely by other hands in an inferior manner. Into the subject of Pericles he entered with manifest delight; but he could be content to see his "Marina" wedged in between the rough and coarse work of another writer. In The Two Noble Kinsmen the degradation of Shakspere's work by the unclean underplot of Fletcher is painful, and almost intolerable. And in Henry VIII. all artistic and ethical unity is sacrificed to the vulgar demand for an occasional play and for a spectacle.

Yet it is not to be wondered at that Shakspere now should feel delivered from the strong urge of imagination and feeling, and should write in a more pleasurable, more leisurely, and not so great a manner. The period of the tragedies was ended. In the tragedies Shakspere had made his inquisition into the mystery of evil. He had studied those injuries of man to man which are irreparable. He had seen the innocent suffering with the guilty. Death came and removed the criminal and his victim from human sight, and we were left with solemn awe upon our hearts in presence of the insoluble problems of life. There lay Duncan, who had "borne his faculties so meek," who had been "so clear in his great office," foully done to death; there lay Cordelia lifeless in the arms of Lear; there, Desdemona, murmuring no word, upon the bed; there, Antony, the ruin of Cleopatra's magic; and last, Timon, most desperate fugitive from life, finding his sole refuge under the oblivious and barren wave. At the same time that Shakspere had shown the tragic mystery of human life, he had fortified the heart by showing that to suffer is not the supreme evil with man, and that loyalty and innocence, and self-sacrifice, and pure redeeming ardour, exist, and cannot be defeated. Now, in his last period of authorship, Shakspere remained grave—how could it be otherwise? —but his severity was tempered and purified. He had less need of the crude doctrine of Stoicism, because the tonic of such wisdom as exists in Stoicism had been taken up, and absorbed into his blood.

Shakspere still thought of the graver trials and tests which life applies to human character, of the wrongs which man inflicts on man; but his present temper demanded not a tragic issue,—it rather demanded an issue into joy or peace. The dissonance must be resolved into a harmony, clear and rapturous, or solemn and profound. And, accordingly, in each of these plays, The Winter's Tale, Cymbeline, The Tempest, while grievous errors of the heart are shown to us, and wrongs of man to man as cruel as those of the great tragedies, at the end there is a resolution of the dissonance, a reconciliation. This is the word which interprets Shakspere's latest plays—reconciliation, "word over all, beautiful as the sky." It is not, as in the earlier comedies—The Two Gentlemen of Verona, Much Ado about Nothing, As You Like It, and others—a mere *dénouement*. The resolution of the discords in these latest plays is not a mere stage necessity, or a necessity of composition, resorted to by the dramatist to effect an ending of his play, and little interesting his imagination or his heart. Its significance here is ethical and spiritual; it is a moral necessity. . . .

When a man has attained some high and luminous tableland of joy or of renouncement, when he has really transcended self, or when some one of the everlasting, virtuous powers of the world,—duty or

sacrifice, or the strength of anything higher than oneself—has assumed authority over him, forthwith a strange, pathetic, ideal light is
shed over all beautiful things in the lower world which has been
abandoned. We see the sunlight on our neighbour's field, while we
are pre-occupied about the grain that is growing in our own. And
when we have ceased to hug our souls to any material possession, we
see the sunlight wherever it falls. In the last chapter of George Eliot's
great novel, Romola, who has ascended into *her* clear and calm solitude of self-transcending duty, bends tenderly over the children of
Tito, uttering in words made simple for their needs, the lore she has
learnt from life, and seeing on their faces the light of strange, ideal
beauty. In the latest plays of Shakspere, the sympathetic reader can
discern unmistakably a certain abandonment of the common joy of
the world, a certain remoteness from the usual pleasures and sad-
nesses of life, and at the same time, all the more, this tender bending
over those who are like children still absorbed in their individual joys
and sorrows.

Over the beauty of youth and the love of youth, there is shed, in
these plays of Shakspere's final period, a clear yet tender luminous-
ness, not elsewhere to be perceived in his writings. In his earlier plays,
Shakspere writes concerning young men and maidens, their loves,
their mirth, their griefs, as one who is among them, who has a lively,
personal interest in their concerns, who can make merry with them,
treat them familiarly, and, if need be, can mock them into good
sense. There is nothing in these early plays wonderful, strangely beautiful, pathetic about youth and its joys and sorrows. In the histories
and tragedies, as was to be expected, more massive, broader, or more
profound objects of interest engaged the poet's imagination. But in
these latest plays, the beautiful pathetic light is always present. There
are the sufferers, aged, experienced, tried—Queen Katharine, Prospero, Hermione. And over against these there are the children absorbed in their happy and exquisite egoism,—Perdita and Miranda,
Florizel and Ferdinand, and the boys of old Belarius.

The same means to secure ideality for these figures, so young and
beautiful, is in each case (instinctively perhaps rather than deliberately) resorted to. They are lost children,—princes or a princess,
removed from the court, and its conventional surroundings, into some
scene of rare, natural beauty. There are the lost princes—Arviragus
and Guiderius, among the mountains of Wales, drinking the free air,
and offering their salutations to the risen sun. There is Perdita, the

shepherdess-princess, "queen of curds and cream," sharing with old and young her flowers, lovelier and more undying than those that Proserpina let fall from Dis's waggon. There is Miranda (whose very name is significant of wonder), made up of beauty, and love, and womanly pity, neither courtly nor rustic, with the breeding of an island of enchantment, where Prospero is her tutor and protector, and Caliban her servant, and the Prince of Naples her lover. In each of these plays we can see Shakspere, as it were, tenderly bending over the joys and sorrows of youth. We recognise this rather through the total characterization, and through a feeling and a presence, than through definite incident or statement. But some of this feeling escapes in the disinterested joy and admiration of old Belarius when he gazes at the princely youths, and in Camillo's loyalty to Florizel and Perdita; while it obtains more distinct expression in such a word as that which Prospero utters, when from a distance he watches with pleasure Miranda's zeal to relieve Ferdinand from his task of log-bearing:—
"Poor worm, thou art infected."

It is not chiefly because Prospero is a great enchanter, now about to break his magic staff, to drown his book deeper than ever plummet sounded, to dismiss his airy spirits, and to return to the practical service of his Dukedom, that we identify Prospero in some measure with Shakspere himself. It is rather because the temper of Prospero, the grave harmony of his character, his self-mastery, his calm validity of will, his sensitiveness to wrong, his unfaltering justice, and with these, a certain abandonment, a remoteness from the common joys and sorrows of the world, are characteristic of Shakspere as discovered to us in all his latest plays.

G. WILSON KNIGHT
1897-

THE SELECTION WHICH follows is a portion of a booklet which Knight published in 1929 and incorporated with additional notes in his *The Crown of Life* (1947), a collection of essays on Shakespeare's final plays. From it his later work flowed.

Whatever we may think of the mystical language and thought of Knight's essay, he there directed the attention of our generation to aspects of the plays which had been almost wholly overlooked: their religious atmosphere, the symbolic significance of storms and music, the theme of resurrection. His view of the plays as having mythic significance has been corroborated by the anthropological study of Elizabethan folk festivals and their relation to Shakespeare's last plays in R. Wincor's "Shakespeare's Festival Plays," *Shakespeare Quarterly*, I (1950).

MYTH AND MIRACLE

THE STORIES OF *Pericles*[1] and *The Winter's Tale* are remarkably alike. In both the hero loses his wife and daughter just after the birth of his child; in both the idea of a child's helplessness is synchronized with a sea-storm of the usual Shakespearian kind; in both the wife and child are miraculously restored after a long passage of time; and the revival of Thaisa, and the restoration of Marina and Hermione are accompanied by music. These plays are throughout impregnated by an atmosphere of mysticism. The theology is pseudo-Hellenistic. The Delphic oracle and a prophetic dream occur in *The Winter's Tale*; Hermione is restored to Leontes in a 'chapel' to the sound of music, Thaisa to Pericles in the temple of Diana, with the full circumstance of religious ceremonial. The goddess Diana appears to Pericles. A reader sensitive to poetic atmosphere must necessarily feel the awakening light of some religious or metaphysical truth symbolized in the plot and attendant machinery of these two plays.

Cerimon, who raises Thaisa from the dead, is a recluse and visionary:

"Myth and Miracle" is from G. Wilson Knight, *The Crown of Life* (Methuen, 1958), pp. 14–28. By permission of the publisher.
[1] In a note to my original text I showed that I was not necessarily regarding *Pericles* as Shakespeare's work throughout.

> I held it ever,
> Virtue and cunning were endowments greater
> Than nobleness and riches: careless heirs
> May the two latter darken and expend,
> But immortality attends the former,
> Making a man a god.   (III. ii. 26)

The body of Thaisa, supposed dead, is cast ashore by the tempest in a coffin. Cerimon, by his magic, and with the aid of fire and music, revives her:

> Well said, well said; the fire and cloths.
> The rough and woeful music that we have,
> Cause it to sound, beseech you.
> The viol once more: how thou stirr'st, thou block!
> The music there;—I pray you, give her air.
> Gentlemen,
> This queen will live; nature awakes; a warmth
> Breathes out of her; she hath not been entranced
> Above five hours. See how she 'gins to blow
> Into life's flower again!   (III. ii. 87)

This incident, with the exquisite conception of the character of Cerimon, and the reviving of Thaisa, is one of the pinnacles of Shakespeare's art: this scene and those of the restoration to Pericles of his long-lost daughter and consort which follow, are alone sufficient to establish my thesis that the author is moved by vision, not fancy; is creating not merely entertainment, but myth in the Platonic sense. Now the theme of music again occurs in the meeting of Pericles with Marina:

Pericles.   Now, blessing on thee! rise; thou art my child.
          Give me fresh garments. Mine own, Helicanus;
          She is not dead at Tarsus, as she should have been,
          By savage Cleon: she shall tell thee all;
          When thou shalt kneel, and justify in knowledge
          She is thy very princess. Who is this?
Helicanus. Sir, 'tis the governor of Mytilene,
          Who, hearing of your melancholy state,
          Did come to see you.
Pericles.   I embrace you.
          Give me my robes. I am wild in my beholding.
          O heavens, bless my girl! But, hark! what
              music?

> Tell Helicanus, my Marina, tell him
> O'er, point by point, for yet he seems to doubt,
> How sure you are my daughter. But, what
>   music?

Helicanus.   My lord, I hear none.

Pericles.   None!

> The music of the spheres! List, my Marina.

Lysimachus. It is not good to cross him; give him way.

Pericles.   Rarest sounds! Do ye not hear?

Lysimachus.   My lord, I hear.   (*Music*)

Pericles.   Most heavenly music!

> It nips me unto listening, and thick slumber
> Hangs upon mine eyes: let me rest.   (*Sleeps*)
>   (v. i. 215)

The blindness of past Shakespearian criticism is at no point more completely in evidence than in the comments in this play. To the discerning mind it will be evident that we are here confronted with the furthest reach of Shakespeare's poetic and visionary power: if we except *The Tempest,* the latter half of *Pericles* has no equivalent in transcendental apprehension in all Shakespeare but the latter half of *Antony and Cleopatra* which on the plane of myth and symbolism it may be considered to interpret.

Almost of an equal beauty is the restoration of Thaisa in the Temple of Diana.

Cerimon.   . . .   Look! Thaisa is

> Recovered.

Thaisa.   O, let me look!

> If he be none of mine, my sanctity
> Will to my sense bend no licentious ear,
> But curb it, spite of seeing. O! my lord,
> Are you not Pericles? Like him you speak,
> Like him you are: did you not name a tempest,
> A birth and death?

Pericles.   The voice of dead Thaisa!

Thaisa.   That Thaisa am I, supposed dead

> And drown'd.

Pericles.   Immortal Dian!

Thaisa.   Now I know you better.

> When we with tears parted Pentapolis,
> The king, my father, gave you such a ring.
>   (*Shows a ring*)

> *Pericles.* This, this: no more, you gods! your present
>   kindness
> Makes my past miseries sport. . . .
>
> (v. iii. 27)

The last thought of Pericles is to be echoed again, with clear religious and universal significance, in the Vision of Jupiter in *Cymbeline*. Now if, as is probable, the greater part of *Pericles* is the work of Shakespeare grafted on to an earlier play of different authorship, of which signs are apparent in some of the early scenes, it is not surprising that, after his composition of these supreme latter acts, he found another plot of the same kind for his next play; nor is it surprising that that next play, *The Winter's Tale,* though more perfect as a whole, lacks something of the paradisal radiance of *Pericles*. The great artist does not well to repeat himself: in *Pericles,* as the writer handles an old theme, some mystic apprehension of a life that conquers death has sprung to vivid form, as it were, spontaneously: a shaft of light penetrating into the very heart of death. The studied repetition that follows is less vital.[2] It will be sufficient here to point the recurrence of the themes of birth, restoration, tempest, and music, and to speak shortly of their significance in both plays.

In *The Winter's Tale,* the plot turns on Leontes' distrust of Hermione's conjugal loyalty. Now too much stress cannot be laid on the importance attached to infidelity in Shakespeare. The horror at the passing of love's faith is twin to the horror of death: the difficulty is quite as much a metaphysical as a moral one—Troilus cannot understand the patent fact of its existence. In *Hamlet* and *Troilus* these death and love problems are given dramatic form, and leave us distressed; in *Othello* the faithlessness-theme is crystallized into a perfected classic mould and makes a great play, but, since Desdemona dies untrusted, leaves us still pained. In *Antony and Cleopatra,* though the love of the protagonists is shown to us as untrusting and untrustworthy, a spiritual and passionate thing tossed tempestuously on the waters of temporal existence, yet, by the synchronizing of faith with death, we are left with a vision of a timeless instantaneous ascension in death to love, which is life. This tragic apprehension is

---

[2] One's past, 'critical' (as opposed to interpretative) pronouncements are apt to make poor reading fifteen years later. I cannot remember ever having seriously held the opinion here expressed. *The Winter's Tale,* which I had known well for years, was, I think, shadowed for the moment by my recent discovery of *Pericles.*

explicated in narrative form in the parables of *Pericles* and *The Winter's Tale*. Leontes is guilty of Othello's distrust, and thinks Hermione dead. He suffers years of remorse, but at last she is restored to him, in a temple, with ceremony, and to the sounds of music. In Shakespeare the failing of love's faith is essentially a metaphysical difficulty, and one with the difficulty of loss in death: conversely, 'perfect love casteth out fear.' The infidelity-theme of *The Winter's Tale* is thus not essentially different from the loss of Thaisa at sea. In both we see the tempests of temporal conditions seemingly at war with the otherness of a purely spiritual experience.

In both these plays we have the theme of a child bereft of its mother and threatened by storm and thunder. The emphasis on tempests is insistent, and the suggestion is clearly that of the pitiful-ness and helplessness of humanity born into a world of tragic conflict. That the tempest is percurrent in Shakespeare as a symbol of tragedy need not be demonstrated here at length. Its symbolic significance is patent from the earliest to the latest of the plays—in metaphor, in simile, in long or short description, in stage directions. The individual soul is the 'bark' putting out to sea in a 'tempest': the image occurs again and again. For instance, we have in *Macbeth*,

> Though his bark cannot be lost,
> Yet it shall be tempest-toss'd (I. iii. 24),

and in *Timon of Athens* (v. i. 205), we hear of

>   . . . other incident throes
> That nature's fragile vessel doth sustain
> In life's uncertain voyage. . . .

and in *Pericles,* which contains perhaps the finest of Shakespeare's profuse storm-poetry in III. i., Marina says (IV. i. 17):

>   Ay me! poor maid,
> Born in a tempest, when my mother died,
> This world to me is like a lasting storm,
> Whirring me from my friends.

Numerous other references could be given. The theme of helpless childhood synchronized with storm in *Pericles* and *The Winter's Tale* (III. i.; III. iii.) is significant, just as the tempests in *Julius Caesar, Macbeth* and *Lear* are significant: poetic symbols of the storm and stress of human life, the turbulence of temporal events reflecting and causing tempestuous passion in the heart of man. Lastly, in these two plays we have the music which accompanies resurrection and re-union. This music may seem to perform a dual function: first, to suggest, as a symbol of pure aesthetic delight, the mystic nature of the act being performed; second, to anaesthetize the critical faculty, as does the overture in a theatre, and prepare the mind for some extra-ordinary event. But these are in reality twin aspects of the same func-tion: for music, like erotic sight, raises the consciousness until it is in tune with a reality beyond the reach of wisdom. 'Music, moody food of us that trade in love,' says Cleopatra (II. v. I.). Music in Shake-speare is ever the solace and companion of love, and love in Shake-speare the language of mysticism. For this reason the mystic happen-ings in these plays are accompanied by the theme of music. I will now pass to the third of the mythical plays, *Cymbeline*.

Many of the former elements recur in *Cymbeline*. We have the faithlessness-theme in which Posthumus distrusts Imogen, and Iago is resuscitated in the deceiver Iachimo. Posthumus' very name sug-gests the birth-theme of the two former plays: like Marina and Per-dita he is cast unprotected into a hostile world. Cymbeline's long-lost sons, Guiderius and Arviragus, remind us of the lost children of Pericles and Leontes. We have again the idea of the apparently dead found to be alive. Guiderius and Arviragus think Imogen is dead, and even prepare to bury her. Solemn music sounds at her supposed death. Posthumus, too, is led to think Imogen dead independently. The same themes are evidently running in the poet's mind, but it is as though the artist tries hard to control them, to control the more directly religious apprehension that is beginning to make the writing of a normal play an impossibility. And this repressed instinct—if repressed it was—certainly has its revenge. In the Vision of Jupiter we have Shakespeare's clearest statement in terms of anthropomorphic theology of the significance of the themes I have been analysing in the final plays. Without analysis of the sequence of tragedies and myths the scene will appear dramatically unnecessary and crude: with knowledge of Shakespeare's state of mind in the writing of this play, when his imagination must have been burningly conscious not alone of human life, but of the mystic significance of it, which he had already touched in *Antony and Cleopatra* and *Pericles,* we shall find it quite reasonable that he should attempt a universal statement in direct language concerning the implications of his plot. The scene becomes, in fact, a priceless possession to the interpreter of Shakespeare. It has been often allotted in the past to the 'incompetent coadjutor.' I will shortly notice this, the central and, for the purpose of this paper, by far the most important, scene in the play.

Posthumus, in the depth of his misery and remorse, sleeps in prison. He has prayed to heaven to take his life, and finally called on his love, whom he has mistrusted, whom he believes dead through his fault:

> O Imogen!
> I'll speak to thee in silence.   (v. iv. 28)

There is next a lengthy stage direction, with a three times iterated mention of music. Posthumus' father, mother, and two brothers appear. And these figures chant, to a haunting dirge-like tune of words, a piteous complaint to Jupiter. It is important to observe the universal significance of their words, and its direct bearing on the troubles and trials of Posthumus, who has endured the same kind of suffering as Shakespeare's other heroes. Jupiter is the 'thunder-master' who shows his 'spite on mortal flies.' The helplessness of Posthumus' birth is remembered:

> *Mother.*   Lucina lent not me her aid,
> But took me in my throes;
> That from me was Posthumus ript,
> Came crying 'mongst his foes,
> A thing of pity!   (v. iv. 43)

If we consider that Iachimo is of the same kin as Iago and that both are embodiments of the spirit of cynicism and devitalised intellectual energy which blights the faith of Hamlet and Troilus in human kind and the purposes of eternity, we can find a poignant and universal note that is generally missed in Sicilius' stanza:

> *Sicilius.*   Why did you suffer Iachimo,
> Slight thing of Italy,
> To taint his nobler heart and brain
> With needless jealousy;
> And to become the geck and scorn
> O' the other's villainy?   (v. iv. 63)

I am not suggesting that Shakespeare intentionally allegorizes here: but that Iago and Iachimo are products of the same potentiality in his mind or soul, and that it is exactly that potentiality that rings in the pain, the cynicism, and the loathing of the problem plays. The family of Posthumus end their chant with fervent cries that justice be done. It is man's complaint to God on behalf of those he loves. Jupiter appears and answers their complaints as follows:

> *Jupiter.* No more, you petty spirits of region low,
>   Offend our hearing; hush! How dare you ghosts
> Accuse the thunderer, whose bolt, you know,
>   Sky-planted batters all rebelling coasts?
> Poor shadows of Elysium, hence, and rest
>   Upon your never-withering banks of flowers:
> Be not with mortal accidents oppressed:
>   No care of yours it is; you know 'tis ours.
> Whom best I love I cross; to make my gift,
>   The more delay'd, delighted. Be content;
> Your low-laid son our godhead will uplift:
>   His comforts thrive, his trials well are spent.
> Our Jovial star reign'd at his birth, and in
>   Our temple was he married. Rise and fade.
> He shall be lord of lady Imogen,
>   And happier much by his affliction made.
> This tablet lay upon his breast, wherein
>   Our pleasure his full fortune doth confine:
> And so, away: no further with your din
>   Express impatience, lest you stir up mine.
> Mount, eagle, to my palace crystalline.
>   (*Ascends*)   (v. iv. 93)

As Jupiter vanishes, Sicilius makes majestic comment:

> *Sicilius.* He came in thunder; his celestial breath
>   Was sulphurous to smell: the holy eagle
>   Stoop'd, as to foot us; his ascension is
>   More sweet than our blest fields; his royal bird
>   Prunes the immortal wing, and cloys his beak,
>   As when his god is pleased.   (v. iv. 114)

Now, whatever we may think about the imaginative impact of this scene as we read—we must remember that we miss the heightened consciousness of the music that is indicated, and the visual accompaniment of grouping and dance—two things are certain: first, that there is nothing whatever in the style to justify a critic who knows his Shakespeare in enlisting the services of the incompetent coadjutor; second, that, coming as it does before the usual reunions at the end of the play, it clearly points the necessity of my thesis in dealing with the similar plots of *Pericles* and *The Winter's Tale,* that these miraculous and joyful conquests of life's tragedy are the expression, through the medium of drama, of a state of mind or soul in the writer directly in knowledge—or supposed knowledge—of a mystic and transcendent fact as to the true nature and purpose of the sufferings of humanity. My primary intention here is not to insist on the truth of the immortality shadowed forth in these plays; but simply to indicate that they are of this mystic kind, so that we may allot them their proper place in our assessment of Shakespeare's achievement.

To-day we hear from theologians that immortality is a matter of quality and value rather than something which can be measured by time. Canon Streeter asserts that its truth can only be expressed by myth or metaphor. Now the supreme value to man is always love. What more perfect form, then, could such a myth take than that of the restoration to Pericles of his Thaisa and Marina, so long and so mistakenly supposed lost? It is, indeed, noticeable that these plays do not aim at revealing a temporal survival of death: rather at the thought that death is a delusion. What was thought dead is in reality alive. In them we watch the fine flowers of a mystic state of soul bodied into the forms of drama. The parables of Jesus, which, through the medium of narrative, leave with the reader what is preeminently a sense of quality rather than a memory of events, are of the same kind. *Pericles* and *The Winter's Tale* show us the quality of immortality in terms of victorious love welling up in the beautiful plot of loss and reunion; and in *Cymbeline* an anthropomorphic theology is introduced to attempt an explanation and a valuation of the mystic fact.

The artist expresses a direct vision of the significance of life, and for his materials he uses, for purposes of imitation, the shapes, the colours, the people and events of the world in which he finds himself. But in course of the spiritual progress to which he is dedicated it may happen that the implements of outward manifestation in the physical universe become inadequate to the intuition which he is to express. Art is an extraverted expression of the creative imagination which, when introverted, becomes religion. But the mind of man cannot altogether dispense with the machinery of objectivity, and the inwardness of religion must create, or discern, its own objective reality and name it God. Conversely, the artist, in process of growth, may be forced beyond the phenomena of actuality into a world of the spirit which scarcely lends itself to a purely artistic, and therefore objective, imitation. In *Cymbeline* Shakespeare is forced by the increasing inwardness of his intuition to a somewhat crude anthropomorphism in the Vision of Jupiter: and this anthropomorphic theology is inimical to artistic expression. *Cymbeline* contains a personal god called in to right the balance of a drama whose plot, like that of *Pericles* and *The Winter's Tale,* is incompatible with the ordinary forms of life; but this god, true enough to the religious intuition of the author, yet comes near to exploding the work of art in which he occurs. The form of dramatic art is necessarily extraverted and imitative; and Shakespeare has passed beyond interest in imitation. If a last work of pure art is to be created there is only one theme that can be its fit material. A prophetic criticism could, if *The Tempest* had been lost, have nevertheless indicated what must be its essential nature, and might have hazarded its name: for in this work Shakespeare looks inward and, projecting perfectly his own spiritual experience into symbols of objectivity, traces in a compact play the past progress of his own soul.[3] He is now the object of his own search, and no other theme but that of his visionary self is now of power to call forth the riches of his imagination.

Let me recall the outline of the Shakespearian progress. In the problem plays there is mental division: on the one side an exquisite apprehension of the spiritual—beauty, romance, poetry; on the other, the hate-theme—loathing of the impure, aversion from the animal kinship of man, disgust at the decaying body of death. This dualism is resolved in the tragedies: the hate-theme itself is finely sublimated in *Timon* by means of the purification of great passion, human grandeur, and all the panoply of high tragedy. The recurrent poetic symbol of tragedy in Shakespeare is 'storm' or 'tempest.' The third group outsoars the intuition of tragedy and gives us plays whose plots explicate the quality of immortality: the predominating symbols are loss in tempest and revival to the sounds of music. It is about twelve years from the inception of this lonely progress of the soul to the composition of *The Tempest.*

[3] I would now repudiate the unnecessary use of such words as 'spiritual' and 'soul,' which do little to advance our understanding.

Now on the island of *The Tempest* Prospero is master of his lonely magic. He has been there for twelve years. Two creatures serve him: Ariel, the 'airy nothing' of poetry; and the snarling Caliban, half-beast, half-man; the embodiment of the hate-theme. These two creatures are yoked in the employ of Prospero, like Plato's two steeds of the soul, the noble and the hideous, twin potentialities of the human spirit. Caliban has been mastered by Prospero and Ariel. Though he revolts against his master still, the issue is not in doubt, and the tunes of Ariel draw out his very soul in longing and desire, just as the power of poetry shows forth the majesty of Timon, whose passion makes of universal hate a noble and aspiring thing. These three are the most vital and outstanding figures in the play: for Shakespeare had only to look inward to find them. But there are other elements that complete the pattern of this self-revelation.

Prospero's enemies are drawn to the magic island of great poetry by means of a tempest raised by Prospero with the help of Ariel. In Alonso, despairing and self-accusing, bereft of his child, we can see traces of the terrible end of *Lear*; in Antonio and Sebastian, the tempter and the tempted, plotting murder for a crown, we can see more than traces of *Macbeth*. But, driven by the tempest-raising power of tragic and passionate poetry within the magic circle of Prospero and Ariel, these hostile and evil things are powerless: they can only stand spell-stopped. They are enveloped in the wondrous laws of enchantment on the island of song and music. Caliban, who has been mastered by it, knows best the language to describe the mystic tunes of Ariel:

> Be not afeard; the isle is full of noises,
> Sounds and sweet airs that give delight and hurt not.
> Sometimes a thousand twangling instruments
> Will hum about mine ears, and sometimes voices,
> That, if I then had waked after long sleep,
> Will make me sleep again; and then, in dreaming,
> The clouds methought would open and show riches
> Ready to drop upon me, that, when I waked,
> I cried to dream again.   (III. ii. 147)

The protagonists of murder and bereavement are exquisitely entrapped in the magic and music of Prospero and his servant Ariel. So, too, were the evil things of life mastered by the poetry of the great tragedies, and transmuted into the vision of the myths. The spirit of the

Final Plays also finds its perfected home in this last of the series. Here the child-theme is repeated in Miranda, cast adrift with her father on the tempestuous seas; here the lost son of Alonso is recovered, alive and well, and the very ship that was wrecked is found to be miraculously 'tight and yare and bravely rigg'd' as when it 'first put out to sea.' (v. i. 224). Prospero, like Cerimon over Thaisa, revives, with music, the numbed consciousness of Alonso and his companions; and, as they wake, it is as though mortality were waking into eternity. And this thought makes necessary a statement and a distinction as to the dual possible approaches to the significance of *The Tempest*.

First, we can regard it as the poet's expression of a view of human life. With the knowledge of Shakespeare's poetic symbolism in memory, we will think of the wreck as suggesting the tragic destiny of man, and the marvellous survival of the travellers and crew as another and more perfectly poetic and artistic embodiment of the thought expressed through the medium of anthropomorphic theology in *Cymbeline* that there exists a joy and a revival that makes past misery, in Pericles' phraseology, 'sport.' According to this reading Prospero becomes in a sense the 'God' of the *Tempest*-universe, and we shall find compelling suggestion as to the immortality of man in such lines as Ariel's when Prospero asks him if the victims of the wreck are safe:

> Not a hair perish'd;
>   On their sustaining garments not a blemish,
>   But fresher than before.   (I. ii. 217)

So, too, thinking of sea-storms and wreckages as Shakespeare's symbols of human tragedy, we shall find new significance in Ariel's lines:

> Nothing of him that doth fade,
> But doth suffer a sea-change
> Into something rich and strange.   (I. ii. 397)

Especially, if we remember that the soul's desire of love in Shakespeare is consistently imaged as a rich something set far across tempestuous seas, we shall receive especial delight in the song:

> Come unto these yellow sands,
>   And then take hands:
> Curtsied when you have, and kiss'd
>   The wild waves whist.   (I. ii. 375)

Commentators divide into two camps and argue long as to the syntax and sense of those last two lines: is 'whist,' or is it not, they say, a nominative absolute? And if not, how can waves be kiss'd? A knowledge of Shakespeare's imagery, however, is needed to see the triumphant mysticism of the dream of love's perfected fruition in eternity stilling the tumultuous waves of time. This is one instance of many where the imaginative interpretation of a poet, and a knowledge of his particular symbolism, short-circuits the travails and tribulations of the grammarian or the commentator who in search for facts neglects the primary facts of all poetry—its suggestion, its colour, its richness of mental association, its appeal, not to the intellect, but the imagination.

The second approach is this, which I have already indicated. *The Tempest* is a record, crystallized with consummate art into a short play, of all the themes I have discussed in this paper, of the spiritual progress from 1599 or 1600 to the year 1611, or whenever, exactly, *The Tempest* was written. According to this reading Prospero is not God, but Shakespeare—or rather the controlling judgement of Shakespeare, since Ariel and Caliban are also representations of dual minor potentialities of his soul. From this approach three incidents in the play reveal unique interest. First, the dialogue between Prospero and Ariel in I. ii. where Ariel is tired and cries for the promised freedom, and is told that there is one last work to be done—which is in exact agreement with my reading of the faltering art of *Cymbeline*:[4] second, Prospero's well-known farewell to his art, where commentators have seldom failed to admit what Professor Saintsbury calls a 'designed personal allegory,' and where I would notice that Prospero clearly regards his art as pre-eminently a tempest-raising magic, and next refers to the opening of graves at his command, thereby illustrating again the sequence from tragedy to myth which I have described; and third, Prospero's other dialogue with Ariel in v. i. where Ariel pities the enemies of his master and draws from Prospero the words:

> Hast thou, which art but air, a touch, a feeling
> Of their afflictions, and shall not myself,
> One of their kind, that relish all as sharply,
> Passion as they, be kindlier moved than thou art?

> (v. i. 21)

[4] A strange error: whatever our personal likes and dislikes, there is nothing 'faltering' in *Cymbeline*.

In poetic creation 'all is forgiven, and it would be strange not to forgive'; but the partial and fleeting flame of the poet's intuition may
light at last the total consciousness with the brilliance of a cosmic
apprehension. This speech suggests the transit from the intermittent
love of poetic composition to the perduring love of the mystic.

Now these two methods of approach considered separately and in
sequence are not so significant as they become when we realize that
they are simultaneously possible and, indeed, necessary. Together
they are complementary to *The Tempest*'s unique reality. For it will
next be seen that these two aspects when considered together give us
a peculiar knowledge of this act of the poet's soul in the round: so
that the usual flat view of it which reads it as an impersonal fairy
story—corresponding to my reading of it as an objective vision of
life—becomes a three-dimensional understanding when we remember
the implicit personal allegory. Only by submitting our faculties to
both methods can we properly understand the play to the full. *The
Tempest* is at the same time a record of Shakespeare's spiritual progress and a statement of the vision to which that progress has brought
him. It is apparent as a dynamic and living act of the soul, containing
within itself the record of its birth: it is continually re-writing itself
before our eyes. Shakespeare has in this play so become master of the
whole of his own mystic universe that that universe, at last perfectly
projected in one short play into the forms and shapes of objective
human existence, shows us, in the wreck of *The Tempest,* a complete
view of that existence, no longer as it normally appears to man, but
as it takes reflected pattern in the still depths of the timeless soul of
poetry. And, since it reveals its vision not as a statement of absolute
truth independently of the author, but related inwardly to the succession of experiences that condition and nurture its own reality, it
becomes, in a unique sense beyond other works of art, an absolute.
There is thus now no barrier between the inward and the outward,
expression and imitation. God, it has been said, is the mode in which
the subject-object distinction is transcended. Art aspires to the perfected fusion of expression with imitation. *The Tempest* is thus at the
same time the most perfect work of art and the most crystal act of
mystic vision in our literature.

J. DOVER WILSON
1881-

THIS LECTURE OF J. Dover Wilson's has something of an old-fashioned quality. Although it sees *The Tempest* as containing personal allegory (its biographical speculation is in the manner of the Victorians) and perceives the symbolic import of the opening scene and of Ferdinand's and Miranda's chess game, it does not get lost in mazes of esoteric symbolism as do such modern critics of the play as Colin Still. It has the great virtues of lucidity and of a simple and unpretentious eloquence in presenting the sensitive insights of the author.

Speaking seven years after the publication of Knight's "Myth and Miracle," which he did not seem to know, he points out the importance of the tempest as a symbol of life and (this was unperceived by Knight) of the ship as a symbol of human society. Although he does not show himself aware of the omnipresence in Shakespeare's plays of tempest imagery and its symbolic opposition to music imagery (the significant discovery of Knight) he perceives the relationship between the symbolic storm in *King Lear* and that in *The Tempest*.

Unlike Wilson, Knight regards Prospero as suggestive of the deity. This idea had already been broached by J. Churton Collins in "Poetry and Symbolism: A Study of *The Tempest*" (1908). Harold S. Wilson in "Action and Symbol in *Measure for Measure* and *The Tempest*" (1953) finds Prospero to be like Duke Vincentio, whose "arrangements are compared with the operation of Divine Grace," as Ariel speaks of himself and his fellow spirits as "ministers of fate." One might also point out that immediately after Gonzalo exclaims "The wills above be done" and after Miranda says that if she were a "god of power" she would not permit the ship to sink, Prospero gives assurance that no harm will come to it, speaking with the authority of such a "god of power" whose will governs events. If Dover Wilson does not, however, see Prospero as at times taking on the aspect of divine providence, his description of Prospero's initial appearance as an irascible father and harsh taskmaster is perhaps significant in this regard. As Harold S. Wilson states, Prospero has, Dover Wilson to the contrary, resolved on his course of forgiveness prior to the beginning of the play, his guiding of Alonso to penitence through affliction and his bringing together of Ferdinand and Miranda and strengthening of their love by his supposed opposition being part of his design of reconciliation. Nevertheless, if he has been guided by a beneficent purpose, he has assumed the appearance of severity; and the revelation of the benevolence behind that appearance may be said to be a revelation that suffering is part of the scheme of divine providence by which the guilty are cleansed and the good tested.

However, if the suffering of the good is nullified, as it is not in the tragedies, the vision of evil of the tragedies is, as Dover Wilson says, contained but transcended in *The Tempest*. He uses Lytton Strachey, whose observations are themselves a development of what was presented in passing by Dowden, as a corrective, exaggerated though it be, for the correspondingly false emphases of the followers of Dowden. In so doing, he arrives at a more balanced presentation of the effect of *The Tempest*.

THE MEANING OF THE TEMPEST

IN WHAT MOOD was *The Tempest* written? No sooner had the order of the plays been more or less determined by nineteenth-century criticism, and it had become generally accepted that *The Tempest*

"The Meaning of *The Tempest*" is from J. Dover Wilson, *The Meaning of* The Tempest (1936). By permission of the author.

was probably in some sense Shakespeare's last play, than the capital importance of this question was seized upon. Moreover, the Victorians returned an unequivocal and almost unanimous answer to it. The play seemed to them the culmination of Shakespeare's last phase in drama, a phase which succeeded the storm and stress of the tragic period and included *Cymbeline, The Winter's Tale* and *Pericles.* Reconciliation and forgiveness formed the theme of all four plays; but in *The Tempest* above all they found the atmosphere of serenity, grave benignity, peace. And they tended also to identify Prospero with the dramatist, so much so in fact that Shakespeare became for many a kind of grand old man of literature, though he was actually under fifty at the time of his retirement.

In 1906, however, Victorianism was on the wane, and the leader of the reaction, Lytton Strachey, administered a rude shock to this interpretation in an essay entitled *Shakespeare's Final Period,* which since its re-issue in the volume called *Books and Characters,* published in 1922, has exercised a very wide influence. After speaking of *Timon* as "for sheer virulence of foul-mouthed abuse . . . probably unsurpassed in any literature" he continues:

"From this whirlwind of furious ejaculation, this splendid storm of nastiness, Shakespeare, we are confidently told, passed in a moment to tranquillity and joy, to blue skies, to young ladies, and to general forgiveness. . . . This is a pretty picture, but is it true?"[1]

He then notes that while some of the principal characters, such as Florizel and Perdita, are charming figures, while Prospero is "grave" and Hermione "serene," the Victorian critics omitted to point out that these last plays of Shakespeare "contain a series of portraits of peculiar infamy, whose wickedness finds expression in language of extraordinary force." Whereupon, after quoting at length from the jealous speeches of Leontes and the tirades of Paulina, he asks, "What traces do such passages as these show of 'serene self-possession,' of 'the highest wisdom and peace,' or of 'meditative romance?' "[2] On the contrary, he declares, "Nowhere are the poet's metaphors more nakedly material: nowhere does he verge more often upon a sort of brutality of phrase, a cruel coarseness."[3] These plays, moreover, he

1 *Books and Characters,* p. 45.
2 *Ibid.,* pp. 46–7.
3 *Ibid.,* p. 47.

observes, show a marked decline in Shakespeare's interest in character. The minor characters, e.g. Polixenes, Camillo, Sebastian, Gonzalo, Belarius, "have not even the life of ghosts; they are hardly more than speaking names, that give patient utterance to involution after involution. What a contrast to the minor characters of Shakespeare's earlier works!" Further, the indication of declining powers, evident in character-drawing, is also seen in looseness of structure in three out of four of this last group of plays.

"Attention has never been sufficiently drawn to . . . the singular carelessness with which great parts of them were obviously written. Could anything drag more wretchedly than the *dénouement* of *Cymbeline?* And with what perversity is the great pastoral scene in *The Winter's Tale* interspersed with long-winded intrigues, and disguises, and homilies!"[4]

Lastly he notes that, while Shakespeare's plays up to the final period are "essentially realistic,"

"all this has now changed: we are no longer in the real world, but in a world of enchantment, of mystery, of wonder, a world of shifting visions, a world of hopeless anachronisms, a world in which anything may happen next."[5] And "in *The Tempest* unreality has reached its apotheosis. Two of the principal characters are frankly not human beings at all; and the whole action passes, through a series of impossible occurrences, in a place which can only by courtesy be said to exist. The Enchanted Island, indeed, peopled, for a timeless moment, by this strange fantastic medley of persons and of things, has been cut adrift for ever from common sense, and floats, buoyed up by a sea, not of waters, but of poetry."[6]

The conclusion he draws from all this is that in his final period Shakespeare was just *bored*—"bored with people, bored with real life, bored with drama, bored in fact with everything except poetry and poetical dreams." So he imagines him in these last years of his life as "half enchanted by visions of beauty and loveliness, and half bored to death; on the one side inspired by a soaring fancy to the singing of ethereal songs, and on the other urged by a general disgust to burst occasionally through his torpor into bitter and violent speech."[7] How different from the Victorian picture of the benign seer breathing benediction upon the world he is about to leave!

[4] *Ibid.,* p. 51.
[5] *Ibid.,* pp. 49–50.
[6] *Ibid.,* p. 53.
[7] *Ibid.,* p. 52.

I have spent some time over these criticisms by Lytton Strachey, because, as I say, they have been widely accepted and also because the main premises upon which they rest cannot be controverted. We owe Strachey a real debt for insisting upon the seamy side of the texture of Shakespeare's last plays, and if we take this into account we may arrive at a juster estimate of the final period and of the meaning of *The Tempest,* even if we find that estimate differing materially from his. But first one or two weaknesses may be noted in Strachey's argument. I hesitate to say so, but it is clear to me from some of the passages just quoted that Strachey does not rightly understand what poetry, and especially dramatic poetry, really is. He speaks of Shakespeare being bored "with everything *except* poetry and poetical dreams." What do we know of Shakespeare "except poetry and poetical dreams?" And are not Hamlet and Falstaff and Cleopatra every whit as much poetical dreams as Caliban and Ariel? He speaks, too, of the action of *The Tempest* occurring "in a place which can only by courtesy be said to exist," and of the Enchanted Island being "cut adrift from common sense" and "buoyed up by a sea not of water but of poetry." Are the walls of the castle at Elsinore built of stones or of poetry? Is there much common sense in *A Midsummer Night's Dream* or in the forest of Arden? Surely, *all* Shakespeare's plays take place in the world of imagination. What is true is that in his last period Shakespeare chose to imagine a different kind of world to anything given us in his earlier plays.

As to the violent language, Strachey oversimplifies the problem by confining it to the last period. There is no doubt that in 1608 or 1609 a change came over the art and temper of Shakespeare as profound as that which took place about 1601. But what Strachey takes as a special characteristic of this final phase, the coarseness and naked metaphors of certain speakers, is an overflow from the tragic period. There is nobody in the last plays in any way so foul-mouthed or disagreeable as Thersites in *Troilus and Cressida,* and he probably belongs to 1600, right at the beginning of the tragedies. Moreover, though the strain is still there in the last plays—in Leontes, in Iachimo, in Cloten and in Posthumus—it is visibly weakening; and in *The Tempest* is confined to Caliban and the two traitors, Antonio and Sebastian. Thus, if it be (as I think it is) an indication of some touch of morbidity or strain of disillusionment and disgust in Shakespeare, it is clearly working itself out, until in *The Tempest* Prospero-

Shakespeare has embodied it in the sub-human creature Caliban and chained it up beneath his cell. One is reminded of the reply of the aged Sophocles to one who inquired what he felt in old age about sexual passion, which is reported by Plato at the beginning of *The Republic*. "To my great delight," he said, "I have escaped from it, and feel as if I had escaped from a savage and frantic monster." It is a sentiment we can very well imagine coming from the author of the sonnets on the Dark Lady.

Much the same answer may be given to Strachey's criticism of the technique of the romances. *The Winter's Tale* and *Cymbeline* are loosely constructed and at times carelessly written. But no one can say this of *The Tempest,* which is technically one of the most perfect of all Shakespeare's plays. Is it not, therefore, common sense to suppose that, having decided to attempt a new kind of drama—what may be called fairy-tale drama, as contrasted with the drama of real life, which he had generally (though not always) written up to that time, Shakespeare had to experiment before he accomplished just what he aimed at? *Cymbeline* and *The Winter's Tale* are clearly experiments; *The Tempest* is the success that crowned his efforts. As for the so-called decline in Shakespeare's interest in character, that is part of the new technique, and I shall have something more to say upon it in a moment or two.

Having set forth Strachey's point of view, and criticized it a little, let me spend the rest of my time by frankly and dogmatically giving you my own interpretation of the mood in which the last and greatest of the romances was composed. In the first place, *The Tempest* is not a play for the Lytton Stracheys of this world, but for fathers! We see Miranda and Ferdinand through a father's eyes. They are Prospero's eyes, of course, you will say. Yes, but inasmuch as we also see Perdita and Marina in the same light, the eyes must be Shakespeare's too. We have only to compare the lovers in these final plays with those of earlier ones, with Romeo and Juliet or with Antony and Cleopatra for example, to see that the atmosphere in which they move depends upon the time of life of their creator. It is possible to identify Romeo with the young Shakespeare, or Antony with the mature Shakespeare, but not Ferdinand. And Shakespeare communicates his attitude to his audience. We say that the spectacle of Ferdinand and Miranda making love is "delightful"—an epithet impossible to apply to Romeo and Juliet or to Antony and Cleopatra.

They appear to us as children, moving in a kind of subdued light of tenderness and compassion. Not that they are unreal, as Lytton Strachey avers, but that we are not inside them, as we are inside Romeo and Juliet. In *Romeo and Juliet,* the play, which is full of old people, we watch them, the Capulets and the Montagues, through the eyes of the young. In *The Tempest* we contemplate them pityingly ("Poor worm, thou art infected" or " 'Tis new to thee!"), lovingly, and with anxiety. At times, indeed, Prospero's paternal solicitude becomes a little too much for some of us. I refer particularly to his twice repeated warning in Àct IV, scene i, against pre-nuptial unchastity. Yet the very strangeness of this, together with its lack of all apparent dramatic point, make its personal reference the more likely. And it is certainly remarkable that both Shakespeare himself and Anne Hathaway in 1582 and their daughter Judith and Thomas Quincy in 1616 appear to have been guilty of the very lapse which the dramatist here condemns so pointedly. He had reason to fear the "savage and frantic monster."

However this may be, we can hardly doubt that the paternal attitude towards love in these last plays is a personal trait, or that Prospero is in some sense Shakespeare himself. The story of *The Tempest* is not his, as I have said, but the spiritual experience of the exiled duke almost certainly symbolizes similar experiences of his own. "Shakespeare led a life of Allegory," wrote Keats: "his works are the comments on it." And of none of his works is the observation truer than of the play we are now dealing with. As Dr. Mackail has pointed out, the allegory has affected the whole movement of the drama. Prospero is not merely the central figure of *The Tempest:*

"the action is throughout, down to its smallest details, planned and ordered" by him. "He is the magician—one might almost go further and say the playwright—and the other figures are his puppets. . . . The dramatist has projected himself bodily into the drama. For once, and once only, he lets us see him actually at work. It is perhaps this double consciousness—as though we were simultaneously in front watching the play as spectators, and behind seeing it being handled—that makes *The Tempest* not in fact . . . highly effective on the stage. The illusion or hallucination to which, in seeing a play acted, we are asked to abandon ourselves, has not its full chance. But when we read it, if we read it carefully enough, it brings us nearer than almost anything else to understanding Shakespeare's art."[8]

[8] *The Approach to Shakespeare,* by J. W. Mackail, pp. 104, 106.

Is not this a more persuasive explanation of the comparative "un-reality" of *The Tempest* than Strachey's theory of the bored Shake-speare?

Yet Prospero is a mask, or shall we say a "player's part," and not the man himself. For one thing, he is old, which Shakespeare was far from being in 1611. He is Lear over again, Lear in another world, a better world, though still to some extent a purgatory. The play might be called "The Purification of Prospero," if the original title were not apter because more symbolic. Why did Shakespeare call it *The Tempest,* when the storm is confined to the brief opening scene and all that follows is calm and enchantment? His opening scenes generally give us in broad and simple statement the main theme of the drama that follows. Thus we have a glimpse of the warring factions in the first scene of *Romeo and Juliet,* turbulent crowds of citizens at the beginning of *Julius Cæsar* and of *Coriolanus;* the witches introduce us to *Macbeth* and the Ghost to *Hamlet.* But with *The Tempest* matters are different. Here the first scene serves as a contrast, not as an initiation. The storm that rages through *King Lear* is now shut up into an episode of seventy lines, in which we see a human society with its gradation of rank—its king lurking un-seen in his cabin, its quarrelsome nobles cursing the fate that hangs above their heads, and its men of action vainly struggling against it— brought to sudden and seemingly irretrievable disaster, as the ship splits and plunges into the gulf, amid the anguished cries of all on board. As a picture of appalling catastrophe there is nothing elsewhere in Shakespeare to touch it; and when Lytton Strachey asks for realism, here it is in full measure! So overwhelming is the realism and so convincing, that the dramatist has us completely at his mercy for the wonders he means later to put upon us; and that, no doubt, is in part the purpose of the scene. But it has other and more profound uses. It serves as a kind of back-cloth to the Enchanted Island, which we contemplate in all its serenity, magic and detachment in deliberated contrast with the world of reality, the world in which the quarrelsome, brawling, cursing, despairing human race is for ever foundering upon the rocks. It is as if Shakespeare had packed his whole tragic vision of life into one brief scene before bestowing his new vision upon us, as if he reminds us first of the old vision that we may the better appreciate the new. Certainly our sense of the island owes much to our coming upon it with the storm in mind. *The Tempest* begins with the stage-direction "A tempestuous noise of thunder and lightning heard"

and ends with Prospero's promise of "calm seas, auspicious gales."
But between these two points lie many descriptions of the island itself.
"The air breathes upon us here most sweetly," exclaims Gonzalo to
his rescued comrades; and again, "How lush and lusty the grass looks!
how green!" Only to the cynics, Sebastian and Antonio, does it seem
otherwise. Even Caliban is moved to poetic utterance by its loveliness:

> The isle is full of noises,
> Sounds and sweet airs that give delight and hurt not:
> Sometimes a thousand twangling instruments
> Will hum about mine ears; and sometimes voices,
> That, if I then had waked after long sleep,
> Will make me sleep again—and then in dreaming
> The clouds methought would open, and show riches
> Ready to drop upon me, that when I waked
> I cried to dream again.

The change from tempest to calm possesses, however, another
purpose also, a psychological purpose. Just as the storm in *King Lear*
symbolizes the spiritual and mental condition of the mad old king,
so the allaying of the waters about the island is paralleled by a
change in Prospero himself. In Act I, scene ii, he is a terrible old man,
almost as tyrannical and irascible as Lear at the opening of his play.
He loves his daughter dearly; but how sharply he speaks to her, when
he suspects her of not giving him her full attention. As if he himself
were not the cause of her wandering thoughts and eyes! For it is
not, I think, sufficiently appreciated that Miranda when we first
see her is in a state of violent emotion. The ship has just gone to the
bottom, as she believes, before her very eyes,

> a brave vessel,
> Who had no doubt some noble creature in her,

and, as her father tells his lengthy tale, her mind constantly reverts to
thought of that "noble creature" and her eyes to the sea which has
swallowed up her hopes and her dreams. The shadow of Ferdinand
has already fallen across her! So little, however, does her father
understand all this, that he sees before him nothing but an inattentive
pupil. Ariel too he rates as "malignant thing" (even "dull thing!")
and when the spirit dares to ask for liberty he threatens him thus:

> If thou more murmur'st, I will rend an oak
> And peg thee in his knotty entrails, till
> Thou hast howled away twelve winters.

There is little difference between this language and that addressed to Caliban:

> Hag-seed, hence!
> Fetch us in fuel, and be quick, thou'rt best,
> To answer other business: Shrug'st thou, malice?
> If thou neglect'st, or dost unwillingly
> What I command, I'll rack thee with old cramps,
> Fill all thy bones with achës, make thee roar,
> That beasts shall tremble at thy din.

Prospero shows, indeed, the natural feelings of a father when Ferdinand, a very presentable young man, falls in love with his daughter, an event all the more welcome that he had carefully planned it himself. But he quite evidently enjoys tyrannizing over him with his magic power and laying menial tasks upon him. And how savage he shows himself towards his enemies at the beginning of Act IV! The recollection of Caliban's plot moves him to fury.

> *Ferdinand.* Your father's in some passion
> That works him strongly.
> *Miranda.* Never till this day
> Saw I him touched with anger so distempered.

And his fury finds its satisfaction at the end of the scene, as follows:

A noise of hunters heard. Enter diverse spirits, in shape of dogs and hounds, hunting them about; Prospero and Ariel setting them on.

Prospero. Hey, Mountain, hey!
Ariel. Silver! there it goes, Silver!
Prospero. Fury, Fury! there, Tyrant, there . . . hark, hark!
  Caliban, Stephano and Trinculo are driven out.
> Go, charge my goblins that they grind their joints
> With dry convulsions, shorten up their sinews
> With aged cramps, and more pinch-spotted make them
> Than pard or cat o' mountain.
Ariel. Hark, they roar!
Prospero. Let them be hunted soundly. At this hour

> Lie at my mercy all mine enemies:
> Shortly shall all my labours end, and thou
> Shalt have the air at freedom: for a little
> Follow and do me service.

Thus ends Act IV without a hint that Prospero means to spare Antonio, Alonso and the rest. On the contrary, the gleeful observation that all his enemies now lie at his mercy, shows that real mercy is far from his thoughts. He is clearly in the same mood of vengeance at the opening of Act V. But we here approach the crisis of the play, and I must beg you to follow closely while I read you Shakespeare's own words.

> *Enter Prospero in his magic robes, with Ariel.*
> *Prospero.* Now does my project gather to a head.
> My charms crack not; my spirits obey; and time
> Goes upright with his carriage. How's the day?
> *Ariel.* On the sixth hour; at which time, my lord,
> You said our work should cease.
> *Prospero.*   I did say so,
> When first I raised the tempest. Say, my spirit,
> How fares the king and's followers?
> *Ariel.*   Confined together
> In the same fashion as you gave in charge,
> Just as you left them; all prisoners, sir,
> In the line-grove that weather-fends your cell;
> They cannot budge till your release. The king,
> His brother and yours, abide all three distracted,
> And the remainder mourning over them,
> Brimful of sorrow and dismay; but chiefly
> Him that you termed, sir, "The good old lord, Gonzalo";
> His tears run down his beard, like winter's drops
> From eaves of reeds. Your charm so strongly works 'em
> That if you now beheld them, your affections
> Would become tender.
> *Prospero.*   Dost thou think so, spirit?
> *Ariel.* Mine would, sir, were I human.
> *Prospero.*   And mine shall.
> Hast thou, which art but air, a touch, a feeling
> Of their afflictions, and shall not myself,
> One of their kind, that relish all as sharply,

> Passion as they, be kindlier moved than thou art?
> Though with their high wrongs I am struck to the quick,
> Yet with my nobler reason 'gainst my fury
> Do I take part: the rarer action is
> In virtue than in vengeance: they being penitent,
> The sole drift of my purpose doth extend
> Not a frown further. Go release them, Ariel:
> My charms I'll break, their senses I'll restore,
> And they shall be themselves.

The conversion of Prospero is sudden, like other conversions in Shakespeare: the age believed in sudden conversions. But it is none the less real on that account, and takes Prospero himself as much by surprise at it takes us. At the beginning of the scene he boasts that his "charms crack not"; thirty lines later he is declaring, "My charms I'll break." What is it that causes his "fury" thus magically, almost involuntarily, to subside like the raging sea when the tempest has ceased to vex it? There is no hint of moral compunction, no reminder, as in Portia's famous speech, of the promptings of religion. The conversion is an æsthetic one; it is made at the suggestion of Ariel, who is surely the genius of dramatic poetry; and is brought about by the force of imagination, which compels Prospero to put himself in the place of his enemies, to "passion as they." Shakespeare, in fact, anticipates dramatically the principles enunciated by Shelley in his *Defence of Poesy*. Shelley is meeting, you will recollect, the objection, common in his day, that poetry is immoral, or as we should put it to-day a-moral, in its influence; an objection which, he maintains, "rests upon a misconception of the manner in which poetry acts to produce the moral improvement of man." Ethical science and moral precepts have their uses.

But poetry acts in another and diviner manner. It awakens and enlarges the mind itself by rendering it the receptacle of a thousand unapprehended combinations of thought. . . . The great secret of morals is love; or a going out of our nature, and an identification of ourselves with the beautiful which exists in thought, action, or person, not our own. A man, to be greatly good, must imagine intensely and comprehensively; he must put himself in the place of another and of many others; the pains and pleasures of his species must become his own. The great instrument of moral good is the imagination; and poetry administers to the effect by acting upon the cause. . . . Poetry strengthens the faculty which is the organ of the moral nature in man, in the same manner as exercise strengthens a limb.

It is significant that Strachey makes no reference at all to this scene in his essay, and that while he describes Prospero as "unpleasantly crusty," "self-opinionated and sour,"[9] he fails to notice that his whole manner changes in the last act. To him the *dénouement* of the play is what he calls the "gorgeous phantasm of a repentance from the mouth of the pale phantom Alonso"[10] in Act III, scene iii, but the far more interesting repentance of Prospero in Act V altogether escapes him. In short, he has missed the point of the play, which culminates not in Act III but in the unexpected scene of forgiveness and reconciliation that brings it to its close. Indeed, he overlooks the significance of the last scene in all four plays of Shakespeare's Final Period. In each it is a scene of reconciliation, from which the note of bitterness, which he has rightly emphasized elsewhere, has been altogether excluded. This oversight is a grave error on Strachey's part. In the theatre, the last scene is all-important, since it is the scene of which the audience carry away the most vivid recollection and which therefore determines for them the dominant impression of the whole. And that in *The Tempest,* at any rate, Shakespeare bent all his energies to the strengthening of this parting impression cannot be disputed. It begins with the embrace between the inveterate foes Prospero and Alonso, and culminates in the discovery of the lovers at chess, itself a lovely piece of symbolism. The ancient feud between Milan and Naples has softened into the mimic war of ivory armies who shed no blood, played out by the representatives of the two houses, united in love. The injurers and usurpers "lie all at the mercy" of the injured, and are overcome not through punishment or revenge, but by means of forgiveness and reconciliation; a reconciliation sealed by love, by the blessed union of innocents from both families, too young to have inherited the wrongs or the guilt of either.

This atmosphere is so all-embracing that it includes and transforms even Stephano, the drunken butler, and Caliban, the moon-calf, whom Prospero had addressed at the beginning of the play as

> abhorred slave,
> Which any print of goodness wilt not take,
> Being capable of all ill!

[9] *Books and Characters,* pp. 54–5.
[10] *Ibid.* pp. 53–4.

When Stephano enters, driven in by Ariel, with Trinculo and Caliban, all decked out in their ridiculous stolen apparel, he is still "reeling ripe." But what *veritas in vino* comes from the mouth of this philo-sophic trencher-shifter! "Every man shift for all the rest, and let no man take care for himself; for all is but fortune." It is often Shake-speare's sly way to set his profoundest observations upon the lips of his meanest creations; and there is no finer example of it than this. If *The Tempest* has any moral, the words of tipsy Stephano express it. For what hope is there for us poor human creatures, how can we save from shipwreck the storm-tossed barque in which we are con-demned to pass our days huddled close together, except by service and self-forgetfulness? As to Caliban, Shakespeare has final words for him that are almost comical in the mouth of so reprobate a cur-mudgeon:

> I'll be wise hereafter,
> And seek for grace.

When Caliban talks of grace, we cannot be far from heaven. And that heaven, indeed, keeps close watch over the doings of those who take part in these final scenes is conveyed in all four of Shakespeare's romances. "Look down, you gods," exclaims good old Gonzalo,

> And on this couple drop a blessed crown!
> For it is you that have chalked forth the way
> Which brought us hither.

It is an echo of Hermione's in *The Winter's Tale:*

> You gods, look down
> And from your sacred vials pour your graces
> Upon my daughter's head!

Or of the Soothsayer's in *Cymbeline:*

> The finger of the powers above do tune
> The harmony of this peace.

There are similar passages in the last scene of *Pericles,* while they all hark back, though in a different mood, to Lear's

> Upon such sacrifices, my Cordelia,
> The gods themselves throw incense.

What then? Are the Victorian critics in the right after all? Does Shakespeare end "on the heights" of wisdom and serenity, like some

Hebrew prophet looking back in benediction before stepping into
the chariot which is to bear him heavenward? The picture is too
Christmas-cardy and makes no allowance for the bitterness, the
violence, the savage indignation that (as Strachey has taught us)
bursts forth at times even in these last plays, though less in *The
Tempest* than in the others. Shakespeare found salvation, we may
believe, as by fire, but not by way of a fiery chariot. It misinterprets
also the final mood of Prospero. Fifteen or sixteen years earlier the
merciless Elizabethan Londoners had listened to Portia's great hymn
in praise of Mercy; they now witnessed a wronged man showing
mercy to his enemies, though he might have tortured them Eliza-
bethan-fashion and sunk them to the bottom of the sea, with none
to hinder or reprove. But it is no self-complacent Olympian who
does this. The Prospero we see at the end of the play is a very
humble person, still a little stern with Caliban, Stephano and Trinculo,
but pardoning even them, and with a mind that looks forward with
penitence rather than exultation to the future.

"We do pray for mercy," said Portia,

> And that same prayer doth teach us all to render
> The deeds of mercy.

Having rendered his deeds of mercy, Prospero bethinks him of the
mercy he stands in need of himself. Once Naples is reached he will
but wait to

> see the nuptial
> Of these our dear-beloved solemnized;
> And thence retire me to my Milan, where
> Every third thought shall be my grave.

The same note is repeated in the Epilogue, which by your leave I will
read again, and read in full.

> Now my charms are all o'erthrown,
> And what strength I have's mine own,
> Which is most faint: now, 'tis true,
> I must be here confined by you,
> Or sent to Naples. Let me not,
> Since I have my dukedom got
> And pardoned the deceiver, dwell
> In this bare island by your spell;
> But release me from my bands

With the help of your good hands:
Gentle breath of yours my sails
Must fill, or else my project fails,
Which was to please. Now I want
Spirits to enforce, art to enchant,
And my ending is despair,
Unless I be relieved by prayer,
Which pierces so that it assaults
Mercy itself and frees all faults.
As you from crimes would pardoned be,
Let your indulgence set me free.

We know nothing of Shakespeare's private life, but if, as I have asked you to believe with me, these lines were uttered from the stage by the poet in his own person, they breathe a very different mood from that imagined by the Victorian critics. The Shakespeare we last catch sight of is no prophet upon the heights, but a penitent on his knees.

And though the concluding scene of the play leaves with us an impression of serenity and peace only paralleled by that conveyed in some of Beethoven's latest compositions, it is of peace after storm, a peace which comes to some battered vessel which makes port with difficulty after many perils. Yet it is far more than rest and escape and self-congratulation. It is the culmination of the life-long experience of one of the greatest spirits that ever walked this earth; and, because of that, it altogether outsoars personality and seems to express the secret intimations of the universe itself. But feeble words of mine are not needed to describe what has already been described by the wisest of modern English thinkers. "At the heart of the nature of things," writes Alfred Whitehead in the concluding paragraph of his *Adventures of Ideas,* "there are always the dream of youth and the harvest of tragedy. The Adventure of the Universe starts with the dream and reaps tragic Beauty. This is the secret of the union of Zest with Peace—That the suffering attains its end in a Harmony of Harmonies. The immediate experience of this Final Fact, with its union of Youth and Tragedy, is the sense of Peace." Whitehead makes no reference to *The Tempest,* and as far as I know had no thought of Shakespeare in mind as he wrote. Yet what better summary of Shakespeare's spiritual development, as mirrored in the plays, could be found than an adventure which begins with the dream of youth, reaps tragic beauty, and attains its end in a harmony of harmonies? *The Tempest* is the inevitable sequel of *King Lear,* but it looks back also to *Romeo and Juliet,* even to *Venus and Adonis.* It is the harvest of tragedy, but it includes the dream of youth; and is thus the fruit of the union of Zest and Peace.

BIBLIOGRAPHY

Previous anthologies of Shakespearean criticism include *Eighteenth Century Essays on Shakespeare,* edited by D. Nichol Smith (Glasgow: J. MacLehose, 1903); *Shakespeare Criticism, 1623–1840,* edited by D. Nichol Smith (London: Oxford University Press, 1916; 15th ed., 1961); *Shakespeare Criticism, 1919–1935,* edited by Anne B. Ridler (London: Oxford University Press, 1936); *Shakespeare: Modern Essays in Criticism,* edited by Leonard F. Dean (New York: Oxford University Press, 1957); *Shakespeare Criticism, 1935–1960,* edited by Anne B. Ridler (London and New York: Oxford University Press, 1963). Shakespearean criticism has also been collected in the New Variorum editions of the plays. The recent editions issued as a Modern Language Association of America project are especially helpful.

For a history of Shakespearean criticism, the reader is referred to Charles F. Johnson's *Shakespeare and His Critics* (Boston and New York: Houghton, 1909). It needs to be revised, however, in the light of current knowledge and brought up to date. Augustus Ralli's two-volume *A History of Shakespearian Criticism* (Oxford: Clarendon Press, 1932), although useful to the scholar, is in reality more of a series of précis than a history. F. E. Halliday's *Shakespeare and His Critics* (London: Duckworth, 1949) is both a historical sketch and a compilation of Shakespearean criticism.

The most convenient bibliography of Shakespearean criticism is contained in *The Cambridge Bibliography of English Literature,* edited by F. W. Bateson (London: Cambridge University Press, 1940) and its supplement, edited by George Watson (1957). For criticism from 1936 to 1958, there is *A Classified Shakespeare Bibliography, 1936–1958,* edited by George Ross Smith (University Park: Pennsylvania State University Press, 1963). Also, there are annual bibliographies in *Shakespeare Quarterly, PMLA, The Year's Work in English Studies* and *Studies in Philology.* The annual volumes of *Shakespeare Survey* review the year's work and from time to time have articles surveying the criticism within a given field. A more cursory survey of contemporary criticism is the chapter "Shakespeare and His Times" in *Contemporary Literary Scholarship,* edited by Lewis Leary (New York: Appleton-Century-Crofts, 1958).

SPECIAL ASPECTS OF SHAKESPEARE'S DRAMAS

Abercrombie, Lascelles, "A Plea for the Liberty of Interpreting Shake-
    speare," *Proceedings of the British Academy*, XVI, 1930. A warn-
    ing against the restrictions of historical criticism.
Bradbrook, Muriel C., *Elizabethan Stage Conditions: A Study of their
    Place in the Interpretation of Shakespeare's Plays*, 1932. Hamden,
    Conn.: Archon Books, 1962. Criticism in the light of dramatic con-
    ventions of the time.
Bradbrook, Muriel C., "Fifty Years of the Criticism of Shakespeare's
    Style: A Retrospect," *Shakespeare Survey* (Cambridge: Cambridge
    University Press, 1954), vol. VII. Analytical review.
Campbell, Oscar James, "Shakespeare and the 'New' Critics," *J. Q. Adams
    Memorial Studies,* ed. James G. McManaway, *et al.,* Washington,
    D. C.: Folger Shakespeare Library, 1948. An attack on G. Wilson
    Knight and other "new" critics.
Clemen, Wolfgang, *The Development of Shakespeare's Imagery*, Cam-
    bridge, Mass.: Harvard University Press, 1951. Chronological study
    of the plays discussing imagery in relation to other elements.
Crane, Milton, *Shakespeare's Prose*, Chicago: University of Chicago
    Press, 1951. Shakespeare's prose compared with that of other Eliza-
    bethan dramatists.
Empson, William, *The Structure of Complex Words*, London: Chatto
    and Windus, 1951. The multifold implications of the key word of
    a play. *King Lear, Timon of Athens, Othello* and *Measure for
    Measure.*
Evans, B. Ifor, *The Language of Shakespeare's Plays,* London: Methuen,
    1952. Survey of the dramas examining dramatic effectiveness of the
    language.
Kirschbaum, Leo, *Character and Characterization in Shakespeare*, De-
    troit: Wayne State University Press, 1962. Characterization in Shake-
    speare's poetic drama.
Kolbe, F. C., *Shakespeare's Way*, London: Sheed & Ward, 1930. The
    significance of repetitive words within a play.
Mahood, M. W., *Shakespeare's Wordplay*, London: Methuen, 1957.
    Shakespeare's artistic use of puns.
Morozov, M. M., "The Individualization of Shakespeare's Characters
    through Imagery," *Shakespeare Survey,* Cambridge: Cambridge
    University Press, II, 1949. Metaphors used by each of characters
    have certain definite themes.
Price, H. T., "Mirror Scenes in Shakespeare," *J. Q. Adams Memorial
    Studies,* ed. James G. McManaway *et al.,* Washington, D.C.: Folger
    Shakespeare Library, 1948. Scenes that symbolically focus the mean-
    ing of the play.

Prior, Moody E., *The Language of Tragedy*, New York: Columbia University Press, 1947. Includes study of Shakespeare's language.

Rylands, George, *Words and Poetry*, London: L & V Woolf, 1928. The development of Shakespeare's style.

Stewart, J. I. M., *Character and Motive in Shakespeare*, 1947. New York: Longmans, Green, 1949. Apparent inconsistencies in characterization explained by Freudianism.

Stoll, E. E., "Symbolism in Shakespeare," *Modern Language Review*, XLI, 1947. Takes issue with the "New Criticism."

Wilson, F. P., "Shakespeare and the Diction of Common Life," *Proceedings of the British Academy*, XXVII, 1941. Puns and proverbs in Shakespeare.

GENERAL CRITICISM

Baker, George Pierce, *The Development of Shakespeare as a Dramatist*, 1907. New York: Macmillan, 1929. Study by a great teacher of drama written before modern knowledge of Elizabethan dramatic conventions.

Boas, Frederick S., *Shakspere and his Predecessors*, 1896. New York: C. Scribner, 1904. Criticism by historical scholar in late nineteenth century.

Bradbrook, Muriel C., *Shakespeare and Elizabethan Poetry*, London: Chatto & Windus, 1951. The plays in relation to the attitudes and conventions in Elizabethan poetry.

Bush, Geoffrey, *Shakespeare and the Natural Condition*, Cambridge, Mass.: Harvard University Press, 1956. The meaning of nature in the plays: the hierarchical universal order has been overemphasized.

Craig, Hardin, *An Interpretation of Shakespeare*, New York: Dryden Press, 1948. Survey of dramas by an outstanding Renaissance scholar.

Duthie, G. I., *Shakespeare*, London: Hutchinson's University Library, 1951. Condensed survey of the dramas.

Harbage, Alfred, *As They Liked It*, New York: Macmillan, 1947. Moral significance of the dramas.

Knights, L. C., *Some Shakespearean Themes*, Stanford, Calif.: Stanford University Press, 1960. Time and change, appearance and reality, fear of death and fear of life, meanings of nature, etc.

Mackail, J. W., *The Approach to Shakespeare*, Oxford: Clarendon Press, 1930. Survey of the dramas.

Moulton, R. G., *Shakespeare as a Dramatic Artist*, 1885. 2nd rev. and enl. ed., Oxford: Clarendon Press, 1888. Plot construction.

Muir, Kenneth, "Fifty Years of Shakespearian Criticism: 1900–1950," *Shakespeare Survey*, Cambridge: Cambridge University Press, IV, 1951. Analytical review.

Murry, John Middleton, *Shakespeare*, New York: Harcourt, Brace, 1936. Survey of the dramas by neo-romantic critic.

Nicoll, Allardyce, *Shakespeare: An Introduction*, New York: Oxford University Press, 1952. Survey of the dramas by the outstanding historian of British drama.

Pettet, E. C., *Shakespeare and the Romance Tradition*, London: Staples Press, 1949. Shakespeare's use of the material of medieval and Renaissance romance.

Quiller-Couch, Arthur, *Shakespeare's Workmanship*, 1918. Cambridge: Cambridge University Press, 1931. Survey of the dramas by a well-loved lecturer.

Schucking, L. L., *Character Problems in Shakespeare's Plays*, New York: Holt, 1922. Dramatic conventions in characterization.

Stauffer, Donald A., *Shakespeare's World of Images*, New York: Norton, 1949. The development of Shakespeare's moral ideas.

Sewell, Arthur, *Character and Society in Shakespeare*, Oxford: Clarendon Press, 1951. Characterization and moral vision in Shakespeare.

Swinburne, A. C., *A Study of Shakespeare*, 1880. London: W. Heineman, 1918. Rhapsodic essays by the Victorian poet.

Traversi, D. A., *Approach to Shakespeare*, 1938. 2nd rev. and enl. ed., London: Sands, 1957. Survey of the dramas by a critic concerned with close analysis of the language and verse.

Van Doren, Mark, *Shakespeare*, New York: Holt, 1939. Brief essays on the plays by a poet-critic.

SHAKESPEARE'S HISTORY PLAYS

Bethell, S.L., "The Comic Element in Shakespeare's Histories," *Anglia*, LXXI, 1952. Comic element serves to express governing ideas of plays.

Courthope, William J., *A History of English Poetry*, New York and London: Macmillan, IV, 1903. The history plays contain an epic unity.

Craig, Hardin, "Shakespeare and the History Play," *J. Q. Adams Memorial Studies*, ed. James G. McManaway *et al.*, Washington, D.C.: Folger Shakespeare Library, 1948. The evolution of Shakespeare as a writer of history plays.

Jenkins, Harold, "Shakespeare's History Plays, 1900–1951," *Shakespeare Survey*, Cambridge: Cambridge University Press, VI, 1953. Analytical review of criticism.

Law, Robert A., "Links between Shakespeare's History Plays," *Studies in Philology*, L, 1953. Plays not written in accordance with grand conception but independent entities loosely linked.

Law, Robert A., "Shakespeare's Historical Cycle: Organism or Compilation?" *Studies in Philology,* LI, 1954. Takes issue with Tillyard. Reply by Tillyard in same issue.

Ribner, Irving, *The English History Play in the Age of Shakespeare,* Princeton: Princeton University Press, 1957. The history plays in the light of a study of the Elizabethan genre and of Elizabethan historiography.

Henry IV, Parts I and II

Bradley, A. C., "The Rejection of Falstaff," *Oxford Lectures on Poetry,* 1909. London: Macmillan, 1950. Falstaff an endearing character because his amorality carries us into an atmosphere of perfect freedom.

Brooks, Cleanth and Heilman, Robert B., *"Henry IV, Part I,"* *Understanding Drama,* 1948. New York: Holt, Rinehart & Winston, 1961. Organic unity of the play.

Morgann, Maurice, "An Essay on the Dramatic Character of Sir John Falstaff," *Eighteenth Century Essays on Shakespeare,* ed. D. Nichol Smith, Glasgow: J. MacLehose, 1903. Falstaff no coward.

Schaaber, Matthias, "The Unity of *Henry IV,*" *J. Q. Adams Memorial Studies,* Washington, D.C.: Folger Shakespeare Library, 1948. Takes issue with Wilson and Tillyard.

Sprague, Arthur Colby, "Gadshill Revisited," *Shakespeare Quarterly,* IV, 1953. Takes issue in part with Wilson.

Stewart, J. I. M., "The Birth and Death of Falstaff," *Character and Motive in Shakespeare,* 1947. New York: Longmans, Green, 1949. Adds another mythic function to Falstaff in addition to those of Wilson: that of redeeming scapegoat.

SHAKESPEARE'S ROMANTIC COMEDIES

Barber, C. L., *Shakespeare's Festive Comedy,* 1957. Princeton: Princeton University Press, 1959. The contribution of the social form of Elizabethan holidays to the dramatic form of the comedies.

Brown, John Russell, "The Interpretation of Shakespeare's Comedies: 1900–1953," *Shakespeare Survey,* Cambridge: Cambridge University Press, VIII, 1955. Analytical review.

Charlton, H. B., *Shakespearean Comedy,* London: Methuen, 1938. The evolution of the form of Shakespearean comedy.

Coghill, Neville, "The Basis of Shakespearian Comedy," *Essays and*

Studies, New Series, III, 1950. The influence of the medieval conception of comedy.

Evans, Bertrand, *Shakespeare's Comedies,* Oxford: Clarendon Press, 1960. Shakespeare's management of the differences in awareness between the audience and the dramatic characters.

Palmer, John, *Comic Characters of Shakespeare,* London: Macmillan, 1946. Berowne, Touchstone, Shylock, Bottom, Benedick and Beatrice in relation to their plays.

Parrott, Thomas Marc, *Shakespearean Comedy,* New York: Oxford University Press, 1949. Discussion of the comedy in each of the plays.

The Merchant of Venice

Gollancz, Israel, *Allegory and Mysticism in Shakespeare: A Medievalist on The Merchant of Venice,* London: G. W. Jones, 1931. Christian allegory of trial scene.

Lewalski, Barbara K., "Biblical Allusion and Allegory in *The Merchant of Venice,*" *Shakespeare Quarterly,* XIII, 1962. Patterns of Biblical allusion and imagery precise and pervasive.

Siegel, Paul N., "Shylock and the Puritan Usurers," *Studies in Shakespeare,* ed. Arthur D. Matthews and Clark M. Emery, Coral Gables, Fa.: University of Miami Press, 1952. Shylock's character and manners designed to recall Elizabethan Puritan usurers.

Small, S. A., *Shakespearean Character Interpretation: The Merchant of Venice,* Baltimore: Johns Hopkins Press, 1927. Contains summary review of previous Shylock criticism.

Tillyard, E. M. W., "The Trial Scene in 'The Merchant of Venice,' " *Review of English Literature,* II, 1961. Portia a partially allegorical representation of Justice and Mercy reconciled.

SHAKESPEARE'S SATIRIC COMEDIES

Brown, John Russell, "The Interpretation of Shakespeare's Comedies: 1900–1953," *Shakespeare Survey,* Cambridge: Cambridge University Press, VIII, 1955. Analytical review.

Lawrence, W. W., *Shakespeare's Problem Comedies,* New York: Macmillan, 1931. Plays not realistic in use of folk elements.

Tillyard, E. M. W., *Shakespeare's Problem Plays,* 1938. Toronto: University of Toronto Press, 1949. Links *Hamlet* with these comedies as sharing interest in religious dogma, abstract speculation and psychological analysis.

Measure for Measure

Battenhouse, Roy W., "*Measure for Measure* and the Christian Doctrine of Atonement," *PMLA*, LXI, 1946. Christian interpretation.

Bradbrook, Muriel C., "Authority, Truth and Justice in *Measure for Measure*," *Review of English Studies*, XVII, 1941. The conflict of justice and mercy.

Coghill, Neville, "Comic Form in *Measure for Measure*," *Shakespeare Survey*, Cambridge: Cambridge University Press, VIII, 1955. Study of comic form confirms Christian interpretation.

Lascelles, Mary, *Shakespeare's Measure for Measure*, London: University of London, 1953. Examination of play in light of possible sources and analogues. Takes issue with Chambers.

Leech, Clifford, "The Meaning of *Measure for Measure*," *Shakespeare Survey*, Cambridge: Cambridge University Press, III, 1950. Christian coloring only intermittent.

Pater, Walter, "*Measure for Measure*," *Appreciations*, 1889. London: Macmillan, 1890. Play concerned with the tyranny of nature and circumstance over human action.

Siegel, Paul N., "*Measure for Measure:* The Significance of the Title," *Shakespeare Quarterly*, IV, 1953. Title signifies the workings of both justice and mercy.

Wilson, Harold S., "Action and Symbol in *Measure for Measure* and *The Tempest*," *Shakespeare Quarterly*, IV, 1953. Two plays deal with theme of forgiveness but use different dramatic methods.

Troilus and Cressida

Ellis-Fermor, Una, "Discord in the Spheres: The Universe of *Troilus and Cressida*," *The Frontiers of Drama*, London: Methuen, 1948. The theme of chaos.

Harrier, Richard C., "Troilus Divided," *Studies in the English Renaissance Drama*, ed. Josephine W. Bennett *et al.*, New York: New York University Press, 1959. Troilus evokes as much admiration as disapproval.

Muir, Kenneth, "*Troilus and Cressida*," *Shakespeare Survey*, Cambridge: Cambridge University Press, VIII, 1955. Play fuses themes of betrayal of values and the destructiveness of passion and time.

Nowottny, W. M. T., " 'Opinion' and 'Value' in *Troilus and Cressida*," *Essays in Criticism*, IV, 1954. Social stability vs. creative imagination represented by Ulysses and Troilus.

Tatlock, J. S. P., "The Chief Problem in Shakespeare," *Sewanee Review,* XXIV, 1916. The play studied in the light of the literary tradition.

SHAKESPEARE'S TRAGEDIES

Campbell, Lily B., *Shakespeare's Tragic Heroes, Slaves of Passion,* 1930. New York: Barnes and Noble, 1961. The heroes of the great tragedies in the light of Elizabethan psychology.

Campbell, Lily B., "Bradley Revisited: Forty Years After," *Studies in Philology, XLIV,* 1947. Criticism of Bradley.

Charlton, H. B., *Shakespearian Tragedy,* 1948. Cambridge: Cambridge University Press, 1952. Bradleyan criticism.

Charney, Maurice, *Shakespeare's Roman Plays,* Cambridge, Mass.: Harvard University Press, 1961. The dramatic function of the verbal and stage images.

Farnham, Willard, *Shakespeare's Tragic Frontier: The World of his Final Tragedies,* Berkeley: University of California Press, 1950. The heroes of the later tragedies more deeply flawed.

Harrison, G. B., *Shakespeare's Tragedies,* London: Routledge & K. Paul, 1951. Chronological survey of the tragedies.

Leech, Clifford, *Shakespeare's Tragedies and Other Studies in Seventeenth-Century Drama,* London: Chatto & Windus, 1950. Tragedies reveal a universe incompatible with Christian faith.

MacCallum, M. W., *Shakespeare's Roman Plays and their Background,* London: Macmillan, 1910. The Roman plays examined in relation to their sources.

Myrick, Kenneth O., "The Theme of Damnation in Shakespearean Tragedy," *Studies in Philology,* XXXVIII, 1941. Guilt, repentance and damnation in *Hamlet, Macbeth* and *Othello.*

Ribner, Irving, *Patterns in Shakespearean Tragedy,* London: Methuen, 1960. Development of Shakespearean tragedy in relation to inherited dramatic forms and ideas.

Siegel, Paul N., "In Defense of Bradley," *College English,* IX, 1948. Takes issue with L. C. Knight's attack on Bradley.

Speaight, Robert, *Nature in Shakespearian Tragedy,* London: Hollis & Carter, 1955. Nature and Grace in the tragedies and *The Tempest.*

Stirling, Brents, *Unity in Shakespearian Tragedy: The Interplay of Theme and Character,* 1956. New York: Columbia University Press, 1957. Leading ideas in relation to structure and motivation.

Weisinger, Herbert, "The Study of Shakespearian Tragedy since Bradley," *Shakespeare Quarterly,* VI, 1955. Analytical review.

Wilson, Harold S., *On the Design of Shakespearian Tragedy,* Toronto: University of Toronto Press, 1957. Tragedies divided into three categories: those governed by Order of Faith, by Order of Nature and by both.

Romeo and Juliet

Dickey, Franklin M., *Not Wisely But Too Well*, San Marino, Calif.: Huntington Library, 1957. *Romeo and Juliet* in the light of Elizabethan attitudes toward love. Takes issue with Dowden.

Evans, B., "The Brevity of Friar Lawrence," *PMLA*, LXV, 1950. The function of Friar Lawrence in the final scene.

Siegel, Paul N., "Christianity and the Religion of Love in *Romeo and Juliet*," *Shakespeare Quarterly*, XII, 1961. Interplay and tension between two sets of ideas. Takes issue in part with Dowden.

Hamlet

Alexander, Peter, *Hamlet: Father and Son*, Oxford: Clarendon Press, 1955. Attacks notion of a tragic flaw in Hamlet.

Battenhouse, Roy W., "Hamlet's Apostrophe on Man: Clue to the Tragedy," *PMLA*, LXVI, 1951. Hamlet, lacking in grace, lives without faith and dies without hope.

Eliot, T. S., "Hamlet and his Problems," 1919. In his *Selected Essays 1917–1932*, New York: Harcourt, Brace, 1950. *Hamlet* an interesting artistic failure.

Elliott, G. R., *Scourge and Minister*, Durham, N.C.: Duke University Press, 1951. Hamlet's flaw is pride.

Fergusson, Francis, "*Hamlet, Prince of Denmark:* The Analogy of Action," *The Idea of a Theatre*, Princeton: Princeton University Press, 1949. Analogous stories, situations and relationships.

Hankins, John Erskine, *The Character of Hamlet and Other Essays*, Chapel Hill, N.C.: University of North Carolina Press, 1941. Hamlet and Elizabethan ideas about revenge.

Johnson, S. F., "The Regeneration of Hamlet," *Shakespeare Quarterly*, III, 1952. Hamlet's trust in providence after ocean voyage.

Jones, Ernest, *A Psycho-analytic Study of Hamlet*, 1922. London: Vision, 1947. The Oedipus complex cause of his delay.

Lawlor, J. J., "The Tragic Conflict in Hamlet," *Review of English Studies, New Series*, I, 1960. Hamlet and Elizabethan ideas about revenge.

Leech, Clifford, "Studies in *Hamlet*, 1901–1955," *Shakespeare Survey*, Cambridge: Cambridge University Press, IX, 1956. Analytical review.

Mack, Maynard, "The World of *Hamlet*," *Yale Review*, XLI, 1952. The imaginative environment of the play.

Murray, Gilbert, *Hamlet and Orestes*, New York: Oxford University Press, 1914. Both have ultimate origin in primitive myth.

Raven, A. A., *A Hamlet Bibliography and Reference Guide,* Chicago: University of Chicago Press, 1936. Lists 2167 items.

Schucking, L. L., *The Meaning of Hamlet,* London: Oxford University Press, 1937. Historical criticism.

Waldock, A. J. A., *Hamlet: A Study in Critical Method,* Cambridge: Cambridge University Press, 1931. Summarizes principal critics and polemicizes with them.

Walker, Roy, *The Time Is Out of Joint,* London: A. Dakers, 1948. Criticism by a Knight disciple.

Othello

Heilman, Robert B., *Magic in the Web,* Lexington: University of Kentucky Press, 1956. Imagery and structure. Notes furnish summary of previous criticism.

Hubler, Edward, "The Damnation of Othello," *Shakespeare Quarterly,* IX, 1958. Takes issue with Siegel. Reply by Siegel in same issue.

Elliott, G. R., *Flaming Minister,* Durham, N.C.: Duke University Press, 1953. Scene by scene examination. Pride Othello's flaw.

Gardner, Helen, "The Noble Moor," *Proceedings of the British Academy,* XLI, 1955. Takes issue with Siegel.

Leavis, F. R., *The Common Pursuit,* London: Chatto & Windus, 1952. Essay on *Othello* attacks traditional concepts of hero, sees him as self-dramatizing sentimentalist.

Nowottny, W. M. T., "Justice and Love in *Othello,*" *University of Toronto Quarterly,* XXI, 1952. Love vs. Justice. Love, like faith, should not require legal evidence.

Spivack, Bernard, *Shakespeare and the Allegory of Evil,* New York: Columbia University Press, 1958. Iago in light of the Vice of the morality plays.

Weisinger, Herbert, "Iago's Iago," *University of Kansas City Review,* XX, 1954. Othello and Iago incomplete men who complement each other.

Macbeth

Brooks, Cleanth, "The Naked Babe and the Cloak of Manliness," *The Well Wrought Urn,* New York: Reynal & Hitchcock, 1947. Clothes imagery and child symbolism.

Fergusson, Francis, "*Macbeth* as the Imitation of an Action," *English Institute Essays, 1951,* New York: Columbia University Press, 1952. The governing idea is the violation of nature.

Knights, L. C., *Explorations,* London: Chatto & Windus, 1946. Contains essay on *Macbeth* attacking Bradley.
Spargo, John W., "The Knocking at the Gate in *Macbeth,*" *J. Q. Adams Memorial Studies,* ed. James G. McManaway *et al.,* Washington, D.C.: Folger Shakespeare Library, 1948. Takes issue with De Quincey.
Walker, Roy, *The Time is Free,* London: Dakers, 1949. Imagery, irony and the tragic pattern.

King Lear

Bickersteth, G. L., "The Golden World of *King Lear,*" *Proceedings of the British Academy,* XXXII, 1946. The effect of classical and Christian concepts in transmuting suffering into beauty.
Campbell, Oscar James, "The Salvation of Lear," *ELH,* XV, 1948. Lear achieves salvation through Cordelia as in the morality plays.
Danby, John F., *Shakespeare's Doctrine of Nature: A Study of King Lear,* London: Faber & Faber, 1949. The Hooker-Bacon view of nature vs. the Hobbesian view in *Lear.*
Frost, William, "Shakespeare's Rituals and the Opening of *King Lear,*" *Hudson Review,* X, 1958. The effect of the ritualistic formality of the first scene.
Heilman, Robert B., *This Great Stage,* Baton Rouge, La.: Louisiana State University Press, 1948. Imagery and the interlinked themes.
Kernodle, G. F., "The Symphonic Form of *King Lear,*" *Elizabethan Studies in Honor of G. F. Reynolds,* Boulder: University of Colorado Press, 1945. Repetition of patterns and motifs in accordance with inherited medieval principles of aesthetic organization.
Muir, Edwin, "The Politics of *King Lear,*" *Essays on Literature and Society,* London: Hogarth Press, 1949. The conflict between two concepts of society.
Stampfer, J., "The Catharsis of *King Lear,*" *Shakespeare Survey,* Cambridge: Cambridge University Press, XIII, 1960. Denies play concludes with vision of salvation.

SHAKESPEARE'S TRAGI-COMIC ROMANCES

Danby, John F., *Poets on Fortune's Hill,* London: Faber & Faber, 1952. Takes issue with symbolic interpretations of last plays.
James, D. G., *Scepticism and Poetry,* London: G. Allen & Unwin, 1937. Myths of final plays inadequate as means for communicating Shakespeare's apprehensions.

Tillyard, E. M. W., *Shakespeare's Last Plays,* London: Chatto & Windus, 1938. Romances complete the tragic pattern of prosperity, destruction and re-creation.

Traversi, D. A., *Shakespeare: The Last Phase,* 1954. New York: Harcourt Brace, 1955. Symbolic unity of the romances.

The Tempest

Bowling, L. E., "The Theme of Natural Order in *The Tempest,*" *College English,* XII, 1951. Violation of natural order and readjustment to it.

Collins, J. Churton, "Poetry and Symbolism: A Study of *The Tempest,*" *Contemporary Review,* 1908. Early Christian symbolic reading.

Dobree, Bonamy, "*The Tempest,*" *Essays and Studies, New Series,* V, 1952. Appearance and reality, free will and destiny.

Gilbert, Allan H., "*The Tempest,* Parallelism in Characters and Situations," *Journal of English and Germanic Philology,* XIV, 1915. The two conspiracies and other parallels.

Still, Colin, *Shakespeare's Mystery Play,* London: C. Palmer, 1921, reissued in altered form in 1936 as *The Timeless Theme.* Highly symbolic reading.

Stoll, E. E., "*The Tempest,*" *PMLA,* XLVII, 1932. Takes issue with symbolic interpretations.

INDEX

This is an index of topics, critics, and Shakespearean plays. In order to avoid cumbersomeness, it does not list instances in which critics and plays receive only passing mention. The subordinate phrases under each heading are arranged in the order of their appearance in the text except that characters are listed alphabetically under "characters, dramatic."

432

Index

mances, (Dowden) 377–381; of
Tempest, (Wilson) 401–402
tragedy: dramatic inevitability in,
(Dowden) 105–106; characterization in, (Dowden) 106–107; morality in, (Frye) 123; romantic criticism on 203; neo-classical criticism
on, 203; Victorian criticism on, 203;
modern criticism on, 203; Bradley
on, 207–221; heroes in, (Bradley)
207–210; fate in, (Bradley) 212–
215; justice in, (Bradley) 215–217;
order in, (Bradley) 217–221; imagery in, (Spurgeon) 221–249; Siegel on, 251–266; changes from Bradley, (Siegel) 251–252; divine providence in, (Siegel) 252–256; and
Christian humanism, (Siegel) 256–
263; heroes in, (Siegel) 263–266.
See also comedy in tragedy
tragi-comic romances: See romances
Troilus and Cressida: Hazlitt on, 152;
Coleridge on, 152; a comical satire,
(Campbell) 159–160; satiric conclusion of, (Campbell) 160; a dramatic
experiment, (Spencer) 193–202;
theme of order in, (Spencer) 194–
195, 200–202; choric comment in,
(Spencer) 196, 200; imagery in,
(Spencer) 196–197, 202n; character
of Trolius, (Spencer) 198–199
Twelfth Night: multi-consciousness in,
(Bethell) 51–52; romance and

comedy in, (Gordon) 116–117;
"green world" in, (Frye) 126; opening scene of, (Coleridge) 284
Two Gentlemen of Verona, The:
"green world" in, (Frye) 125–126

unities: See laws, dramatic

Van Doren, Mark: on *Measure for
Measure,* (Campbell) 154, 156
versification: Hazlitt on, 42; in *As You
Like It,* (Bethell) 53–55
Victorian criticism: concerns of, 4, 6–
7; on romantic comedies, 103; on
"dark" comedies, 152; on tragedies,
203; on romances, 376; and Wilson,
396
Voltaire: Johnson on, 25; Coleridge
on, 25, 28, 29

Werder, K.: on *Hamlet,* 290
Whiter, Walter: on imagery, 221
Wilson, Harold S.: on *Tempest,* 396–
397
Wilson, J. Dover: on Falstaff, 80–102;
on *Measure for Measure,* (Chambers) 162–163; on *Tempest,* 396–
412. *See also Henry IV, Part I;
Tempest, The*
Winter's Tale, The: compared with
tragedies, (Bradley) 208; Knight on,
385–387; carelessness in, (Wilson)
401

J1